ORDER IN SPACE AND SOCIETY

ORDER IN SPACE AND SOCIETY

Architectural Form and its Context in the Scottish Enlightenment

Edited by THOMAS A MARKUS

Essays by
Thomas A Markus
Peter Reed
Frank A Walker
Andrew Noble

Assistant editor Honor Mulholland

MAINSTREAM

First published by
MAINSTREAM PUBLISHING COMPANY (EDINBURGH) LTD.
25a South West Thistle Street Lane
Edinburgh EH2 1EW

ISBN 0 906391 29 6

The publisher acknowledges the financial assistance of the Scottish Arts
Council in the publication of this volume.

Designed by James Hutcheson 1982

Typeset, printed and bound in Great Britain by
Spectrum Printing Company, Edinburgh.

TABLE OF CONTENTS

List of Illustrations

Essay 3

Essay 4

    (b) elevation and ground floor plan for a Village School

    (c) elevation and ground floor plan for a 'Small Training School' with Master's house

    (d) alternative ground and first floor plans for (c) when site is limited.

4.32 Stow school in Sherbone (sic, Sherborne?) Dorset, 1849; architect R.J. Withers, elevation and ground floor plan.

4.33 David Stow's design for the London and City Moral Training Schools, 1853, elevation, ground, first ('ground'?) floor and roof plans.

4.34 Motto of the Training System on heraldic emblem in entrance hall of the Glasgow Normal Seminary.

4.35 New Glasgow Normal Seminary, 1845: architect Charles Wilson(?).

4.36 Design for a school for eighty children, 1839-40; Committee of Council on Education.

4.37 Design for a school for three hundred juveniles and one hundred and fifty infants, 1839-40; Committee of Council on Education.

4.38 Poor Law Commissioners' proposal for a workhouse school, 1839,

    (a) isometric

    (b) ground floor plan.

4.39 Poor Law Commissioners' proposal for an 'Orphan House and Normal School' (workhouse) for four hundred and fifty children, 1841.

Essay 5

5.1 Engraving of a painting by D. Octavius Hill of Mossgiel, the farm rented by Burns and his brother in 1784.

5.2 Engraving of a painting by D. Octavius Hill of the Braes of Ballochmyle.

Errata

List of Illustrations	Fig 1.11—1742 should read 1752
Page 36—Caption	Fig 1.11—1742 should read 1752
List of Illustrations	Fig 1.63—Elliott's should read Elliot's
Page 83—Caption	Fig 1.56—Elliott's should read Elliot's
Page 90—Caption	Fig 1.63—Elliott's should read Elliot's
Page 79—Caption	Fig 1.53(a)—roof plan should read basement plan
Page 186—Line 5	Omit (Figure 3.16)
Page 320—Line 18	LE COURBOUSIER should read LE CORBUSIER
Page 4—Line 28	Quatremere should read Quatremère
Page 85—Line 22	Salpetriere should read Salpetrière
Page 321—Line 54	Quatremére should read Quatremère

Introduction

Thomas A. Markus

The essays in this collection deal with aspects of Scottish society and culture primarily in the century from about 1730 to 1830—a period which allows us to study not only aspects of the Enlightenment but especially its response to the two revolutions. The effects of the French Revolution and of the Industrial Revolution combined in Britain to produce interactions between technical progress, political reform movements, the new entrepreneurial class, working class ferment and harsh repression. In the many excellent social and technical histories of this period architecture and even urban development play minor roles. Yet in these fields the revolution was no less marked and gave rise to dislocation of a pattern which for some four hundred years had been dominant. Not only did the rapid rate of urbanisation create entirely new problems of housing, health, education and sanitation but it resulted in new town forms and spatial structures. In the production of buildings, there were formal innovations so abrupt that Kaufmann[1] in fact refers to the neo-classical designers as 'revolutionaries'. There were technical revolutions too: the coming of iron as a structural material, the introduction of lifts and hoists, heating, ventilation and sanitary systems, 'fireproof' and glass-and-iron construction. Almost overnight completely new building types were called for, not only in the direct service of the Industrial Revolution, such as mills, warehouses and, towards the end of our period, railway stations but for new classes, new commercial processes, new urban functions and new patterns of legal and institutional control. Examples of developing types in these latter areas are clubs and Mechanics' Institutes, banking and insurance offices, town markets, and prisons, hospitals and asylums on an altogether new scale and with new modes of organisation. The emerging towns and new building types were clearly different in their forms and styles—that is in their appearance. But they also 'felt' different in the organisation of the spaces they contained. The hierarchy, sequence and permeability of public urban space and its interface with private housing or institutional building space—that is to say its structure—changed. So did the structure of space within buildings, following new rules in accordance with changing social functions within families and organisations (public and private) on the one hand and the interaction of these groups with society itself on the other. What was the nature of the society of which these towns and buildings were an integral part?

Scotland at this time presents many of the paradoxical new phenomena present in Europe as a whole. But in many respects it also has a unique, but equally new face. Much of its political dynamic was the outcome of the 1707 Act of Union and the failed Jacobite risings of 1715 and 1745. For the social class which wielded political power the attempt to achieve national identity and, at the same time, maintain the closest of links with Westminster as the only security for both trade and the maintenance of its controlling position, created immense conflicts. The effects of these are seen throughout society and are relevant to many of the issues discussed in these essays. The battle between the old class of landed privilege and the new bourgeoisie was fought not only along the orthodox Tory-Whig dimension but in the Kirk (Evangelicals against Moderates); in the Universities, the professions and in the arts. The Scottish Tories, and their leaders such as Henry Dundas lacked the ability of the English Tories to adapt and present a face other than that of reaction. The Whigs were able to espouse the causes of Parliamentary reform, popular education, reform of the Burgh elections, repeal of the Corn Laws and even to establish some common ground with trade unions and radicals. The transfer of power from the old to the new party in the 1820s and '30s meant the transfer of mechanisms for the defence of property and position. The development of Radical and critical challenge and the reactions they caused was focused around a few remarkable magazines, notably the *Edinburgh Review* founded in 1802 by Henry Brougham a Scottish emigré to England, Francis Jeffrey and others, which became an overt Whig political organ after 1808, and the Tory *Blackwood's Magazine* set up in 1817 to fight the pro-reformist *Scotsman* which also first appeared in that year.

We shall see in several of these essays the power of such organs not only overtly to attack or to diffuse social and political ideas—as in the cases of popular education, the poor law and electoral reform—but to operate as covert political instruments through literary comment of a type which occasionally even crossed the party lines. An example of such a united front was the damning of English Romantic poets and their language in the name of criticism, for the purpose of repressing the real or imagined insurrectionary power of such literature.

There can be no doubt that the intellectual achievements of the Scottish Enlightenment were enormous. The work of William Adam and his sons was of a quality to render Scottish architecture for a time equal to any in Europe; in philosophy and in economic thought David Hume and Adam Smith established international supremacy. Figures of comparable distinction arose in science, medicine and technology: Joseph Black, discoverer of carbon dioxide, William Smellie, outstanding obstetrician; the brothers William and John Hunter, the latter becoming the most eminent surgeon in Britain by the time of his death in London in 1793 and James Watt, who, with support from Joseph Black and others, developed the separate condenser and then the rotary steam engine and thus enabled industry to move from remote rural, water-powered sites to the urban

2

centres. In Scotland there was concentrated, therefore, both in theory and practice an extraordinary amount of the energy which was to be so formative in changing western society. In spite of this, however, much Scottish thought in the eighteenth century seems to have been subject to a paradox at least as vitiating as that propounded by Professor Daiches in his account of the decay of the native language among the educated classes in the same period.[2] The elements of this paradox can only be outlined here. Broadly, it could be said that these, and subsequent Scottish thinkers— despite the formative role of their thought particularly in politics and economics through the radical ideas of Hume and Smith—could only envisage such ideas as leading to the world remaining a stable, rural, albeit more prosperous one or, alternatively, leading to a gradual form of progressive evolution which entailed, in Hume's case, the growth of small scale and highly civilizing cities.

Of course, Hume and Smith were intellectuals and not prophets; nor could they have the benefit of our hindsight regarding the harsher consequences of the incorporation of their theories into society. Even so, curious dualisms, contradictions and perhaps a degree of wilful blindness exist in their thought. Despite Hume's demolition of causation and his sceptical, anti-rationalist stance which made his epistemology into what Bruce Lenman has recently described as 'a time bomb . . . ticking away underneath it (the Scottish Enlightenment)',[3] he did not see those ideas as leading to social upheaval. On the contrary his social essays envisage the growth of general prosperity created by the entrepreneurial energy of a liberalising 'middling class'. His *History of England,* on which his contemporary reputation was founded, is a justification of the Glorious Revolution, a celebration of the Constitution and as conservative in its view of society as his *Treatise on Human Nature* (1740) is radical in its philosophy.[4] Smith's *The Wealth of Nations* (1776) laid the foundations for the English (!) school of economists—a cornerstone of whose theoretical stand was the rational division of labour and limited popular education. Smith's model was devised for agriculture as he had hardly yet seen the beginnings of mechanised factory production and, in fact, unlike Hume regarded the city as inimical to 'the original destination of man'.[5] His ideas, of course, were later applied by economists to the industrial, mechanical and labour system, and, as we shall see, to various models of education and the poor law in which division of labour was interpreted as a mechanical principle and therefore appropriate to utilitarian, mechanised systems for intellectual formation and institutional care.

These essays deal with the period when the theories of the Enlightenment start to bear tangible fruit. Certainly such ideas created change and growth but by no means with the exclusive, felicitous general prosperity which had been postulated. We can at best speak of the ambiguity of progress in that age. In these essays aspects of that ambiguity in architecture and, in one case, in literature are explored. In exploring these we are asking questions about the history of society. Professor Hobsbawm[6] has outlined the methods which can be used to transform social history into the history of society '. . . which is still being constructed'. In this transformation he sees the fruitful influence of workers in disciplines outside history; specifically he lists anthropology, sociology, political science, '. . . not to mention students of literature and religions'. Architecture is notably absent from his list compiled more than a decade ago. It is true that since that time the work of Girouard[7], Evans,[8] King,[9] and Rykwert,[10] in Britain, and Thompson and Goldin[11] in America have moved towards placing the interpretation of buildings in a social context; whilst Jetter's [12] continuing work in Germany had already done so. Much of this work is either specific to a single building type, such as the hospital or country house, or is indirect social history, making the link through the *ideas* which permeate both the philosophy and the architecture of a period. A handful of French scholars influenced by Foucault's work on the history of ideas have focused on the social and political content of planning and architecture: Chouay[13] in the field of planning myths and Utopias had already followed such a path; more recently Demengeon and Fortier[14] on the naval arsenals in eighteenth century France as 'urban laboratories' for the development of techniques for urban zoning, classification, hygiene and administration and Teyssot[15] on the production of vast numbers of civic buildings starting in Napoleon's First Empire have also done so. In America through the pages of such journals as *Oppositions* and *Lotus International* Vidler and others have been exploring the relationship of the formal planning solutions of such industrial settlements as the Royal saltworks at Chaux by Ledoux[16] to production techinques and ideologies. They have also been exploring the idea of 'type' especially in French architectural theory of the nineteenth century in the work of Durand, Quatremere de Quincy and Viollet le Duc.[17] Nevertheless it is to be doubted whether, were Professor Hobsbawm writing today, he would yet feel ready to include architecture in his list of contributing disciplines. The reasons have to do with the nature of architectural discourse—that is, with the difficulty of finding a level of meaning which integrates the fragmented discourse*s* to architecture. This difficulty is never clearer than when trying to develop a building typology.

The question of 'type' raises the issue that in order to classify buildings as objects—that is in order to fit them into a framework which makes consistent analysis possible—characteristics have to be identified. What these will be depends on individual perspective—that is, the boundary of an individual discourse. 'Discourse' as used here includes everything said, written or done in the field. ('Doing', in architecture, includes all that is designed and built). Discourse also includes silence—those *possible* things which are not said, written or done. In order to identify the silent parts of discourse, boundaries have to be defined—otherwise silence is infinite. The discourses of intentions in architecture seem to be of three kinds— yeilding three sets of characteristics and three ways of classifying or 'typing' buildings.

The first discourse is that of form—that is one that deals with the formal properties of space and of the boundaries which define it. These boundaries have expressive, physiognomic surfaces, whose properties traditionally are analysed in terms of style. The form and composition of spaces, in three dimensions, generally represented in two-dimensional drawings such as plans and sections, is analysed by reference to geometrical methods. So the two concerns of formal discourse are the symbolic, semiotic and abstract content of style and that of geometry. The analytical tools are those of art history and criticism, coupled to formal analysis of such properties as axial composition, proportion, scale, rhythm, regularity and articulation.

The second discourse is that of function—the analysis which allows the purposes of buildings to be described. Functional discourse is often initially verbal—descriptions by society of what is required in a building programme. Today we refer to these as 'briefs'. In any culture these 'use categories' are rich and complex—for instance the words 'museum', 'parlour', 'back court' or 'bathroom' are each shorthand names for a complete set of social functions and carry images of physical form and properties. This verbal part of the discourse is then transformed by designers into formal and spatial solutions which embody the functional statement. So a transformation process takes place within the functional discourse. The language employed, the meaning of categories, the items about which there is silence and the statements about the use and users of spaces are matters of social intention. Design techniques which purport to analyse function and to produce solutions employ methodologies which themselves carry social meaning and are thus *part* of this discourse.

The third discourse is that of space, treated in an a-formal manner. The methods of analysis go back to the abstract morphological systems of Durand and his pupils at the École Polytechnique in Paris at the very end of the eighteenth century. Alexander's *A Pattern Language*[18] deals in similar spatial entities; but the most rigorous methods are those developed by Hillier.[19] The matter for analysis, whether in towns, settlements or buildings, concerns the structure of space, the sequences and the permeability between one space and others adjacent to it. Whether the entry from the street into a courtyard is through a Gothic or a Baroque gateway, and whether the courtyard itself is square or oblong, are issues which, in spatial terms, are irrelevant. Spatial intentions are, however, the basis of all architectural decisions and can be analysed in terms of topological relationships and measured by such properties as 'depth'—that is, the number of layers of space one passes through from the outside of a building to reach an internal location. Moreover these spatial structures can be shown to relate to characteristic social structures—they map society.

Although the analytical methods in each of the three discourses may be abstract, the phenomena of each are concrete and matters of daily experience. These discourses deal with architectural intentions—that is *ends*. The *means* of achieving these brings into play other discourses especially those dealing with technology and resources, fields which even more obviously are interwoven with social and economic forces.

Clearly, then, the three discourses of form, function and space will yield three sets of independent characteristics—for instance the hospital function can be achieved in a great variety of formal compositions and styles; moreover it can have a number of different spatial structures which are independent of form but which will express quite different relationships between staff, patients, visitors and the wider, urban social group. The problem then remains of discovering interdependency not at the level of the phenomena themselves but at the level of meanings.

A focus on social relationships and the analysis of social structure appear to provide the links between the analyses and aid the discovery of meaning. For this purpose 'social' is used to define three levels of relationship in each of which the self appears directly or by empathy. The first relationship is that of self to self; the relationship which answers the universal questions 'who am I?', 'where am I going?' and 'what am I becoming?'. The second level is that of the relationship of self to others and, hence, others to others. The third level is that of self (or others) to Other—the cosmic order and meaning whose presence is not only at the core of creation stories, philosophical and religious systems and historical analysis but is equally present in the foundation rites of cities, the symmetries of settlements and the geometries of domes. At some times the Other is divine; at others it is Reason, Science or Society. Or it may be merely the sound of the Piper in the willows. These three authentic relationships of self to self, others and the Other, when frustrated, become the three forms of alienation described by Marx—from self, others and nature. The mechanism which controls these relationships, and is able to frustrate them, is social structure.

*   *   *

In these essays we have tried to explore the significance of certain Scottish developments, mainly in Edinburgh and Glasgow, by methods drawn from each of the three discourses. The distinction between each discourse is not always sharply made—in part because of technical difficulties and in part because the blurring often helps to maintain connections. The spatial analysis in particular is generally implicit and therefore the explicit methods described later in this introduction have to be 'read into' the architectural designs.

Thus these discourses enable buildings to become transparent; that is, instead of erecting an opaque and reflective surface behind them, which fixes the interaction between observer and object, it allows them to speak of a larger world of ideas, society, values and relationships. It is precisely thus that Blake's sick rose attacked by its worm enables the listener to see quite universal aspects of beauty and evil—its transparency in no way diminishes either the beauty of the poem or of the rose.

In Andrew Noble's essay on Scottish pastoral imagery in the literature and criticism of the Enlightenment these techniques are not of course appropriate. In literary analysis the relationships between form and content and the social meaning of both have been explored over a much longer time and hence Professor Hobsbawm was able to see it as a discipline capable of contributing to social history. Had Raymond Williams' *The Country and the City*[20] been published at the time he would have surely done so with even greater emphasis. But Andrew Noble's essay also raises the issue of a silent discourse. For it not only analyses the reasons for the sentimentality and heroic nationalism of the fabricated Scottish pastoral world inhabited by a quiet, sturdy peasantry synthesised to extol the virtues of rural order, but it also approaches the question as to why Scotland produced no literature of *urban* imagery. The disruptions of rural enclosure and of urban concentration were not only achieved by economic, social and legal mechanisms, but their effects were camouflaged in both explicit literary images and by the use of silence.

The literary focus on scenes and characters of harmony and romance and the silence with regard to conflict, dislocation and degradation are one aspect of the programme of order. The title of this collection of essays indicates that they are concerned with order and society—with special architectural focus. But in moving from literature to architecture we are confronted with different phenomena and a variety of 'orders' which form the linking themes between the four architectural essays and also between them and the literary analysis. As a way of making the various connections it will be useful first to summarise the various perspectives, each of which reveals a different aspect of order.

The first is that which deals with order in form. The ubiquitous grid as a planning principle for new town developments, the radial, centric geometries which appear in total institutions such as prisons and also in Utopian industrial settlements, the classical system of the Edinburgh New Town palace fronts—all these have compositional, geometric and stylistic principles which represent, in different degrees, meta-orders which had long been established in the European tradition.

The perspective on formal order may be concerned to display character —a concern which caused the French neo-classical architects to refer to *une architecture parlante* which directly transmitted ideas to the observer through the use of metaphoric forms.

In addition to these formal perspectives there is that which focuses on the functional programme of the Enlightenment buildings and this represents a second type of order. The diffused, almost invisible threats of disease, crime and insanity, coupled to the loss of the productive capabilities of the persons afflicted, required concentration, visibility and classification as a means of control—and a whole range of building types was developed to achieve these aims. The dangers of ignorance, as had been foreseen by Adam Smith, and of early vice and unruliness, were countered with a programme of conformist education carried out in another new type of building.

A third type of order is that found in the spatial structures used in the new types of towns and buildings—structures which enabled the functions to be firmly defined and the corresponding structure of society to be reproduced in the town and its buildings.

But order in architecture is not only a matter of its pure, abstract creations; it is also evident in the way in which nature, as given or created, is incorporated into the city. The peaceful juxtaposition of built order and nature had already been achieved in the paintings of Poussin and Claude. This arcadia had its architectural counterpart. The picturesque, the farm, cottage and rural idyll also each appear in the subjects of these essays.

Reference has been made both in general, and in the particular case of literature, to the discourse of silence, which can be seen as an ordering device. In Enlightenment architecture it takes the form of almost total inactivity in consideration of working class urban housing. It was not until the publication of the Report of Chadwick's Royal Commission on the Sanitary Conditions of the Labouring Population in 1842, well after the end of the period of these essays, that the silence was first broken—and it was another thirty years before legislative and planning action began to be significant.

Peter Reed and Frank Walker explore the growth and meaning of the urban grid and housing in late eighteenth and early nineteenth century Edinburgh and Glasgow respectively. Although the surprising link of Craig's involvement in both developments emerges, in most respects the two represent quite different attitudes to geometrical order. Craig's New Town was planned as a finite, bounded scheme, with the suggestion of 'gates' and with marked edges. It was placed on a hill, with alignment of its main axes along its contours and with a grid *within* it which allowed subdivision and localised order. The linking of two major squares by the central axis of George Street, the proposal for a church at each end of the two squares (though one, St. Andrew's, was replaced by means of a land deal which enabled Sir Laurence Dundas to build his house at this point on the axis) and the proposal to include a Register House for recording all of Scotland's land holdings gave the scheme a unity and cosmic validation which in many ways follows from the European tradition of planned cities. The New Town was a suburb in which the political and professional rulers of Edinburgh, and indeed Scotland, could establish a self-conscious image removed from the density, social mix and increasing squalor of the Old Town. Its eminence on a hill equalled the equivalent topographical eminence of the Old Town and castle on Castle Rock. On the extension of the New Town eastwards, towards Calton Hill, were to be built the Bridewell and prisons, a school and a number of public monuments, with housing and the Register House beneath the hill. One image which emerges is that of the twin power of the Capital—*tradition* and power (in the form of the castle) on one side balanced by *progress* and power (major institutions, élite housing and the Register House) on the other. The image of the old and the new seats of power is well captured in Ewbank's

painting of the entry of George IV into Edinburgh in 1822 (Figure 1); an event for which the monarch was draped in tartan and to which Andrew Noble refers in his essay. The painting also shows Register House, an office in which the whole of Scotland's territory and its legal ownership could be recorded—in fact mapped by a regular system of location of documents under Robert Adam's dome. This cosmic form used to cover the cylindrical projection of national territory is a particularly significant part of the New Town's ideology.

In contrast Glasgow's grid, with one possible exception, is used as a neutral, open-ended medium through which the dynamic growth of middle class housing could be accommodated more or less indefinitely. The one exception is the location of Stark's St. George's church and the possible plan for a Blythswood mansion on the same axis—which, if it was ever intended, was abandoned. Although the legal framework of land division and feuing both in Edinburgh and in Glasgow was best achieved by a regular grid, one has the feeling that in the former case land law was used as a *means* for controlling the overall desired effect, which was inward-looking, whilst in the latter its mechanism, within the vigorous mercantile context of Glasgow society, became an *end* in itself, and the planning principle, which was outward-looking, was designed as a subservient form to suit the workings of the law.

The grid is, of course, as old as architecture itself. In many classical cities it was firmly bounded by an outer wall with gates and, as Rykwert has shown,[21] this outer edge had its special sacred character—the line where man's creation and that of the gods met. The grid appears over and over again in military camps and formations where it enabled the hierarchical organisation of an army to be expressed. It became the standard way of

9

dividing fortified towns and colonial settlements. In these cases therefore it was an expression of a meta-order, imposed by imperial or military power. Its adaptation to serve the housing needs of mercantile growth in Glasgow, as *system* rather than as an *object,* represents a shift in the mode of thinking. Stability is now gained not by finite marks on the *ground,* but by finite legal and economic rules enshrined in *documents,* whose outcome is a pattern with unpredictable limits. This formal system then became adapted to other classes of housing such as tenements and has survived well into this century in local authority and developers' grids.

The inward-looking nature of the Edinburgh New Town, its spacious-ness and low density, its separation by a wide strip of open land—some of it marsh—from the Old Town also had sanitary motivation. The constant danger of disease and the vaguely understood connection between it and the contamination of water supply by sewage was as formative in such schemes as it was in the planning of hospitals with complex peripheral moats and drainage channels, running water supply and internal drainage systems. Separation of buildings for access of fresh air was also considered fundamental for health and this belief has survived well into our present times in the form of building and planning regulations designed to achieve optimal layout and to limit maximum densities. At various times the principles of fresh air, light and space were actually held to be embodied in the human brain; Charles Fourier's disciple Jean-Baptiste André Godin (1817-1888) for instance drew on phrenology (Figure 2) to justify his palatial factory settlement forms (based on Versailles and on a new 'science' of human relationships). Paradoxically, the 'Four Functions' model of the CIAM Athens Charter of 1933 propounded a similar principle.

In contrast to the grid, especially in its Edinburgh version, was the centric, radial project. The dome, and the centric plan of which it is almost invariably a part, is first and foremost a symbol of the cosmos. It was thus in the Pantheon and in the Panopticon. My essay on Scotland's insti-tutional buildings shows the connection between much European ideal and Utopian town and building design and some of the executed schemes in Scotland, notably Robert Adam's semi-circular Bridewell in Edinburgh, based on Jeremy Bentham's Panopticon, and William Stark's four-armed radial lunatic asylum in Glasgow. In such instances the idea of central surveillance—by both the inspector or director and God (as the chapel was often juxtaposed on the inspection tower or located around its base)—is fundamental. But this is less obvious in settlements or buildings which are not actually circular or radial in plan. In the same essay, as well as that on the early nineteenth century schools, Robert Owen appears as a significant figure. There is no essay devoted specifically to his best known practical achievement—the New Lanark mill complex. Its history and description are already well studied and recorded.[22] Those studies show the develop-ment of the complex after Owen acquired a controlling interest in the mills in 1799 and at the same time married the daughter of one of its founders,

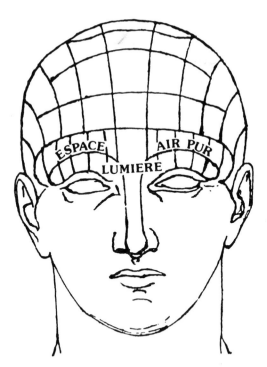

2 *Godin's use of phrenology to justify the principles of space, light and fresh air.*

David Dale (the other original partner was Richard Arkwright). The extreme difficulty of the site topography in the steep Clyde valley, and the need to locate the mills linearly along the river for water power, made it impossible to adopt a centric *form*. However, in *spatial* structure this could be, and was, achieved: the production areas along one edge, the workers' housing along another and, in the centre, the manager's house (occupied by Owen after his marriage) and Dale's own house. The New Institution for the Formation of Character and, later, the school, were also located in this central zone. Thus the central surveillance of production and the embedded location of the elements which controlled social life and early education continued the tradition already established in much more formal factory towns such as Ledoux's Royal saltworks at Chaux (1774 to 1776) where both the Director's house and the Chapel were in the central building of the extended circle. When Owen was able to plan *ideal* forms, untramelled by site or water-power exigencies, he designed square or rectangular settlements (Figure 3) in which the central building was an institution with social and educational functions, around it were the production areas and at the outer edge a wall of houses for the workers which separated the village from the open countryside. Although neither circular nor radial, schemes such as Owen's villages must be seen as having the same intention of a central focus. However, during the Industrial Revolution the form also acquired another meaning—that of the

11

3 *Ideal Community for 2000*
persons by Robert Owen, 1832.

THE CRISIS,

OR THE CHANGE FROM ERROR AND MISERY, TO TRUTH AND HAPPINESS

1832.

IF WE CANNOT YET   RECONCILE ALL OPINIONS

LET US ENDEAVOUR   TO UNITE ALL HEARTS

IT IS OF ALL TRUTHS THE MOST IMPORTANT, THAT THE CHARACTER OF MAN IS FORMED FOR—NOT BY HIMSELF

Design of a Community of 2,000 Persons, founded upon a principle, commended by Plato, Lord Bacon, Sir T. More, & R Owen

EDITED BY
ROBERT OWEN AND ROBERT DALE OWEN.

London.
PRINTED AND PUBLISHED BY J. EAMONSON, 15, CHICHESTER PLACE
GRAY'S INN ROAD
STRANGE, PATERNOSTER ROW, PURKISS, OLD COMPTON STREET
AND MAY BE HAD OF ALL BOOKSELLERS

machine. Owen's 'parallelograms' of Utilitarian order came to symbolise to the English Romantics the mechanistic rationalism they deplored and associated particularly with Scotland. Cobbett, Coleridge, Hazlitt and Southey, each from his own political standpoint, attacked the systematising principle of which they saw New Lanark as a prime example.[23]

The water wheel and, later, the steam engine, provided a single power source for a vast number of machines. The power generated was distributed by shafts, cogs and belts through space, vertically and horizontally. The motion was constant, and steady. To utilise the power without a break was, as E.P. Thompson has shown,[24] the motive behind shift work and the organisation of time as well as space in the industrial settlement. Not only was the motion distributed from a centre, but in accordance with the laws of mechanics, it was hierarchical, being broken down into major lines, branches and finally individual machines. The human organisation was similarly hierarchical and systematic—a director, various ranks of managers and finally the individual workers (mainly women and children at first) who were attached to each machine at the tip of the hierarchically branching tree. The machine model appears in various design solutions. First, as has been shown, in the industrial settlement. Then, as is shown in my essay on the school, in the design of its

12

organisation with its single master, its rank of monitors and its children divided into classes down to the paired interaction of one idiot child with one genius. Stow in Glasgow actually describes the motion of children from the main schoolroom, to the gallery, to the smaller classroom, to the playground ('the outdoor schoolroom') and back by a different route into the schoolroom, continuously surveyed by the master, as being a 'rotary' movement. In the hospitals, prisons and asylums there is a similar decomposition into major wings, by sex, further by 'class' (often of economic status and hence ability to pay), then by crime or symptom, down to the individual bed or cell. The supervisory staff are broken down into a similar hierarchy—so a social structure that in pre-industrial times might be held to have reflected the cosmos now became a model of the machine. Machine and cosmos were however united and no more fitting architectural symbol for that unity could be found than the central location of church or chapel (or in the case of the rationalist Owen, the social and educational building) in institutions or factory settlements. Moreover the institution was seen as a machine for producing character.

Since the production of character was the objective of the institution there had to be, and indeed there was, an explicit belief in the *formability* and *re*-formability of human nature. This was shared by Owen with Utilitarians, Rationalists and Radicals as well as with the leaders of philanthropy such as John Howard. It was part of much religious thought, especially of the various Dissenting movements. Its roots lay in Locke and in the psychologies of Priestley, Helvétius and Hartley the 'associationist'. The monitorial schools of Bell and Lancaster, Stow's 'model' schools in Glasgow, Owen's New Institution, Bentham's Panopticon and the prison and asylum régimes were all built upon it. There were however strange contradictions within this belief. On the one hand it was thought that society, especially the developing urban society, was an evil influence on the child. If the child could be removed early enough and surrounded from infancy with good, or rational ideas and influences it could be brought up to become a naturally good human being. If this was not done from the start it would, later, be hopeless. Yet, on the other hand, adult criminals and the insane were put into institutions where discipline, introspection in isolation and the new 'moral' treatment were supposed to cause fundamental changes in the mal-formed character. Belief in the reformability of the criminal and curability of the madman represents a contradiction with the educational philosophy, in that the environment is seen as both determining, and at the same time as having only superficial effect. What both views however share is a fundamental pessimism about *society*, since it was either malevolent or irrelevant, and a fundamental *optimism* about the individual. Hence, action was based on gathering individuals into large groups and separating them from contamination. The refusal to recognise the potential for healing *within* society was not only an affirmation of its increasingly destructive nature but a ratification of public and private philanthropy. Thus it was neither necessary nor possible to focus on the formation or re-formation of society itself.

Not only in plan but also in three dimensions the forms used on the surfaces of the elements enclosing space—that is their stylistic treatment—are invested with metaphorical or symbolic meaning. Ledoux is probably the outstanding exponent of *une architecture parlante.* By direct metaphor, allegory or symbol he addressed the spectator or user. The River Surveyors' house at Chaux was in the form of a semi-cylinder through which the river falls and crashes onto a base in the form of a cataract. The surveyors' control over the power supply is thus dramatically portrayed although Kaufmann reads additional sensuous meanings into the design. The House of the Lumbermen is a pyramidal structure composed of logs. Boullée, in his Palace of Justice, explicitly states the aims of the grand project:

> It seems to me that if I placed this august Palace above the shadowy lair of Crime, I should not only show to advantage the nobility of the architecture on account of the resulting contrast, but I should also have an impressive metaphorical image of Vice overwhelmed by the weight of Justice.[25]

During the Enlightenment and the French Revolution the building of a rational, noble and logical *legal* structure for society was seen in precisely these metaphoric terms. Jeremy Bentham's mammoth enterprise in jurisprudence was a rationalist and radical programme with such an aim. The popular view of law and order is well summarised by an early nineteenth century commentator who, immediately after describing the prisons of Liverpool in 1825, comments on the *penal* laws of England which '. . . require to be digested into one complete code, which, *built* on the immutable principles of substantial justice and unerring wisdom, *should present to the eye of contemplation a structure founded on reason and truth*' (my italics).[26] The visions of Rousseau, Bentham, and the whole Enlightenment now takes a Boullée-esque, architectural form in reverse metaphor—not the building representing ideas but ideas represented as buildings.

In the physiognomic treatment of facades the most marked phenomenon is, of course, the survival and expansion of the classical language. Both Peter Reed and Frank Walker look in detail at how these forms were adapted to the planning and social structures of the new housing projects and the stresses that arose between facade composition—as for instance the Edinburgh 'palace front'—and the legal and functional entities of individual houses divided by vertical party walls or by floors where multiple ownership on the same plot of ground occurs. Naturally one finds the expression of such social distinctions in the identification of main and servants' entrances and servants' and children's floors, on the one hand, and the main family and public rooms on the other. Predominant both in houses and public buildings is the use of major orders often rising through the two main floors—the first and second—built on a rusticated base and capped by some sort of attic. Rustication is a decorative treatment which permits, and should receive, many interpretations. At its simplest it can be seen as nothing more than giving 'weight' to the bottom of a composition

14

—analogous to making the *passe partout* surround to a print wider at the bottom than on the top and the two sides. Sometimes it refers back to the arcaded piazza of shops or agora. Often it should also be read as the image of a fortified, strong wall, with arched forms suggesting gates or dungeon windows. This can be seen in a number of the prisons. It also carries a suggestion of rough-hewn 'natural-ness' implied by its immediate adjacency to the ground. (Though in fact this adjacency was sometimes only apparent and not real; for instance in many of the urban terraces there was an ashlar basement sunk below the ground floor and thus invisible in its well). Rustication relates to what is part of nature, activity, society—that is the 'given' on the ground. Its surface therefore often has the deliberate marks of processes of decay such as de-laminating layers of stone or worm-eaten wood. But the facade structure should also be seen as reproducing the origins of classical architecture—the temple on the rock.

By an act of pure cosmic imagination or human reason a superstructure is erected on the rocky platform of the Acropolis. Human creation draws a horizontal line over the natural base—in the form of a paved platform with ascending steps—or merely a string course in classical house facades—and on this a fresh start is made from which columns and their entablature rise and enclose the essential functions of buildings, those dedicated to the most abstract principles of order. Whether this order is cosmic, or that of the law, or of universal healing, or of the public image of important families, is a secondary matter; it is always the embodiment of those ideas which give meaning and structure to society.

The adoption of anything other than mainstream classical facades before the end of the eighteenth century is surprising. Of course, the Gothic revival was already in its formative stages in England, under the influence of men like Horace Walpole. In Scotland Robert Adam was developing the castellated style not only in water colour whimsy but in his extensive country house practice albeit still organised in classical compositions. These designs may be the architectural correlate of Walter Scott's reference to the Country's heroic and military past. Even so, it is a break with all precedent for Adam to have given the Edinburgh Bridewell in 1791 a Scottish baronial facade when all the other competitors for the project used classical compositions. Possibly the prominence of the site at the foot of Calton Hill facing the Castle prompted this; perhaps, too, the emphasis on castles, rather than that of the more conventional temple front, more easily created the image of a keep or jail. There are also features of the facade which have ecclesiastical connotations. In the early nineteenth century working class school, inspired by religious philanthropy, the Tudor and Gothic image soon developed into a serious rival to the classical which became associated with higher levels of learning and more elevated sectors of society. There was a deliberate attempt to make certain kinds of buildings more accessible by the use of new metaphors.

The most startling inventiveness of the architects of the half century from about 1780 to 1830 is that shown in the development of new

15

functional types. It is true that the institutional buildings had a long history in the European Renaissance and earlier. But these had never been on this scale, nor had they ever demanded this degree of functional specialisation and technical organisation. Almost overnight architects were planning accommodation for hundreds instead of dozens of inmates; they were coping with anatomy theatres, corridors, vast kitchens and complex mass feeding arrangements. At the same time iron structures, ventilation, fireproofing, drainage and water supply were tackled in technically highly innovatory ways. In this enterprise architects, engineers, industrialists and philanthropists worked together; we shall see for instance how the Bentham brothers, Arkwright, the Strutts, Owen and architects adopted certain common innovations in warm air heating and fireproof construction. Technological 'transfer', through such bodies as the Birmingham Lunar Society and various learned societies was much faster than it is today. It was a common characteristic of Utopian, Rationalist and Utilitarian thinkers to leave no nut undesigned—hence Bentham's Panopticon designs of 1787-1791 include every detail of sanitation, listening tubes and iron construction. David Stow's Glasgow model school even had specifications for the kinds of flowers to be planted in the beds in the playground and the teaching 'gallery' was drawn and dimensioned to the nearest half inch.

Other types not dealt with in the present essays were being 'invented' at the same time. They include town markets; towards the end of our period, railway stations and hotels; Mechanics' Institutes; art galleries and museums; and, of course, a highly specialised range of industrial buildings —mills, foundries, warehouses, dock buildings, canal structures—and hothouses and urban arcades. Whereas the period starts with a handful of types mostly based on the country house, the church or temple and a few derivatives such as guildhalls, it ends with dozens of new ones or older ones so transformed that they bear little resemblance to their functional predecessors. The typological explosion is an important mechanism for vastly increased specialisation of role and function in society.

In the development of types for these new functions a critical area for decision was the organisation of space. Many of the institutional buildings acquired great 'depth'—that is, there was a controlled sequence of penetration from street to inner spaces and the innermost—for instance the prison cell—was now often found ten or more 'layers' in. Moreover the portions of buildings for inmates, visitors and staff began to acquire characteristic structures—either tree-like and branching or connected by alternative routes to form rings. Typically changes in staff-inmate relationship can be seen in detailed planning too. For instance, in comparing the spatial structure of William Adam's Edinburgh Infirmary (1738) with that of the London Hospital (1752) and Manchester Royal Infirmary (1797) we can trace the development of *en filade* wards, partial corridor systems to a complete, double-banked corridor. The spatial maps (Figure 4) show the increasing freedom given in the choice of routes to the ward beds. Of

16

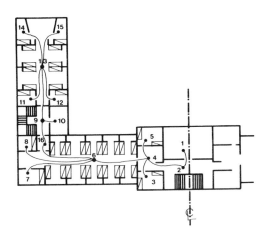

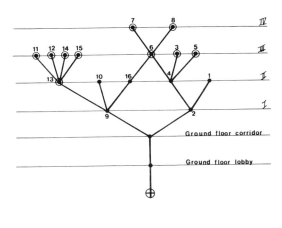

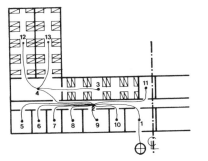

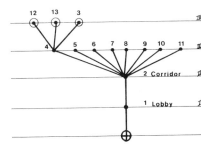

4   Schematic plans and space-
structure maps of three eighteenth
century hospital ward blocks,
  (a) Edinburgh Infirmary 1738
  (b) the London Hospital 1752
  (c) Manchester Infirmary
      1797.
The progression is from beds at
various layers, and great depth, to
beds at the deepest layer only
and decreasing depth. All space
with beds marked ⊙ and each map
starts at lobby on the same floor as
all the spaces, although spaces
further 'out' are also indicated.
Detailed plans given in 1.4, 1.11
and 1.13.

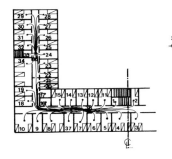

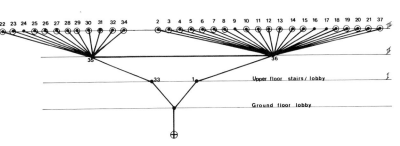

17

5 *Schematic plan of a Panopticon prison (e.g., Edinburgh Bridewell) and space-structure map, showing connection from central inspection tower (1) to exercise yard inspection tower (13) by underground tunnel. Detailed plans given in Figures 1.51 to 1.55.*

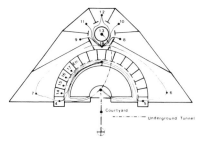

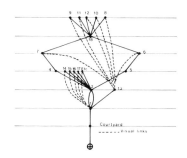

course, as the relevant essay points out, part of the change can be accounted for in terms of increased emphasis on preventing cross infection.

Some of the most interesting and recurring spatial structures are seen on analysis of very dissimilar buildings. For instance my essay on institutional buildings shows several examples of prisons and asylums where the need to have continuous central surveillance both in the outdoor exercise yards and within the main building resulted in centrally located outdoor watch towers, approached by a separate *underground* route from the inspection zone of the main building which crosses the yards themselves but makes, topologically, a direct and separate connection between the outdoor and indoor inspection points. This connection appears on the map (Figure 5). In some of the most prestigious housing in Edinburgh New Town a similar phenomenon occurs. In the squares there were central gardens, which were privately owned by the residents. Therefore entering the square from one of the streets and continuing round its sides on public space, one was surrounded on both sides by private property—on one side, of individual persons, on the other, by shared property in which each of the same individuals had a stake. No more powerful spatial arrangement for emphasising proprietorial rights could be imagined; for it is unlike the experience of the ordinary street where the houses on each side belong to *different* individuals and proprietorial rights in space are more distributed.

18

Greater emphasis could be given only by making a direct and separate link between the two private spaces to cross the public street in a way which, topologically, was direct. This could only be by a change in level—such as an underground tunnel analogous to those in the prisons and asylums. This is precisely what is found in at least one example—not a square but a street—Queen Street on the northern boundary—where a house had a tunnel to connect its servants' basement to the private ground on the other side of the street.[27]

Another method of emphasis was to use 'embedment' of the less significant or more startling features behind or within conventional forms. This can be seen in the location of the small houses probably intended for artisans and tradespeople in Craig's plan (Figure 6) and in the placing of the cell blocks in Adam's Bridewell and in the designs by all three competitors for Glasgow's new jail. Such 'embedment' can be described both formally and spatially.

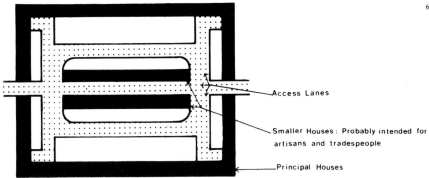

Access Lanes

Smaller Houses: Probably intended for artisans and tradespeople

Principal Houses

6 *'Embedment' of the small houses probably intended for artisans and trades people within the principal houses in Craig's Edinburgh New Town. Schematic plan of one block. Detailed plan given in 2.1.*

It is rewarding to examine the principles of order applied to natural and man-made landscape. In Craig's Edinburgh New Town design for example the entire scheme was bounded and set in a broader landscape of the valley and Castle Rock on the south and the Firth of Forth and Fife on the north. In this sense, perhaps, the Poussin analogy applies; but certainly not to the town itself, with its rigid forms and gardens in geometrical shapes. Gradually however, as Peter Reed shows, landscape was treated in a looser, more picturesque way, especially as the development spread around Calton Hill and the marked change in topography made it necessary to change the whole approach. The architect most influential in this was William Stark who in 1813, just before he died, wrote the report which recommended a radically new approach to the layout of streets and the use of natural features and of topographical formations. It was his ideas

19

which influenced the next phase of the development by Playfair. There is evidence that Stark was undergoing a profound personal revolution in the last few years of his life. In my essay on asylums and other building types I show how in the last six years of his life Stark designed three asylums. The first for Glasgow in 1807 (not built till later); the second for Gloucester in 1811 and the third for Dundee in 1812. The Glasgow scheme was a rigid, hierarchically classified, four-armed radial scheme with complete and continuous central surveillance. Tuke and others likened it to a prison. The Gloucester scheme had a crescent-shaped front wing for paying patients and a straight, rearward projecting, pauper wing, but central inspection and hierarchical classification was abandoned. The Dundee scheme was single-story over most of its area; it had the cottage image and Stark is supposed to have modelled it on the idea of a farm. It was permeated by gardens throughout. Although Stark had been a strict classicist in his architecture, as for instance in his Glasgow University Hunterian Museum, it seems that during his experience of applying the most rigid formal and spatial ordering principles to large institutions he shifted his view towards the romantic and picturesque in both landscape and buildings.

The new emphasis on the cottage, the farm and rural idyll contained the seeds of a gross sentimentality which, in the case of asylums for instance, was used as a new method of control in place of physical force and harsh discipline. Stow also had the view of the Scottish peasant as being heroically sturdy and peaceful and his aim in the urban school for the children of the working class was to re-create an environment with the quality of rural order and to create citizens with the virtues of the peasant. Andrew Noble's essay shows that at the same time the *literati* were busy creating a similar historically rooted image of the country and the peasant stock. The idea of gardens, self-sufficiency, farming and landscape formed a central part even of such mechanistic Utopias as Robert Owen's Villages of Unity and Mutual Co-operation. The use of the rural image combined fruitful productivity, stability and retreat and was to permeate much of the garden city and New Town movements in nineteenth and twentieth century British planning.

It is perhaps the relationship of Scottish Enlightenment and industrial innovation to English Romanticism which highlights the essential features of the pervasive drive to order. Andrew Noble shows the fierce attack by both Whig and Tory writers and literary organs on Wordsworth, Coleridge and others. This arose from the conjunction of rationalism, Calvinism, sentimentality and, above all, an obsessional fear of the release of inner forces which might present a challenge to a social structure built on developing capital. It was an attack *outwards*, from Scotland to England. But as has been mentioned, another, and reverse attack was proceeding. This was by the same English Romantics on a variety of utilitarian and mechanistic systems in industry, education and philosophy—notably Robert Owen's New Lanark and socialist utopianism. The Scottish educated character is often parodied as for instance when, later, Dickens gives a Scottish name, McChoakumchild, to his pupil teacher who had been ' . . . turned at the same time, (as one hundred and forty others) in the same factory, on the same principles, like so many pianoforte legs . . . ' and who had 'at the ends of his ten chilled fingers . . . Orthography, etymology, syntax and prosody, biography, astronomy, geography, and general cosmography, the sciences of compound proportion, algebra, land surveying and levelling, vocal music, and drawing from models'[28] In fact everything but humanity. This was the attack *inwards*, into Scotland, but the battle lines were the same. The issue was whether the stable institutions of state, religion and classical art, forming an alliance with new modes of production, could offer scope for personal development and freedom or whether these systems were increasingly suppressive by placing on society a great load of utility, reason, science and technology, backed by forces of law and order. At the end of my essay dealing with, amongst other issues, prisons, I suggest that in architecture and planning one has to see the creation of superstructures of order as products designed, like Boullée's Palace of Justice, to sit on an underworld. But this underworld, unlike his, should not be read as one of vice, but of human feeling and spiritual growth, inevitably rooted in conflict and apparent chaos. I use Piranesi's *Carceri* etchings to make the point; his were inventions that express the antithesis within architecture itself—that is that its search for order and light suppresses a darkness which contains a deeper order of nature and human personality and thus makes it the inevitable and tragic ally, except at rare moments, of those forces which oppose individual freedom by society's order. Insofar as this process can be seen at work in the Scottish Enlightenment we shall gain an insight into architecture itself.

REFERENCES

1. Kaufmann, Emil, *Architecture in the Age of Reason; Baroque and Post-Baroque in England, Italy and France,* New York, 1968, reprint of first edition, Cambridge, Massachusetts, 1955.

2. Daiches, David, *The Paradox of Scottish Culture,* London, 1964.

3. Lenman, Bruce, *Integration, Enlightenment, and Industrialisation,* London, 1981, p. 25.

4. Stewart, John B., *The Moral and Political Philosophy of David Hume,* New York and London, 1963.

5. Smith, Adam, *The Wealth of Nations,* Andrew Skinner, Ed., London, 1979, p. 281.

6. Hobsbawm, E.J., From Social History to the History of Society, in Flinn, M.W. and Smout, T.C., Eds, *Essays in Social History,* Oxford, 1974.

7. Girouard, Mark, *Life in the English Country House,* New Haven, 1978.

8. Evans, Robin, *The Fabrication of Virtue; English Prison Architecture 1750-1840,* Cambridge (forthcoming 1982).

9. King, A.D., Ed., *Buildings and Society; Essays on the Social Development of the Built Environment,* London, 1980.

10. Rykwert, J., *The Idea of a Town,* London, 1976; and *The First Moderns—the Architects of the Eighteenth Century,* Cambridge, Massachusetts and London, 1980.

11. Thompson, J.D. and Goldin, G., *The Hospital: A Social and Architectural History,* New Haven and London, 1975.

12. Jetter, Dieter, *Geschichte des Hospitals,* Wiesbaden, Vol. 1. Westdeutschland von den Anfängen bis 1850, 1966; Vol. 2. Zur Typologie des Irrenhauses in Frankreich und Deutschland (1780-1840), 1971; Vol. 3. Nordamerika (1600-1776) (Kolonialzeit), 1972.

13. Choay, Francoise, *L'Urbanisme, Utopies et Réalités: Une Anthologie,* Paris, 1965.

14. Demengeon, A. and Fortier, B., The Politics of Urban Space, *Architectural Design,* Nos. 8-9, 1978, pp. 8-13.

15. Teyssot, G., Citta-servizi; La Produzione dei Bâtiments Civils in Francia (1795-1848), *Casabella,* 424, April 1977, pp 56-65.

16. Vidler, A., Architecture, Management and Morals, *Lotus International,* 14, March, 1977.

17. For instance Vidler, A., The Idea of Type; and Porphyrios, D., The End of 'Styles', *Oppositions,* 8, Spring 1977.

18. Alexander, C.A., *A Pattern Language*, New York, 1977.

19. Hillier, W.R.G., *The Social Logic of Space*, Cambridge (in the press 1982).

20. Williams, Raymond, *The Country and the City*, London, 1973.

21. Rykwert, J., The Idea of a Town, from *Lectura Architectonica* pub. by G. van Saane, Hilversum (distributors in the UK., St. George's Gallery, London), 1963.

22. See for instance: Butt, J., Ed., *Robert Owen, Prince of Cotton Spinners*, London, 1971; and Silver, H., Ed., *Robert Owen on Education*, Cambridge, 1969.

23. Noble, Andrew, *English Romanticism and Robert Owen's New Lanark*, unpublished essay, 1980.

24. Thompson, E.P., Time, Work-discipline, and Industrial Capitalism, in Flinn and Smout, op. cit.

25. Rosenau, Helen, *Boullée and Visionary Architecture, including Boullée's 'Architecture, Essay on Art'*, London and New York, 1976, p. 98.

26. Smithers, H., *Liverpool, its Commerce, Statistics etc.*, Liverpool, 1825, p. 74.

27. The Royal Commission on the Ancient Monuments of Scotland, *An Inventory of the Ancient and Historical Monuments of the City of Edinburgh with the Thirteenth Report of the Commission*, HMSO, Edinburgh, 1951, p. 198, referring to No. 8 Queen Street.

28. Dickens, Charles, *Hard Times*, London, 1853.

Buildings for the Sad, the Bad and the Mad in Urban Scotland, 1780-1830

Thomas A. Markus

The half century span of the title embraces the political, social and technological changes which largely shape European society today. It was the period of the 'dual Revolution'—the French and the Industrial Revolutions. Both of them brought in their wake upheavals of social structure of the most profound kind. The completion of land enclosures; the rise of the factory system; the innovations of power sources, machines and transport; the ascendancy of the middle class in France and of the new entrepreneurial class in Britain; the foundation of working class movements; and the growth of social welfare legislation in Britain—all these inevitably were accompanied by a new dynamic. The difficulty in controlling the direction of these movements, and predicting their consequences, made it natural for the conservative elements to seek stability by increased emphasis on order. The opening year of this period saw the Gordon Riots in London when mobs temporarily gained control and were only suppressed with great loss of life. The French Revolution nine years later showed the whole of Europe the immense power which such mobs could wield and gave rise to new fears and a demand for instruments of control against radical movements, which can be seen at work during and immediately after the Napoleonic wars. And certainly, in England at least, there was plenty of evidence of the pent-up forces—the Spa Fields Riots in 1812, the outbreaks of workers' risings in Lancashire and Yorkshire, the Peterloo massacre in Manchester in 1819; the continuous Luddite machine-breaking in town and country—all these indicated the presence of a wide and deep disorder which was channelled and controlled by a combination of liberal reform, repression, philanthropy and economic development.

The persuasive and long tradition of Whig Scottish historical writing makes it difficult even today to establish whether Scotland was, as is implied by that writing, really less prone to these popular disturbances than England and, if so, whether that was due to lower expectations, to better conditions in some respects or to a more authoritarian social tradition. On the one hand Smout, whilst he describes how, as soon as Tom Paine's *The Rights of Man* was banned by the Government in 1792, its sales in various parts of Scotland rocketed, ascribes the urban riots in Aberdeen, Perth, Dundee and Lanark to specific land or industrial issues rather than to the contemporary view of their cause as 'an almost universal spirit of reform and opposition to the established government and legal administrators which has wonderfully diffused through the manufacturing towns'.[1] And it seems to be generally agreed that the three Conventions of the Friends of the People in 1792 and 1793 attracted little genuine working class support, even though the middle ranks of society from which their support came did not prevent the Braxfield trials from reaching corrupt convictions and passing fierce sentences. On the other hand Logue[2] has described riots not dissimilar in their causes and nature from those in England. Perhaps on account of the effectiveness of the post-1745 repressions and of the suppression of radical movements at their earliest stages, and hence the delay in the emergence of organised urban or rural working class movements, Scotland gave the *appearance* of relative quiet. Nevertheless the image of the French Revolution, the sporadic riots in Scotland and the much publicised ones south of the Border, the Napoleonic wars and their economic and social repercussions, the miseries of the rural poor dispossessed by land enclosure and the rapid rate of urbanisation in the last quarter of the century all caused considerable nervousness. This fear was not only manifested in the political, educational, literary and architectural forces which are central themes in several of these essays, but also, more specifically relevant to this essay, in the passing of a host of Acts and Town Council resolutions concerning prisons, Bridewells and the police. At the same time philanthropy, advances in medicine and fear of the spread of contagious and infectious diseases became united in a significant effort to cope with physical and mental illness by means of institutional care.

Physical, moral and mental disorder—that is the disintegration of the personality in its various aspects—represented, in microcosm and symbolic form, disorder in society itself. Although religion, law—including Scotland's own Poor Laws[3]—science and the power of reason as the main tool of the Enlightenment were the primary mechanisms of control, buildings for institutional care and restraint were the concrete instruments of these invisible mechanisms. First, they were able to convey in their style and physiognomic, expressive form images which linked these enterprises to the Classical tradition of learning and order; or sometimes, as in Adam's Edinburgh Bridewell, to the more Scottish imagery of castle, baronial supremacy and a suggestion of validation by reference to mediaeval ecclesiastical forms. Second, these buildings served vast numbers of inmates, through régimes completely new in their size and degree of organisation and this required completely new functional programmes. Third, the organisation of space in and around these buildings had to map the social relationships between two sub-sets of society—the inmates and the custodians—and society itself, as present in the surrounding city. So their forms, functions and spatial structures are capable of analysis in terms of the relationships and order in society.

In other essays we shall see how eighteenth and nineteenth century Glasgow and Edinburgh in their middle class housing created what might be interpreted as monuments to stable order in contrast to the rural disruptions which surrounded the cities and the rising tide of urban squalor and deprivation which was embedded within them. In parallel the great institutional monuments can be seen as not dissimilar but more explicit statements of the essential ingredients of order: visibility, light, classification, unity and clear, stable boundaries. The presence of disease, crime and madness throughout the city, invisible, diffused and undifferentiated within it, was threatening and unacceptable. The application of legal constraints, clinical experiments and even philanthropic aid required their subjects to be observable, available, concentrated and in a setting where these processes would be seen as part of the total institutional framework. Also, the professions and the Enlightenment conscience required their own 'laboratories' in which law, medicine and philanthropy could obtain the subjects for their fulfilment: Elizabeth Fry needed the female wards of Dance's Newgate prison as much as the wretched inmates in them needed her ministrations.

The bringing of order into the organisation and buildings of these total institutions is the Enlightenment's way of continuing the tradition of Utopian design based on cosmic and ideological concepts,[4] which had its roots in the Roman Vitruvian model city, re-interpreted in various Neoplatonic forms in the fifteenth and sixteenth centuries such as Filarete's Sforzinda and military towns such as Palmanova. The Neoplatonic ideas of institutions had been kept alive in the middle ages by Augustine's City of God and City of Man, the unification of which here on earth seemed to be the aim of such great monastic settlements as St. Gall. The tradition was continued in the sixteenth and seventeenth century secular and hermetic Utopias such as Doni's and Campanella's in which the physical form was always a centric, radial city with a church or domed secular 'temple'[5] at its centre, into the eighteenth century ideal industrial city such as Ledoux's Chaux[6] and finally into the emerging nineteenth century schemes such as Robert Owen's 'Villages of Unity and Mutual Co-operation'[7] and his ideal factory towns.[8] The shift was from community, defence and philosophical or theological microcosmos, to production, idealised housing and social welfare of a more or less radical kind. The unifying thread throughout the middle ages and Renaissance was the institution—a vehicle which in a special way always allows the imagination freedom to invent a new world within which a pure structure of healing or moral improvement could evolve isolated, as it were, from the contaminating disorder of urban reality. So mediaeval and later prisons, hospitals and leper-, plague-, and pest-houses were designed in a manner which shared forms with the ideal town plans, using a variety of greek-cross, courtyard, radial and pavilion plans, enclosed by walls and moats, entered through a few gates, and often located at the edges of the town.[9] It was these same forms which the Enlightenment took up, in the name of scientific and rational order, for its own institutional buildings and the tradition upon which it was able to build was already rich in both executed and imaginary public schemes.

Developers were realising another kind of perfect order in new housing forms for middle class professionals and merchants, as in Bath and Edinburgh's New Town. In the former, as in some later spas, the town was a new invention, catering mainly for leisure and fostering social connections, including marriage, and was seasonal in use. In the latter the intention was to separate from the existing Old Town, a zone of order, luxury and visible status for the permanent use of the ruling élite. Here at first there were no businesses, shops or markets[10]—simply an intention of calm purity. One way of achieving it was to establish a fresh and separate settlement on a hill, strongly contrasting with the dense disorder of the Old Town. Another was to purify the existing society by removing from it those elements which most tended to chaos and which, through the systems of law, reason and philanthropy, most required help or correction. The three types of institution to cater for them—the hospital, prison and asylum—had developed the variety of grand and complex models, already mentioned and described below, which were capable of being developed into the new, 'pure' forms. In Scotland it was, characteristically, science and medicine coupled to philanthropic charity which gave the impetus for the first specialised, functional type—a hospital—in Edinburgh.[11]

Edinburgh had a long established Incorporation of Surgeons, which was first given recognition in 1505. Surgeons, apothecaries and barbers were at first in a single group, to be gradually separated. The surgeons erected the Surgeons' Hall (Figure 1.1) in 1697, of which a part still exists. They were traditionally in conflict with the physicians the setting-up of whose College they opposed; this was however finally achieved in 1681, when the physicians in turn received their Royal Charter, though they were specifically debarred from setting up their own medical school. The difference in the approach and tradition of the two groups can be summarised briefly: the surgeons were primarily practical, apprenticed empirical men; the physicians prided themselves on a theoretical, abstract approach, with practical training as a subsequent stage of formation.

The art of anatomy as the theoretical basis of medicine was advanced by the physicians who modelled their teaching from the beginning of the eighteenth century on that at Leyden where, under Boerhaave who had arrived in 1701, a world centre of medical education was established. The

1.1 *Surgeons' Hall, Edinburgh, 1697.*

A Perspective View of the Surgeons Hall

links between Scotland and Holland were strong and it was not therefore surprising that the Leyden example should become the model for the Edinburgh physicians. They worked for the incorporation of medicine as a University subject, a goal which they achieved with the appointment of Alexander Munro as the first Professor of Anatomy in the City and Town's College in 1722 and his confirmation in a Chair by the University. By 1726 medical teaching had become incorporated into the University structure and became one of its strengths, drawing students from every part of Europe. The relative fortunes of the physicians and surgeons was changing and by 1729 a small teaching hospital was opened in a converted house in Robertson's Close, off Cowgate, with four beds, a resident housekeeper and servant, mainly on the initiative of the College of Physicians although a few surgeons did play a part in its establishment. McGill, an Edinburgh architect, was responsible for the conversion. The surgeons in turn set up their own hospital in College Wynd, again on a small scale with six beds, in 1736 in which year the Infirmary received its Royal Charter. It would appear that the rivalry between the physicians and the surgeons was resolved, temporarily at least, by their agreeing to join in the venture to build a new Royal Infirmary for which, in 1738, William Adam—father of John, Robert, James and William—was appointed architect. The project for the Infirmary resulted from the coincidence of the medical pressures described and Lord Provost George Drummond's vision of a new Edinburgh. Lord Provost six times, during which the New Town proposals were formulated, Drummond also pressed for the development of the Town's College (later the University), many public buildings, bridges and parks.

Before this agreement was reached the surgeons decided to build their own new hospital and a scheme was submitted to the Dean of Guild and approved in 1738. The drawings may be by William Adam (Figure 1.2).[12]

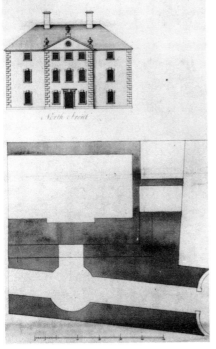
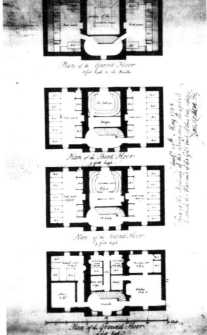

1.2 *Proposed Surgeons' Hospital, Edinburgh, 1738; architect William Adam,*
   (a) site plan and front elevation
   (b) floor plans.

29

They show a compactly planned building with wards around a central space in which the surgical theatre is located, opening directly off the surgeons' council room. The scheme may have been devised more as a bargaining tool than as a realistic proposal—in any case it was abandoned.

William Adam as far back as 1727 started the project for publishing a collection of his designs by subscription. However it was only in 1810, long after his death in 1748, that this, the *Vitruvius Scoticus* was realised and included designs by one of his sons, John. However, by the 1730s Adam was well known, especially for his country house designs. As William Edgar's plan of 1742 (Figure 1.3) shows, the new Royal Infirmary was built just within the 1513 town wall between the College and the Surgeons' Hall on a site acquired in 1737 from George Watson's Hospital. Adam adopted a straightforward U plan—a simple enough solution, it might be thought, where the site was limited and where it was desired to avoid the evils of enclosed courtyards, with their lack of ventilation; this was a problem for which some of the older London hospitals were by now being severely

1.3 *Edinburgh Royal Infirmary; site plan from William Edgar's plan, 1742.*

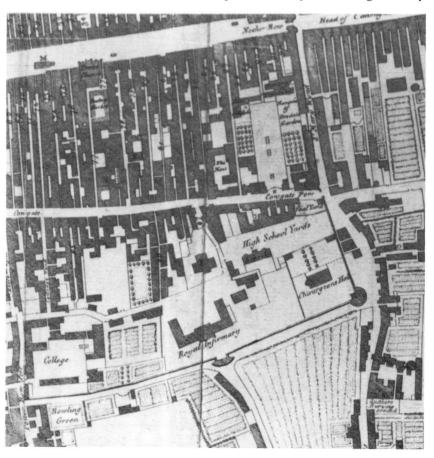

30

criticised. Yet the use of this U form for a hospital (Figures 1.4 and 1.5) was, as we shall see, quite original in Britain; it really brought together the Palladian country house with certain military and utilitarian buildings. He must have worked quickly for, though '. . . many plans were presented to the Managers' the foundation stone was laid in 1738; the first patients were admitted in 1741 and the project was complete by 1748.

He was asked to make the building '. . . solid and erected of the most durable materials, not slovenly yet that very little or no expense should be paid in useless ornament'.[13] He made no professional charges and Dunbar-Nasmith suggests that he was not put off by this rather restrictive brief because a group of subscribers also made it a condition that their contribution go towards '. . . making the central block more dignified and attractive to the eye'.

Adam knew London well and may have been informed of Continental precedents so before describing the building it is worth seeking the possible influences of earlier hospitals and institutions against which he may have been reacting. The mediaeval tradition of both monastic and public infirmaries was of long 'naves', with beds ranged along the long walls, and an altar at one or both ends for observation of daily Mass.[14] Often this would serve a double purpose of infirmary and church altar, with the church and hospital axes pivoted on the same point at 90° or 180°. The greek-cross plan with a central altar or church was an extension of the principle, and was widely popularised by Filarete's design for his hospital for the ideal town of Sforzinda; it consisted of two greek-crosses with central altars and a central church in the courtyard between them (Figure 1.6). It was designed between 1461 and 1465 and actually built as the Ospedale Maggiore in Milan; the central church was moved to the rear, but still on one of the two major axes.[15] Thus his design established several important spatial and formal principles. First, the use of symmetry as signifying not only a formal desire for balance and unity but as symbolising the totality of human society—for one side was for men, the other for women. Second, the centre, without and above gender, represented cosmic unity. Third, the few entrances were located on the two major and two minor axes. Fourth, the whole was firmly bounded by what was effectively a moated wall; and finally, the sequence of spaces from street to patient was through a series of public rooms or courts, then offices and staff quarters and finally the wards in the crosses. In Hillier's sense the inmate was at the 'deepest' point of the plan structure, even though he may have been, in later schemes, physically adjacent to an outside wall.[16]

Combinations of such greek-crosses, with linking courts, and finally spoked radial plans were developed in the sixteenth, seventeenth and eighteenth centuries.

The British tradition during that period and up to the 1720s was less absolutist and less heavily loaded with cosmic imagery. The post-Reformation London Royal hospitals which preceded the eighteenth

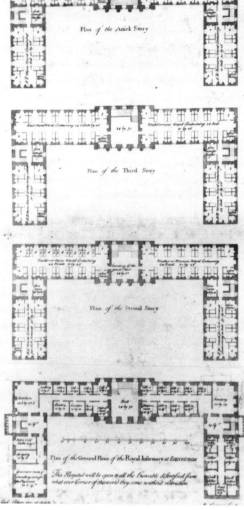

1.4 *Edinburgh Royal Infirmary,*
1738; architect William Adam,
floor plans.

1.5 *Edinburgh Royal Infirmary, front*
elevation.

The North Front of the Royal Infirmary facing the City of Edinburgh

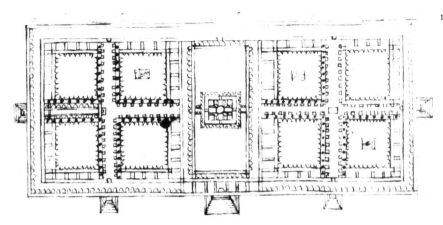

1.6 *Filarete, Hospital for Sforzinda,*
1461-1465, plan.

century voluntary hospitals were based on courts. St. Thomas's developed
as a complex of courts, started in the sixteenth century and substantially
altered and added to in the seventeenth. St Bartholomew's, designed by
James Gibbs in 1729 (Figure 1.7), was a late example of the courtyard plan
although here, under the influence of ventilation 'theorists' it was formed
of four independent blocks. The only other major hospital was the
Bethlehem hospital for lunatics, which survived the Reformation but was
rebuilt in Moorfields in 1676 (to be followed by London's other major
asylum, St. Luke's, founded in 1751 and re-housed in new buildings by
George Dance the Younger in 1786).

Guy's, a voluntary hospital set up in 1722, followed the same court
pattern; it is usually however not classed as a genuine voluntary hospital
since its funding was almost entirely from the wealth of a single individual,
Thomas Guy who was a governor of St. Thomas's and founded his own
hospital of four hundred and thirty-five beds, to cater for the chronic sick
and, perhaps, lunatics. It is interesting to note that the main entrances of
both Guy's and Bart's (Figures 1.8 and 1.9) consisted of a pedimented
'temple' front, with major orders rising through two or three floors, set
upon a heavily rusticated base. This feature recurs in numerous Scottish
hospitals and other institutions. It can be read as the application to public
institutions of the temple, villa and palazzo ideal plane—the analogue of
the Acropolis platform or base of earth, rock and reality, upon which the
pure and abstract new start can be made.

The first genuine, public subscription voluntary hospital in Britain was
probably the Westminster, founded in 1720 and accommodated in a
converted house; from dissensions and factions amongst its managers
grew both St. George's, founded in 1733 in a converted house in Hyde
Park Corner, and the London Hospital, founded in 1740 but with no
purpose-built building till 1752. In the English provinces too a number of
voluntary hospitals were established in the first decades of the century, but
initially in converted houses.

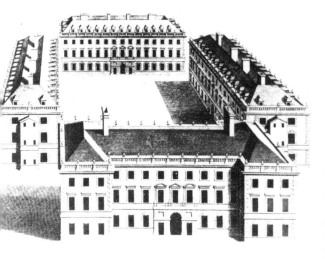

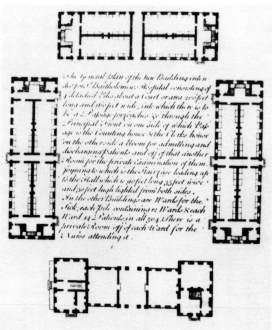

1.7 *St Bartholomew's Hospital,*
London 1729; architect James
Gibbs,
   (a) bird's eye view
   (b) ground floor plan.

Adam may also have seen Wren's prophetic design (1696-1702) for Greenwich Hospital,[17] which was never built in that pavilion form and which became so favoured amongst French Academicians, doctors and scientists in the last quarter of the eighteenth century and was executed hundreds of times during the nineteenth. But as for his own solution for Edinburgh Infirmary this represented scientific functionalism and order in a more modest way, and his rejection of the grander Continental and pragmatic English plans is itself innovatory.

The four floors contained a total of two hundred and twenty-eight ward beds, symmetrically disposed around the central axis for men and women, together with a further sixty in the 'garrets'. The ground floor had various offices and twelve 'cells' for lunatics which by 1778 had been converted to other uses as had the garret since it could not be properly heated. The first and second floors had medical wards, whilst the third ('attic') contained surgical and lying wards, the former located on either side of the great central operating theatre, so that patients did not have to be moved up and down stairs. This theatre was covered by a dome and it could accommodate over two hundred spectating students and '. . . is also a convenient *Chapel'.*[18] The cupola was designed also to be usable 'sometimes' as an astronomical observatory. This combination of practical, clinical function, religious worship and cosmic science was a peculiarly Scottish Enlightenment response by Adam to the established European practice of locating a church, chapel or altar at the centre.

34

The 'distinct' beds for each patient in the wards were planned in pairs, probably separated by partitions, between the windows; behind each bed was '. . . a press (cupboard) at its head, for containing medicines, clothes, or other necessaries, belonging to the respective patients.'[19] The layout is not dissimilar from some of the recent, twentieth century designs, which have followed the so-called Nightingale wards of the nineteenth. Great attention was paid to ventilation by means of carefully located windows, doors, chimneys and staircases; and there was also 'artificial ventilation' to some of the less accessible spaces, probably in the form of fresh air ducts.

A little later than Adam's scheme in 1742 came the design by George Tully and/or William Halfpenny for Bristol Infirmary (Figure 1.10) also in the form of a shallow U; followed shortly by Boulton Mainwaring's similar 1752 scheme for the London Hospital (Figure 1.11). The London Hospital had corridors alongside the wards in the main block, and parallel wards, separated by a spine wall and separately entered in the two wings, unlike the Edinburgh plan where circulation was, except on the ground floor, *through* wards both in the main block and the wings. As shown in the Introduction to these essays, this is an important change in spatial structure.

The application of the U-plan to hospitals represents a step in the institutionalisation of medical practice and education. Fleming suggests that Adam's precedent lay in the Ordnance Board's barracks;[20] but it was also a form commonly used at this time for other institutional buildings such as 'poor', 'charity' and 'work' houses. Edinburgh's own Poor House (later Charity Workhouse) of 1740 was planned thus, although the two

1.8 *Guy's Hospital, London, 1722, main entrance.*

1.9 *St Bartholomew's Hospital, London, 1729, main entrance.*

35

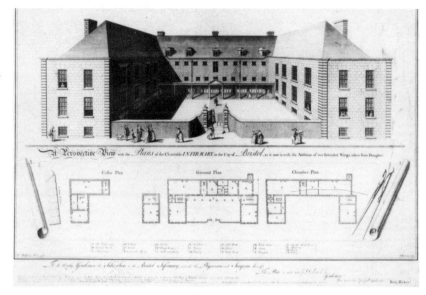

1.10 *Bristol Infirmary, 1742; architect George Tully and/or William Halfpenny.*

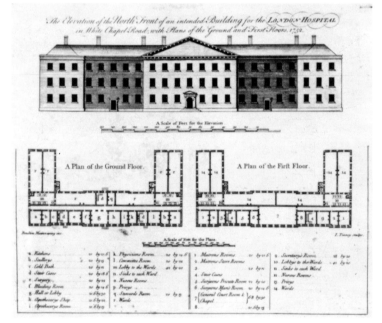

1.11 *The London Hospital, 1742; architect Boulton Mainwaring, front elevation and floor plans.*

wings were incomplete till about 1753 (Figure 1.12). We shall see that Glasgow's 1733 'Town's Hospital' had a similar plan with a 'reflection' to the rear, creating an H.

London Hospital and Adam's project became nationally and internationally known and copied, mainly through the medium of *medical* régimes which were admired and of which the built form was an accepted part. By the end of the eighteenth century some forty English and Scottish Infirmaries were established, many with Royal Charters, and most following the Edinburgh and London plan. A late example (1797) was

36

The Charity Work Houſe.

Manchester Royal Infirmary (Figure 1.13).

The Edinburgh 'medical' site developed for about one hundred years after the Infirmary was built. The High School, built in 1777, was converted to the Surgical Hospital in 1832 (when the school moved to Calton Hill) and still stands (now part of the University). The Surgeons' Hall was converted to a fever hospital and in 1853 David Bryce designed

1.12 Edinburgh Poor House (later Charity Work House) 1740, shown in 1753 engraving.

1.13 Manchester Royal Infirmary, 1797, upper floor plan.

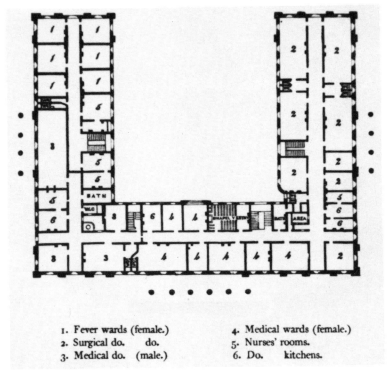

1. Fever wards (female.)
2. Surgical do.   do.
3. Medical do.   (male.)
4. Medical wards (female.)
5. Nurses' rooms.
6. Do.   kitchens.

the new surgical hospital as an extension to the old Surgical Hospital (old High School). Also at this time Lock (VD) and Burn Hospitals were added to the site. Finally the new Royal Infirmary, in Lauriston, was designed by Bryce in 1872.

Glasgow was some way behind Edinburgh both in medical achievement and hospital design, although it did set up a *joint* Faculty of Physicians and Surgeons as early as 1599. A 'Town's Hospital' (Figure 1.14) was founded in 1731 and built in 1733 on Clyde Street, near the site of the present Catholic Cathedral. It was a mixture of workhouse, hospital, lunatic asylum and poorhouse. Since most of its inmates were old, weak or sick, its function for productive work was never fulfilled. It was built by public subscription, both private and corporate. Amongst the subscribers were the Town Council, Merchants' House, Trades' House and the Kirk Session.[21] Members of the Glasgow Faculty gave their services free and probably taught apprentices and students. By 1766 there were only twenty beds in the Infirmary. The régime not only made Sunday services obligatory, but allowed '. . . liberty and encouragement to attend the several week-day sermons'.[22] Its planning organisation is not known in detail. Cleland[23] describes its plan as quadrangular, with a large court in the centre 'for an airing ground for paupers', and having a centre block with two three-storey projecting wings. The centre block contained the great hall where the inmates assembled for family worship, committee room and other charity offices. The buildings at the rear of the quadrangle had accommodation 'for the sick and fatuous' (mentally handicapped?); the lunatics were not removed to Stark's new Asylum till 1814. All eighteenth and early nineteenth century Glasgow maps show an H-shaped block, *behind* which an open court was formed by an L-shaped block and some plain rectangular ones (Figure 1.15). This is probably what Cleland refers to.[24]

The movement for a public, voluntary hospital gained ground in the 1780s; in 1787 the Magistrates and Council were debating the desirability of the project and themselves subscribed the funds for an infirmary '. . . for relief of the indigent in the west of Scotland labouring under diseases'.[25] A Royal Charter, obtained in 1791, emphasised the essentially philanthropic nature of the project: ' . . . for the relief of persons labouring under poverty and disease . . . more necessary at present than any former period, on account of the prosperous state of manufacturers in Glasgow and its neighbourhood, and the increased population of those classes of manufacturers and labourers of every kind, who are most likely to require charitable assistance'.[26] A site was acquired and architects appointed in 1792.

According to some accounts both Robert and James Adam were appointed as architects; but since Robert died in March 1792 there must be doubt about this and Bolton believes the drawings in the Soane Museum are probably by James.[27] In any case his (or their) design follows some of William's principles. It consisted of a single straight block, with a

1.14 *Glasgow Town's Hospital, 1733.*

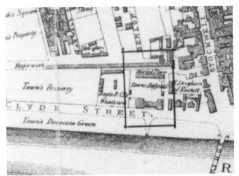

1.15 *Glasgow Town's Hospital shown on McArthur's 1778 map.*

pedimented projecting centre block, its major orders rising through two floors and projecting pavilions at each end whose windows rose through two floors. The whole was raised on a heavily rusticated base, and the centre capped by a substantial dome some 14 metres in diameter (Figure 1.16).

The accommodation was divided symmetrically, as usual, about the centre on the four floors according to sex. There were nineteen beds in each of the eight wards and under the domed central structure an operating theatre to seat two hundred, under which was a central Director's room. There was no chapel. On the ground floor, under the entrance floor, various offices were arranged along a double-banked corridor, as well as some 'cells' for lunatics. Whilst the exterior was far more elaborate and polished than that of the Edinburgh Infirmary, the interior planning had not really advanced much further in spite of the half century of experience which separated them.

In 1814-15 a north-facing ward block was added, shown in Figure 1.17, turning the building into a T; it contained offices for the matron and

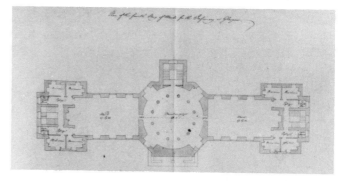

1.16 *Glasgow Infirmary 1792;*
architect(s) James (and Robert?)
Adam,
  (a) fourth floor plan
  (b) third floor plan
  (c) second floor plan
  (d) first ('entrance') floor plan
  (e) ground floor plan

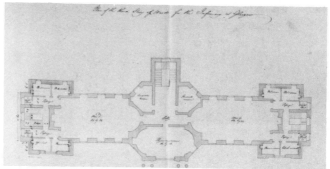

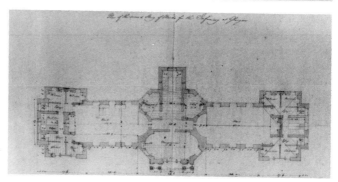

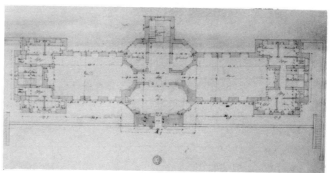

40

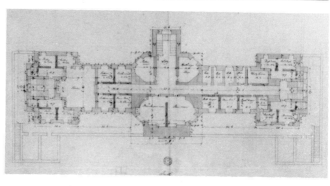

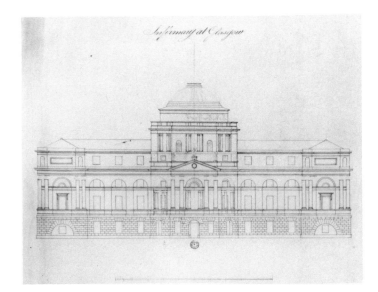

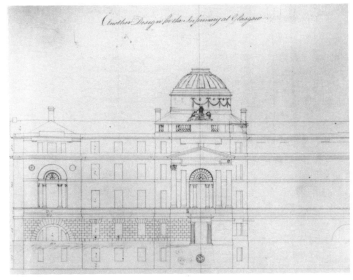

(f) elevation (as executed)
(g) alternative elevation
(h) exterior from 'Swan's Views'.

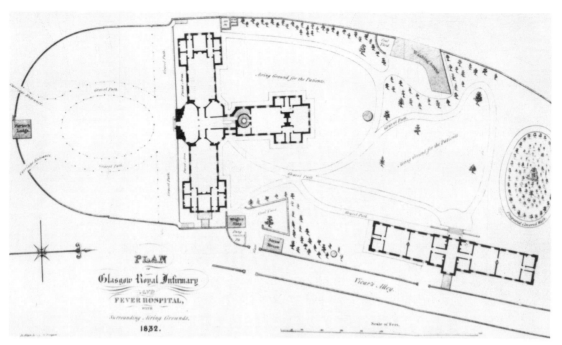

PLAN
of
Glasgow Royal Infirmary
AND
FEVER HOSPITAL,
with
Surrounding Airing Grounds.
1832.

1.17 Glasgow Infirmary, plan in 1832 showing added wing and Fever Hospital.

apothecary, and sleeping rooms for clerks and servants on the ground floor; on the four floors above a total of eighty new beds became available. The Figure also shows the Fever Hospital, built in 1825-26 for one hundred patients, (increased to two hundred and twenty in 1832); although it is later in date it reverts to the simpler institutional facade characteristic of the early eighteenth century, with a plain pedimented centre-piece on orders enclosing the upper three floors and standing on a projecting base of one and a half storeys.

As was the case in Edinburgh, for the same reasons, these buildings were demolished during the nineteenth century to make room for more substantial and medically advanced types. It is an interesting question, however, why in the half century since William Adam's scheme so little change in design standards had taken place. This was the period of greatest advance (on a theoretical plane at least, since no significant projects were *built*) in France and more widely on the Continent. In the 1770s and '80s the French Academy of Sciences, Tenon and others were developing a whole range of new pavilion types, in which diseases were classified by type in each pavilion, and enormous (claimed) advances in ventilation and sanitation were being made. These had been preceded by large radial projects—such as Petit's in 1774 and Poyet's in 1785 (Figures 1.18 and 1.19). Moreover from as far back as 1765 the naval hospital at Stonehouse, Plymouth, had been built on a pavilion plan; it was well known on both sides of the Channel, Tenon and Coulomb finding it the outstanding hospital in Europe at the time; Howard had also commented on it in 1782; and Durand included it in his panoramic catalogue of types in 1801. Of course it may be argued that the constrained site in Glasgow, and in other British cities which were building similar hospitals at the time, did not allow for a fully fledged radial or pavilion plan. But more

42

probably there was opposition to these types from the more pragmatically oriented English and Scottish physicians and surgeons whose clinical classification was based on practice rather than theory, and who seemed to reject the absolutist over-centralisation of the radial types. We shall see however that for lunatic asylums and for prisons, where surveillance was a more fundamental consideration, the radial and central forms *were* adopted at this time and predominated in Scotland, to the first quarter of the nineteenth century. In one case the same architect, Robert Adam, worked simultaneously on a centralised prison and a rectilinear hospital.

However, in another respect too Glasgow Infirmary was less developed than others—it had wards entered from one end, directly from a lobby or stairs, without any linking corridors—a planning change which had already taken place, as we have seen, in the fourteen years between the designs for Edinburgh Infirmary and the London Hospital. There were of course still arguments on both sides; the corridor-less type involved circulation through wards by both staff and patients from other wards. The plans with corridors certainly allowed more separation of patients, but provided an air channel for the transmission of infection. It was precisely to overcome this conflict that later the pavilion type became so favoured.

It was not for the physically but for the mentally sick that plans were invented during this period that carried a much greater weight of formal classification and surveillance. Before, however, considering the earliest lunatic asylums in Scotland we have to turn to the penal institutions, first because the forms and ideas found in the asylums sprang from these and second because there was in the eighteenth century, as indeed there is today, a good deal of confusion between assessment of moral and social culpability, which was punishable, and of mental sickness, which was treatable albeit sometimes compulsorily. But a class of 'defect' which overlapped lunacy and crime was that of poverty—especially idle poverty.

The sixteenth century saw the establishment of laws and institutions to cope with the increasing number of vagrants, petty criminals, paupers, beggars and homeless—and, as Evans[28] points out, a link was made for the first time between systematic labour and morality. Idleness was considered to arise from old age, sickness or thriftlessness. Provision was made for the first two in almshouses and hospitals; the third were to be sent to Bridewell, the palace originally built by Henry VIII in 1522 but shortly afterwards deserted and crumbling. Archbishop Ridley asked Edward VI to reopen the Bridewell Palace for the reception of the idle poor, to be engaged in productive work. Throughout the first half of the sixteenth century legislation to control and punish vagabonds and the idle was passed, culminating in the passing of an Act in 1576 which allowed Justices of the Peace to build Houses of Correction which were modelled on Bridewell, by now used for this purpose for almost twenty years. They were commonly referred to as 'Bridewells', even at the beginning of the nineteenth century. A London Quaker, John Bellers, in 1696 proposed raising the title of such an establishment to a 'Colledge of Industry'—'. . .

1.18 *Petit's radial hospital, 1774, plan.*

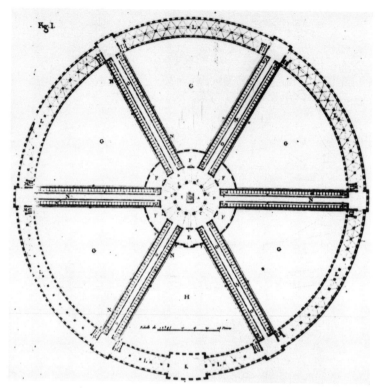

1.19 *Poyet's hospital for Paris, 1785,
block plan.*

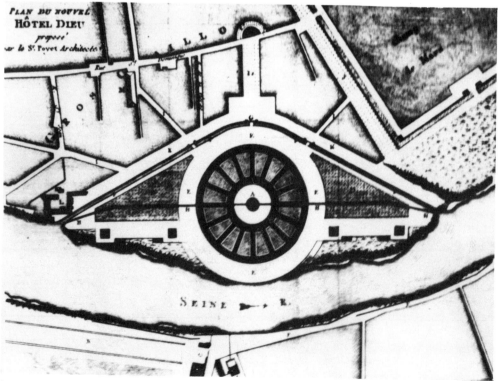

with profit to the rich, a plentiful living for the poor, and a good education for youth'! When Robert Owen was pressing upon Parliament his industrial Utopian 'Villages of Unity and Mutual Co-operation' in 1817 he reprinted Bellers' tract as a useful model[29] and the educational significance of this model is further discussed in essay 4. The Amsterdam Rasphuis (where the labour was, literally, wood-rasping), set up in 1595, was an early Continental institution of this kind.

Evans sees the conversion of the Bridewell Palace to workhouse as an 'ironic inversion'. But Jean Genet, in his *The Thief's Journal* sees the Royal Palace and the prison identical in their unity, splendour and symbolism.[30]

> Prison offers the same sense of security to the convict as does a Royal Palace to a King's guest. They are the two buildings constructed with the most faith, those which give the greatest certainty of being what they are—which are what they meant to be, and which remain. The masonry, the materials, the proportions and the architecture are in harmony with a moral unity which makes these dwellings indestructible so long as the social form of which they are the symbol endures. The prison surrounds me with a perfect guarantee. I am sure that it was constructed for me—along with the Law Court, its annex, its monumental vestibule. Everything therein was designed for me, in a spirit of the utmost seriousness. The rigour of the rules, their strictness, their precision, are in essence the same as the etiquette of a royal court, as the exquisite and tyrannical politeness of which a guest at that court is the object. The foundations of the palace, like those of the prison, inhere in the fine quality of the stone, in marble stairways, in real gold, in carvings, the rarest in the realm, in the absolute power of their hosts; but they are also similar in that these two structures are one the root and the other the crest of a living system circulating between these two poles which contain it, compress it and which are sheer force.

It is aspects of this unity and defined order which are striking in the Scottish penal buildings of the late eighteenth and early nineteenth centuries.

The sixteenth, seventeenth and eighteenth century legislation both in England and Scotland which dealt with vagrants, paupers and criminals gradually blurred the distinctions, so purpose-built Bridewells by the end of the eighteenth century house prisoners of various classes—but the offences for which they were sentenced were not felonies and they were almost without exception associated with forced work of some kind. But work, even if only on tread-wheels, was also becoming a feature of gaols.

Glasgow had its House of Correction 'for dissolute females', established under Scottish legislation, in 1635.[31] John McArthur's 1778 map (Figure 1.20) shows the Correction House and its garden. It was in a converted manse belonging to the Prebend of Douglas, on the south side of Drygate; in 1782 it was still used mainly for women who were held in two large rooms and provided with work.[32] By 1785 the magistrates had ordered substantial repairs and extensions to the 'town's workhouse' which was, it seems, the same building, including the addition of cells.[33] This House of Correction was now a legal institution for commitment of

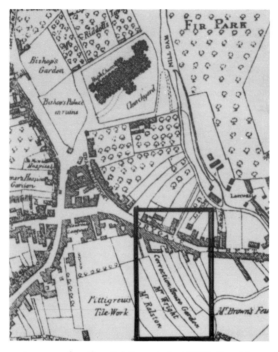

prisoners for 'hard labour'. In 1788 the Council approved the conversion
of the south side of the granaries near the mealmarket, leased from the
Town's College (University) into a Bridewell.[34] It initially contained
fourteen rooms, with two houses, one for a keeper and one for a person
who would provide and supervise the work for these 'idle and disorderly
persons'. All the rooms were for women and boys, but in the same year it
was decided to build cells for men.[35] But the problems were clearly
becoming too great for small institutions like the House of Correction, this
small *ad hoc* Bridewell, and the few cells for petty criminals that also
existed in the 1733 Town's Hospital in Clyde Street.[36] The Trades House
petitioned the Council in 1788 to provide a Bridewell 'upon an extensive
scale' and donations and bequests for it were already coming in from
merchants, such as James Coulter's £400.[37] In 1790 a 'memorial (from) a
number of very respectable citizens' was submitted to the magistrates and
Council for the establishment of a Bridewell, and a committee was set up
to examine the proposals.[38] Between 1792 and 1794 the Council had
decided to sell back to the College the granaries containing the small
Bridewell and adjacent land[39] and to purchase from the College other
lands for the erection of a Bridewell and barracks, all this activity of a penal
and military kind being given a great sense of urgency by the feared effects
of the French Revolution.

However it was found that the barracks would consume too much of the
land so the decision was made to build a new and substantial Bridewell in

46

the grounds of Drygate House of Correction to which were added certain other adjacent properties.[40] In 1795 the plans were still incomplete and the old mealmarket Bridewell's lease was extended by the College.[41] That same year the Council commissioned John Paterson to design the new Bridewell which initially had one hundred and twelve separate cells on six double-banked floors. Each floor was said to have twenty one cells, so two, and sometimes three cells on each floor must have been dedicated to keepers, offices and similar accommodation (Figure 1.21). The front and rear facades show simple centre-pedimented structures and *three* rows of apparent windows—these were however recesses in the masonry wall, with small window apertures at the top and bottom, thus each served two floors as shown by the section. This was a characteristic use of a classical window facade to camouflage the functional divisions behind. Heating was by ducted warm air from two central stoves and drainage was along the central spine corridor, collected at the two gable ends. A variant of the design of the same date, also by Paterson, exists but the differences are minute, and it is not known which was the executed scheme.[42]

William Horn, a member of the Council, later in the same year presented a design for extending the Bridewell by two projecting wings in front of the main block. This was accepted[43] and added to the main contract. A few months later he produced new plans, to accommodate the 'shape and situation of the ground'—suggesting a somewhat inadequate original survey![44] It is assumed that Horn's drawings (Figure 1.22) together with Paterson's earlier ones, represent the revised and executed design. With these additions the Bridewell now contained additional apartments, possibly the chapel and work rooms, almost doubling its original floor area. The two wings had turnpike stairs at the ends nearest the centre block. Horn had difficulty in being reimbursed for his design and supervision fees, but eventually the Council made him an *ex gratia* payment three years later.[45] The creation of the Bridewell followed immediately upon the laying out of George Street and Duke Street. The Town Council decided on this project in 1790[46] and an enabling Act of Parliament was passed in 1791.[47] The street(s) were first to be called Glasgow Street; but by 1794 the section east of High Street was re-named Duke Street.[48] Fleming's 1808 map (Figure 1.23) shows the completed U-shaped Bridewell. In 1821 James Cleland, surveyor, shows proposed additions: day (work) and night (sleeping) rooms, as well as a Governor's house (Figure 1.24), these developments presumably being considered desirable to bring the Bridewell into line with the 'separate system' which required night *and* day separation between prisoners, whilst still requiring work. This scheme was probably never executed as by this time legislation and plans for a completely new City and Lanark County Bridewell, considered later, were in hand.

Prisoners were received in the Bridewell in 1798 when the old meal-market building was finally abandoned for this purpose, although it was now re-used for its original purpose and the lease extended.[49] At the same

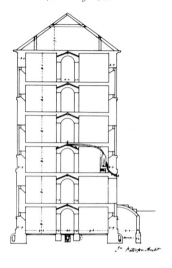

Nᵒ 3.
Section of A Bridewell for the City of Glasgow with Section of Drains and Warm air pipes for heating the Cells

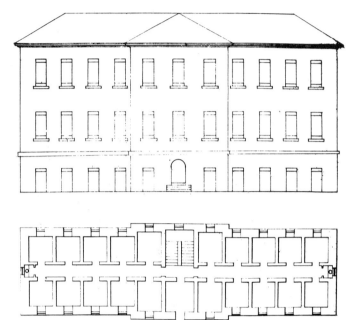

1.21 *Glasgow Bridewell 1795;*
architect John Paterson,
  (a) cross section
  (b) elevation
  (c) ground floor plan
  (d) plan with warm air ducts
  (e) drainage plan.

Second floor of A Bridewell for the City of Glasgow with the Furnaces and manner of laying the Warm air pipes for heating the Cells

North,

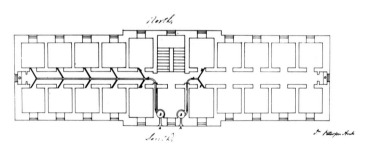

South,

Ground floor of A Bridewell for the City of Glasgow with the Plans of the Drains

North,

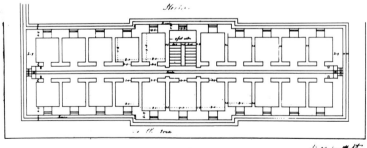

48

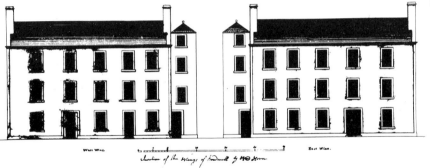

1.22 *Glasgow Bridewell, 1796;*
architect William Horn (second
design for extensions),
(a) elevations
(b) ground floor plan.

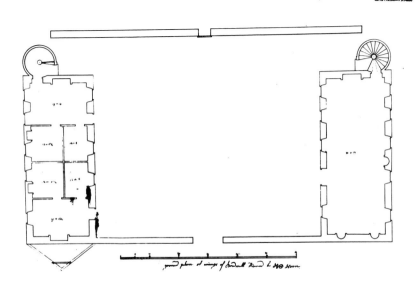

time legal proceedings were begun to declare the Bridewell a legal prison for felons (for whom the Tolbooth Jail, described below, was now inadequate) so that unused parts could be used for convicted criminals. In the same year the decision was made to close and dispose of the House of Correction. The petition for prison use was not successful till 1805.[50] Almost immediately pressure began for a new jail.[51]

The Old Tolbooth in Trongate Street (Figure 1.25) contained originally the Town Council Chamber, Dean of Guild Court, court hall, collectors' offices and related civic accommodation and was built in 1626 to replace the mediaeval 'Pretorium' (sic) on the north east corner of the Trongate, which had combined town hall, or court house and prison. The Tolbooth also had prisons entered by a stair in the steeple. The Town Hall in Trongate, designed by Allan Dreghorn and John Craig in 1737 and

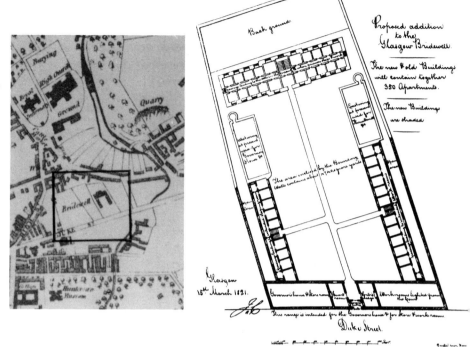

1.23 *Glasgow Bridewell shown on Fleming's 1808 map.*

1.24 *Cleland's proposed additions to Glasgow Bridewell, 1821, ground floor plan.*

completed in 1760, was first occupied in 1740 and the Justiciary Court was moved to an adjoining building in the High Street in 1795. The spaces thus vacated in the Old Tolbooth were converted to prison cells for felons and debtors. In 1796 there were eleven rooms for male debtors, ten cells for male criminals and six for women. It was this converted and insecure accommodation which had caused the magistrates to seek to take over part of the 1795 Bridewell and also, only ten years later, to start the movement for a completely new courthouse and jail.

Architects were to be sought, a site to be found and estimates obtained.[52] James Cleland, the City Surveyor, was sent on a journey to England and Ireland in 1808 to see the 'principal jails' and report back[53] and by the end of that year it was decided to build on a site in Saltmarket.[54] In 1809 three architects were asked to submit designs—Robert Reid and William Stark of Edinburgh (the latter having by then moved from Glasgow) and Glasgow's David Hamilton. Reid produced two designs, Hamilton three and Stark also produced two since the first was deemed to be 'upon too great a scale' and he responded by submitting a second scheme which was accepted.[55] In 1812 the old court, jail and public offices were ordered to be disposed of— they were in fact sold to Cleland for £8000 by public roup (auction) on the express stipulation that he would demolish and rebuild on the site a project designed by David Hamilton. Cleland was also appointed to supervise the erection of Stark's new building and published a detailed specification for its construction and materials.[56]

The drawings for Reid's and Hamilton's schemes exist, more or less intact. Those for Stark's second scheme have only partly survived,

50

1.25 *The Old Tolbooth and Steeple, Trongate, Glasgow (on right) and Dreghorn and Craig's Town Hall (on left).*

although some dating from 1814, by an unknown draftsman, also exist; none are known for his first design.

Reid's first design, (Figure 1.26) from 1809, shows a U-shaped block, with one wing departing from axial symmetry on account of the site; a central portico of Tuscan coupled columns in four pairs, rising through two floors approached by a broad flight of steps; council chambers and smaller courts on the ground floor, with the main court room on the first floor rising through to the second on the central axis. The end pavilions of the front block contain various offices on the upper two floors. The jail is divided into two main parts, on three floors—the debtors occupying the two rearward projecting wings, and the felons a separate straight block between the wings, with single-banked cells, a central keeper's room on the ground floor and chapel over it on the upper two floors, occupying the full depth of the block from front to rear. Each class of prisoner has a yard, symmetrically disposed on the axis, with the two felons' yards directly observable through windows from the keeper's room.

Reid's second design, of the same year (Figure 1.27) was far more elaborate, in both planning and in its two alternative elevations. The first had a front with a central dome and a smaller one over each end pavilion and was limited to two main floors. The second had three floors, with the upper two raised over a heavily rusticated base and with Ionic substituting for the earlier Tuscan. The plan consisted of a front block with symmetrical wings, containing on the ground floor the magistrates' court on the central axis, which was at right angles to the Clyde, and the main court above it, with smaller courts and legal offices on either side. Behind this was a

1.26 *Glasgow Judiciary Buildings;*
Robert Reid's first design, 1809,
  (a) elevation
  (b) first floor plan
  (c) ground floor plan.

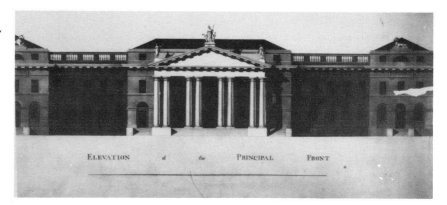

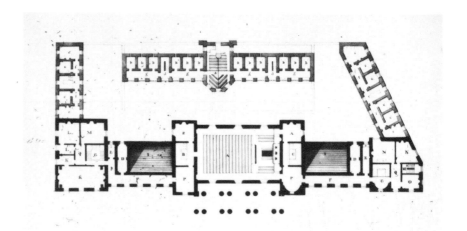

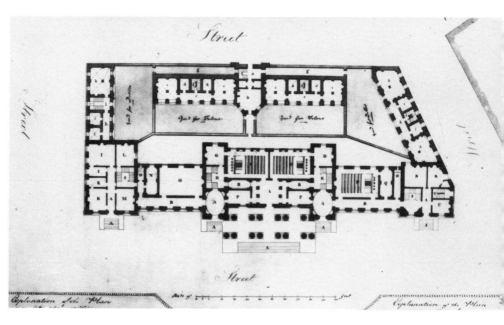

courtyard, three sides of which contained felons' day rooms and cells above, the fourth, at the rear, the debtors' day and night rooms. In the middle of this fourth wing was the keeper's apartment with windows looking into each of four yards from his kitchen, and the chapel above it. Further back still, on the same central axis, was the execution platform. So entrance, judgement (court), surveillance, worship and death were on one, central line (which also lined up with the new Saltmarket bridge) thus mapping out a unified and inevitable chronology and cosmology.

David Hamilton's first design (Figure 1.28) is simpler and more severe than either of Reid's. The main entrance has four Doric columns rising through the two floors. The symmetrical plan (with the same concession to the site as Reid's on the northern side) has the main court on the central axis, flanked by two courts, one for felons and one for debtors. The felons' cells are embedded on the south by legal offices, so they have no external windows—only openings into the internal gallery. There is no evidence in the surviving drawings of a chapel. His second design (Figure 1.29) was completely asymmetrical internally but with a symmetrical main facade. The main court lay to one side of the centre; on the other a courtyard with a jail around its sides; and two minor courts, one above the other, on the front. Women felons had their own day rooms and, instead of cells, a common dormitory above it. Again, no chapel was provided nor do we know what was intended for the elevations. Hamilton produced yet a third design, still dated 1809 (Figure 1.30); it is, once again, symmetrical, with a central pavilion containing the main court, flanked by two courtyards for the jail—felons and debtors. The building is three storeys high with a rusticated base and major Doric orders spanning the upper two—with a flat dome over the centre. The dome was actually designed in two versions which appear on the drawing one over the other in the form of a fold-down flap!

The scheme actually built—by William Stark—has unfortunately the most incomplete set of drawings and we know nothing of his first design. The main neo-Greek front had a double row of Doric columns, with giant Doric pilasters on each end pavilion (Figure 1.31). We can get some idea of the plan from the drawing dated 1814 showing the first uses of the rooms at first floor level (Figure 1.32). The main court occupied the centre of the totally symmetrical plan, under which, as seen from a block plan at ground level made by William Kyle the surveyor in 1810 (Figure 1.33), was the entrance approached through a double row of Doric columns. The gaoler's quarters separated the two jail courtyards each of which had cells on two sides—felons at the rear and first or second class debtors on the other, at right angles to the felons. All cells had external windows and it is quite likely that this, amongst other features, recommended itself to the Council, in view of the immense post-Howardian emphasis on fresh air and ventilation which was by this time current in medical and institutional circles. Above the gaoler's quarters was an infirmary and above that the chapel, whose detailed planning is shown in Figure 1.34. The main court

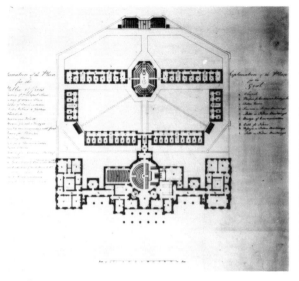
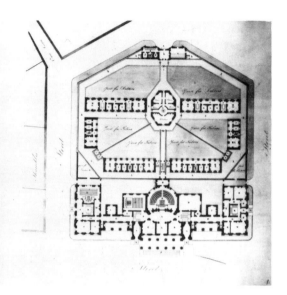
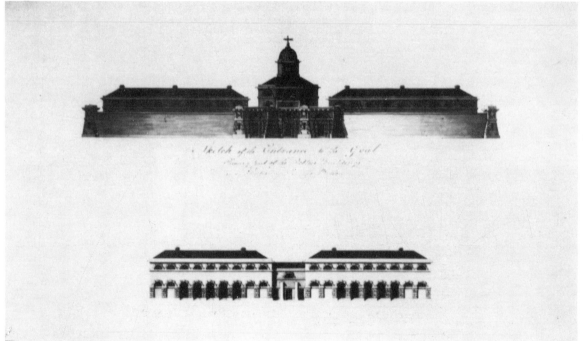

1.27 *Glasgow Judiciary Buildings;*
  Robert Reid's second design,
  1809,
  (a) first floor plan
  (b) ground floor plan
  (c) sections

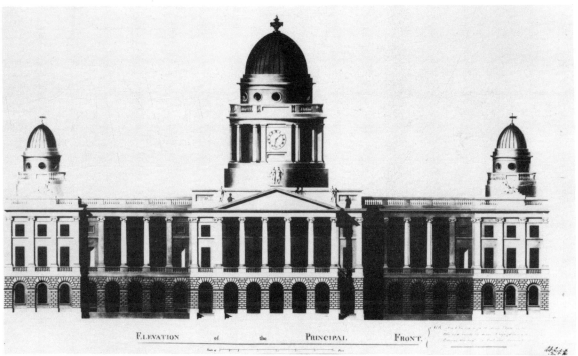

(d) front elevation
(e) alternative front elevation.

55

1.28 *Glasgow Judiciary Buildings;*
David Hamilton's first design,
1809,
 (a) front elevation
 (b) first floor plan
 (c) ground floor plan.

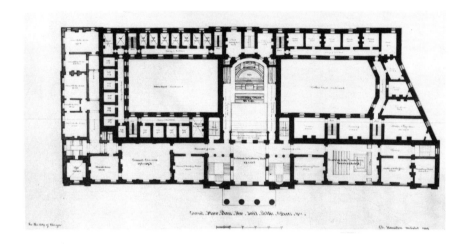

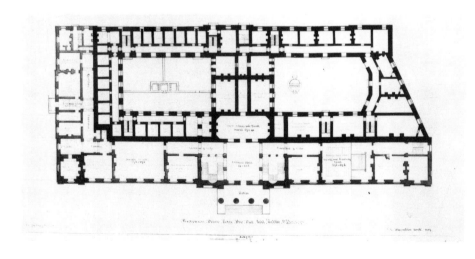

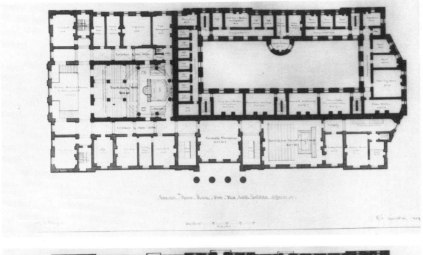

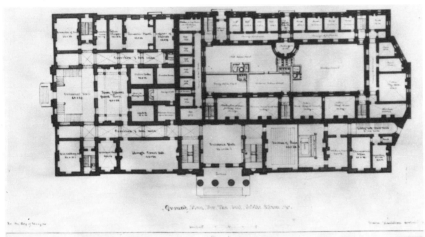

1.29 *Glasgow Judiciary Buildings;
David Hamilton's second design,
1809,*
(a) first floor plan
(b) ground floor plan.

had a gallery supported on Doric columns as the section (Figure 1.35) shows. The judge sat in a kind of apse, and a roof plan shows that there were large skylights. The debtors' cells were heated by individual fireplaces whose flues discharged into grouped stacks (Figure 1.36). The cells were barrel vaulted and each had a central ventilation porthole over the door. The west elevation (Figure 1.37) was an extraordinary exercise in neo-classical severity. The only windows belonged to the central block containing the gaoler's quarters, infirmary and, possibly, the chapel; the felons' cells were without any openings on this side, thus giving a monumental four-storey-high wall with corner pavilions.

Before the opening of the new Saltmarket jail the Bridewell in Duke Street was legalised for housing convicted felons in its spare capacity; but despite this, and although the new jail had a capacity of seventy-four cells

57

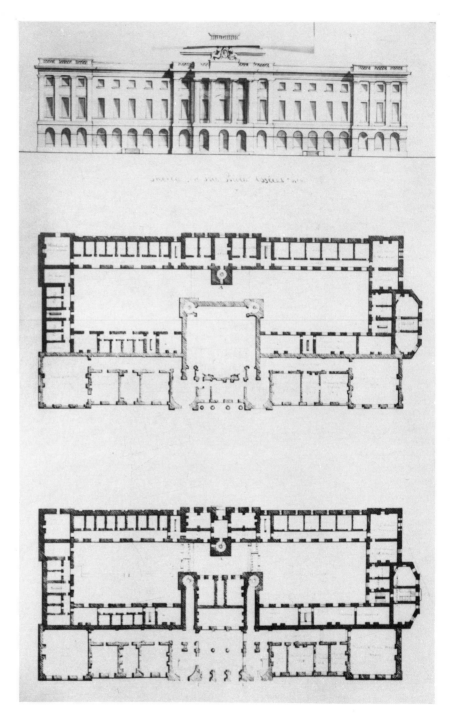

1.30 *Glasgow Judiciary Buildings; David Hamilton's third design, 1809,*
    (a) front elevation
    (b) ground floor plan
    (c) first floor plan.

1.31 *Exterior photograph of William Stark's 1809 design for Glasgow Judiciary Buildings taken in about 1900 before the substantial rebuilding in 1910.*

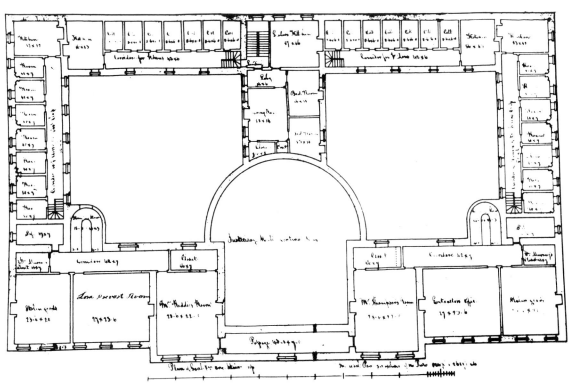

1.32 *Glasgow Judiciary Buildings, William Stark's plan, 1809 (drawing from 1814).*

59

1.33 *William Kyle's site plan of Stark's Judiciary Buildings, 1810.*

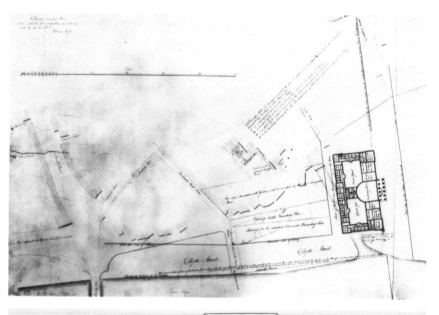

1.34 *Stark's Judiciary Buildings, sections and plan of chapel.*

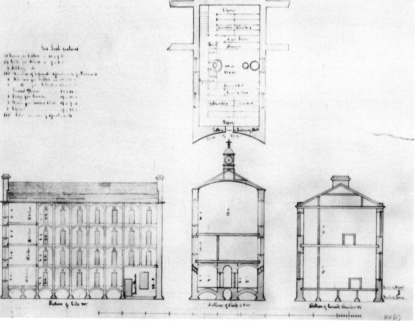

for debtors; fifty-eight felons' cells, as well as day rooms and condemned cells (thirty-five prisoners were transferred from the Tolbooth in 1814) its accommodation was inadequate and there was a demand for a new jail. By 1823 the assimilation of Bridewells and jails, which had been proceeding throughout the previous century, was recognised in the Gaol Act[57] under which the two could be 'united or (in a) contiguous building' and the distinction was finally eliminated by Parliament in 1865. Glasgow used a private Act of 1822, the need for which was recognised as far back as 1819[58], and built a new Bridewell completed in 1825, which overcame one of the noted deficiencies of Stark's jail—whose 'construction is unfortunately such, as to retard, if not entirely to prevent the great purpose of solitary confinement and distinct classification'.[59] David Smith's map of 1828 shows the new Bridewell on Duke Street with two cell wings radiating at 120° to each other from a central circular block and the old Bridewell still intact to the north of it (Figure 1.38). Maps of the thirties and forties continue to show the same blocks; however by the time of the 1:500 Ordnance Survey map of 1860 (Figure 1.39) and a block plan of 1862 (Figure 1.40) the wings of the eighteenth century Bridewell have gone, and new blocks of various sizes and shapes have been added. One set of undated mid-century drawings by Thomas Brown shows the old Bridewell intact; another of the same period shows it with its wings demolished to make way for three extra wings of which, apparently, only one was built.[60] An aerial photograph of the mid-twentieth century (Figure 1.41) shows the prison shortly before its demolition. What is known of its detailed planning and design has to be deduced from the 1860 O.S. Map (Figure 1.39). Its first two wings were 'on the radiating principle',[61] and contained some one hundred and sixty cells; but there was no open gallery and no direct connection to the central tower, hence little real surveillance was possible.

This prison, like Stark's and those of his two competitors, as well as the eighteenth century Bridewell, was curiously behind the times in its conception. By the time the 1795 Bridewell was built a number of greek-cross, radial prisons had been built in England.[62] Moreover, four years earlier Jeremy Bentham had published his designs for the circular Panopticon which, as we shall see, was influential in the thought of Robert Adam when he designed the Calton Bridewell in Edinburgh, in the same year (1791). When the Saltmarket schemes were prepared in 1809 the ideas of classification, solitary confinement and central surveillance had become far advanced in England and in America. It seems that economy, conservatism and the desire to keep prison buildings hidden by various methods of camouflage to some extent blinded the builders to advances made south of the border. After all, Cleland was sent on an official mission in 1808 and would, or should, have seen Ipswich, Gloucester, Salford and John Orridge's Bury St. Edmunds' Gaol. The camouflage took two main forms—one of style, a method seen at work in all the 1809 schemes which used neo-Palladian and neo-Classical compositions—and the other of

1.35 *Stark's Judiciary Buildings, two sections.*

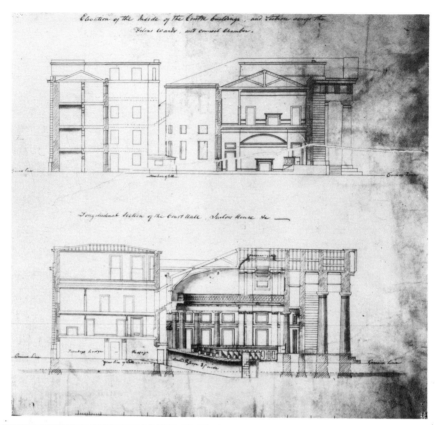

1.36 *Stark's Judiciary Buildings, section showing flues in debtors' cells.*

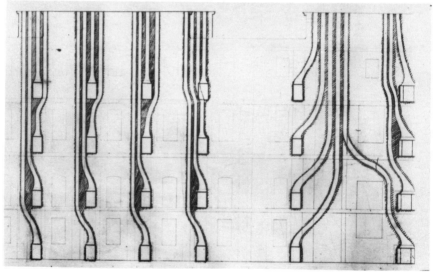

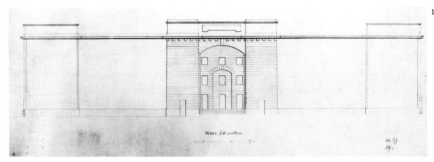

1.37 *Stark's Judiciary Buildings, west (rear) elevation.*

1.38 *David Smith's 1828 map showing the Bridewell with two radiating wings.*

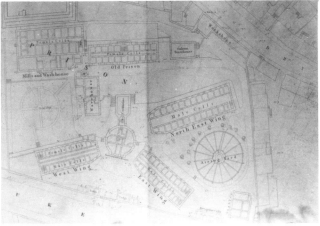

1.39 *1860 Ordnance Survey map showing new Bridewell and old Bridewell without its wings.*

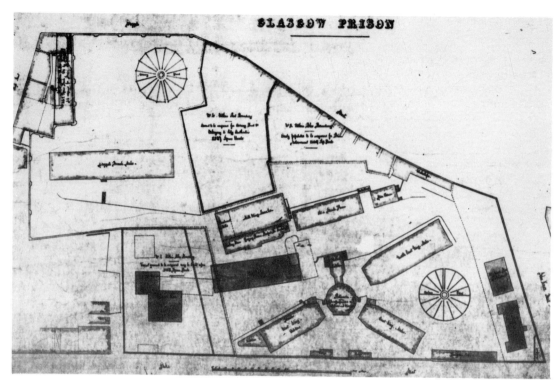

1.40 *1862 block plan of Glasgow Bridewell.*

1.41 *Mid-twentieth century aerial photograph of Glasgow Bridewell.*

64

screening and 'embedment' whereby the prison buildings proper were fronted, or even surrounded, by court, town council and office buildings.

As in the case of hospitals, it seems that Edinburgh, perhaps more directly under Continental and English influences, was more advanced in its thinking. Towards the end of the eighteenth century it had the same awareness of urban paupers and criminals as Glasgow and other cities and began to consider replacing some of its mediaeval and sixteenth century institutions and buildings. In 1782 a remarkable plan was published by Lord Provost David Steuart and the Sheriff Depute of the County, Archibald Cockburn *For Erecting a New Prison and Bridewell in the County of Edinburgh*.[63] Although they acknowledge a debt to John Howard, whose first prison design was published five years earlier, the first English radial prison at Ipswich (Figure 1.42) by John Blackburn was still four years away, although Blackburn had won, in 1782, the premium offered by the newly appointed Commissioners for Penitentiary Houses. Steuart and Cockburn make no mention of this competition, and it is not known whether Blackburn's design was ever published, even in England, nor indeed what form it took, although it is almost certain to have been of the Ipswich type. So the authors almost certainly invented this version of the radial prison plan (Figure 1.43) from first principles. The first was 'that the Jail and Workhouse, or Bridewell, should be *united* (the italics and subsequent ones are the present author's) and laid out in divisions, in such a manner as to afford one for the reception of felons, with a suitable area and court belonging to it; another for young offenders, with a court and area; a third for debtors with the same conveniencies; and, lastly, a Bridewell, consisting of separate accommodations for men and women, with proper courts and areas: And, that there may be no communication between the refractory and incorrigible, and such as are less hardened, distinct places of abode are to be prepared for each'.[64] Classification, separation so moral contagion is avoided, and open visibility through the system of courts—this was a thoroughgoing programme, well beyond what Howard had spelt out. They also detailed the construction of cells, wall thicknesses, vaults and the design of the outer wall for security.

But their ideas of surveillance were startlingly novel; '. . . The jailor's house is to be placed in the centre of the whole, and to consist of three storeys . . . The situation of this house being *centrical*, will enable him (the jailor), from the second storey, *to look into all the different subvisions*, and discover immediately if anything amiss is going on'.[65] They suggest that had Akerman, the keeper at Newgate, had his house in the centre the riots could have been defeated (these were the Gordon Riots of 1780 when Newgate was set on fire). On each of the four turrets of the outer wall there were to be swivel guns, to shoot either outwards or inwards in case of riots. Nine years before Jeremy Bentham set out the aim of surveillance in his Panopticon as being the creation of 'the sentiment of an invisible omniscience', and the minimisation of skilled, or supervisory labour, they argue that '. . . The centrical situation of the Governor's house, and the precautions already described, for strength and security, will render the number of inferior officers and servants much smaller than would otherwise have been necessary'. They insist on the appointment of a surgeon and of a chaplain 'to preach every Sunday to the people in the House'—just where is not clear as there are no large rooms for use as a chapel. The plan shows a three-winged radial prison, with some single-banked wings and one for the felons, with a double row of cells, back-to-back, with outer galleries. There had been no previous statement as clear as this of the *principle* of central inspection (although in practice the plan does not permit central surveillance) and it fell to Bentham, nine years later, to spell it out again and to show its full architectural consequences.

Although this project was not executed, the movement was pursued and resulted in the passing of an Act of Parliament in 1791[66] for building a Bridewell and Correction House. The Act is curiously detailed in the specification both of the organisation and the building. It nominates the Calton Hill site for its '. . . air, dryness and healthiness'; it requires a Lazaret for prisoners with infectious or contagious diseases; an infirmary; baths; a wash-house for clothing; provisions for labour; it demands strict separation of the sexes and classes of prisoners and continuous day and night separation of each prisoner even during work if possible, the only exception is during attendance at religious services, meals and exercise. It lays down a minimum distance for future developments on Calton Hill, and also foresaw the building of a gaol for debtors and felons adjacent to the Bridewell—a project that was not to be realised for about twenty five years.

The choice of the Calton Hill site was preceded by public debate and contention, mainly couched in practical and sanitary terms. But it is clear that the issue really was whether a jail could and should occupy a visible, central city site, or be peripheral—in the tradition of earlier institutions; even William Adam's Infirmary was built hard up against the Town Wall, in more or less open countryside. Calton was a compromise and can be seen as the acceptance of *social* surveillance *of* the prison by the city as an analogue of the internal system of surveillance *by* the gaoler of the inmates. Its presence would be both a reminder of the order being achieved and a deterrent. Of course this gave the architect the problem of finding a suitable *formal* expression for such a central, civic site.

The building erected was designed by Robert Adam, and was chosen as a result of a competition in 1791. Before describing the evolution of his alternative designs it is interesting to look at those of two unsuccessful competitors. The first (Figure 1.44) is that by James Wardrop, a Glasgow architect who had clearly absorbed the lessons of Blackburn's designs in England but had six instead of four radiating blocks, each with a double-banked corridor of cells for one class of prisoner, including one for 'vagrants'. On the central, entrance axis was located the apsidal chapel and the keeper's quarters. The axes of the four central wings met at a point which was also the centre of the apse!

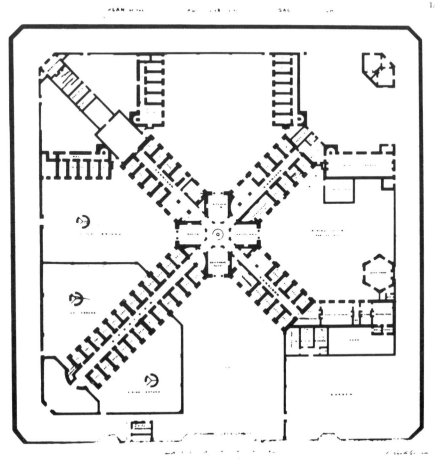

1.42 *Ipswich Gaol, 1786; architect John Blackburn.*

The second unsuccessful design in two variants (Figure 1.45) was by John Baxter. Both consisted of a central building with four radiating cell wings, each double-banked with cells on each side but, unlike Wardrop's plan, the corridors were directly connected to the central building and clear lines of surveillance were possible. It contained on the various floors, the keeper's 'rendezvous', chapels (a separate one for males and females, on separate floors) and a 'laboratory' (workroom). In one version the T blocks at the end of each wing had oval central halls; in the other rectangular. The latter version also shows a detached entrance block on the central axis containing the turnkey's offices and a court room above. 'Workhouses' are included and in this respect the design goes somewhat further than the Act. In most respects the plan is a copy of Blackburn's Ipswich Gaol, designed five years earlier, and is the first example North of the Border of this widely used, *surveyable* greek-cross radial principle.

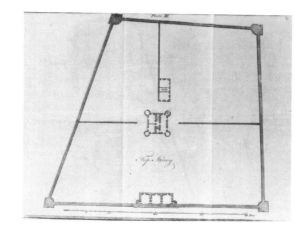

1.43 *Steuart and Cockburn's proposal*
for a Bridewell in Edinburgh,
1782,
    (a) second floor plan
    (b) first floor plan
    (c) ground floor plan.

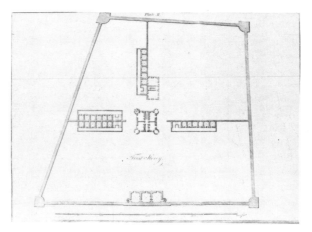

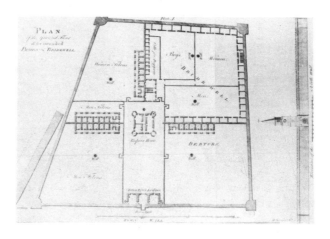

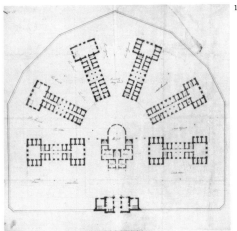

1.44 *Wardrop's entry for Edinburgh Bridewell Competition, 1791, ground floor plan.*

However it was Robert Adam who was successful and was commissioned. He must have had considerable debate with the sponsors, for no less than five different designs were produced, with some further variants. The first two, which are difficult to place in chronological sequence, were not very different from some of the continental prisons which Howard had visited, admired and published—typically the House of Correction in Milan (Figure 1.46) and, to a lesser extent, Howard's own Ideal Penitentiary published in 1789 (Figure 1.47).[67] In one of the two designs (Figure 1.48) there was a detached chapel at the front on the entrance axis, two great courtyards surrounded by cells facing an internal cloister, two further courtyards with segmental, curved outer boundaries, and two lateral wings—one for a substantial infirmary and the other for a Bedlam. This latter provision was certainly not part of the Parliamentary brief, but by this time provision for lunatics was a subject of public debate in Scotland. The elevations and sections are a curious mixture of heavy classicism (on the north, prison entrance side) and utilitarian with Palladian features (on the rear, south side). The other variant (Figure 1.49) has eight courts with a similar cell-cloister-entrance sequence—a spatial structure which involved entry into some courts through a corner space from the main passages. The chapel here occupied a dominant, free-standing position deep inside the complex and was, presumably, domed, although no elevation exists.

It seems that whilst he was working on this scheme, Adam heard of Jeremy Bentham's Panopticon ideas, which were first published in the same year—1791[68]—although from 1786 onwards Bentham had been corresponding with his father, publishers and even William Pitt to propagate the concept. The circular 'Elaboratory' or 'Inspection House' was invented by his brother Samuel to allow the few skilled supervisors to oversee a large number of men in the naval arsenal at Kritchev.[69] Jeremy read of the Penitentiary Act of 1779, saw the designs submitted by

69

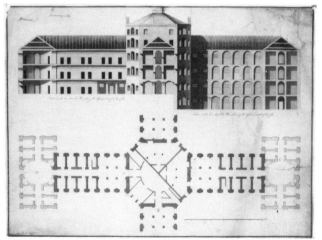

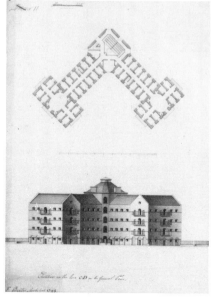

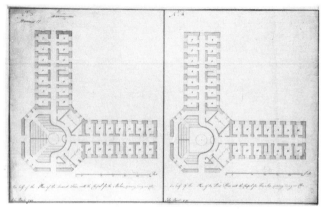

1.45 *Baxter's entry for Edinburgh*
Bridewell Competition, 1791,
(a) plan and sectional elevation
of centre block
(b) plan and sectional elevation
of chapel and two wings
(c) plans at two levels of two
wings with male and
female chapels
(d) alternative plan, elevation
and section.

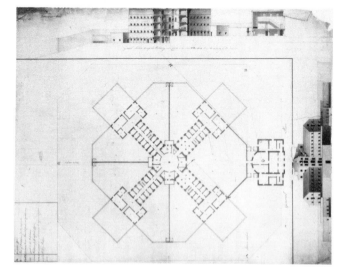

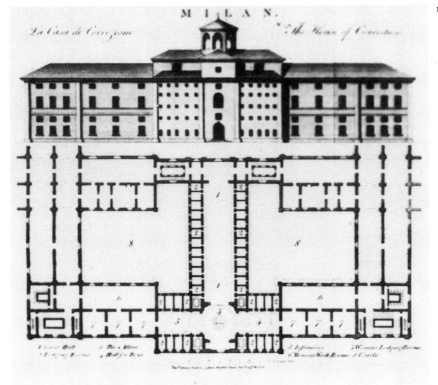

1.46 *Milan House of Correction.*

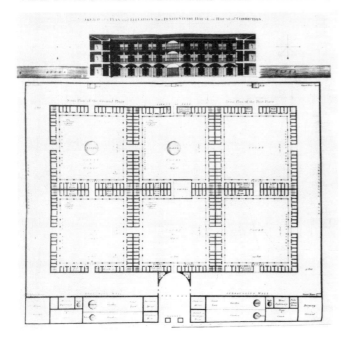

1.47 *Howard's Ideal Penitentiary,*
1789.

71

architects for a competition arranged under the Act in 1782 and considered his solution superior. Figure 1.50 shows the first and second variants of the Panopticon, both published in 1791 although the first was said to have been drawn in 1787. The former is four and the latter six storeys high. The central inspection tower, with a chapel on top in the first design, was designed for night and day surveillance of the cells on the periphery. In the second scheme the floor of the open space in the circular ring around the tower is proposed as the chapel. The daylighting was carefully designed to give one-way vision from the centre; and one-way *listening* was also proposed through special listening tubes.

In May 1791 Jeremy's friend Reginald Pole Carew wrote to him after a meeting with Robert Adam saying that he had mentioned to the latter 'an ingenious Friend' who had invented a building highly suitable for the purpose of the 'Penitentiary House' he (Adam) was then designing for Edinburgh.[70] He did not reveal Bentham's name, fearing that somehow the use of the idea in Scotland might interfere with its novelty, and hence acceptance, in England. By the end of May, Bentham is in correspondence with Adam, asking him to suggest architectural improvements to his proposal; commenting that the building '. . . will be more difficult to represent upon a flat surface than perhaps any other that was ever yet imagined.' He refers derogatorily to Blackburn's plan; to James Stirling, then Lord Provost of Edinburgh and David 'Steward' (Steuart) whose 1782 publication he knew; and suggests meeting Adam in London.[71] Adam replies that he does not wish to publicise the Panopticon widely as every 'Lord and Gentleman' in Scotland imagines himself to be an architect, and they will produce '. . . a million Panopticons, fraught with every kind of absurdity' and the one to be built would be the worst of the cluster. He therefore proposes to work on it quietly and to prepare a scheme, with a model, for Bentham's comments. Significantly he already claims to be working on the 'principle of invisible inspection.'[72]

The third design, which appears to have been Adam's first Panoptical design (Figure 1.51) must date from about June 1791; it shows a semicircle of cells four storeys high, with a central inspection tower, and open annular space, top lit, a central gaoler's house between the main entrance and the outer gatehouse and two minor, three-storey Panoptical wings, containing a Bedlam and an infirmary. The chapel is in the semi-circular open space, as currently proposed by Bentham with tiered concentric pews, where the minister was presumably intended to officiate from the foot of the inspection tower. The slit windows of this tower are already carefully slanted so as to give one-way vision from the centre out. An alternative plan varies the bastions in the outer walls; both have an outdoor inspection tower, approached by an underground tunnel, which views into each of the seven exercise yards. The main north and rear, south, elevations show the characteristic castle style with three stepped gables, corner turrets and battlements which Adam had by this time developed. It is instructive to compare it with the garden-front of his Culzean (Figure 1.52).

1.48 *Robert Adam's first Edinburgh*
Bridewell project, 1791,
   (a) front elevation
   (b) rear elevation
   (c) section
   (d) first floor plan
   (e) ground floor plan.

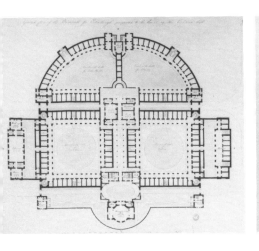

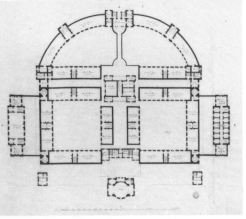

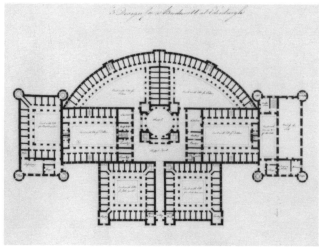

1.49 *Robert Adam's second Edinburgh Bridewell project, 1791, ground floor plan.*

1.50 *Jeremy Bentham's Panopticon Prison,*
    (a) first design, 1787
       (published 1791)

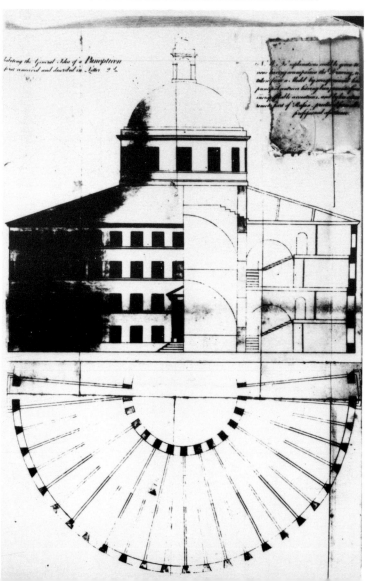

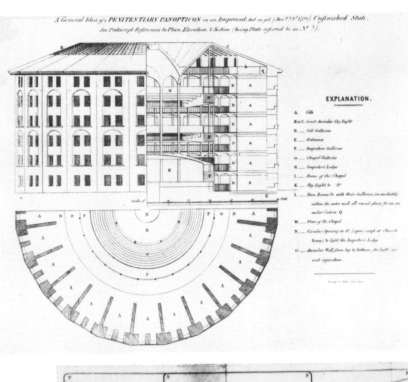

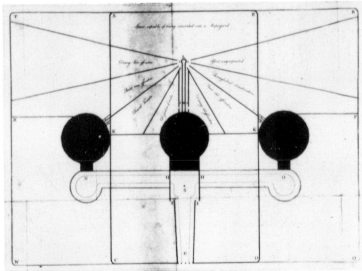

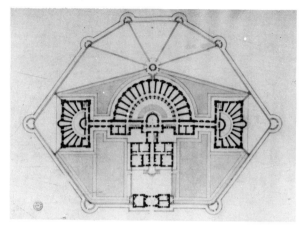

1.51 *Robert Adam's third Edinburgh*
Bridewell project 1791,
    (a) ground floor plan
    (b) section
    (c) section
    (d) section

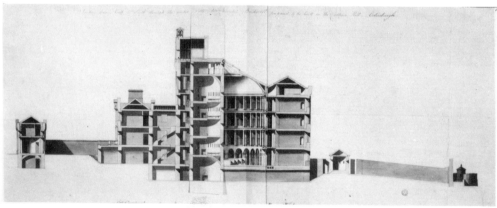

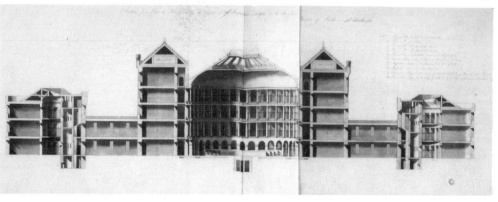

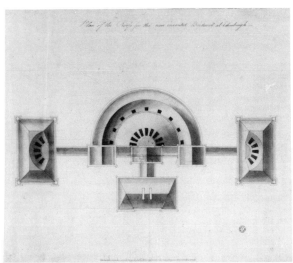

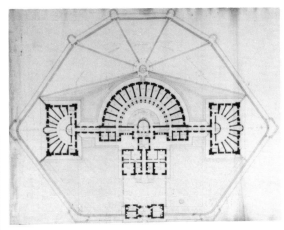

(e) rear elevation
(f) front elevation
(g) roof plan
(h) alternative plan.

A second Panoptical scheme, Adam's fourth design, (Figure 1.53) quickly followed. The wings were omitted, the ground floor of cells which were arcaded in the earlier scheme is now similar to the upper three, which have rectangular openings and the cell gallery no longer has the coupled column-pier supports, but simple square piers. The wings are marked as 'gardens' and it is probable that all these changes were a response to instructions for economy. In both these schemes, however, an essential Benthamite notion is present—group cells, for day and night use, with continuous, twenty-four-hour surveillance from the centre.

A big change occurs with the fifth design, the third Panoptical design (Figure 1.54). The Infirmary and Bedlam re-appear, in wings with double-square courtyards. The peripheral, single cells are now for sleeping only; they are separated from the larger, day (work) rooms by a corridor and it is these latter which are visible from the central tower. The day rooms were designed for two or more prisoners. In other essentials the design is similar to the earlier ones. On the main elevation the central gable has disappeared; the side blocks have received their own, conical corner turrets; and the gaoler's house retains its former position.

The scheme which was eventually built is shown on the 1852-54 Ordnance Survey map (Figure 1.55) and on Shepherd's prints dating from 1831 (Figure 1.56). The main cell block has the same plan as in the fifth design but the gaoler's house has now been lopped off. The wings and the eleven complex yards were not built—but the outer wall, gatehouse and corner turrets are in keeping with the original concept. In July 1792 Jeremy Bentham wrote to James Adam,[73] who had taken over the project upon Robert's death in March 1792, to ask for an urgent meeting. It seems that he had become aware through his brother Samuel that the plan was not according to his principles in that the day rooms prevented night-time surveillance of the cells. He also appears at this time to be accusing Robert Adam of claiming to have *invented* the Panopticon principle for his Edinburgh Bridewell.[74] The Bentham brothers' battle with James to restore

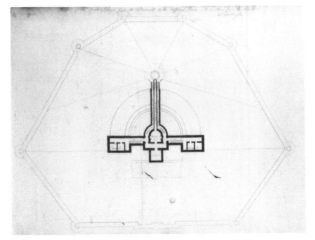

1.53 *Robert Adam's fourth Edinburgh Bridewell project, 1791,*
    (a) roof plan
    (b) first floor plan
    (c) ground floor plan
    (d) section.

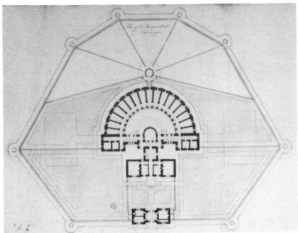

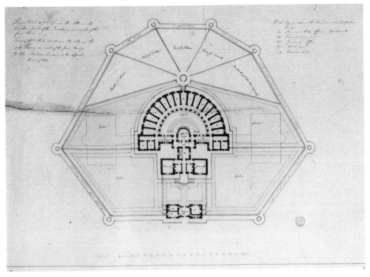

1.54 *Robert Adam's fifth Edinburgh
Bridewell project, 1791,*
(a) roof plan
(b) ground floor plan

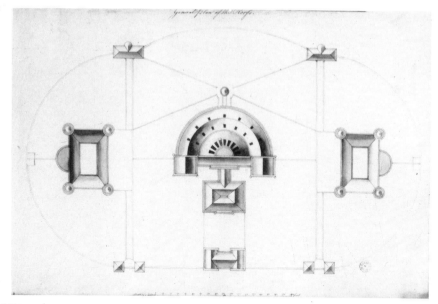

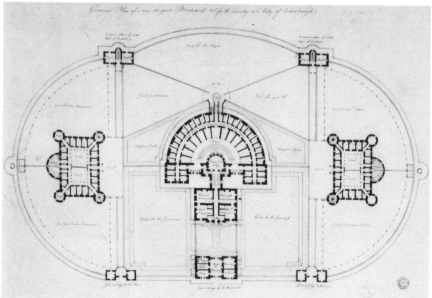

the design was now a lost cause; Samuel, writing to Lord Elgin, seems to hold James responsible, for refusing to abandon Robert's last design, which '. . . if not actually spoiled (the idea), have very much impaired (it)'. Bitterly he complains that 'Neither the late Mr Adam ever took any notice of my Brother afterwards' (i.e. his first enthusiasm for the Panopticon) '. . .

80

(c) rear elevation
(d) front elevation
(e) section.

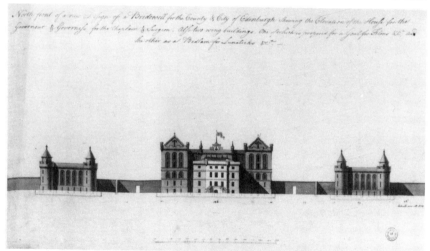

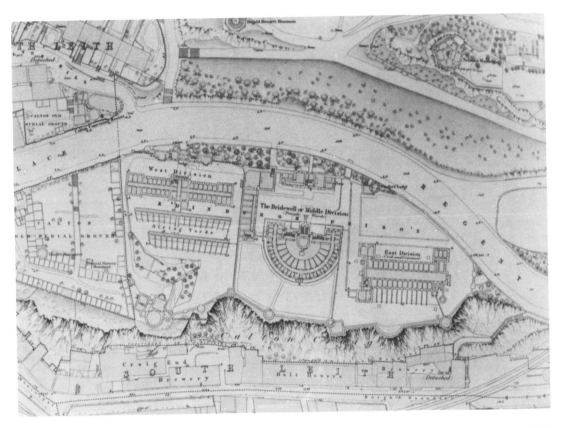

1.55 *Edinburgh Bridewell complex shown on the 1852-54 Ordnance Survey Map.*

nor his brother till now that my Brother called on him'.[75] But the July 1792 meeting achieved nothing.

The abandonment of the single row of cells, and hence of night-time surveillance, was commented on by Samuel Romilly in an illustrated letter to Bentham written during construction in September 1793;[76] in it he particularly draws attention to the fact that the doors of the day and night rooms are not opposite each other hence the arrangement defeats Bentham's principles of rear illumination of the cells, and also essential through-ventilation. It was a serious disappointment to Bentham that the only British prison design which came anywhere near a strict interpretation of the Panopticon was, in its execution, a departure from it.

The Bentham brothers did persuade the Government to build the National penitentiary on Panopticon lines in 1794; but after years of discussion, debate and dubious site deals the scheme was eventually abandoned in 1811 and £23,000 compensation paid to them. The following year the new Millbank Penitentiary, on the site of the present Tate Gallery, was designed and its supporters claimed Benthamite influences but in fact it was far removed from their idea. Other prisons which superficially at

82

least resembled the Panopticon were built in America—such as Benjamin Latrobe's 1797 State Prison at Richmond, Virginia, inspired by Jefferson and, through him, by grandiose French neo-classical circular designs,[77] and the Western Penitentiary, Pittsburgh, designed by William Strickland in 1818.

Henry Cockburn writing in the early 1850s deplores the choice of site for the Bridewell and the later prisons erected on each side of it in the nineteenth century. These, like the first Lancasterian school also built on Calton Hill, confirmed his view that it was the place '. . . where it was then the fashion to stow away everything that was too abominable to be tolerated elsewhere.'[78]

The new jail, to the west of the Bridewell was started in 1815 to the designs of Archibald Elliot (Figure 1.57). It contained in a straight block fifty-eight cells, double-banked, with a chapel in the centre and closely followed the castle style of the Bridewell. It eventually came to be called the 'West Division'; the surviving plans shown in Figure 1.58 are drawn by Thomas Brown for alterations proposed in 1829.[79] Thomas Brown and his firm of Brown and Wardrop became the prolific prison designers of Victorian Scotland; in the twenty-five years from 1840 at least eighteen Scottish prisons are their creation and probably a number of the unattributed ones in addition.[80]

Brown was almost certainly responsible for the mid-century 'East Division' block which closely followed Elliot's 1815 jail in both plan and elevation.[81] He also proposed alterations to the Adam Bridewell, including the removal of the offending day-rooms and extension of the cell party-walls (to increase the number of prisoners in each cell?)[82]—but it appears

1.56 *Shepherd's prints of Edinburgh Bridewell published 1831 (a) rear elevation with Elliott's Governor's House (1815)*

(b) front elevation from Calton Hill.

from the evidence of the 1852–54 map that these were not carried out as the building is then still almost as the Adam brothers had designed it. It had always been envisaged that the site would contain a debtors' jail—and an early nineteenth century scheme survives (Figure 1.59) whose designer is unknown. Here the airing grounds for each of the five classes of debtors (three male, two female) radiate from a chapel dedicated to this block; the elevation is gothic-baronial.

By 1881 the Bridewell was demolished for a new central prison block (Figure 1.60) and today nothing remains except for the romantic cluster of round turrets which Elliot designed for the governor's house as part of his 1815 project (Figure 1.61).

In 1820 Elliot also designed Jedburgh Castle (Jail) which, for its time, is a remarkably conservative three-pronged radial Bridewell and jail combined, two storeys in height and with limited inspection possible from the central governor's house (Figures 1.62 and 1.63). The style is now frankly that of a keep, with little of the classicising influence which had been present in all the earlier examples.

Having traced the development of a few of the more important hospitals and prisons it remains to see how these influences converged in a type where there was, and still is, considerable confusion as to whether the inmates were sick or morally culpable—the lunatic asylum.

We have seen that in both infirmaries and prisons some provision was made for lunatics at the end of the eighteenth century, as also in many poor houses, workhouses and similar institutions. Foucault proposes that with the gradual disappearance of lepers by the end of the seventeenth century, the horror which society had concentrated upon them was transferred to the insane.[83] This makes itself felt in the establishment of

84

institutions in which the fear of madness is coupled to the fear of unreason (to the Enlightenment mind this is the most corrosive attack on society and thought). Instead of superstitious punishments the régime now has confinement and cure as its aim and, since anti-reason is seen as the animal-in-man, when it takes over the behaviour of the mad person, to treat mad people *as* animals, is seen not as a punitive, but as a rational response. Hence the seventeenth and eighteenth century conditions of chains, kennels, locks, bars, fences and constraint devices with which the descriptive and pictorial literature is filled. It was only gradually that a *clinical* and scientific view of madness, coupled to philanthropy, overtook the institutions. They now became centres in which the emphasis is on order, silence, cleanliness, fresh air and good sanitation. This coincided with a period when architecture itself was searching for images of perpetual order and tranquility.

Europe already had its great asylums from the seventeenth century on; the foundation in 1656 of the Hôpital Général in Paris created a whole family of institutions for the sick, mad, orphaned, pauper and senile.[84] Productive work was a central theme for all those capable of it and the Paris police were the instruments of administration.[85] It is thought that near the end of the seventeenth century one percent of the population of Paris had been removed from the streets into the two main institutions of the Hôpital—Salpetriere (for women) and Bicêtre (for men). Each housed between three and six-thousand patients, with the insane in separate blocks of 'loges'. By the late eighteenth century these were ranged in rectilinear patterns and sub-divided by class of disease—or rather by symptom: the senile; recent agitated (curable); agitated (incurable); melancholics; and idiots, escapees and sowers of discord. The latter were

1.57 Edinburgh 'New Jail', 1815; architect Archibald Elliot, as shown on Shepherd's print 1831.

85

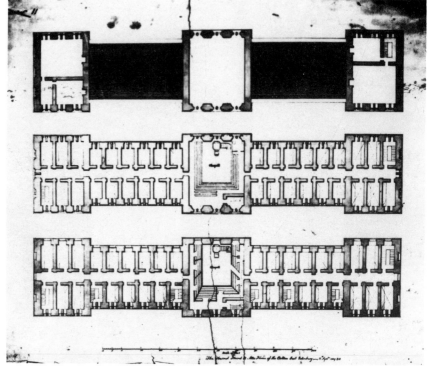

1.58 *Edinburgh 'New Jail', 1815 as shown on Thomas Brown's drawings in 1829; architect Archibald Elliot,*
    (a) third floor plan
    (b) second floor plan
    (c) first floor plan
    (d) ground floor plan.

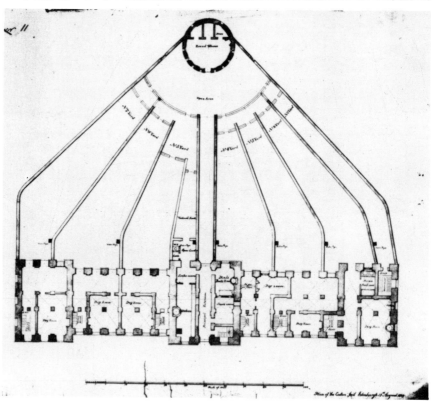

86

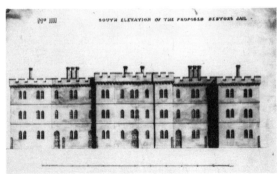

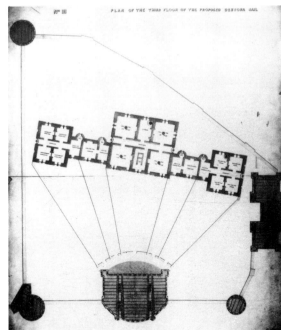

1.59 *Proposed Debtors' Jail for*
Bridewell site, Edinburgh; early
nineteenth century, architect
unknown,
    (a) front elevation
    (b) second ('third') floor plan
    (c) first ('second') floor plan
    (d) ground floor plan.

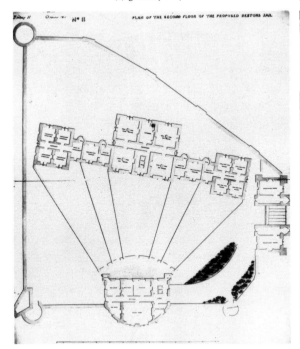

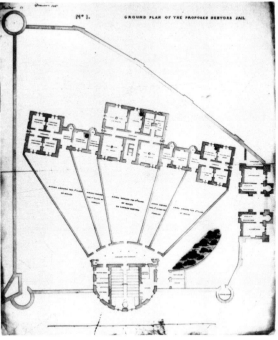

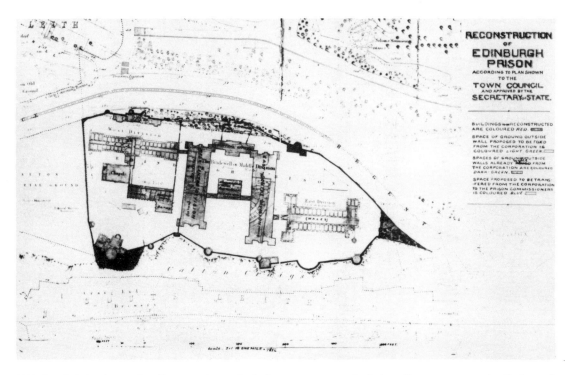

RECONSTRUCTION
OF
EDINBURGH
PRISON
ACCORDING TO PLAN SHOWN
TO THE
TOWN COUNCIL
AND APPROVED BY THE
SECRETARY OF STATE.

BUILDINGS TO BE CONSTRUCTED
ARE COLOURED RED.

SPACE OF GROUND OUTSIDE
WALL PROPOSED TO BE FEUED
FROM THE CORPORATION IS
COLOURED LIGHT GREEN.

SPACES OF GROUND OUTSIDE
WALLS ALREADY FEUED FROM
THE CORPORATION ARE COLOURED
DARK GREEN.

SPACE PROPOSED TO BE TRANS-
FERED FROM THE CORPORATION
TO THE PRISON COMMISSIONERS
IS COLOURED BLUE.

1.60 *1881 plan of Edinburgh Bridewell site with Adam's building demolished.*

in the most central loges, surrounded by the more controlled and controllable classes. At Celle, in Germany, a prison (1711) and an asylum (1731) were combined into quadrangles, united at the centre by the church. It is interesting to note, in this instance that the prisoners' cells are on the outside of a cloister, whilst the lunatics face inwards, with an outer passage: the prisoner's return to society was through the contemplation of nature; the madman's through observation of his colleagues.

In 1784 Joseph II (having recently returned from a visit to his sister, Queen Marie Antoinette) commissioned Canevale to design a 5-storey, cylindrical asylum, the Narrenturm, in Vienna (Figure 1.64). He saw the Hôtel Dieu and no doubt also the grandiose circular designs of the Royal Academicians. Although the structure has a castle-fortress appearance, the medical and surveillance régimes were advanced for the time, for Joseph had not only created an Absolutist centralised hospital for the whole of Vienna, of which the Narrenturm was a part, but collected in it the most advanced physicians and surgeons in Europe.

London had its major institution, the Bedlam in Moorfields in 1676; it was not until 1786 that George Dance designed the next new asylum for St. Luke's, which was founded in 1751. Accounts of both in the eighteenth century reveal mainly harsh physical restraints with chains and instruments; classification was not by diagnosis but by ability to pay and an assessment of 'curability'. Symmetry in layout was generally used for

88

1.61 *Governor's House, 1815 as seen today; architect Archibald Elliot.*

1.62 *Jedburgh Jail, 1820; architect*
  Archibald Elliot
    (a) ground floor plan
    (b) upper floor plan

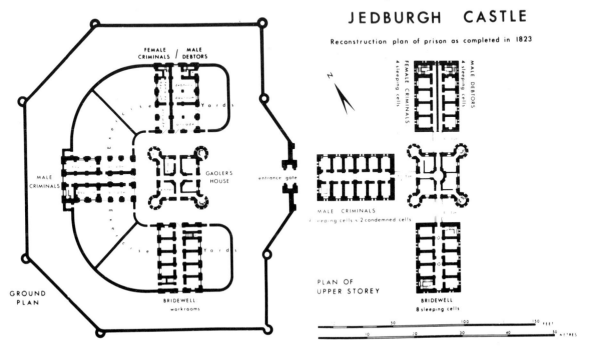

JEDBURGH CASTLE

Reconstruction plan of prison as completed in 1823

FEMALE CRIMINALS / MALE DEBTORS

Yards

MALE CRIMINALS

GAOLERS HOUSE

entrance gate

Yards

GROUND PLAN

BRIDEWELL
workrooms

N

FEMALE CRIMINALS
4 sleeping cells

MALE DEBTORS
4 sleeping cells

MALE CRIMINALS
sleeping cells x 2 condemned cells

PLAN OF UPPER STOREY

BRIDEWELL
8 sleeping cells

50   100   150 FEET

10   20   30   40   50 METRES

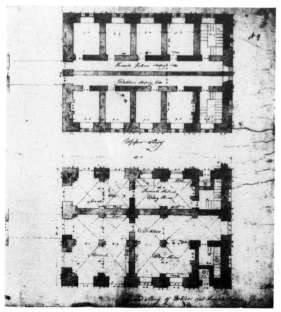

1.63 *Archibald Elliott's drawings of Jedburgh Jail, 1820,*
(a) ground and upper floor of debtors' wing, with central wall on upper floor dividing debtors from female felons
(b) typical elevation section and window details.

division between men and women. However, by the end of the century remarkable experiments in new ways of treating lunatics by a *moral* régime were in existence. The Retreat in York was founded in 1796 and run by three successive generations of Tukes, the grandson, Samuel, writing a good description of it in 1813.[86] Its first purpose-built building had a simple plan and domestic elevation (Figure 1.65) in keeping with the founder's régime—'moral persuasion', reward but no punishment, no physical force and the formation of small social groups. Others too were experimenting with this approach at the time—notably Fox in Bristol and Ferriar in London. By 1807, when the Parliamentary Committee on the State of Lunatics[87] was making its enquiries these establishments were giving evidence; and Tuke's book was reviewed in the *Edinburgh Review* in 1814. The ideas must therefore have been well known in Scotland.

The movement for an asylum at Edinburgh goes back to 1792.[88] By 1806 the state of care for lunatics in the Charity Workhouse raised an outcry and reforms were instituted; and by 1807 a Royal Charter was received authorising the building of an asylum; in the same year Robert Reid's designs for it were first published (Figure 1.66).[89] It was a bi-axial, bi-symmetrical courtyard scheme, having on each face a three-storey centre block, a pair of two-storey wings, and two, three-storey, end pavilions which returned and repeated the theme on the adjacent face. The ground floor had recessed and round-headed openings, with the suggestion of an arcade; the upper two were as plain as could be, as was the simple central pediment. The central block contained the keeper's house, where he shared his dining room with the convalescent male patients' day room;

90

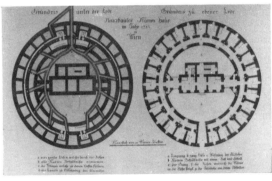

above that his apartments, and above that the female equivalent of the ground floor room but now dedicated to patient use alone. The wings were occupied symmetrically, men on one side, women on the other. Patients were divided not only by income and sex, but also by symptom—'furious, melancholic, curable and incurable'. The cells in the centre were double-banked and unheated; those in the pavilion blocks at the end were larger and had individual fireplaces and were intended for 'patients of the higher rank'—that is those whose relatives could pay. There was similar accommodation for them in detached blocks in the front gardens, shown on the block plan.

The four keepers' houses had individual sunken passages to the centre of the exercise courtyards which were divided into four and surveyed from a central inspection room where the four passages met.

The building was erected on a site in Morningside, just within the walls at the Braid gate, in what was still more or less open country as Kirkwood's map of 1817 (Figure 1.67) shows. This also indicates that only the east wing was built; it was not until about 1823 that the entire block was complete.[90] Reid apparently gave his services free. Although the intention from the start was to cater for poor lunatics, the lack of public response in the subscription appeal and other reasons limited its early intake mainly to paying patients. In 1827 Reid prepared a further design for one hundred and sixty 'pauper patients' of the 'humbler classes'. This aim was not however achieved until the erection of a completely new building for three hundred and fifty patients, designed by William Burn, in the 1840s.[91]

From the start Morningside Asylum modelled its régime on that practised at the Retreat at York, with the banning of 'chains, stripes, and every other rough mode of treatment, (using) mild treatment with proper confinement'. Reid himself was sent on a tour of the latest asylums during his initial project, and received comments from the leading experts of the time—including Sir George Onesipherous Paul, Governor of Gloucester Gaol (the first to instal a complete 'separate system' in 1792) who had also given expert evidence to the Parliamentary Committee in 1807[92] that Gaols

1.64 *Joseph II's 'Narrenturm' at Vienna General Hospital, 1784; architect Canevale*
    (a) exterior view
    (b) basement and upper floor plans.

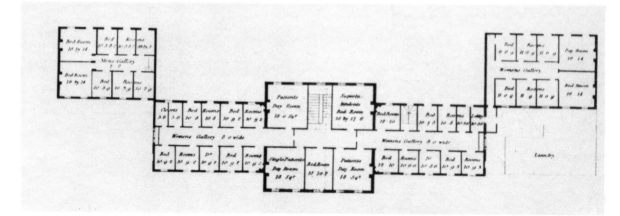

1.65 *The Retreat, York, 1796*
   (a) upper floor plan
   (b) exterior view.

were improper places for the confinement of lunatics. Paul was involved with the setting up of the Gloucester County Lunatic Asylum, as a prime promoter in 1792—the same year in which both Edinburgh and York asylums were first promoted. A design for Gloucester, probably by John Nash, was prepared in 1794, but remained unexecuted on account of legal and financial difficulties. These were not resolved till 1811[93] when the Scottish architect William Stark was appointed to prepare a new design which is considered in detail later. The Managers evidently intended Reid's design to be widely circulated and used as a model so that 'similar establishments . . . may therefore be built'. In fact the wide circulation of the designs at home and abroad (subscriptions were received from India, Ceylon, the West Indies and America) was more of a publicity than a scholarly device.

Clearly by this time Westminster was moving towards action; the 1807

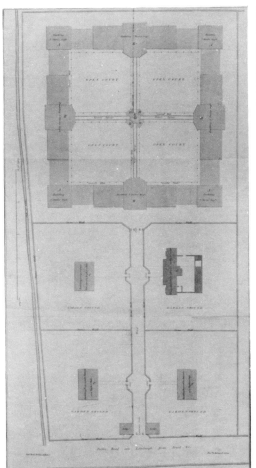

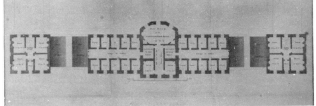

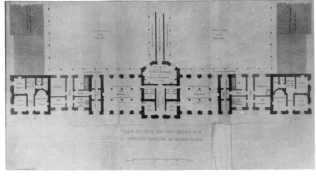

1.66 *Edinburgh Lunatic Asylum,*
Morningside, 1807; architect
Robert Reid
  (a) site plan
  (b) elevation
  (c) second ('third') floor plan
  (d) first ('second') floor plan
  (e) ground floor plan.

93

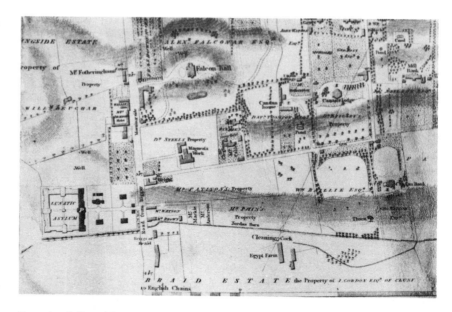

1.67 *Edinburgh Lunatic Asylum, Morningside shown on Kirkwood's 1817 map.*

Enquiry followed substantial but largely ineffective legislation on criminal and pauper lunatics, going back for fifty years. Public rate support for new asylums was recommended; apart from evidence by Paul and the Keeper of St. Luke's, they also heard from John Nash of designs he was working on for Hereford, Exeter and Gloucester; of the need for a 'hall of inspection' and cost estimates. Scotland was also covered in the review. The Enquiry was followed by the passing of the *Lunatic, Paupers and Criminals Act* in 1808 (48 Geo.IIIc.96) under which a County rate could be raised for building asylums. It also specified separation between male and female wards and between convalescent and incurable patients. These ideas found their way into official thinking within a few years as we shall see, but they had already been preceded in what was probably the most 'pure', classified and formalised asylum design of the whole period—in Glasgow.

In 1807 William Stark produced his radial asylum plan in a pamphlet published in Edinburgh, but addressed to 'A Committee of the Inhabitants of Glasgow'.[94] He was critical of designs then current, both in the 'metropolis' and in England—he was presumably referring to Reid's Edinburgh project, of the same date, for which he may have been an unsuccessful contender. He emphasised the need to classify the insane patient by 'rank of life' (i.e. ability to pay), sex, degree of insanity and the degree of liberty he ought to enjoy. The complexity of plans to achieve this together with 'ease and simplicity of superintendence peculiarly required in Lunatic Asylums' was, he reckoned, insoluble save by the strict geometry of the radial plan with central inspection. His proposal (Figures 1.68 and 1.69) is for four wings—two for males and two for females. Each

94

1.68 *Glasgow Lunatic Asylum from Swan's Views.*

pair is further sub-divided into one wing for 'higher' and one for 'lower' rank patients. A further sub-division takes place—the ground floor contains the incurable, nearest to the centre and, further away, the 'frantic'; the first floor the convalescent; and the second those 'in the ordinary state'. Even the explanatory key to this plan is set out as a hierarchically de-composed tree of classes (Figure 1.70). Special detached blocks were to be built for the totally unruly and there were eight courtyards, one for each class, each approached by separate stairs and passages. Thus each individual had access to the enclosure assigned to him '. . . while it may be completely out of their power to go beyond their own boundary, or to meet with, or even see, any individuals belonging to the other classes'. This coupled with an awareness '. . . that an unseen eye is constantly following them, and observing their conduct' describes the perfection of the absolute order which Genet sees as that of the Royal Court: rational, safe, predictable, class- and space-divided mirroring the stable, classified structure of society itself.

Stark introduced a number of improvements and enlarged the scale of the project before he died in 1813, and the building was started in 1820 on the Parliamentary Road site. His concept was clearly influential. The 1815 Parliamentary Committee on Madhouses published four Reports in 1819.[95] Attached were designs by the architect James Bevans for a 7-winged, enormous project prepared in 1814 for a London Asylum (Figure 1.71). Tuke had attacked the radial idea by 1819 remarking that Stark's scheme was 'nearly a copy of the excellent prison at Ipswich, built under the direction of the benevolent Mr Howard, and it appears to me, that W. Stark

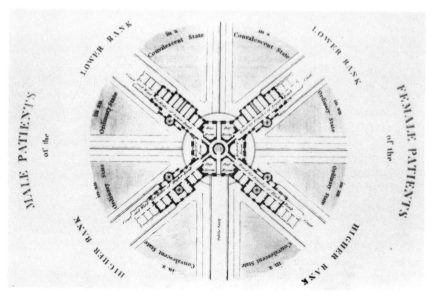

1.69 *Glasgow Lunatic Asylum, 1807; architect William Stark, ground floor plan.*

1.70 *Glasgow Lunatic Asylum; Stark's Hierarchical Table of Classes of Patients.*

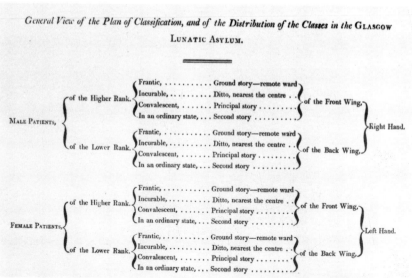

General View of the Plan of Classification, and of the **Distribution of the Classes** in the GLASGOW LUNATIC ASYLUM.

did not sufficiently consider the different objects of the two establishments';[96] the former had classification as a *permanent* structure, the latter allowed for movement between classes according to the inmate's progress. Whilst Tuke admits that easy 'superintendence . . . by overseers and supervisors is of the greatest importance', he thinks that it is carrying inspection too far '. . . to adopt some of the panopticon plans, in which a

96

centre room lighted from above, and enveloped on all sides by the apartments of the patients, is appointed to the master or mistress of the *family*' (the present author's italics; a notable new concept, for the analysis of which in contemporary literature and religion there is no space here). Tuke also adds '. . . Whatever lessens the prison like appearance of these abodes deserves attention.'[97] He had shifted his view since 1813 when he was still admiring Stark's project (as yet unbuilt) as the panoptical design afforded better supervision.[98]

Bevans was obviously sensitive to Tuke's views (which had been expressed before the 1819 publication) for, in the same year as he proposed his seven-winged London radial scheme he submitted, with thirty-nine others, a design for the 1815 Wakefield Pauper Asylum Competition, which was also published in the 1819 Parliamentary Reports (Figure 1.72). Although he did not win, in principle it resembles the winning design by Watson and Pritchett (Figure 1.73) in having two main cruciform wings, one for each sex, joined in the centre by the 'Governor's' and Matron's quarters, with central inspection possible between double rows of rooms within each wing. But in the winning scheme the central block contained committee rooms and a chapel. Bevans really did not see the difference between prisons and asylums; his London radial asylum is not much different from the model prison he submitted to the 1819 Select Committee on the State of Gaols (Figure 1.74).[99] He was a truly Benthamite, universalist character, who even applied his skills in 1816 to the design of a twelve-sided school in Bentham's own back garden at Queen Square, for nine hundred boys! This is further discussed in another essay. Bevans more than Adam, or indeed any other architect, fully absorbed Bentham's obsessions and applied them in England and Ireland for all kinds of institutions on the whole having about as little success in the translation of ideas into execution.

William Stark was also designer of at least one English asylum—the revived Gloucester scheme of 1811. The plan and exterior view in Figure 1.75 show a combination of Regency crescent, radial and courtyard elements, but with a more domestic scale and character than in his Glasgow scheme of 1807. Upon Stark's death in 1813 John Wheeler was appointed and is said to have 'enlarge(d) the scale of the drawing' to increase the accommodation.[100] Wheeler also died shortly after and the project was completed under Collingwood in 1823. The back-to-back cells for pauper lunatics in the central, axial wing was in harsh contrast to the arrangements in the commodious front crescent for paying patients. This was severely criticised by both British and foreign visitors to what became, otherwise, a much admired model.[101]

However, the Wakefield competition and the Tuke and Parliamentary debates were even more clearly foreshadowed in another Scottish scheme of an innovatory, even prophetic kind. This was also by Stark—still regarded as Scotland's leading asylum architect—for Dundee, where he was asked to design the Royal Lunatic Asylum in 1812. By that time he was

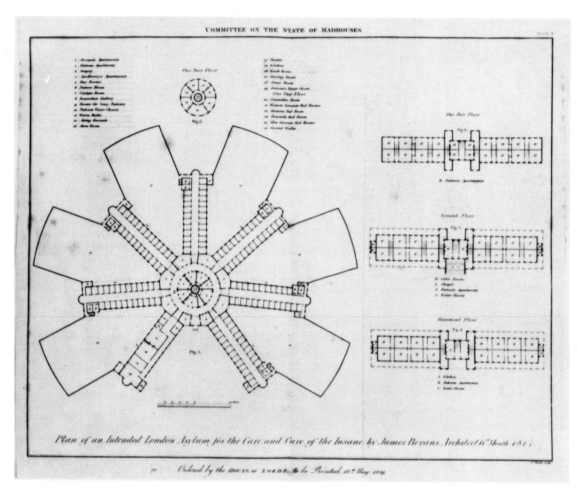

Plan of an Intended London Asylum for the Care and Cure of the Insane, by James Bevans, Architect 6.ᵗʰ Month 1814.

Ordered by the HOUSE of LORDS to be Printed 18.ᵗ May 1814.

1.71 *Radial Lunatic Asylum, 1814,*
architect James Bevans.

a dying man—but this, his third and last asylum design, represented nevertheless a vigourous and conscious effort to depart from his two radial and centralised layouts. He produced a symmetrical H plan (Figure 1.76) with administration in the cross bar and four rows of single-banked rooms in the four legs, classified in a standard way and originally of single storey, with a matron's and keeper's room centrally placed at each end of the cross piece. Later, storeys and pavilions were added to the four legs. After Stark's death in 1813 the Edinburgh architect William Burn was asked to take over in 1824. He abandoned Stark's cellular system and converted the cells to dormitories; by 1839 the project was stopped, half completed. It was said by contemporaries that the Stark design was laid out on the principle of a rural farm; certainly he had by then visited York, Montrose and Bristol and the ruralised, domestic-scale had become the new architectural image of the asylum to correspond to these new 'moral'

98

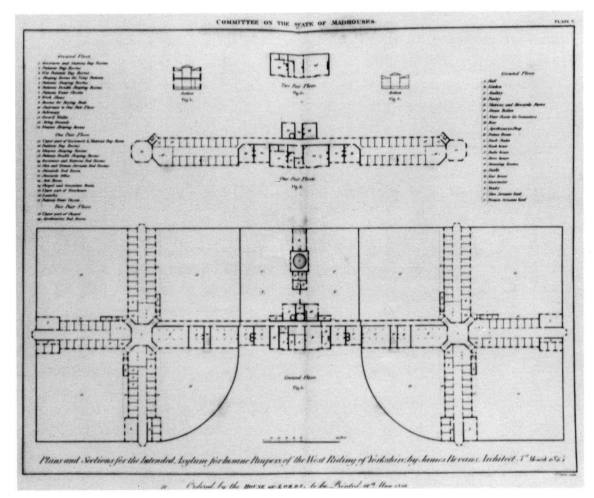

1.72 *Bevans's submission for Wakefield (West Riding of Yorkshire) Pauper Lunatic Asylum Competition, 1815, ground floor plan.*

régimes. Burn now became the Scottish expert *par excellence*; we have mentioned his addition to Morningside in Edinburgh in 1840; but his chief achievement was the Crichton Royal Asylum in Dumfries where he applied the lessons he had learnt from Stark and the Wakefield projects.

Dumfries had a wing for the insane attached to its Infirmary in 1790; but by 1834 after years of planning and fund-raising a site had been acquired and William Burn was appointed architect. His project (Figure 1.77) was remarkably like Bevans' submitted and Watson and Pritchett's executed Wakefield designs. The two greek-cross blocks for men and women were to be joined by the keeper's and matron's quarters with a central inspection hall in each of the crosses. In fact only one half (that is one cross) was built, with considerable changes to the planned classification which had been intended to be like Stark's in Glasgow. In 1847 a new

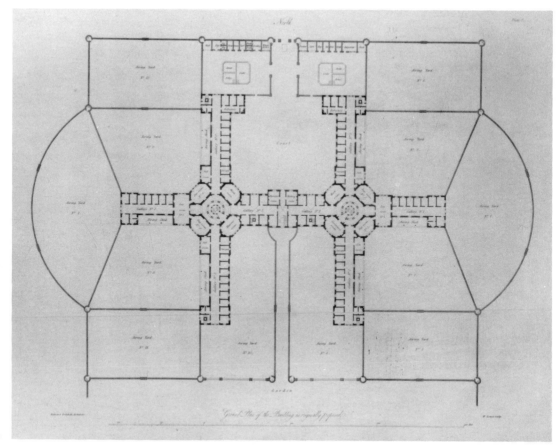

1.73(a)

1.73(b)

A PERSPECTIVE VIEW OF THE PAUPER LUNATIC ASYLUM FOR THE WEST RIDING OF THE COUNTY OF YORK, ERECTED AT WAKEFIELD IN 1816.

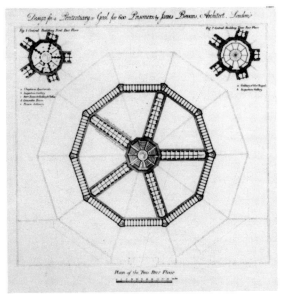

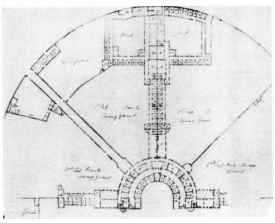

asylum for 400 patients, designed by W. McGowan, a Dumfries architect, was added.[102]

The first superintendent of the Crichton, W.A.F. Browne, was appointed in 1834; he had previously held the same post at what was, even by so late a date, still recognised as one of the most advanced asylums in Scotland, Montrose. Whilst still there he had delivered five lectures on asylums—the fifth entitled 'What asylums ought to be'.[103] The contents summarise: 'A

1.73 *Wakefield (West Riding of Yorkshire) Pauper Lunatic Asylum, winning design by Watson and Pritchett (architects), 1815,*
   (a) ground floor plan
   (b) perspective view.

1.74 *Radial prison, 1819; architect, James Bevans, first floor plan.*

1.75 *Gloucester Lunatic Asylum, 1811; architect William Stark,*
   (a) exterior perspective
   (b) plan

101

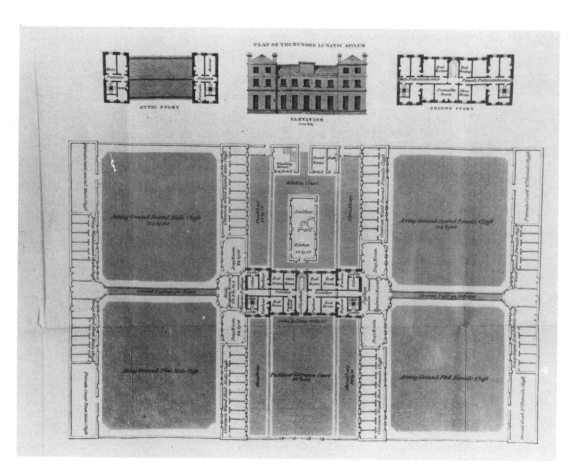

PLAN OF THE DUNDEE LUNATIC ASYLUM

1.76 *Royal Lunatic Asylum Dundee, 1812; architect William Stark, ground floor plan.*

perfect asylum a Utopia—. . . Benevolence, conscientiousness, courage— . . . Houses of one storey— . . . Shrubberies—Gardens—Farm-employment of patients—Payments for labour—Classification—Religious worship and instruction—Fallacies in moral treatment— . . . Dancing— . . . Library' etc. He elaborates:

> Conceive a spacious building resembling the palace of a Peere, airy and elevated, and elegant, surrounded by extensive and swelling grounds and gardens. The interior is fitted up with galleries and workshops, and music rooms. The sun and the air are allowed to enter in every window, the view of the shrubberies and fields and groups of labourers is unobstructed by shutters or bars; all is clean and attractive . . . The inmates all seem to be actuated by the common impulse of enjoyment, all are busy, and delighted by being so. The house and all round appears a hive of industry. All are anxious to be engaged, toil incessantly, and in general without any recompense than being kept from disagreeable thoughts and pains of illness. They literally work in order to please themselves . . . There is in this community no compulsion, no chains, no whips, no corporal punishment,

102

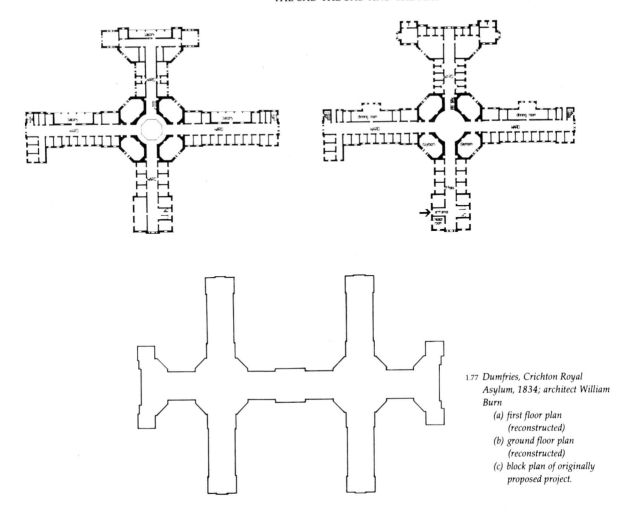

1.77 *Dumfries, Crichton Royal*
Asylum, 1834; architect William
Burn
    (a) first floor plan
        (reconstructed)
    (b) ground floor plan
        (reconstructed)
    (c) block plan of originally
        proposed project.

simply because these are proved to be less effectual means of carrying any point than persuasion, emulation and the desire for gratification.[104]

Browne's version of Utopia and the juxtaposition of the images of the palace and asylum recall the actual juxtaposition at Bridewell Palace and stands at the opposite pole, the view from 'outside' so-to-speak, from Genet's 'inside', experiential interpretation of an identical image, learnt through experience as an inmate. All the elements we have observed in earlier enterprises are present: peace and quiet; order; joy; productive labour without coercion; internal compulsion to good behaviour replacing external force; greenery and pastoral idyll.

*   *   *

103

1.78 *Adjustable wind resistance on a treadwheel.*

1.79 *Hand-turned crank in a prison cell.*

There have been at least five interpretations in recent literature of the medical, penal and mental institutions of the Enlightenment and the nineteenth century. First, Foucault's analysis, penetrating as it is in terms of the imposition of the discourse of Reason over disorder, is an abstraction; both his medical and prison analysis lack concrete evidence in terms of the actual régimes, the laws and the buildings which were the social instruments through which intentions were achieved. But he has significantly shifted the interpretation to a level at which the acts as well as the silences can be seen as reflecting the whole new mode of rational thought about society and the universe.

Second, a number of social and political historians see the institutions wholly in terms of repression, a secret world of alienated inmates and keepers, supporting each other in a dialogue essential for both, and given legitimacy by a reactionary society through the whole weight of its legal, juridical and medical systems. But this interpretation, whilst it clearly has a basis, cannot adequately account for the similarity of the institutions across a wide range of political systems (for instance France, Britain and post-Revolutionary America) nor their survival over such long periods of time.

The third view sees them as parts of an economic system which, prior to the Industrial Revolution, had to cope with large-scale unemployment and poverty, as well as the protection of craft guilds; and after it with massive urbanisation and the sheer economic necessity of somehow making institutionalised care pay for itself. It also had to impose a general work-morality which equated idleness with sin. This view, too, has of course substance; but it ignores the large number of cases, some of which we have noted in Scotland, where the inmates really could not work on account of age, infirmity or handicaps and where they were, nevertheless supported for many years on public and private funds. It does however account for the imposition of totally unproductive labour in the prisons—groups of prisoners working treadwheels attached to a fan (Figure 1.78) whose wind resistance could be adjusted to grade the difficulty of the labour; or hand-turned cranks, again with variable resistance (Figure 1.79) on which counters were fixed to record the ten- to twelve-thousand revolutions per day which the régime demanded.

The fourth interpretation emphasises the basically philanthropic intentions—as for instance Tuke's 'moral treatment' asylum; but this, in the light of Foucault's analysis of the nature of moral coercion, is too simplistic; it accepts uncritically the good as defined by the philanthropists and fails to penetrate the disguise under which they operated.

Fifth and last is the explanation in terms of the progress of reason and science—the evolutionary view which sees society becoming more reasonable and skilled in its diagnosis and treatment; the kind of optimism which was actually expressed by some of the leading figures of the time and which led to the conviction that given enough experiment, control and patience, not only would society gradually be changed, so that fewer sick, insane and criminals would be *produced*, but that the shrinking numbers which were nevertheless inevitable could, on the whole, be *'cured'*.

In the light of concrete social and architectural analysis, none of these, nor even a combination of them, seems to be a complete explanation of the phenomena. Though they all have specific relevance in the Scottish Enlightenment context—reason, Whig rationalism, scientific medicine and a refined legal system designed to defend the social structure—they fail to focus on a deeper phenomenon. That is that the control mechanisms were not only designed to repress social forces which threatened the class structure, but also to suppress those growth points which accompany the dark face of personality and society: precisely those germinal forces which caused the Scottish establishment to attack Wordsworth and the English Romantics with the unprecedented vehemence described in another essay. Those same forces had been suppressed for centuries by ascribing their manifestations to the devil and, in our day, to the independent life of the unconscious which can be 'explained' through psychoanalysis. The erection of a superstructure of order, light and reason over a secret dark and chaotic netherworld never had such a good architectural exponent as Piranesi. His Carceri etchings really have nothing to do with prisons as such, although the *concept* of prison was a convenient shorthand for a whole new imaginative experience and was a theme commonly represented in his day; the massive world of arches, vaults, stairs and bridges leading to the undefined, paradoxical, or infinite spaces, his chains and pulleys which could be instruments of *con*struction or torture (human *de*struction) are often surmounted by a glimpse of an upper world of radiant light and classical order (Figure 1.80).

Like the film *Metropolis* the etchings suggest that the psychological reality upon which architecture as a phenomenon of order is built is architecture's own antithesis—disorder and darkness. Rykwert has recently suggested that the underworld, at least in the redrawn versions, represents the corruption of Hellenistic law as contrasted with the purity of Roman law glimpsed in the world above.[105] But this underworld is not represented by Piranesi merely as a scene of fear or confusion—rather he presents the paradox of something dignified and strong in its own right. By the end of the eighteenth century Burke's notion of the 'Sublime' and the first Romantic poetic images—dealing powerfully with death, decay, the accidental in nature and the secret forces of the mind, had prepared the imagination for this new kind of reality.

So these great formalised institutions can be seen as models of the architectural programme of purity and order in a particularly clear form; it is a legitimate reading which finds a correspondence between these spatial structures and forms and alienating social structures. After all in early nineteenth century prisons not only were prisoners isolated from each other day and night, they paraded into chapels through underground passages to emerge into individual, wooden cubicles so arranged that each could only see the preacher; if they had to move in the silence of the prison they did so with hoods over their heads with slits for the eyes; and,

1.80 *Piranesi's Carceri, No. V, first edition.*

as Rothman shows,[106] the literature was filled with discussions of cell party-wall thicknesses and transmission of voices (and hence moral contagion) through drains running under the cells. But the separation of this architecture into a class of its own is too easy; Piranesi saw that all formal architecture was, potentially at least, alienating in this way—its organised forms and static divisions of space denying, through the power of light, reason and order, the force of individual freedom, feeling and germination in the darkness of a deeper order. Thus the Carceri are not *eccentric* architecture but the *essence* of architecture itself; a representation of a contradiction—it is the light of order and not the darkness of chaos which is truly imprisoning. Whether we can bear to follow Piranesi's insight is a question that confronts us with ever-increasing insistency during the nineteenth and twentieth centuries—when we follow the progress of local authority housing, garden suburbs, new towns, the Ville Radieuse and Brasilia. But to answer that question would take us well beyond the confines of this essay.

REFERENCES

1. Smout, T.C., *A History of the Scottish People, 1560–1830*, Glasgow, 1969.

2. Logue, K., *Popular Disturbances in Scotland, 1780–1815*, Edinburgh, 1979.

3. Cage, R.A., *The Scottish Poor Law*, Edinburgh, 1981.

4. Rosenau, H., *The Ideal City*, London, 1959, 2nd Edition 1974; Müller, W., *Die Heilige Stadt*, Stuttgart, 1961; Markus, T.A., The 18th Century Roots of the 19th Century Industrial Town, presented at Symposium: *Architecture of Industrial Towns in the Second Half of the 19th Century; its Historical and Contemporary Problems*, Łodz, Poland 28–30 September 1981; and Tod, I. and Wheeler, M., *Utopia*, London, 1978.

5. Doni, A., *Les Mondes Célestes, Terrestre et Infernaux*, Lyon, 1578; Campanella, Thomas, *The City of the Sun* (Civitas Solis), Frankfurt, 1623.

6. Kaufmann, E., Three Revolutionary Architects, Boullée, Ledoux, and Lequeu, *Trans. of the American Philosophical Society*, New Series, 42, Part 3, 1952.

7. Owen, R., Report to the Committee on the Association for the new Relief of the Manufacturing Poor, March 1817, in *The Life of Robert Owen* etc. Vol. 1A, London 1858; and *Report to the County of Lanark of a Plan* etc., Glasgow, 1821.

8. Tod and Wheeler, op. cit.

9. Thompson, J.D. and Goldin, G., *The Hospital: A Social and Architectural History*, New Haven, 1975; Jetter, D., *Geschichte des Hospitals*, Band 1, Westdeutschland von den Anfängen bis 1850, Wiesbaden, 1966; and Markus, T.A., The Pattern of the Law, *Architectural Review*, CXVI, October 1954, pp. 251-256.

10. The stages by which such elements found their way into the New Town are described in Peter Reed's essay in the present collection.

11. Turner, A. Logan, *Story of a Great Hospital; the Edinburgh Royal Infirmary, 1729-1929*, Edinburgh, 1937; and Stott, Rosalie, The Battle for Students: Medical Teaching in Edinburgh in the First Half of the Eighteenth Century, in *Edinburgh's Infirmary, A Symposium* etc., Edinburgh, 1979.

12. These are bound in a volume of original drawings in the archives of

the History of Medicine and Science Unit, Department of History, Edinburgh University. I am particularly obliged to Dr. Stephanie Blackman for making them available.

13. Dunbar-Nasmith, J.D., Designs for Health: The Architecture of the Royal Infirmaries of Edinburgh, in *Edinburgh's Infirmary, A Symposium* etc., op. cit.

14. These designs are discussed in detail in Thompson and Goldin, op. cit.

15. Filarete, *Treatise on Architecture*, Ed., Spencer, J.R., New Haven, 1965.

16. Hillier, W.R.G., develops this concept in greater detail in *The Social Logic of Space*, Cambridge, (in the press 1982).

17. The plan is illustrated in Fürst, V., *The Architecture of Sir Christopher Wren*, London, 1956.

18. *The History and Statutes of the Royal Infirmary of Edinburgh*, 1778, p. 10.

20. Fleming, John, *Robert Adam and His Circle*, London, 1962, (reprinted 1978), p. 62.

21. Duncan, A., *Memorials of the Faculty of Physicians and Surgeons of Glasgow, 1599-1850*, Glasgow, 1896, pp. 91-2 and 136-7.

22. ibid., p. 137.

23. Cleland, J., *Annals of Glasgow*, Glasgow, 1816, Vol. 1, pp. 76-7.

24. Maps by McArthur (1778), Denholm (1797) and Fleming (1808) all show the layout described.

25. *Extracts from the Records of the Burgh of Glasgow*, (hereafter referred to as 'Extracts'), Vol. VIII 1781-95, Glasgow, 1913, p. 222, meeting of 8th March 1787.

26. Christie, J., *The Medical Institutions of Glasgow; a Handbook*, Glasgow, 1888, p. 42.

27. Bolton, A.T., *The Architecture of Robert and James Adam*, 2 Vols., London, 1922, Index of Adam Drawings, Vol. 2, p. 14.

28. Evans, R., Regulation and Production, in *Lotus International*, September 1976, pp. 6-14.

29. Bellers, J., Proposals for Raising a Colledge of Industry, (1696) reprinted in Owen, R., *New View of Society*, London, 1818, in Supplementary Appendix to the First Volume of the *Life of Robert Owen*, London, 1858, Vol. 1A, Appendix L.

30. Genet, Jean, *The Thief's Journal,* trans. Bernard Frechtman, London, 1967, pp. 71-2.

31. Cleland, J., *Statistical Facts* etc., (bound-in with), *Glasgow Bridewell or House of Correction*, Glasgow, 1837, p. 1; and Cleland, J., *Statistical Facts and Population Tables* etc., 3rd edition, Glasgow, 1828, p. 176.

32. *Extracts*, Vol. VIII, p. 64, meeting of 18th September 1782.

33. ibid., p. 172-3, meeting of 29th June 1785.

34. ibid., p. 248, meeting of 28th February 1788; and p. 267, meeting of 29th October 1788.

35. ibid., p. 268.

36. ibid., p. 386, meeting of 29th November 1790, records the decision of the Councillors to inspect the prison House, the House of Correction, Bridewell and 'Cells at the Town's Hospital' once a week.

37. ibid., p. 260, meeting of 25th September 1788 and p. 277, meeting of 10th December 1788.

38. ibid., p. 342, meeting of 30th January 1790.

39. ibid., p. 452, meeting of 22nd March 1792.

40. ibid., pp. 551-2, meeting of 12 May 1794; and p. 598, meeting of 1st June 1795.

41. ibid., p. 585 meeting of 13th March 1795.

42. The original drawings are all in the Strathclyde Region Archives; the variant design, not illustrated here, is indexed under D-TC 13 438 G and H.

43. *Extracts*, Vol. VIII, pp. 607-8, meeting of 11th August 1795.

44. *Extracts*, Vol. IX, 1796-1808, Glasgow, 1914, p. 7, meeting of 21st March 1796.

45. ibid., p. 142, meeting of 7th February 1799.

46. Renwick, R., *Glasgow Memorials,* Glasgow, 1908, p. 26, referring to Council Reg. xxxii p. 280.

47. 31 Geo. III c. 107.

48. Renwick, op. cit., p. 28.

49. *Extracts,* Vol. IX, p. 49, meeting of 1st December, 1796; p. 103, meeting of 8th May 1798; p. 278, meeting of 13th November 1801; and p. 349, meeting of 7th February 1803.

50. ibid., p. 477, meeting of 10th September 1805.

51. ibid., p. 550, meeting of 5th February 1807.

52. ibid., p. 557, meeting of 13th February 1807.

53. ibid., p. 662, meeting of 1st September 1808.

54. ibid., pp. 673-4, meeting of 15th December 1808.

55. ibid., Vol. X, 1809-1822, Glasgow, 1915, pp. 43-4, meeting of 20th February 1810.

56. Cleland, J., *Specification of the Manner of Building and Furnishing a Set of Public Offices and a Prison* etc., Glasgow, 1810.

57. 4 Geo. IV, ch. 64, 1823.

58. *Extracts,* Vol. X, pp. 651-2, meeting of 11th February 1822.

59. Cleland, J., 1828, op. cit., p. 97.

60. Scottish Records Office, Edinburgh Drawings Collection RHP 21478 and 21479.

61. Copies of the *Reports Made to His Majesty's Secretary of State for the Home Department Respecting The Gaols in Scotland,* London, 1835, pp. 201-2.

62. Markus, The Pattern of the Law, op. cit.

63. Steuart, D. and Cockburn, A., *General Heads of a Plan for Erecting a New Prison and Bridewell in the City of Edinburgh,* (Edinburgh?), 1782.

64. ibid., p. 7.

65. ibid., p. 8.

66. 3 Geo. III ch. 57, 1791.

67. Howard, J., *An Account of the Principal Lazarettos in Europe,* etc., London, 1789.

68. Bentham, J., *Panopticon; or the Inspection House,* London, 1791, (another edition appeared in the same year in Dublin); and *Panopticon; Postscript,* 2 Vols., London, 1791.

69. Bentham's seminal letter, from Russia, to George Wilson, is in Bowring, J., Ed., *The Works of Jeremy Bentham,* 11 Vols. London 1843, Vol. 4 p. 40; and the relevant letters on the Panopticon, from 1786 onwards, in *The Correspondence of Jeremy Bentham,* Ed. Christie, I.R., Vol. 3, January 1781 to October 1788, London, 1971. esp. letters 582, 584, 590 and 593.

70. I am indebted to Professor J.H. Burns for making available to me before its publication the material referred to here and in the next six notes, in galley form, from *The Correspondence of Jeremy Bentham,* etc., Milne A.T., Vol. 4, October 1788 to December 1793, London, 1981, Letter 771.

71. ibid., Vol. 4, letter 789.

72. ibid., letter 792.

73. ibid., letter 848.

74. ibid., letter 850.

75. ibid., letter 848, note 1. referring to Samuel Bentham's correspondence.

76. ibid., letter 922.

77. Peterson, C.E., Early Prisons, *J. of the Soc. of Architectural Historians,* XII, 4 December, 1958, pp. 26-30 illustrates the plan by the Lyon architect, Bugniet, dating from 1765.

78. Cockburn, H., *Memorials of His Time,* Edinburgh, 1856, pp. 271-2.

79. Original drawings in the Archives of Edinburgh District Council. I

am indebted to Mr R. Kilgour and Mrs C. Brooke of that Department for access to these drawings and those shown in Figures 1.58 and 1.62.

80. Scottish Records Office, Edinburgh, Drawings Collection RHP 21327-21489 (from Rowand Anderson Kininmonth and Paul Collection).

81. ibid., items No. 21432-21435 show Brown's scheme.

82. ibid., item No. 21436.

83. Foucault, M., *Madness and Civilization; a History of Madness in the Age of Reason,* trans. Howard, R., from *Histoire de la Folie,* Paris, 1961; London, 1971.

84. Thompson and Goldin, op. cit., pp. 54-9.

85. Williams, A., *The Police of Paris, 1718-1789,* Baton Rouge and London, 1979.

86. Tuke, Samuel, *Description of the Retreat,* London, 1813.

87. *Report of the Select Committee of the House of Commons Appointed to Enquire into the State of Lunatics,* London, 1807. (Hereafter referred to as *State of Lunatics).*

88. *Report of the Treasurer's Committee etc. on . . . The Best Means of Obtaining Immediate Accommodation for Pauper Lunatics,* Edinburgh, 1837.

89. Some account of the Plan for establishing a Lunatic Asylum at Edinburgh, attached to *Address to the Public Respecting the Establishment of a Lunatic Asylum at Edinburgh,* Edinburgh, 1807. The attachment is not dated; the same drawings by Reid appear in *Observations on the Structure of Hospitals for the Treatment of Lunatics* etc . . . *to which is Annexed an Account of the Intended Establishment of a Lunatic Asylum at Edinburgh,* Edinburgh, 1809.

90. Peterson, op. cit., p. 7.

91. The plan is illustrated in *Regulations of the Edinburgh Lunatic Asylum,* Edinburgh, 1840.

92. *State of Lunatics,* op. cit.

93. For a history of the Gloucester County Lunatic Asylum see: Bailey,

Ann, An Account of the Founding of the First Gloucestershire County Asylum, now Horton Road Hospital, Gloucester 1792-1823, *Trans. Bristol and Gloucester Archeological Society*, 1971, pp. 178-191; and Walk, Alexander and Walker, D. Lindsay, Gloucester and the Beginnings of the R.M.P.A., *The J. of Mental Science*, 107, 449, July 1961, pp. 603-632.

94. Stark, W., *Remarks on Public Hospitals for the Cure of Mental Derangement* etc., Edinburgh, 1807.

95. First, Second, Third and Fourth *Reports from The Committee on Madhouses in England, 1815*, London, 1819.

96. Watson and Pritchett, *Plans, Elevations, Sections and Description of the Pauper Lunatic Asylum lately erected at Wakefield for the West Riding of Yorkshire etc., 1819*, York, included Tuke, S., Practical Hints on the Construction and Economy of Pauper Lunatic Asylums; his comments on Stark's asylum, p. 16.

97. ibid., p. 20.

98. Tuke, *Description of the Retreat*, op. cit., p. 14.

99. *Report from the Select Committee on the State of Gaols*, etc., London, 1819.

100. Walk and Walker, op. cit., pp 606-607.

101. For example Crommelinck, C., *Rapport sur les Hospices d'Aliénés de l'Angleterre, de France et de l'Allemagne*, Courtrai, 1842, p. 109: 'Le plus mauvais plan possible a été adopté par l'architecte; . . . un antre de misère et de douleur etc.'!

102. I am grateful to Ian Brebner who, in his Special Study Dissertation, *Madness and Morals*, Department of Architecture and Building Science, University of Strathclyde, Glasgow, June 1981, described the development of Crichton Royal, gave permission for reproduction of his hypothetical reconstruction of the half-plans shown in Figure 1.77 and first drew my attention to Browne's work.

103. Browne, W.A.F., *What Asylums Were, Are and Ought to Be*, Edinburgh, 1837, Lecture V, p. 176.

104. ibid., pp. 229-239.

105. Rykwert, J., *The First Moderns—the Architects of the Eighteenth Century*, Cambridge, Mass. and London, 1980, pp. 374-390.

106. Rothman, D.J., *The Discovery of the Asylum; Social Order and Disorder in the New Republic*, Boston and Toronto, 1971.

Form and Context: a study of Georgian Edinburgh

Peter Reed

The Georgian development of Edinburgh constituted a vast exercise in classical form in monuments, public buildings and housing for the well-to-do; its history has been often told, most comprehensively by Professor Youngson.[1] In this essay one aspect of the phenomenon is considered: the relationship between the form given to housing and its spatial context. This context is established by development plans. The expansion of Edinburgh to the north of the Old Town was, by and large, effected through five plans, still easily distinguishable one from another. Of these, four are discussed for the present purpose, beginning with the eighteenth century scheme that initiated the northward expansion.

It should be recalled that there had been resistance by rural landowners to an extension of government from the City and that not until 1767, after the building of a bridge from the High Street over the depression of the North Loch, was an Act passed that brought the fields to the north within the City's jurisdiction. Work began there at once on James Craig's competition-winning scheme for a New Town (Figure 2.1). After initial hesitation building progressed steadily from east to west for some thirty years on the three great parallel thoroughfares: Queen Street to the north opposed to a prospect of sea and distant hills; Princes Street to the south enjoying the encrusted panorama of the mediaeval city; and the central elevated spine of George Street terminating in ostentatious squares. Subsidiary streets and lanes were laid out to serve this essentially residential development. Ainslie's map of 1804 (Figure 2.2) shows the scheme substantially completed, although in the west work was then still in progress on Charlotte Square.

Craig's plan and its realisation have had a variable press:

> . . . the natural advantages of the situation, joined to the regulation of the whole being built conform to a regular and beautiful plan, gave the extended royalty a superiority over any city in Great Britain . . . The prospect from the New Town is as beautiful as almost any Country can afford. (Arnot)[2]

> What a site did Nature give us for our New Town! Yet what insignificance in its plan: what poverty in all its details! . . . every conception except of straight lines, cut rectangularly into equal spaces, and of every thirty front feet being covered with the plainest and the cheapest house, each exactly like its neighbour, seems to have been excluded. It will take many years, and the cost of building about half of the original New Town over again, to lessen the baseness of the first ideas. We have now some pillars, balconies, porticos and ornament roughening; and money, travelling, and discussion will get us on. (Cockburn)[3]

These commentaries evidence, over fifty years or so, a change in planning critique from regularity, in Georgian classicism, to variety, in Regency picturesque. Cockburn was, no doubt, influenced by the opinion of

William Stark, for him 'the best modern architect that Scotland has produced.'[4] In 1813 Stark had written a report[5] (published posthumously) of central interest to this essay: in it he advocates, with explicit reference to the landscape painting of Claude and Poussin, the mutual enhancement of Nature and Architecture and, in town planning, the exploitation of variety and 'accident of situation' offered in plenitude by the topography of Edinburgh. Scenic principles, he argues

> may injure the symmetry of the *ground* plan, and disturb the harmony and measured allotment of streets, squares and crescents. Yet it were easy to show of how little consequence all this is, except upon paper; how unavailing in execution the minute precision of a mathematical figure; the exact parallelism of lines, equiangularity of divisions, and all the other niceties of square and rule.[6]

This implied criticism of Craig's plan is then made explicit:

> to a stranger occupied in the examination of the present New Town, it would import little to be informed, when looking along George's Street, that it is precisely parallel to Princes Street and Queen's Street, or, if admiring Charlotte Square, to be told that it forms the exact counterpart upon the ground plan to St. Andrew's Square.[7]

Yet Stark's indifference to—or distaste for—classical idealism surely here betrays his appraisal of perceived relationships. Experience of Craig's grid is dominated by the insistent parallelism of the major streets; and awareness of its finite extension demands perception of reflections that pair northern and southern terraces, eastern and western squares. The clarity of this structure is due to the topography of the site: the symmetrical form of the New Town is absorbed directly through the effort of ascent and descent between the central axis and the parallel boundaries of Princes Street and Queen Street.

Above all, however, any ambiguity of orientation is resolved by the eminence of the Old Town, dominating every prospect to the south. From the Castle Rock the ridge, formed in its lee by glacial retreat, declines due east, piled high with the tenements of the then mediaeval city. The New Town and the Old progress in parallel across the divide of the valley of the loch. The contrast between the former—an invention of one time—and the latter—a product of historic growth—is irresistible. The aligned separation of the Georgian and the Mediaeval still provokes comparison between their modes of living; and in this Craig surely realised the ambitions of the prime begetters of the New Town, Provost Drummond and his Town Council. For in proposals[8] indebted to Drummond and published in 1752 the 'steepness, narrowness and darkness' of the Edinburgh wynds, and the 'great want of free air, light, cleanliness and every other accommodation' are compared with the conditions of London, with

> the neatness and accommodation of its private houses; the beauty and conveniency of its numerous streets and open squares, of its buildings and bridges, its large parks and extensive walks.[9]

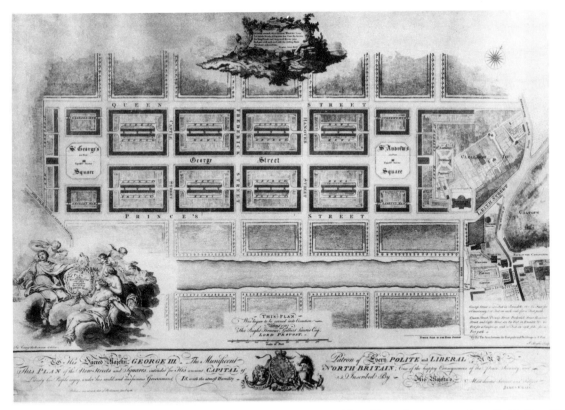

2.1 *James Craig's 'Plan of the new streets and squares intended for the City of Edinburgh; 1767.*

The Town Council comprised in extraordinary assembly thirty-three persons, of whom twenty-five made up the ordinary Council.[10] The membership was exclusively of the merchant and trades classes, though it was not representative of all commercial interests in the city. It was elected by a convoluted system that effectively preserved in power a select coterie. Drummond's council was alarmed by two tendencies in the wealth-dispensing classes. The first was for those who maintained residence in the vicinity of Edinburgh to do so outside the royalty, and therefore to contribute little to the treasury of the city. That this had long been the case is noted by Arnot,[11] but from 1749 the challenge became acute when, on private initiative, houses for the well-to-do were built in the English style on land south of the city limits. But a more important threat to the trade of the city was the steady migration of its wealthy clientele to the southern capital, following the Act of Union of 1707:

> Let us improve and enlarge this city, and possibly the superior pleasures of London which is at a distance, will be compensated, at least in some measure by the moderate pleasures of Edinburgh, which is at home.[12]

The arguments for the extension of the royalty and for making provision for a more fashionable mode of living—to be funded nationally—were couched, appropriately for the interests of the magistrates and councillors, in terms of trade, and with the promise of an economic prosperity that would spread from the capital throughout Scotland:

117

The examples set by the capital, the nation will soon follow. The certain consequence is, general wealth and prosperity; the number of useful people will increase; the rents of land rise; the public revenue improve; and, in the room of sloth and poverty, will succeed industry and opulence.[13]

The detached siting of the New Town is reinforced by the parallelism of Craig's plan; they combine in an unambiguous and dramatic declaration of a new status for the Scottish capital and of new possibilities for a future based upon the prosperity of the bourgeoisie.

The New Town was therefore to be a symbol and a catalyst for a new dynamic in society. There are often-quoted contemporary descriptions of the unique mode of living in the historic northern capital—of the great elevation of its buildings, of the accommodation of all classes off a common staircase, of the congestion, and of the lack of amenity in fresh air, clean water and covered drainage. Serated by its steep wynds, Edinburgh was likened to 'an ivory comb, whose teeth on both sides are very foul, though the space between them is clean and sightly'.[14] The propaganda for the New Town was couched simultaneously in terms of a

2.2 *Ainslie's map of Edinburgh, 1804 (part showing first and second New Towns and the Earl of Moray's property).*

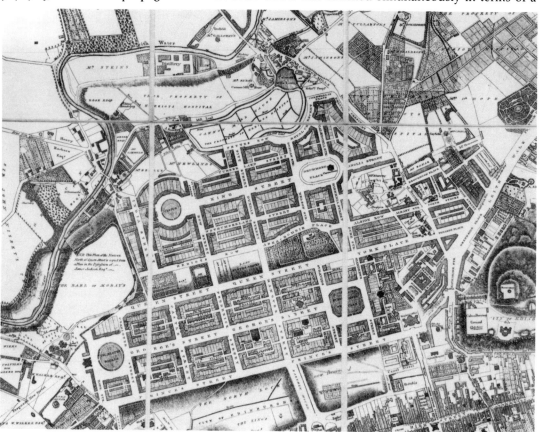

118

different aesthetic and of improved hygiene. Thus Arnot continues his praise for the regularity and beauty of the plan with a note that the declivities of the site afford the 'opportunity of making proper common sewers'. And, significantly, the inscription that Craig himself gave to his project—a quotation from the long poem on Liberty by his uncle James Thomson—apostrophises in the same breath streets for their stateliness and squares 'that court the breeze'. Indeed, given the kinship between Thomson and Craig, and Craig's explicit use of his uncle's work, it is reasonable to interpret the plan for the New Town as a realisation of that prospect of the future revealed by the Goddess of Liberty herself.

In his poetic survey of the course of western civilisation, Thomson identifies libertarian progress with the classical tradition, realised most magnificently in architecture. In Greece this art was 'refined, And . . . to full perfection brought'; its rules there established are so sure

> that Goths of every age,
> Who scorned their aid, have only loaded earth
> With laboured heavy monuments of shame.[15]

In the dark ages the Goddess 'with Arts and Sciences in her train' quits earth; but returns to renaissance Italy and progresses to her ultimate destination, Great Britain. There she inspires in the poet a utopian vision of imposed classical order:

> Lo! vanished monster-land. Lo! driven away
> Those that Apollo's sacred walks profane—
> Their wild creation scattered . . .
> Detested forms! that, on the mind impressed,
> Corrupt, confound, and barbarize an age.
> . . . .
> August around what public works I see!
> Lo! stately streets, lo! squares that court the breeze . . .
> See! long canals, and deepened rivers join
> Each part with each, and with the circling main
> The whole enlivened isle . . . [16]

The ordered geometry of Craig's island settlement is a metaphor for the enlightened society that, it was believed, would come to prevail through-out the kingdom. And, by implication, the Old Town with

> streets which were filthy, . . . causeways rugged and broken, . . . big gurgling gutters in which ran the refuse of a crowded population, and among which the pigs poked their snouts in grunting satisfaction for garbage[17]

represented the forces of corruption, confusion and barbarism.

The eighteenth century private developments in London and Bath, planned as contiguous expansions from established centres, were, like the private initiatives in Edinburgh, motivated by land speculation. The English leasehold system, by which the disposal of the developed plot reverts regularly to the landowner, was the source of vast wealth that accrued—and continues to accrue—to the beneficiaries of the speculation;

it was also the stimulus for repeated refashioning of property to maintain its attraction on the market. Under the Scottish system, though the land was sold outright, the superiority to it was not transferred; which meant that an annual feu-duty was payable to the superior and that the charter of sale might include binding conditions on the use of the land. Craig's extension was planned on land within the extended royalty for which the superiority was possessed by the Corporation or by the Heriot's Hospital Trust. Youngson's careful study[18] of the Town Council's accounts shows that by the end of the century when, with the exception of Charlotte Square, the New Town was substantially complete, the income for the city from land sales and annual feu-duties was still short of total expenditure. For the councillors, making of direct profit—beyond the need for a solvency that was not eventually achieved—was of less interest than maintaining the momentum of the development; on this depended the increased prosperity of the city—as far as it was identified with their own mercantile and trading interests. The regularity of Craig's plan facilitated economical, ordered partitioning into building lots. That the interest of councillors in the successful realisation of the plan was *indirect*—though some speculated personally in its development—may account for the lack of commitment that the *ensemble,* beyond the splendour endowed by the situation, should amount to more than the sum of these parts.

Craig's plan proposed a limited range of urban motifs: the *rue-corridors* of the principal east-west axis and the paired north-south crossings; the eastern and western *places,* five hundred feet square; and northern and southern *boundaries* confronted, respectively, by open landscape and the irregular prospect of the Old Town. But apart from the intended axial location of churches in the squares, neither his plan nor the Acts formulated for its materialisation recognise interdependence of building form and urban space. The Acts of 1767 and 1768 were designed primarily to ensure convenience and uniformity, though in the first there is a tacit admission of the monotony of complete regularity and an incentive for incidental variety:

> . . . those who incline to feu three lots upon the principal street, should be allowed to carry their houses farther back than eight feet, . . . such three lots being in the centre of one of the plots; which the Committee were of the opinion would not hurt the plan, but rather be an additional beauty to it.[19]

This Act therefore envisaged larger houses on George Street symmetrically placed within a block, and set behind a forecourt to which the standard housing would form wings. We see from Ainslie's map (Figure 2.2) that such opportunity was not taken up, but that public buildings—the Assembly Rooms, Physicians' Hall and St. Andrew's Church—occupy central positions in blocks of housing.

A hierarchical arrangement of housing was established on the east side of St. Andrew Square. As Craig's plan shows, Sir Laurence Dundas—apparently with foreknowledge of the proposal—had acquired a plot

120

centred on the proposed axis. In 1767 he obtained the feu of the plot designated for the church and made plans for a town house—begun in 1772 to the design of Sir William Chambers—that encroached on the proposed church site. Consequently the church now stands in George Street. The Council restored symmetrical order to the square in 1781 by offering the adjacent site to the south at a preferential rate on the condition that on it should be mirrored the design of the columnated house that flanked the Dundas property to the north.

Such intervention in the planning process by the Council was rare; generally the Building Acts (of 1781, 1782, 1785) were merely restrictive—limiting storey heights according to location in the hierarchy of streets, limiting the pitch of roofs, forbidding dormer windows. Although prospective feuers were required to submit their proposed designs, no conditions were imposed to integrate the piecemeal development of sites. Moreover lack of security in the venture inhibited architectural ambition. So the earliest housing was generally of the plainest repetitive unit of a standard width, raised in droved ashlar and relieved only by a spare architrave, a modillioned cornice, a stylar doorpiece. Shepherd's view from George Street to St. Andrew Square (Figure 2.3.) shows the character of this early housing, as well as the ensemble around the Dundas House, and the church, denied its axial status.

Craig was not able to integrate the approach from the Old Town into the axial system of his plan because of the private ownership of land on the line of the North Bridge. The comparison, often made, between his plan and that prepared in about 1752 by Emmanuel Héré for the town of Nancy

2.3 *T.H. Shepherd's print of George Street, St. Andrew's Church and Lord Melville's Monument.*

is misleading in points of similarity but illuminating where the schemes differ. Although both include *places* linked on an axis, Héré's scheme penetrates two existing systems: the *ville neuve* and the fortified Old Town. The terminal *places*—the place Royale and the Fer du Cheval—are nodes within, respectively, the new and old urban networks, to which they give access. The new centre bridges the two systems, establishing between them a spatial dynamic; moreover it is introverted. Had St. Andrew Square terminated *both* George Street and the new route from the Old Town it would have been an articulating pivot between the two systems. George Street could then have been generated as the principal thoroughfare of the new scheme in effect as well as in intention. Craig's concern for spatial elaboration at junctions between systems is shown by his 1786 scheme[20] for a *place* to encompass the Tron Kirk at the intersection of High Street and the North Bridge. And his unease about the dignity of George Street is indicated by his unrealised amendment[21] of 1774 that proposed a great circus centred on its mid-point. But it is Robert Adam's Register House at the very edge of Craig's site and barely inflected from the line of Princes Street that closes the vista of the North Bridge. And it is Princes Street, not George Street, that almost from the inception of the project became the principal thoroughfare. Princes Street enjoyed the advantages of southern aspect, and the picturesque prospect (which it was necessary to defend at law) of the mediaeval city—hygienically distanced, but still conveniently near for business interests.

From early prints it is clear that, like most of George Street and St. Andrew Square, Princes Street was built in an austere economical mould and in piecemeal fashion. In the controlled spaces of the street and the square, however, there had been attempts to bring a wider order to the architecture through localised symmetries. But Princes Street and Queen Street are frontages presented by the system as a whole. Each is vast, some 3500 feet in length, and each—Princes Street in particular—is viewed comprehensively. Given the scale of this architecture, and its function as boundary to an environment unmediated by classical principles, Cockburn's plea for 'pillars, balconies, porticos and ornamental roughening' is somewhat beside the point.

Cockburn was writing in the 1820's by which time in London Nash had completed Regent Street and was at work on the even more elaborate classical picturesque of the terraces bounding Regent's Park; and the classical expansion of Bath had run its course. But for Craig and the Town Council of 1767 the precedents to hand for an urban residential ensemble on classical principles were few. In London Edward Shepherd had unified three houses on the north side of Grosvenor Square behind a Palladian facade, and John Symmons had treated the entire east block, somewhat tentatively, as a symmetrical composition, with a centre accented by a small pediment and corners given prominence as pavilions. The imagery is of the aristocrat's town house or palace, fronting an open space, recalling the core of earlier exercises in the speculative settlement of London. This precedent is even clearer in John Wood's original intentions for Queen Square in Bath. A wide parade crosses the south side of the square, which is seen as the forecourt of a 'palace' on the north side, to which the east and west blocks stand as wings. These schemes in London and Bath were completed in the second and third decades of the eighteenth century. In 1754 Wood's design for a residential circus in Bath was begun, to be completed by his son; the son was to begin his own grandiose scheme for a semi-elliptical crescent of houses confronting open landscape and with distant views of the town in 1767—the very year of the Edinburgh competition.

These English achievements were not made at first at the behest of the landowners but through the initiatives of the first lessees, aiming for profit through sub-leasing or tenancy. Edinburgh New Town was, with the seminal exception of Charlotte Square, built according to similar economic principle. Fues were granted both to those building for speculation as well as to intending residents. Apart from the prescriptions of the Building Acts, and rare example of direct local intervention, the Council did not seek to influence the form of housing. Any initiative to integrate units into a wider architectural scheme had to come from speculators; and the mere scale of the blocks in Craig's plan must have precluded a sufficient outlay of capital on a scheme yet to prove viable. Nor, of course, was it known how much in Edinburgh a collective imagery would prove an asset in the fashionable market. Robert Adam's experience with the Adelphi speculation, executed between 1768 and 1772, and which brought him to the verge of bankruptcy, would doubtless have instilled caution north of the Border.

Yet, these economic considerations aside, none of the English examples—not even that of Royal Crescent with its similar relation between building and prospect—could offer a way to the formal resolution of Craig's plan in its boundary conditions. Any classical solution for the street *as a whole* is precluded by its scale—each of the larger blocks of Princes Street alone could accommodate a Royal Crescent. And consider the lateral spread of the great classical complexes at Greenwich (660'), Castle Howard (800'), Blenheim (850'), even Versailles (1350').

Classical order is hierarchial—it embodies reflections and rotations about axes, or translations of elements within some integrating finite geometry. Hence Craig's *plan* is classical; and, as has been argued above—Stark notwithstanding—this is how its structure is experienced. But for the unmodulated vastness of its boundary no hierarchical ordering of *form* is possible; within it, of course, localised order may be achieved. What the plan offers here is the neutrality and extensibility of the grid, within which the elements enjoy an independence denied by classicism. Hence there is a contradiction in the intentions of the plan; and it is possible that Craig recognised this boundary problem, for on the plan he shows the cross-routes tentatively extended to north and south—and then they are simply faded out. It is as if he himself felt that his axial system should properly be embedded in some infinitely extensible network.

The neutrality of the grid renders it freely susceptible to social and economic pressures. Whereas the grid of Princes Street well accommodates its present commercial variety, in its first form the imposed uniformity of function had drear consequences. Possibly for the first time, but certainly not for the last, housing was likened pejoratively to barracks.[22] Craig's plan has been compared with that for the new town built after 1630 by Cardinal Richelieu on his estate south of the Loire. It, too, was planned symmetrically around an axis that connected two squares. But its order and symmetries are contained and inward—like those at Nancy. For defence it was surrounded by fortifications—a moat and a wall studded with look-out towers. Craig's plan, too, seems conceived with boundaries to be viewed from, not looked at. This privilege was, of course, denied by the eminence and exposure of the site.

Cockburn was but a late critic of the nature of Craig's plan and of its bleak realisation; and the Town Council was moved to more direct action than its earlier timid and unsuccessful attempt to encourage focused variety in George Street. By 1790 all but the western square and its immediate environment was complete. Delays here were due to difficulties with the adjacent landowner, the Earl of Moray; and when they were resolved the Town Council entered into a contract with Robert Adam for the unified design of the square, now renamed after Queen Charlotte.

Adam must have been familiar with the New Town project from its inception—his brother and partner, John, was one of the adjudicators of the competition. At an early stage of building he was involved professionally: he was probably the architect of the columnated house built in St. Andrew Square in 1768 north of the Dundas plot; and he was certainly responsible for No. 8 Queen Street, designed in 1770–1 for Lord Chief Baron Ord. Just as the new square was not Adam's first involvement with domestic building in Edinburgh, neither was it his first attempt at integrating housing on a grand scale. There had been the ill-fated project of the Adelphi, with its range of eleven houses fronting the Thames and flanked by the advanced, pedimented gables of lateral terraces; and immediately prior to his Scottish commission he had provided elevations for the square in Colonel Fitzroy's development of his estate north of Oxford Street. In his designs for Charlotte Square Adam introduced to Edinburgh the classical norms through which the further Georgian expansion of the city was to be realised.

Classicism is the least obliging of architectural systems to accommodate conflict between the forces of communal order and individualism. The Georgian urban *ensemble* is a late extension of the renaissance-baroque system that was initiated in the churches and palaces of the *quattrocento*. The system, of course, uses the forms of the classical orders. But, adopting the terms and the argument applied by Emil Kaufmann:

> more important and far more significant than the reintroduction of ancient forms, was the rise of a new compositional principle: the parts now should . . .

124

be differentiated as superior and inferior components. The post-mediaeval composition which emphasised the different values of parts made of the whole a hierarchy of well-disciplined elements. The means by which this goal was reached . . . were concatenation, integration and gradation.[23]

The particular coherence of a design within this system resides in compensations made between these three independently unifying conceptions of form. Thus typically within the comprehensive Georgian scheme there is horizontal concatenation of identities—of bay with bay, of house with house; and a vertical gradation from storey to storey—in the proportions of openings, in the textures of masonry. But the extension of form—potentially infinite—through repetition and transition is delimited by the principle of integration. Horizontal and vertical continuities of classical elements frame and unite bay with bay and storey with storey. Moreover, in response to the spatial geometry of its context, the whole is commanded by symmetries that frequently overlay the cellular aggregation of houses without relation to its spatial divisions. This ordering of repeated like units within a hierarchical structure is the formal correspondence to the identification of individual necessity with the social aspirations of the group.

Adam's plan (Figure 2.4) accommodates the church on the axis of George Street. Both the church to the west and the return of the street to the east are flanked by paired blocks of housing, each of six units. As well as the entrance to the square of the principal thoroughfare, cross-connections with Queen Street and Princes Street are proposed at the four corners, all in accordance with Craig's plan. These cross-streets delimit the extent of the north and south ranges, each of nine houses.

A sketch for the west side (Figure 2.5) shows alternative treatments for the two blocks flanking the church. Each is bilaterally symmetrical, and it will be useful for this study to define the distinction between the two types of symmetry that are represented here. Each has a *dominant* axis of reflection that commands the total composition. There are additional *subsidiary* axes that dictate localised symmetries. In the northern block of this west range the vicinity of the dominant axis is elaborated in a centre-piece; the dominant symmetry is thereby *accented*. In the southern block the dominant symmetry is *non-accented*; between the subsidiary symmetries of the terminal pavilions there is a regular spacing of bays with no concentration of interest towards the centre. Accents can vary in strength, according to which elements from the classical vocabulary are used for the purpose, their scale and the degree to which they are advanced or recessed. A free-standing pedimented portico constitutes the strongest accent. As with the whole so with the part: localised symmetry may be accented or non-accented. In the two designs preferred by Adam the terminal pavilions in the southern elevation are more strongly accented than those in the alternative. Thus in a composition without a dominant accent they have even greater independence in the scheme of things.

The tension created between distanced terminal elements in such

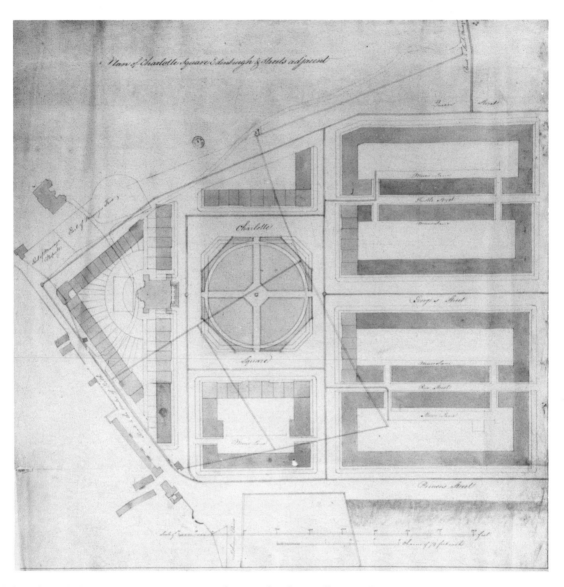

2.4 *Robert Adam's Charlotte Square, plan.*

symmetry may be resolved to effect within a larger composition. This symmetry was used in Paris by Ange-Jacques Gabriel in the two buildings that he designed by 1775 for the north side of what is now the Place de la Concorde. These frame the Rue Royale, and the composition is completed, as Gabriel intended, by the distant prospect of a church—though, of course, the Madeleine was a creation of the nineteenth century. In spite of the close parallels between Gabriel's scheme and his own grouping of church and housing, Adam chose not to follow this powerful neo-classical precedent. For each of the six blocks in the square he adopted a more baroque and dominant-accented composition, even where this conflicted

126

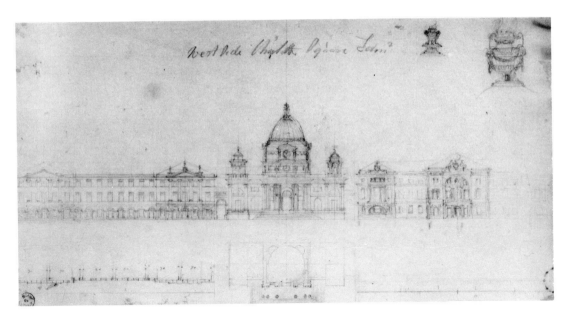

2.5 *Robert Adam's Charlotte Square, sketch for west side.*

with subdivision into an even number of houses.

On each block, therefore, is conferred a relative autonomy; the design is varied from block to block in the details of centrepieces and pavilions, and in their relative proportions in each elevation. Integrating factors are the uniform heights of horizontal elements such as entablatures and string courses, the consistent rustication of the ground storey, and the repetition of the motif of a tripartite window beneath a lunette. This motif, also a feature of the Fitzroy Square elevations, is used at different scales in the western blocks—smaller in the pavilions, larger in the centrepieces where it provides the main accent. In the eastern blocks it is used only in the pavilions; while in each of the long ranges to the north and south (Figure 2.6) it is repeated five times.

The design for these north and south buildings is Adam's classic and influential contribution to the integrated design of urban housing. The relation between advanced centrepiece and pavilions is finely judged in the balance of their relative proportions and in the contrast of their architectural detail. The pavilions are robust, pilastered end-pieces; the centre has a rounded Corinthian order and is itself elaborated into palace form—with a pedimented centrepiece framed by wings. Yet the facade is not disjointed. The centralisation is moderated by regularities in the design—in the rhythm of the fenestration, in the paired spacing of semi-columns in the centrepiece, in the arched rustication at ground level—and by the echo in the pavilions of the first floor alteration of rectangular and lunette-headed windows.

Although the Council had commissioned the designs for Charlotte Square it was not directly involved in building to them. The process was as before: individual lots were offered for development, but feu-charters were granted on the not totally effective condition that elevations should

127

Robert Adam's Charlotte Square, design for north and south sides.

conform with Adam's design. The opportunity was not eagerly seized upon—Youngson notes that not more than six houses, all on the north side, had been built by 1800, and that the south side, completing the square, was not finished until 1820.

Though Craig's plan and Adam's conception were thus brought haltingly to completion, before the turn of the century plans were already underway for further substantial expansion of housing on the land now opened up to the north. For the middle classes the need was still there and for them there was now no alternative to residence away from the Old Town. For there the 'great want of free air, light, cleanliness and every other accommodation' had become even greater as the pressures on urban centres mounted. According to Smout[24] the population of Edinburgh increased from 48,000 by some 18,000 between 1750 and 1801, and by a further 70,000 by 1831— these increases were almost wholly proletarian, and accommodated around the 'steepness, narrowness and darkness' of the Edinburgh wynds. The historic juxtaposition of the Mediaeval and Georgian had now set into a division of social classes. Craig's New Town accommodated only some 7,000 of the well-to-do in an area comparable to that of the Old Town. Though the expense and uncertainties of the Napoleonic Wars might inhibit investment in property, it was clear that with peace there would be renewed and greater demand for quality housing—and plans were made.

The first was prepared in 1802 by two official architects, Robert Reid, the last King's Architect for Scotland, and William Sibbald, Superintendent of Works for the City. The land, north of Queen Street, was largely in the feu of the Heriot Trust, though the City had an interest. Lothian's map of 1825 shows this scheme complete in all but its northern boundary. It also shows that by this time three other large projects were underway: one either side of the road to Queensferry, and the third, the largest of all, east of the road to Leith.

In all these projects the planners were also, at least in substantial part, the executant architects. The plans were therefore drawn with building form in mind; and, extensively the building forms employ the varieties of

128

symmetry explored by Adam in his designs for Charlotte Square.

In the plan for a second New Town by Reid and Sibbald, in the main realised by Reid as architect, these forms are applied to a spatial structure derived from and dimensionally generated by Craig's New Town. Ainslie's map (Figure 2.2) shows the new project, and though it may not represent exactly the original intentions, departures from it as built are minor, except in the forms given to the circus and the southern crescent. The layout has the general structure of the first New Town, with a principal thoroughfare parallel to George Street and, like it, terminated in *places*. The topography does not here point the parallelism between the schemes; and indeed the second plan lacks the stability of the first, balanced about its central ridge. Here the site falls quickly and persistently away from Queen Street and the steepness of the gradients across the plan makes difficult the perception of its overall order.

Certain cross-streets of the first plan are extended into the second, and determine the dimensions of the central blocks. Hence problems of building scale and formal order, unresolved in Craig's plan, are here raised again, but now expressly in terms of the prevailing commitment to symmetry.

The southern boundary, facing Queen Street across a fall of gardens, comprises four blocks, two of them formed into a shallow crescent as Abercromby Place. The juxtaposition of terraces and crescent not within some controlling hierarchical order, but as *alternative* peripheral forms indicates the incipience of the picturesque in Edinburgh planning. By this principle architectural form is incidental rather than definitive. The earlier ensemble in George Street depicted by Shepherd (Figure 2.3) is, by the force of circumstances, picturesque; so too is the free array of crescents that form the north-eastern border of this second plan. To the boundary problem first posed by Craig, this plan offers a tentative solution in terms of sequential picturesque incident, and, by implication, of variety in form. But, in Edinburgh, the time was not yet ripe for the choice of forms to be anything but classical.

Heriot Row includes two blocks of the southern boundary; each is some 600 feet long. To each immense stretch is applied the formal order of the symmetrical palace front. One has sixty-nine elevational bays, seven in each pavilion, nine in the centrepiece—all of three storeys— and twenty-three in each of the two storey terraces that were designed to link them. The north and south blocks of Charlotte Square (Figure 2.6) are each of a mere twenty-seven bays—arranged 3–7–7–7–3—and designed uniformly in three storeys. Some account has been given of the integrative power of Adam's elevations, and this is maintained in spite of built variations from the intended design. In Heriot Row classicism constitutes a weak discipline for elevations limited in height but so expansive in length; and lacking, moreover, in the organic irregularity of Queen Street gardens, a context of geometrical order. What formal structure there was is now lost in the random alterations that have been made, particularly in the *ad-hoc* addition of storeys.

Great King Street is the offspring of George Street, though, it is two blocks long, not four. Like the blocks in Heriot Row these are determined in length by the dimensions of Craig's grid. But each elevation is a storey higher, is more strongly accented, and has fewer bays—arranged 7–15–9–15–7. Centrepiece and pavilions carry an attic; and below an advance in the entablature each has an attached portico of four Ionic pilasters carried through the first and second storeys. The centrepiece also has wings of paired pilasters, in the manner of Charlotte Square. Further accent is provided in attic lunettes on the dominant and subsidiary axes. In the terminal blocks the attic is raised even higher so that in the perspective of the street the tension between the distanced pavilions is a coherent force in the composition. This design is repeated twice on each side of Great King Street so the tension is extended in dualities between like forms along and across the space. These complex spatial relationships confer on it a powerful unity, resistant to depredation.

In this second New Town there is the first use in Edinburgh of terminal pavilions to articulate junctions between one space and another. For Charlotte Square Adam provided side elevations for the north and south ranges, and proposed that the ends should be returned as street frontages (Figure 2.4); but he did not conceive of the pavilion as a pivotal element between two contiguous elevations, and as part of both of them. Neither are the returns into the streets that divide the terraces of Great King Street so elaborated; but at the entrances to the terminal *places* each pavilion is expressed volumetrically. Both of its elevations are advanced in plane and accented by pilastered tetrastyle porticos. The Great King Street elevation is given precedence by its greater breadth and extra accents, including the grouping of arcuated doorways below the portico. These doorways give access to the complex of accommodation above. The orthogonal frontages and restricted rear access afforded by corner sites necessitated departure from the general subdivision of terraces into house lots. The pavilions in Great King Street comprise complexes of two-storey houses over a basement, with flats above. The four-storey centrepieces are similarly arranged; so is much of the accommodation in the cross-streets in the first as well as this second New Town.

As shown in Ainslie's map (Figure 2.2), the crescent of Abercromby Place is asymmetrically divided by the extension into Reid and Sibbald's plan of the line of St. David Street from Craig's St. Andrew Square. In execution, however, the integrating geometry of the crescent prevailed (Figure 2.7).[25] The route from Abercromby Place to Drummond Place is offset so that the crescent is divided symmetrically. Each part is formed as a curved terrace, with terminal pavilions but without a centrepiece. This form implies resolution along the axis of division, though here the route, diverted from direct entry to Drummond Place, is closed only by the bland frontage of Northumberland Street.

Drummond Place is the eastern of the two *places* connected by Great King Street and, like it, is bounded by buildings of three storeys, with attics

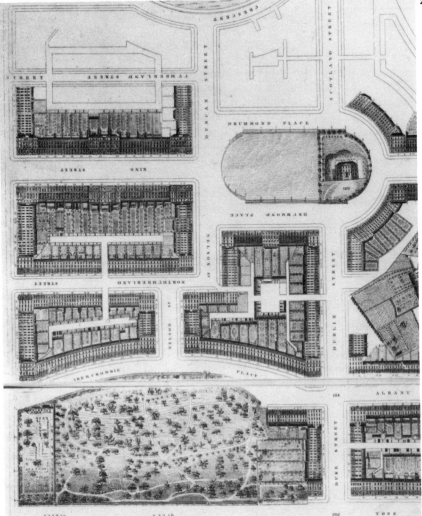

2.7 *Kirkwood's Plan and Elevation of the New Town of Edinburgh, 1819 (part showing Abercromby Place, King Street, Drummond Place).*

raised over centrepieces and pavilions. The north and south blocks, in length determined at a distance by the dimensions of St. Andrew Square, are palace form. The space is rounded to the east in a divided crescent—two quadrants of terraces connecting terminal pavilions frame the east-ward extension of the axis of Great King Street. To the west Drummond Place is bounded by terraces extended from adjacent cross-streets. These terraces are articulated to form the pilastered returns of pavilions from Great King Street and again, similarly accented, to mark the corners of Drummond Place.

The buildings through which the plan of Reid and Sibbald was realised evidence the application of a *formal code* through which the parts of a plan are articulated and status given to each part. The rules of the code are: urban spaces are of two kinds, *place* and *route*; the spaces are continuously bounded by buildings; the buildings are symmetrical; those buildings in which the dominant axis is accented signify a *place*; those with terminal pavilions but no centrepiece signify a *route*, in pairs they flank the *entrance* to a *route*; a *route* terminates in a *place* and on the centrepiece of a building bounding that *place*; terminal pavilions of contiguous buildings are integrated volumetrically, and articulate the junctions between the urban spaces.

Thus the status of Drummond Place is signified by the palace form symmetry of the north and south blocks; the axial route that intersects with it is framed to east and west by terraces—respectively curved and straight—accented only in their pavilions; and these pavilions are returned into the terraces that define the route. Royal Circus, designed by William Playfair in 1820, is signified as a *place* by the centralised symmetry of two opposed crescents, even though the terminal building proposed by Reid and Sibbald is replaced by paired pavilions that signify the further westward extension of the *route*.

That the code is not applied consistently by Reid is due to the derivation of the plan from Craig's scheme and the exigencies of steep gradients that preclude symmetrical order. The inherited dimensions on occasion extend symmetry beyond its ordering power. Cross streets continued from the earlier development intersect the plan and open up vistas that are not resolved in built form. Moreover the treatment of *boundaries* is not accommodated by the formal code; except for the provision of entrances to *routes* a spatial system generated by the code is self-enclosed. To see it more consistently applied in the genesis of a plan we must turn to the neighbouring and later development designed by James Gillespie Graham for the Earl of Moray.

With the completion of the first and the near-completion of the second plan—and in a period of peaceful economic prosperity—the property owned by the Earl of Moray contiguous to them both (Figure 2.2) had promising speculative possibilities. In 1822 the Earl instructed his architect to prepare plans for a high class residential area.

The awkward shape of the site, the slope to the north, and the final fall of a hundred feet to the Water of Leith would have offered challenging opportunities to a picturesque-minded designer. Instead, Gillespie Graham chose to follow the now established system of urban order. The appeal of unmediated Nature is resisted, and a controlled, introverted environment is created on a plateau, carried by heavy retaining walls high above the water. From Queensferry Street an axial sequence of crescent, ellipse and polygon is expanded almost to fill the site (Figure 2.8).[26] The margins with the earlier development are blocked out; four connections with the adjacent networks are made through streets that are angled to enter the scheme at positions dictated by its geometry.

The standard elevational bay is of three storeys over a basement, and surmounted by the plainest of entablatures and a blank parapet. The common distinction is made between storeys. In each bay the ground floor has a flat-headed opening and carries channel-jointed rustication. Above the ground floor the ashlar is dressed. The first floor, the *piano nobile*, has the largest window, the opening elaborated with a moulded architrave; the second floor has the smallest window, treated more plainly. Further distinction is given here to the first floor window by its individual balcony, a cast decoration of anthemion and palmette. This is the matrix from which are formed by concatenation the terraces—straight or curvilinear—that link the accented elements in the design. These have attic storeys above the entablature, arcuated openings in the ground storey, and an expressed Tuscan order integrating the first and second floors.

The quadrants of Randolph Crescent signify entrance to the estate and the *route* that is manifested in the two short sections of Great Stuart Street. The buildings of the crescent and the street are bounded by pavilions, but none has centralised accent. The status of Ainslie Place, however, is confirmed by the advanced centrepiece of its semi-elliptical facade. This centrepiece, symmetrical about the minor axis of the ellipse, opposes the entrance made from the angle projected from Craig's plan; the entrance is marked by paired 'quadrants' of the ellipse, bounded by pavilions.

The geometry of the entrances and terraces of Moray Place (Figure 2.9) is derived from that of the Circus, Bath. These entrances are made mutually at 120°: one from the main route of the scheme; the others by diverting extensions from the Reid and Sibbald plan. A fourth entrance connects (through Forres Street) with extensions from Queen Street and Charlotte Square. The added complication of this entrance, the complexity of the forms used in the terraces, and the present density of planting in the enclosed garden makes it difficult to decipher the underlying geometry. This is based on a regular hexagon which is superimposed on the tri-axial scheme so that entrances are located in the middle of alternate sides and are opposed by continuous facades (the entrance from Forres Street creates exception to the rule). The vertices of the hexagon are splayed off; Moray Place therefore has the form of an irregular dodecagon of alternating long and short sides, and is bounded by buildings with facades cranked successively through angles of 150°. The major facades not only have centrepieces on the axes of entrances, and pavilions that mark and articulate those entrances, but also include across each splay a further localised symmetry in the form of a pedimented portico flanked by wings.

The formal confusion, and hence also the spatial confusion, in Moray Place is due in large measure to the inversion of values given to dominant and subsidiary symmetries. The centrepiece on a dominant axis has a colonnade of Tuscan semi-columns flanked by pilasters, all regularly spaced below a progressively advanced entablature. Even though this motif is more extended than the pedimented palace form given to the splayed subsidiary axes, it is much less strong in accent. The ambiguity in

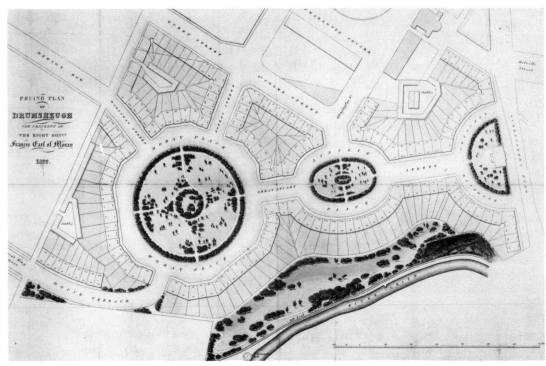

2.8 *Gillespie Graham's feuing plan of Drumsheugh, 1822.*

2.9 *Geometrical analysis of Moray Place.*

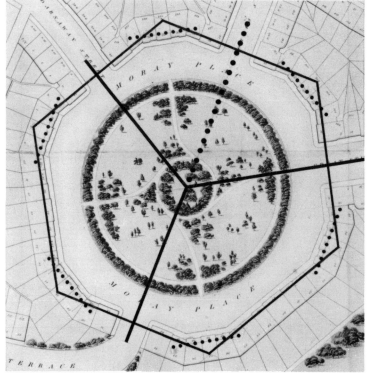

value is compounded, since it is this subsidiary motif that is used for the centrepieces of the shorter buildings that flank the entrance to Forres Street; these centrepieces are, in any case, a contravention of the formal code as previously enunciated. The code is not a guarantee of architectural quality; it is the means by which cognition of this urban space is structured. In default of the code the building forms of Moray Place unfold in a sequence of arbitrary incidents unrelated to spatial context. The exceptions to the code—here in Moray Place and in the *ad hoc* boundaries made with the earlier schemes—confirm its rules.

The last development considered here illustrates the continuing agency of the Town Council, until its reform in 1833, in promoting development of housing for the middle classes across the divide of the North Loch. The City had been one owner of the lands developed north of Queen Street, and indeed the contract between the City and the other owners included a clause that brought the whole of that scheme within the bounds of an extended royalty.

Early in 1811 it was the Lord Provost who moved at a meeting of Governors of the Heriot's Hospital Trust 'that a committee be appointed to draw up an advertisement for plans for feuing the Hospital lands of Quarryholes, in conjunction with the Governors of Trinity Hospital, and any other adjacent proprietors that it may be judged proper to invite'[27] and he made a similar motion at a meeting of the Governors of Trinity Hospital. The two committees, together with the other major landowner concerned (Mr. Allan of Hillside), met under the presidency of the Lord Provost and agreed

> that the ground belonging to Heriot's Hospital, the Trinity Hospital and Mr. Allan, situated between the Easter and Wester Roads to Leith, also a small part of Heriot's Hospital's ground, and a part of Trinity Hospital's ground lying on the east side of the Easter Road to Leith shall be laid out on a joint plan for building ground.[28]

The meeting, no doubt reassured by the Lord Provost of the interest of the Town Council, directed that 'a letter be written to the City of Edinburgh to know if the City would incline to have the Calton Hill ground included in said plan'.[29] Other adjacent proprietors were also invited to attend the next meeting. The joint committee then agreed to have a survey made; this was not ready until June of the following year, when

> the meeting were of the opinion that advertisements should be put into the newspapers inviting persons to give in plans or designs for laying out in streets, squares etc. for building on the grounds belonging to the parties . . . and that premiums should be offered for the best and second best plans as was done in the case of the building grounds north of Queen Street.[30]

The site, advertised as being between two and three hundred acres in area, and 'forming nearly an oblong square' has two parts: the whole of the rugged eminence of Calton Hill, and the extensive undulating lands to the

135

north, stretching as far as the outskirts of Leith. The topographical distinction between the two parts was emphasised in their division by a thoroughfare projected as the new approach to the city from Haddington and beyond. The alignment of this new London Road was fixed as a competition condition; it was to terminate in Leith Walk, which formed the western boundary of the site. The eastern boundary was irregular, following the outline of the included feus. It was also a condition of the competition that recent buildings on the hill should not be altered: the observatory designed by James Craig, the Nelson Monument by Robert Burn, and the Bridewell by Robert Adam. A signal point with its flagstaff was also to be preserved.

The closing date for submissions was set at 1st January 1813. By then thirty-two 'artists' had sent in plans and William Hamilton and Richard Crichton of Edinburgh sent letters of their intention to submit; their plans and another marked 'MB' were accepted, though late. An exhibition was arranged though invitations were limited to 'gentlemen of taste and genius and professional people who have not rendered plans . . . that the general opinion of the public may, if possible, be known'.[31]

When the committee next met it was decided to seek the opinion of eight prominent Scottish architects, or 'at least such of them as choose to accept and have not rendered competition plans'. It was not until one year later that reports were received from Robert Reid, John Baxter, William Burn, John Paterson and James Gillespie. The delay may have arisen from the need to circulate the plans, presumably available only in single copy, among the architects consulted. Gillespie, not yet styled Gillespie Graham, received them in the Highlands, and 'was not able to give them the necessary consideration'. Fees were paid for the other four reports, in which attention was concentrated on four of the submissions. After the lifting of the conditions of anonymity these were revealed as by William Reid, Alexander Nasmyth, Richard Crichton and by 'MB'—the last a joint submission by James Milne and Benjamin Bell. Instructions were given for these plans to be engraved and published; they are reproduced as Figures 2.10, 2.11, 2.12 and 2.13 respectively.[32]

A tabulated abstract of the opinions expressed in the reports was prepared for the committee by Baron Clerk, and, not surprisingly, it is quite inconclusive. The plan by 'MB', for example, while it was placed first by Baxter and Burn, was placed fourth by Paterson and fifth by Reid. Clerk and his associate, Gilbert Innes, expressed their own opinions on the plans incorporating some of the views of the professionals; but it was their conclusion that though

> several of the designs evidence much genius and skill in the artists . . . none of them are fit to be adopted as building plans for the parties concerned; some of them have noble features and parts that would have a good effect in execution, but at the same time they have such defects as to render it unwise to adopt them.[33]

They recommended that Reid, Nasmyth and Crichton should share the first prize, and that the remaining premium should go to 'MB'. In effect all four prizewinners had the same reward. The recommendations, both as to the awards to prizewinners and the non-appointment of any of them, was accepted by the joint committee in July 1815.

One report to the joint committee was not finished, for on 13th October 1813, its author, William Stark, died. Yet his incomplete report was certainly the most influential, both in the decision not to effect any of the submitted plans and in the manner in which it was finally agreed to lay out the site. In the opinion of Clerk and Innes 'the observations offered by the late Mr. Stark deserve the utmost attention and as far as practicable should be assumed as a rule, for forming the plan of the buildings along the Leith Walk'.[34]

At the meeting in July 1815 it was noted that this 'most excellent and well digested report' had 'as far as it goes . . . been printed by the desire of the committee and widely circulated'. The report was introduced as 'observations . . . communicated to a gentleman high in office, sometime after the death of Mr. Stark, by one of his relations'. In a postscript, added by 'a friend', are recorded further opinions ascribed to Stark but not, in the circumstances, included in the report; it is also noted that Stark had begun to make a large drawing to illustrate his observations. The anonymity surrounding the printing of the report, and its circulation before a final decision on the competition had been made, suggests that there may have been influences operating behind the scenes. If so they are likely to have been Whiggish. Cockburn, always interested in the architectural improvement of Edinburgh, certainly knew of the report and admired it, and his high opinion of Stark has already been cited. Within Cockburn's social and political circle was John Playfair, professor of natural philosophy at the University. In 1794 Playfair's nephew, William, came to live with his uncle; later he was to study architecture under Stark. This connection between Stark and Whig society, though tenuous, may be significant in that when at last an architect was appointed to lay out a scheme for Calton Hill it was Stark's ex-pupil who was chosen.

Stark's report makes no particular reference to the competition submissions; instead it is a clear declaration of picturesque principles applied to town planning, and includes detailed proposals of his own. Consistently he argues that the opportunities for variety and beauty afforded by the site should dictate the form of development. He cautions

> against. . . any plan which presupposes the ground being cleared away, and spread out like the paper on which it is delineated. . . (for). . . when the smoothing process is once finished, what remains for (the architect) to do but set off in the plain straight forward course, and to ring a few monotonous changes upon right angles and regular mathematical curves?[35]

And thus he castigates not only Craig's New Town, as has been noted, but also, by implication, its northward extension, and the entries for the present competition. Though he admits the necessity for regularity of form

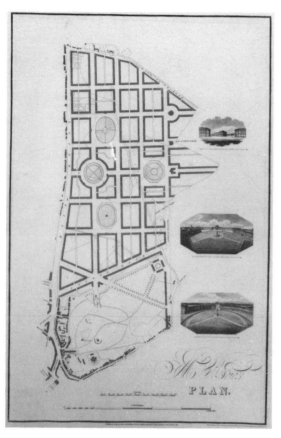

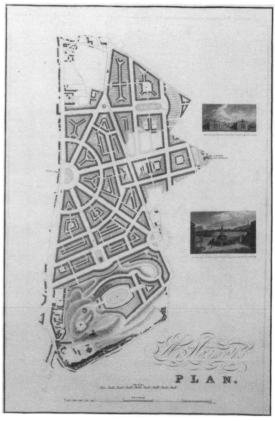

2.10 *William Reid's layout of streets to the north of Calton Hill.*

2.11 *Alexander Nasmyth's layout of streets to the north of Calton Hill.*

'in so far as it can be indulged without harm' he comes near to equate the 'desirable quality of variety' with the 'preservation of positive beauty', and to this end 'accidents of situation' should be exploited. His caution against the straight alignment of streets down steep gradients is extended to an advocacy for 'bending' alignment, made for its 'striking effects'. In such a setting, a public building is seen in immediate perspective, rather than in distant elevation terminating a long straight street; moreover 'swelling acclivities' in the ground might be used 'to give such a building a more commanding site, and more elevation and dignity'.

Among the irregularities and peculiarities of the site Stark gives much attention to the value of existing trees. He mentions in particular elms on the boundary of Mr. Allan's property, not indicated on the survey plan and therefore ignored by all competitors. Here, he argues, the building should be set back, and the trees preserved, particularly as it will mark the point of entry to the new development and 'is likely to stamp the value, tone, and character of every other edifice which may arise on the same quarter'.

The most important specific recommendations concern the layout of

138

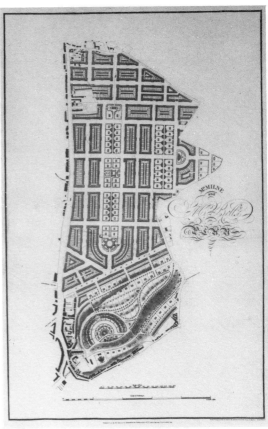

Calton Hill itself. Stark notes:

> The irregular surface of the upper part of the building property has given rise, as might be supposed, to great difference of opinion among the competitors who have given in designs. In some of these, the buildings are carried up to the summit of the Calton Hill, and seem to envelope the sites both of the monument and observatory! In others, they are confined to its more temperate and accessible regions; and in many more it has been overlooked altogether, as if unfit for the purpose of building.[36]

It is the prospect of views from the hill that dictate his own proposal. These views, he argues, are 'finer when seen from a moderate elevation, by skirting the brow of the hill, than when taken from near the summit'. He chooses a level 'not greatly higher than that of Princes Street' and on this contour proposes a continuous terrace—around the south, east and north slopes—from which to enjoy the extensive panorama of the Old Town, Arthur's Seat, and the distant Firth of Forth. It is not his opinion 'that buildings placed higher than this line would form accessible, or in any respect desirable, residences'. From the postscript we learn that Stark

2.12 *Richard Crichton's layout of streets to the north of Calton Hill.*

2.13 *James Milne and Benjamin Bell's layout of streets to the north of Calton Hill.*

139

proposed that the summit should be made into a public walk, and that this whole development of Calton Hill should be made directly accessible from Princes Street by means of a new bridge—a connection soon to be effected by the construction of Waterloo Place.

The decision not to proceed with any of the submitted designs was taken over four years after the first formation of the joint committee, and after expenditure on the survey, the premiums, and the fees to assessors. The landowner Allan immediately intimated his intentions to feu to his own plan, but could not proceed until the exact line and elevation of the proposed London Road was determined. There the matter rested until, on 5th February 1818, a committee representative of Heriot Hospital and Trinity Hospital came unanimously to the opinion 'that an architect of eminence and taste . . . should be employed to prepare a general plan *suited to the varied and picturesque state of the ground'.*[37]

The italics are not, of course, in the original; what they emphasise is the prolonged influence of Stark over this operation. When the full committee met the following week Allan's agent argued that the road should be begun before there was any further expenditure on a plan; but the majority view was that the general principles of the plan should be settled first. What is more the meeting decided then and there that the 'architect of eminence and taste' should be William Playfair, aged twenty-eight.

Playfair gave due attention to the business of the road, and by April 1819 was ready to submit a plan 'for laying out the New Town between Edinburgh and Leith', together with an explanatory report. A reduced copy of the plan was printed (Figure 2.14) along with the report;[38] and the scheme was further publicised through an invitation to 'Noblemen and Gentlemen of Taste' to examine the plan and suggest improvements. Playfair responded to such suggestions in a second report,[39] submitted in August.

It has been suggested and repeated that Playfair's plan merely realises the philosophy of Stark's 'observations . . .', but except where Playfair follows the quite specific advice concerning Calton Hill and Mr. Allan's elms, such comment does not give Playfair's own contribution its due, nor acknowledge possible debts to the competitive designs. We do not know, of course, if Playfair was able to acquire the sketches and drawing made by Stark nor what they contained. He had Stark's report, and the four competition plans that had been rewarded but rejected—he was to make specific comparison between these and his own scheme in respect of their potential for feuing. Important features of his plan take up themes from the earlier proposals. Thus, like Crichton and Nasmyth, Playfair forms a major focus halfway along Leith Walk from which radial routes open up the plan. Like these, too, he maintains the division of the site by the eastern road to Leith and accepts the consequent triangular spaces and wedge-shaped building lots—indeed in his second report he justifies them on grounds of *variety.* The orthogonal layout of symmetrically elevated building lots to the east recalls that aspect of the plan by 'MB', though Playfair is even less

140

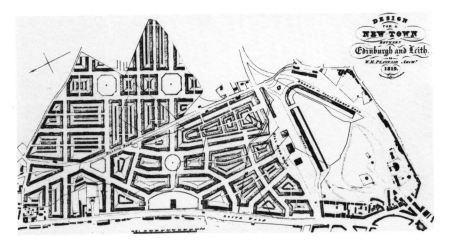

2.14 *William Playfair's design for a New Town between Edinburgh and Leith, 1819.*

mindful of the irregular boundary. Like Reid, Playfair has *places* about an east-west axis, which he uses to connect the disparate parts of his plan.

Playfair follows Nasmyth in forming a crescent on the London Road (renamed by him as Hill Side Road), but reverses its orientation and opens up routes northward from it. Thus in the main triangular plot bounded by the roads to Leith there are two radiating systems—one of them with an axis accented by *places*—and the resulting network is formed by their conflicting influences. Playfair achieves Stark's desired variety of form and incident, and the 'bending alignment' of streets, through the use of competitive geometries, rather than the exploitation of vagaries in the site.

Stark's report makes no mention of social influences on planning. Craig's scheme and that of Reid and Sibbald had secreted in their grand plans minor streets for the accommodation of supportive groups in the population. Playfair proposes a grading of streets from primary to quaternary of diminishing width:

> interspersed with one another in such a manner to afford accommodation to the various classes of society likely to inhabit so large a district.[40]

But the mix is hierarchically ordered;

> The main streets are intersected only by the secondary kind which again are crossed by those of inferior note, and by the openings into meuse lanes, a proper and necessary subdivision.[41]

Playfair was also aware that so large a scheme needed its own centre for trade, and he included in his proposal provision for markets. These were to be located in the complex of streets and buildings that form the angle between his Eastern Road and Hill Side Road. There they would be easily accessible for the delivery of 'cattle and objects of sale . . . without interference to the main part of the town'. Moreover:

> being placed also at the bottom of the Calton Hill it would be no very

difficult matter to contrive a reservoir in such a way that after market hours the whole might be laid under water and completely cleaned.[42]

Though in the 'most respectable and popular part of the town' the markets are deeply embedded within the hierarchy of housing so that 'no nuisance can possibly arise':

> The situation . . . is first surrounded by houses forming principal streets, with the backgrounds and stables. Within this there is a road 30' wide, then a row of 4th rate houses with background, and finally the market places . . .[43]

It should be noted that this progressive enclosure of the lower by the higher in categories of streets and housing is also a feature of the competition plans of Crichton and Nasmyth; both plans show open spaces at the core of such encasements that were intended for what was then considered to be one of the less savoury communal functions. In Crichton's plan two of these spaces are explicitly labelled as markets; Nasmyth has several such spaces marked 'M' (for market?) scattered throughout his scheme.

Playfair indicates formal intentions in his plan by projections from the general building lines; but except where these are dictated by uncompromised geometry (where they then conform to the established formal code) it is not clear that at this time he had any system in mind. Projections occur not only at the centre and ends of terraces but also off-centre and at obtuse and re-entrant angles. In defence of the irregularities of his plan he argues:

> . . . the corners of some streets must be obtuse or acute angles. Fully aware that this is not the most advantageous form for the internal arrangement of houses I have avoided them as much·as possible . . . on the other hand I am confident that the obtuse or acute angle, where it does occur, will form a pleasing variety in the external appearance of the streets, and will do away with the monotonous and tiresome effect that is sure to attend a series of rectangular buildings.[44]

Lothian's map of 1825 (Figure 2.15) shows not only the little of the plan at that time executed, but the full projection of this vast undertaking; it shows also significant revisions to the plan, with more precise indication of intended building forms. No doubt the need to formulate proposals for building elevations was an influence on the regularisation of the plan, particularly in those streets that cut the radial lines emanating from the two crescents. The competitive geometries are now reconciled. Gone is Stark's 'bending alignment', and with it the promise of variety in an unfolding prospect.

In September 1819 the joint committee 'unanimously approved the plan in all its great features', but it was accepted that although the roads east of the eastern road should be laid out as shown, the owners might lay out their grounds for detached villas instead of terraces. This is not the first suggestion for building villas so near to the city: Ainslie's map of 1804 includes a proposal for serried ranks of villas off Pilrig Street, west of Leith Walk.[45] But, more significantly, two of the competition entrants made

provision for villas in their plans. Nasmyth and Crichton had both kept the
eastern road so that their compact centralised systems are separated from
the irregularly bounded and more problematic area further east. Into this
Nasmyth (Figure 2.11) tentatively extended his system of *place* and *route*,
but Crichton (Figure 2.12) changed his system altogether—from the
continuity of terraces to the staccato of detached villas. Reid (Figure 2.10)
and 'MB' (Figure 2.13) both generated extensive orthogonal networks over
the whole of the northern part of the site, ignoring the irregularity of the
eastern boundary. In the assessors' report the scheme by 'MB' is praised
for its 'novelty'. This consists of its combination of terraced blocks and
detached villas; and in the placing of the villas not just—as in Crichton's
scheme and as now proposed by the joint committee—in peripheral
suburbia but also at the heart of the plan, regularly spaced, back-to-back on
a north-south axis aligned on the Nelson Monument. Paterson had pointed
out that the principal axis was given to the stabling of the villas ('a powerful meuse lane from end to end' as the summary puts it); and the doubt is
expressed by Clerk and Innes that the villas, if built, would be magnificent
enough for this prominent position. But 'MB' did not stop there. Villas
were also to be the solution to the topographical difficulties of the even
more magnificent site of the hill itself. There they are regularly spaced

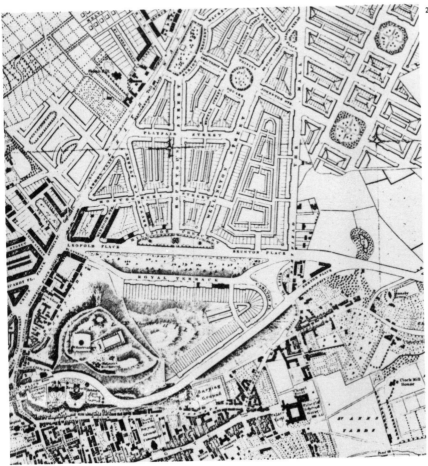

2.15 *Lothian's plan of the City of
Edinburgh and its vicinity, 1825
(part showing Calton Hill and
proposed layout to the north).*

along sinuous curves, and in a tight part-circle at the summit. James Milne was an architect and builder. Benjamin Bell was 'a highly successful surgeon, a farmer and an astute property developer'.[46] It was in this last capacity that, in 1806, Bell began feuing the first of the nineteenth century suburban settlements, at Newington. Although consideration of the villa is beyond the scope of this essay, it should not be overlooked that at this early date it was being proposed as an alternative to the terrace—and not just in suburban arcadia.

In his treatment of Calton Hill Playfair follows closely the most explicit advice given in Stark's report. By the time of Playfair's commission construction of Waterloo Place was underway, thus effecting the connection between Calton Hill and Princes Street that had also been advocated by Stark. In his plan Playfair carries this new access around the cluster of penitentiaries—the subject of a companion essay in this volume—to become the southern extension of that continuous esplanade held by Stark to be the most appropriate development for the slopes of the hill. The wedge of land bounded by this terrace would be laid out as private gardens; these, in Playfair's view 'will present a pleasant foreground to the enchanting landscape which is to be seen from the public walks above'.[47] To criticism that his proposal for the hill was too sparse, and therefore uneconomic, Playfair responds:

> this ground will produce a considerable revenue by the sums that will be paid for permission to walk there . . . and . . . it should be considered that in bringing this ground into the market there is a formidable rival to contend with at the western end of the present new town. There a circle of fashionable and wealthy people has been collected and there, unless some strong inducement elsewhere be held out, they will continue to assemble. This inducement I should hope will be obtained in the magnificent gardens in question—this is the main spring by which the whole may be set in motion. The nature of the ground too, which is so peculiarly unfit for building upon, is particularly well adapted for producing a beautiful effect as a garden. No one surely can deny that the value of the property in Queen Street, Heriot Row and Abercromby Place, is materially improved by the beautiful shrubbery lying between them.[48]

Playfair's argument is an expansion of Stark's view that 'beauty of site will be found most probably a vendible commodity', and it illustrates the highly competitive nature of these Edinburgh projects. Playfair may have had wind of the Earl of Moray's intentions, but the note of rivalry at the 'western end of the present New Town' most probably refers to other private developments—not considered in this essay—already initiated west of Queensferry Street and north of the Water of Leith. As it turned out collectively these speculations rapidly exhausted the market at which they were aimed. In the eastern expansion only the Calton Hill terraces now manifest the grandeur of Playfair's conception. By the time of the Ordnance Survey of 1852–54 even these were not yet complete, and very little of the scheme had been built—or indeed was to be built—north of the London Road.

In their extrovert nature and their extent, the Calton Hill terraces revive the challenge—first clarified in the context of the northern and southern boundaries of Craig's scheme—between formal order in buildings and the unregulated prospect which they enjoy. These are expansive terraces, built to command superb views, but are seen themselves in their entirety against the natural irregularity of the hill that they enclose.

Regent Terrace faces south and confronts, in Stark's restrained words, 'a mountain scene of no despicable kind, with an interesting foreground accompaniment in the venerable pile of Holyrood House'. Thus coolly does the picturesque anticipate romanticism; it is worth noting that Stark (b.1770) and Scott (b.1771) were contemporaries, and that Stark's report was printed in the same year as 'Waverley'.

The terrace is organised in alternating sections of two and three storeys, with the three storey sections given some further accent at each end through slight projections in the elevational plane; but the steady fall from west to east, accommodated in the stepping down of the terrace, blurs these distinctions. Moreover order is hardly imposed by the expression of classical architectural elements. Each section has a crowning cornice, but the irregularities in height deny its integrating function. First floor balconies are similarly dislocated. Horizontal integration is further weakened since Playfair does not here distinguish by rustication the ground storey from those above—this had been the almost invariable pattern in housing from at least as far back as 1770, when Adam produced his design for Baron Ord. The elevation is carried out uniformly in smooth ashlar with little elaboration. The individuality of window openings is emphasised in their moulded architraves; and each doorway is given its own prominence by a projection in the Doric order of semi-columns and entablature. Thus from near and afar Regent Terrace presents an assemblage of houses, connected through repetition of detail, but not otherwise classically disciplined. As in Heriot Row, the looseness of composition has encouraged attic extensions, but here they cannot be destructive of symmetrical order—indeed they contribute to the pragmatic nature of the design.

Royal Terrace is quite a different proposition. A single span of forty houses, it is over 1200 feet long—that is nearly twice the length of the blocks in George Street (and hence of those in Great King Street) and of the progressively canted frontage of the larger terraces in Moray Place; and it is elevated in the one commanding and uncompromising composition. The elevation is an exercise in dominant and subsidiary symmetries conducted on an unprecedented scale. It is articulated into three blocks—the largest in the centre—generally of three storeys. These are expressed proud of a two storey terrace that connects them and extends them. This theme is repeated in the centre on an elevated scale. Here there are three colonnaded units, of Corinthian order, with attic storeys over. The central colonnade has ten columns; each of the flanking pair has seven. These accents are regularly spaced in the elevation of the central block; they are divided by and extended by seven bays of three-storey terracing. The two subsidiary blocks. as befits their compositional role, have less height overall, and no accent on the axis of localised symmetry; each is bounded by pavilions with hexastyle colonnades of Ionic order. Throughout the terrace the ground storey is of rusticated masonry, and all the openings at this level are arcuated; this foundation constitutes a powerful binding force within the complexity of the composition, particularly when it is seen in angled perspective.

The marked conceptual differences between the terraces either side of Calton Hill can be understood only in terms of their context. Over the palace and ruined abbey of Holyrood, Regent Terrace surveys the formidable outcrop of Salisbury Crags and Arthur's Seat. This is its object, immediate and distant—and not to be commanded by generated geometries. Royal Terrace, elevated above London Road, is an integral part of a vast formal construction to be projected over the northward plain. It is exactly the length of the crescent that opposes it below and to the north of the road; the repeatedly tri-partite composition of its elevation is a response to the divisions in that crescent. In Playfair's conception the terrace is a termination of views from the heart of the scheme and a reflective boundary that reinforces his rational ordering of space on geometrical principles.

Facing Royal Terrace and the northern slope of Calton Hill, Hillside Crescent is drawn in a great arc along the chord of London Road. It is cut into segments by the three streets that converge from the north. The east and west segments are returned, in Leopold Place and Brunton Place respectively, as frontages to the main thoroughfare. Only the western parts of the crescent were built to Playfair's designs—as three storey terraced housing raised to four storeys at junctions. To the east are later tenements of four storeys, accented by only small variations in height. A photograph (Figure 2.16), taken before recent demolition and construction, shows the conjunction of the two systems.

Number 11, built in 1823 to Playfair's designs, graphically demonstrates the piecemeal manner in which were executed all the Georgian terraces of Edinburgh, however integrated they might be in elevation. It shows the operation of elevational control effected through conditions imposed on the developer by the superior to the land: features, such as the paired Doric columns, span the division between plots and accordingly the elevational plane is projected beyond the party wall, in anticipation of adjacent building.

The three storey elevation evidences in the vertical dimension that hierarchy of spaces deemed proper for the convenience of a single wealthy family. In the horizontal dimension features of the design emphasise the continuity of the house with its projected neighbours and imply the solidarity of the family with others similarly privileged in contemporary society. The ground floor is raised above a semi-basement which, typically, would have accommodated the service quarters of the household. The

2.16 *Hillside Crescent, No. 11; and Nos. 12-14 (demolished).*

larger windows of the ground and first floors light the important reception rooms; the first floor windows rise from floor height and open behind a trellis balustrade onto a continuous balcony. The smaller windows of the second floor are set on a string course that marks off the private from the more public accommodation. A high parapet of turned balusters masks the pitched roof; in Number 11 this discrete attic space is not used for extra servants' rooms though elsewhere this was common enough practice.

The crowning balustrade carried over a modillioned cornice, the string course, the projecting balcony, and the colonnade with its heavy entablature—these are the integrating elements that, with the regular spacing of openings, would bind the house into a larger, coherent unit. The house elevation is in three bays with the entrance to the left—approached by steps and a bridge over the well that lights and gives access to the service level—but this local ground level asymmetry would be absorbed by the insistent rhythm of the classical order. It is this peristyle that distinguishes the design of Hillside Crescent from that of other integrated terraces of Georgian Edinburgh. The Doric order, traditionally associated with masculine virility, substitutes for the conventional rustication in providing visual support for the upper storeys; the pairwise spacing of columns is finely judged to provide adequate bearing, and at the same time to permit wide openings that give to the ground storey the appropriate appearance of a loggia for the reception and entertainment of social peers.

For over fifty years Number 11 remained isolated. It is shown in Lothian's map of 1825 (Figure 2.15) with the little of Playfair's scheme built at that time. By the 1852–54 Ordnance Survey there had been scant progress. Its nearest neighbours are still the six houses in Brunswick Street, with which it shares rear access. Far to the east four units of Brunton Place are shown completed. There are still gaps even in Royal Terrace. Very little more was to be built according to Playfair's scheme. The grand project to link Edinburgh and Leith in continuous conurbation had been effectively abandoned with the cutting of the North British Railway.

The market for superior houses within the city had collapsed; the rivalry from the west had prevailed. By 1852 the Moray estate was virtually complete, and it maintained an exclusive residential occupation well into the twentieth century. But there remained the need for accommodation at other levels of society. Playfair had recognised this in the hierarchy of housing provided for in his plan, though the balance was envisaged in terms of the district rather than the city at large. But soon after its inception it was realised that this eastern development would need to provide for a more modest scale of residence, even in its more prominent sites. Thus Playfair's first scheme for Calton Terrace—the bow that continues Regent Terrace into Royal Terrace—was designed on three floors with a rusticated ground storey; the drawing is dated 1821. Except for a straight section aligned with Royal Terrace, the houses were, however, all built a few years later on two floors (over a basement) and elevated in plain ashlar. So, too, Playfair's designs for two-storey housing in Windsor Street and Brunswick Street, incongruously framed by the returned pavilions of more pretentious terraces, show that not all of this development was intended to proceed on the exalted scale of Royal Terrace and Hillside Crescent. Yet not even this diminshed scale of development could be sustained from the ranks of the middle classes. When building around Hillside Crescent was to be revived it was no longer for prosperous bankers, merchants or gentlemen of independent means all with servants, but for bank clerks, grocers, and tradesmen.[49]

Hillside Crescent to the east of Number 11, along with the return to Brunton Place, was completed after 1880 to designs by John Chesser. Chesser was substituted for Playfair as controlling designer for the as yet undeveloped lots, and he derived his elevations from Playfair's scheme for Brunton Place—conceived in terms of flats over two-storey houses. Numbers 12 to 14 Hillside Crescent (Figure 2.16), now demolished, comprised pairs of flats at each of the four levels. The eight flats were constructed elevationally as a single unit, with three symmetrically arranged entrances at street level. Each vacant segment of the crescent was built up with four such units, with the ends advanced slightly as vestigial pavilions. The duality of this 1–2–1 rhythm works against the coherence of the block as a whole; the independence of each unit is further emphasised by localised symmetries in the irregular spacing of windows and the arrangement and form of entrances. This conflict between the form of the part and its aggregation should be compared with the integrated balance of Playfair's work; moreover the difference extends to the reading of the crescent as a whole.

To the west the impulse generated by the regular rhythm of bays, the continuity of strong horizontal detail and the doubled emphases of paired pavilions overcome the division of the crescent by the converging streets (though this effect can no longer be appreciated on the site since the demolition of the pavilion east of Brunswick Street). To the east the juxtaposition of just a few large units, in which the linking by already weak horizontal detail is further diminished by the vertical repetition of like window forms, precludes the absorption of intervening space. Thus while the former elevational system maintains the integrity of the crescent against its division, the latter confers on each segment the independence within the crescent that the unit enjoys within the segment.

It is not the purpose here to demonstrate the evident superiority of the Georgian over the Victorian design, nor to make a case for the virtues of classicism. The form in which Hillside Crescent was completed was a metamorphosis of the Georgian system made to accommodate new social forces. But the *context* is not transformed, and there is conflict.

So, too, the classical system fails to articulate the nature of the tenement. The planning of flats is not readily accommodated by regularity from bay to bay; and equality from floor to floor conflicts with finite hierarchical order. Here cornice and string-course divide like from like, and if the attic storey is no different from the floor below, then there is no reasoning in the logic of form to preclude—within the limits of available technology— further vertical extension. The pronounced identity in elevation of grouping around vertical circulation intimates the possibility of further separation into discrete blocks. So the tenement configuration challenges the universality of the classical principle of hierarchical integration; and, viewed with hindsight of course, it prefigures the forms and spatial ordering characteristic of modernist housing: the spaced isolation of the tower and the slab. It is the destruction of traditional urban fabric in the twentieth century by the imposition of this spatial order that has led some theorists to look for a new order in varieties of classicism.

In this current intellectual climate the course of the classical experiment in Edinburgh over sixty years or so may be relevant. Classicism was projected in Craig's plan as an abstract ideal of order that, away from the controlled spaces of the squares, was not sustained by the manner in which it was realised. The scale and nature of boundaries in particular precluded ordering through an applied formal system. In Reid and Sibbald's expansion the boundaries take forms that localise the need for order—order and symmetry are now conceptually synonymous. In those boundary terraces determined in length by Craig's grid the symmetry is found to be over-extended. To the introverted axis of *place* and *route*—a contracted version of Craig's scheme—is applied a formal code, founded in symmetry, by which urban spaces are distinguished and co-ordinated; though its consistency is tested by the insistent topography of the site.

The Moray estate was established on a *tabula rasa*, and within it, with the exceptions noted, the rules of the code apply. That the project was immediately successful—of the three later plans this is the only one to be completed to the original conception and in uniform style—indicates not only that the Earl's judgment of the market was right but also that the architect's exercise of the code articulated the prevailing aspirations of the wealthier Scottish classes. The development is introverted—appropriately for an exclusive closed community, conscious of status; it is clearly demarcated, with imposing entrances inhibiting casual infiltration; its order is pervasive and complete, indicative of a belief in social stability; and it is consistent, as one would expect in a society dictated if not by reason then by rule.

These presumptions came, of course, to be opposed by the forces of social change; but they were always challenged by the proximity of unbounded Nature eminent in Edinburgh. In the Calton Hill scheme the assaults on classical order from Nature and Society were emphatic and effective: the first in the derivation of an alternative principle for planning based on view and incident, the second in the frustration of the completion of the project. The hill manifests a conceptual divide between Playfair's northern and southern terraces just as significant as the separation of the Old Town from the New. Whereas the development of the Moray estate turns away from unregulated Nature, Regent Terrace confronts it and thereby relinquishes control over the wider scheme of things. Royal Terrace, however, is part of a late grand attempt to recover a universal order through the geometric structuring of space; and it was intended to command that order as uncompromisingly as a baroque palace impresses Nature by the extended geometries of its formal gardens. To the north there was no topographical challenge to this ambition, but its achievement assumed a stable society in which the dominant interest would continue to prosper and multiply.

150

REFERENCES

1. Youngson, A.J., *The Making of Classical Edinburgh*, Edinburgh, 1966.

2. Arnot, H., *The History of Edinburgh*, Edinburgh, 1779, p. 319.

3. Cockburn, H., *Memorials of His Time*, Edinburgh, 1856 edition, reprinted in facsimile, 1971, pp. 287–8.

4. ibid., p. 289.

5. Stark, W., *Report to the Right Honourable the Lord Provost, Magistrates and Council of the City of Edinburgh and the Governors of George Heriot's Hospital, &c on the Plans for laying out the grounds for buildings between Edinburgh and Leith*, Edinburgh, 1814.

6. ibid., p. 7.

7. ibid., pp. 7–8.

8. *Proposals for carrying on certain Public Works in the City of Edinburgh*, Edinburgh, 1752.
   This pamphlet, thought to be written by Sir Gilbert Elliot, is quoted at length in Youngson, op.cit., pp. 3–12. The references given here are to the original.

9. ibid., p. 5.

10. Arnot, op.cit., p. 507.

11. ibid., p. 235.

12. *Proposals . . .* op.cit., p. 31.

13. ibid., p. 32.

14. Morer, T., *A Short Account of Scotland*, London, 1715; in Hume Brown, P., *Early Travellers in Scotland*, 1891, reprinted in facsimile, Edinburgh, 1978, p. 280.

15. Thomson, J., *Liberty*, 1738, in *Poetical Works*, London, 1908, p. 335.

16. ibid., pp. 411–412.

17. Grey Graham, H., *The Social Life of Scotland in the Eighteenth Century*, London, 1900 edition, p. 83.

18. Youngson, op.cit., pp.102–110.

19. *Town Council Minutes,* 29 July 1767.

20. Meade, M.K., Plans of the New Town of Edinburgh, *Architectural History: Journal of the Society of Architectural Historians of Great Britain,* 14, 1971, Figures 36a, 36b.

21. ibid., Figures 34a, 34b.

22. Farington, J., *Notebook No.3,* (1788), quoted in Youngson, op.cit., p. 93.

23. Kaufmann, E., *Architecture in the Age of Reason,* Toronto and London, 1968, p. 79.

24. Smout, T.C., *A History of the Scottish People, 1560–1830,* Glasgow, 1972, p. 440.

25. Kirkwood's Map of 1819 combines, in a remarkable feat of draughtsmanship, the plans of the first and second New Towns with elevations of the terraces built by that date.

26. The feuing plan of Drumsheugh, 1822, includes a proposal for a mansion (or assembly rooms?) within the bow of Randolph Crescent; there it would command the entrance to and the extended axis of the development. It was not built.

27. *Minutes of Committees for Feuing Calton Hill Grounds &c.,* 14th January 1811.

28. ibid., 15th February 1811.

29. ibid., 15th February 1811.

30. ibid., 19th June 1812.
    This seems to refer to an earlier competition for plans for the second New Town; if this is the case it is the only such reference known to the writer.

31. ibid., 1st January 1813.

32. These figures are reproduced from Kirkwood's *Plans and Illustrations of the City of Edinburgh,* 1817.

33. Minutes &c. op.cit., 1st July 1815.
    The 'Opinion by Baron Clerk and Gilbert Innes, Esq.' is dated 22nd March 1815.

34. ibid.

35. Stark, op.cit., p. 13.

36. Stark, op.cit., p. 16.

37. Minutes &c. op.cit., 5th February 1818.

38. Playfair, W.H., *Report to the Right Honourable the Lord Provost, Magistrates, and Council of the City of Edinburgh, and the Governors of Heriot's Hospital, &c. on a Plan for the laying out of the New Town between Edinburgh and Leith,* Edinburgh, 1819.
    The report was first presented to the joint committee on 12th April 1819. It is referred to hereafter as Playfair, *First Report.*

39. Minutes &c. op.cit., 30th August 1819.
    This report was not published. It is referred to hereafter as Playfair, *Second Report.*

40. ibid.

41. ibid.

42. ibid.

43. ibid.

44. ibid.

45. This layout is also shown in Lothian's map of 1825 (Figure 2.15).

46. Youngson, op.cit., p. 272.

47. Playfair, *First Report.*

48. Playfair, *Second Report.*

49. Dallman, L. and McNish, D., *The Spatial Order and Social Order of Georgian Edinburgh,* Department of Architecture and Building Science, University of Strathclyde, Unpublished Dissertation, 1981.

The Glasgow Grid

Frank Arneil Walker

It is so ludicrous to imagine anybody actually building the things that I have always assumed that Glasgow's tenements have just always been there.[1]

The tenement is woven into the fabric of Glasgow, held fast in the 'pleached alleys'[2] that cross and re-cross the urban landscape. No-one brought up in the city before the end of the last war can forget a childhood lived out beneath its sandstone cliffs. It has been like that for generations: football, peevers, or 'kick-the-can' in the streets, cries of alarm or admonition ringing across the back courts, washouses to climb, coal cellars to hide in, toilets on the landings, worn pipeclayed steps, wally tiles, the first cuddle in the close. As the *mise-en-scène* of urban life and experience it is the 'foursquare' tenement block that tesselates the mosaic of Glasgow's robust culture. Hind, Sharp, Gray, and others, have all needed something of its security as the grid on which the patterned play of character and narrative might be plotted. The canvasses of Eardley and Morrison have held and honoured its hugely palpable presence. But there is, too, another picture, another reality. A crumbling world of spalling sandstone and damp walls, torn sheets flapping in the grimy drizzle, wind gusting through doorless closes, rats and vagrants picking at the middens, blind and bloody violence or sullen *Weltschmerz* on the street corner—the dilapidated tenements of the slums. In this picture the social reality is one of observed degradation, the harsh aged buildings as brutally implicated in the blame as the capitalist class who erected them 'on a foundation of poverty'.[3] Edwin Muir, fifteen years in Glasgow but still the Orcadian outsider, passes on his journey down Eglinton Street, 'a long and dreary slum'.[4] He does not see in Greek Thomson's Queen's Park Terrace that 'front elevation of startling originality'[5] which makes it perhaps the greatest tenement block of them all. Why should he? It is no more to his purpose to make architectural judgments than it is to romanticise tenement life. But, if Muir avoids this pitfall, there are many who do not.

All too frequently, a roseate view of the tenement's fancied past or a bitter consciousness of the squalor and despair that have sometimes afflicted its old age, has become the basis for appraisals of architecture and townscape as critically fallacious as Ruskin's Victorian moralising that men must be good else they could not paint. Neither indifferent nor irrelevant, such pictures of Glasgow are, nevertheless, partial; one thirled to nostalgia, the other to misery. While some have turned the urban world of nineteenth century Glasgow into a back-court Kailyard of couthy reminiscence and gritty but comforting folk-lore, others have pictured the tenemented streets of the city as prison walls behind which an exploited society exercised its grim existence, 'Denied, adulterated, diluted, cowed.'[6] These are stereotyped and perhaps not unrelated views, romanticising or politicising the evidence they choose to see. As social or architectural history they are not untrue but wholly inadequate, limited, not to say distorted, in their perspective on time and space.

The tenement, after all, has a long record. It is the predominating building type in the fabric of Scottish towns. From mediaeval times to the present it has proved acceptable as 'A Way of Life'[7] to all but the most elevated strata of society. The tenement has accommodated proletarian and professional alike, social distinctions being achieved first by vertical gradation within a single building block and later by district location within the expanding city. But the same building type has consistently prevailed creating a tradition of what might be called socially indifferent architecture which has proved an important factor in forming the urban character of Glasgow.

Yet, although the tenement as building type is by no means a recent phenomenon, its combinational role in providing, as it were, the building blocks for the urban structure of modern Glasgow undoubtedly is. Architecture alone, however, does not make a city. There are also the courts, lanes and streets. Solid and void *together* constitute the matrix of urban living and experience. The problem is, then, to discern in this matrix that more pervasive order in which the intimate cultural bond between people and place subsists.

The architect has come late to the tenement dilemma: first, in a post-war orgy of moralistic cleansing, weeding out the detritus of neglect, damning and demolishing his inheritance; then, in more recent years, at last 'concerned with the blossom',[8] rehabilitating building and concept alike. Only now, as whole street facades are cleaned and back-courts recovered as communal space, do earlier losses seem all the greater, for only now has the significance of that regular chequer-board pattern of solid and void, which unites buildings and streets and which is the pervasive underlying structure of Glasgow's urban form, been fully sensed. In the analysis of the architectural historian, neither the sociological nor the technical critique—however pertinent the first may prove to be in blocking in the broader cultural picture or the second in delineating the details of construction, sanitation, and so on—can ever claim more than secondary validity beside this essentially formal issue. He must first record what Le Corbusier called 'the plastic system'.[9] He must document form. And in this respect, ludicrous as it may also seem to those for whom the tenements 'have just always been there', Glasgow's urban identity antedates, in important part, their dense and massive sandstone permanence. The streets were there first! And while the nineteenth century tenements themselves were not, of course, without their *architectural* precedents in the eighteenth and seventeenth centuries, it was by reinforcing that established *urban form*—a street plan established in the late eighteenth and early nineteenth centuries to a large extent for a quite different building type, the one-family terrace house—that they created a lasting townscape for the rapidly expanding Victorian city. Someone did 'put them up deliberately'. It is not the tenement itself but the given basis for this imputed deliberation—the Glasgow grid—which this essay will seek to explore.

A word may be said first, however, about the architectural reputation of the tenement simply as building type. For more than two generations since the twilight Edwardian years when Gourlay set down his practical design hints for tenement builders,[10] almost nothing was erected and little written which did honour to the tradition. Some cheapskate attempts to revive the form between the wars only accelerated a fall from grace that age and neglect had otherwise ensured. Not until the second half of the century did this bleak view begin to change. No doubt the widespread and at times apparently gratuitous destruction of much of the city's nineteenth century housing stock following the cavalier comprehensive re-development proposals of the 1960s wrought some perverse consequences. The antiquarian appetite is always alerted by scarcity and, in this regard, it is possible, if sadly ironic, to speak of 'beneficial demolitions'.[11] No doubt, too, as confidence in the future has ebbed, a slower tide of conservation and rehabilitation, swelled by the pessimism of recession and a revived stylistic pluralism in architectural theory, has impelled new and less puritanical critiques of the past. At any rate, while belated and tentative, the architectural historian's view of the tenement which has emerged over the last decade or so has been an unusually wide and generous one. In certain respects, however, it is a view which—coloured perhaps by a catholicity of interpretation intent on atoning for sins of both commission and omission—is hardly warranted by the facts. And it is a view which, in its specifically architectural focus, has blurred out the significance of *urban context.*

Some scholars, for example, studying the nature and evolution of housing in Scotland's largest city, have tended to induce a spurious universality for the category *tenement* by applying it to an entire tradition of high urban living. Since this building tradition and particularly its concomitant legal terminology can, of course, be observed in Scotland from mediaeval times to the present, the assumption is tempting and in some sense understandable. The very word *tenement,* like its synonym *land,* simply refers to the plot of ground over which someone exercises tenure and it is certainly true that this initially legal usage has, in the course of time, become more commonly and firmly attached to what was built on such a plot rather than to the land itself. As the bulk of all buildings is housing and the development of such housing proved to be restricted to vertical expansion as a consequence of the constraints of town marches and site size, it is not surprising that, for example, the notorious court or garden infill housing of the early nineteenth century should be known as *backlands,* or that individual blocks of flatted houses should acquire names such as Gibson's Land (Saltmarket, Glasgow; about 1690), Shortridge's Land (Dunlop Street, Glasgow; 1761) and Spreull's Land (Trongate, Glasgow; 1784). In like manner, the word *tenement* attained its ubiquitous and generalised application to all similar flatted property.

157

But to adduce the category *tenement* to each and every instance of urban housing of more than one storey built for more than one tenant is surely a suspect elaboration of usage. To be sure, such a definition cannot but provide the greatest possible evidence and, by implication, historical—or perhaps one had better say, historicist—justification. Thus Worsdall, defining a tenement as 'a domestic building of more than a single storey, built for multiple occupation, access being by a common entrance or stair'[12] was able to include in his important study virtually everything from dormered thatch-roofed terraced cottages to the nearly 300 feet high Red Road flats (Balornock, Glasgow; 1962–64). Robinson, too, in his otherwise more architecturally perceptive examinations,[13] seems to follow this abusage when he suggests that the tenement tradition 'lingers on in the form of the multi-storey flat'.[14]

Such wide-ranging applications are critically attenuated; nor are they supported by local usage. No Glaswegian refers to the two-storey flatted council houses at Penilee (1944) as tenements. Nor is the category thought appropriate for the Kelvin Court 'luxury flats' built privately at Anniesland just before the last war. Still less does he think of applying the word to that inner ring of post-1960 high-rise housing which has so catastrophically changed the face of much of his city. Yet Worsdall's definition permits such extremes so that, paradoxically, the gloss of historical continuity only obfuscates other quite specific qualities of the tenement proper. The assumption that almost all Scottish urban housing from almost any period can be regarded as tenemental is as illegitimate and misleading as the folk myth that 'tenements have just always been there'.

But none of this is meant to suggest that the specifically architectural qualities of the tenement have not been otherwise seriously and valuably examined. Indeed, since Gomme and Walker's pioneering work on the *Architecture of Glasgow*,[15] where the formal problems of the tenement facade were brilliantly and definitively analysed, there have been several studies each adding to a growing corpus of knowledge and interpretation. But while issues such as those of internal planning, of structure and materials, of facade scale and stylistic manipulation, of origins and precedents, have all been scrutinized, the question of urban context—the integrated relationship of building form and street block—has been much less discussed. Yet the Glasgow tenement of the last two hundred years is both building type *and* urban type; it can surely scarcely be said to exist outside the Glasgow grid.

Street and flat belong together. This is something the storyteller knows best.

> . . . Maggie Grierson sat looking at her brother through her tears. She knew exactly what he was seeing. Duke Street's drab width had been her home for nearly forty years, and there was nowhere else she wanted to go. For her it had kept the quality of the old Glasgow, a sense of the street, a realisation that streets were places for living in, not just passing through. She knew a lot of the people in its three-up tenements. She knew who was never out the

158

bookie's, who drank in the Ballochmyle Bar, who ran up a lot of tick in Mulholland's dairy. The places in the street had become as familiar to her as her own furniture.[16]

No doubt anecdote and sentiment are anathema to the scholar, for they so easily fabricate the tissue of false myth. Yet they animate the spirit of the place. And, paradoxically, it is the street singers, the workers of myth 'dancing in the streets' who sometimes see the truth most clearly—even in the fractured and prosaic tones of selective quotation.

> The tenements are built extravagantly of good sandstone . . . Most of them run to four storeys, built in rectangles to enclose the back courts. The back courts are divided by brick walls and brick built washhouses . . . The close leads directly from the street to the back court, and the staircase to the flats above starts in the middle of it . . .[17]

By way of definition little more needs to be said: material, size, configuration . . . A brief paragraph artificially contrived from three pages of droll nostalgia, the words are, of course, uncharacteristically flat for Cliff Hanley. Much is missing: the desperate menace and misery of the tenement slums, dismally degenerate and putrid with the stench of dank decay; the sense of community that tenement life engendered, particularly in adversity; the variation in social status that was possible within a common building type and cityscape; the complex legal and financial background to urban housing development; the nuances of stylistic variation; not least perhaps Hanley's own gallus humanity and humour without which the history of the place can only remain cold or glib. But however limited and unevocative, the words do afford an adequate formal description of tenement building in the Glasgow streets. Not all-inclusive, it is true—there are brick-built tenements; there are tenements whose facades can scarcely be called 'extravagant'; there are tenements of less than four and more than four storeys; not all staircases are embedded in the middle of the plan—not all inclusive, but adequate. What Hanley's words provide is a satisfactorily normative description for the tenement city block—'four storeys, built in rectangles to enclose the back courts'.

The validity of this view, in contrast to other more singularly architectural definitions, is grounded in its identifying beneath such important but secondary aspects as facade scale, close and stair planning, choice of materials, etc., which have so far preoccupied commentators, those more fundamental formal and spatial categories of street block and court. The norm is useful because it does not derive solely from the relationships existing between function and form in the restricted area of building type, as for example the definition which is content with the high-rise flat factor, but, by the elaboration of that building type *within the particular urban context of modern Glasgow*, engrosses the wider socio-spatial relevance implicit in the grid-iron plan.

*   *   *

The characteristic grid-iron plan of modern Glasgow—the urban basis of the tenement street block and court—did not appear until the last quarter of the eighteenth century. Until then, a mediaeval pattern of settlement had prevailed and growth within the bounds of the royalty had taken place principally along the two crossed axes of the city's main streets. By the end of the seventeenth century, however, significant developments in this underlying pattern were already underway.

First of all, the long burgh feus or *lands* behind the gabled facades of High Street, Saltmarket, Bridgegate, Gallowgate and Trongate were more and more built up. The strip fields or 'runrigs' of a self-sufficient 'farmtoun'[18] husbandry gradually disappeared. In their place a tight urban weave emerged in which bands of ill-lit frequently makeshift timber housing of one, two or more storeys alternated with dark narrow vennels threading back through the gloom. Serious fires in 1652 and 1677 had, to some extent, delayed this early *backlands* housing and Denholm, writing at the end of the eighteenth century, records how as a result of these tragic events Glasgow's buildings

> . . . from being gloomy, incommodious and constructed without taste . . . have, in process of time, become rivals to the city buildings in any town in Britain, with regard to whatever is convenient, healthful, or agreeable in human habitation.[19]

Although this view can probably be maintained of those substantial stone-built flatted residences which by then fronted the city's four or five principal streets, a glance at McArthur's map[20] (Figure 3.1), produced twenty years before Denholm's history, immediately reveals the main lines of an intensive and extensive rig development. The legal convenience of *backlands* growth made it an irresistible speculation. For two centuries it was ruthlessly perpetrated producing those fetid channels of disease and despair darkly familiar in Thomas Annan's nineteenth century photographs.[21]

Away from the densely built-up alleys around Glasgow Cross, however, a second pattern of growth—not unrelated to the first in its physical form, equally speculative no doubt, but more far-sighted—had taken shape. By the middle of the seventeenth century a series of parallel streets (Stockwellgait, Old Wynd, New Wynd and Main or Back Wynd) ran north to south between Trongate and Bridgegate. By the early eighteenth century it was possible for McUre to detect the same model at work along each of the city's five main streets; a model which, he observed,

> . . . may be justly compared to a double wooden comb, viz the street, the wood in the middle, and the teeth of each side, the closses or small lanes.[22]

Although these narrow lanes were at times very closely spaced and ultimately as heavily developed as the mediaeval rigs, their appearance could only result from more complex and deliberated negotiations relating to the conveyance and use of land within the burgh. In other words the planned development of the city had begun.

160

In determining the disposition and direction of subsequent development the orthogonal relationships established with Trongate appear especially important for they clearly provided guidelines for later growth, particularly that to the north and west. When King Street was laid down in about 1722, to be followed soon by Candleriggs, these 'New Streets'[23] struck a long perpendicular across Trongate, reinforcing the pattern of the earlier Wynds to the west. Being close to the Cross, they were quickly drawn into the densely mixed commercial and residential nexus of the old town, now booming under the stimulation of the American tobacco trade. But some distance to the west later developments in Virginia Street (1753), Miller Street (1761), Queen Street (1762), Buchanan Street (1771) and Jamaica Street (1751), all fostered by continuing mercantile success, proposed a new and more spacious townscape. Still running at right angles to the Trongate—or rather its westward extension, Argyle Street, begun after the demolition of the West Port in 1749—each of these new streets was to be lined with the graceful restraint of early Georgian architecture. Several elegant mansions in the chaste idiom of Palladian fashion, already evident along the Trongate from the early years of the eighteenth century, were raised by the richer merchant families. The 'handsome buildings of Miller Street'[24] and the scarcely less pretentious villas of Virginia Street and Queen Street each 'occupied by one family from top to bottom as in London',[25] testified to the taste, wealth and aspirations of the bourgeois classes. Away from the claustrophobic squalor of mediaeval streets Glasgow had become, as Defoe had already observed, 'one of the cleanliest, most beautiful, and best-built cities in Great Britain',[26] a planned town in which, by the second half of the eighteenth century, a clearly rectilinear pattern coincident with the tentative lines of seventeenth century growth, was emerging.

Still the grid did not appear. Like a series of parallel ribs strongly articulated at right angles to the backbone of the city's westward development, the new urban structure, albeit rectilinear, maintained for a time a pronounced 'main street' inflection. To the south, where expansion was in any case quickly restricted by the pre-existent curve of the Bridgegate or by the river itself, this simple hierarchy, expressed in street widths and architectural attitudes, could not be threatened. Here, after the sacrifice of the Old Green, further growth was only achieved by an increase in the density of building and population within the limits of the established street pattern. To the north, on the other hand, the potential for planned expansion was greater. The northern extremities of Queen Street, Miller Street and Virginia Street were all somewhat indeterminate with only the old 'narrow country road'[27] known as Back Cow Loan (present-day Ingram Street) seeming to reflect the principal east-west axis of Trongate. Beyond this lane the Ramshorn Croft stretched over flat open country until the ground began to rise against the first of the drumlin ridges characterising the landscape to the north and west. In 1772 the city magistrates bought these fields and, intending to develop, 'got plans of the

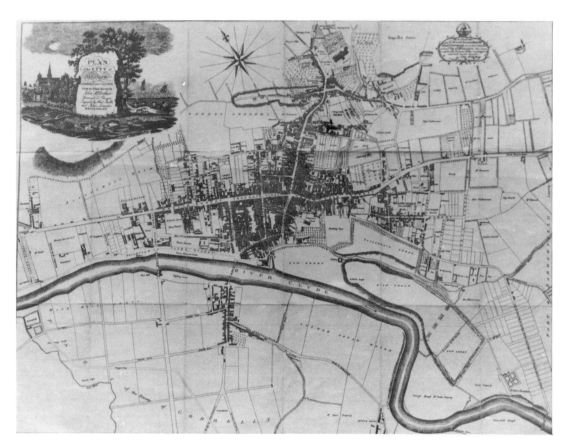

3.1 *McArthur's map 1778.*

said lands drawn out for building on'.[28] Proposals for a street layout and plot feuing were accordingly prepared by James Barry (or Barrie), 'land surveyor in Glasgow' and, although little further seems to have been done for a number of years, it was almost certainly on these lost plans of the 1770s that the putative basis of the Glasgow grid was first delineated.

In 1778, following a survey by John McArthur, the 'first general plan of the City ever published'[29] appeared. The City Council immediately authorised the purchase of ten copies. McArthur's map was not, of course, the first plan of the city to be drawn up. The ever-active James Barry had only the year before been paid for 'a plan of the royalty of Glasgow'[30] which he had been commissioned to produce. Some years earlier, in 1769, there is a record of a council committee walking the march stones with two plans of the city as a basis for their inspection: one of these had also been prepared by Barry, some time in the 1740s; the other, drawn up in 1732 by John Wat (*sic*), a mathematics teacher, was 'a curious map or plan of the 16 merk land of Glasgow, which has cost him great pains and trouble, and taken a long time in the doing thereof . . .'[31] But none of these is extant and

162

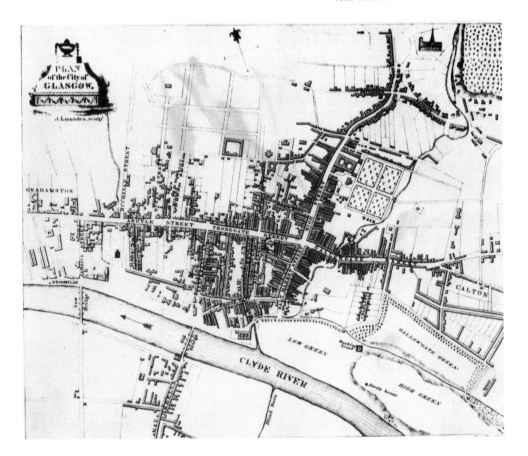

3.2 *McArthur's map 1783.*

none was, in any case, published. McArthur's plan must, therefore, be regarded as the earliest record of what may be termed modern Glasgow.

It did not, however, include the projected network of new streets. Evidently the city fathers had not made Barry's proposals for the Ramshorn lands public. But five years later, on a second edition of McArthur's plan appearing in *The Glasgow Magazine and Review* . . ., a grid is shown (Figure 3.2). The writer of several serialised 'Anagraphs of the Past and Present State of The City of Glasgow' doubtless felt his descriptions would prove appropriate for the future too.

> Every stranger is charmed with the appearance of Glasgow; the streets are clean and well paved . . . several of them, intersecting one another at right angles, have a very fine effect . . .[32]

Parallel to the broadened and straightened line of Back Cow Loan, which had been opened up for feuing as Ingram Street in 1781, the grid depicted two more-or-less equally spaced new thoroughfares running east to west across the Ramshorn ground for a distance of almost half a mile.

163

Crossing these are five new streets drawn south to north: the three most westerly continue the lines of Buchanan Street, Queen Street and Miller Street; the fourth approximates to what is now John Street; the fifth, close to the feu of the North-West or Ramshorn Church, follows the line of the future Montrose Street. Although the particular street alignments of this 1783 McArthur plan had in fact been preceded by the more informed and concrete proposals of a plan published in 1782 from another survey which Barry had made five years before, they exhibit a number of interesting points which are worth noting.

First, a compromise between the abstract attraction of the drawing-board grid and the contingent needs of the site is evident. The three new streets running east-west have certainly been equally spaced. But the dimensions of the blocks have not, however, been *fully* regularised since the locating of the north-south ordinates depends, to some extent, upon an already established street pattern.

A second aspect of the potential implications of the grid plan is also evident. Although tied to the lines of earlier streets to the south, on its north and west margins the new street layout has been left 'open-ended'. It seems likely that, although the royalty had not yet extended its boundary over the lands concerned, further expansion was both anticipated and intended to take place in these directions. At any rate, this proved to be a critical decision for the growth and image of the city. Not only did the logic of the grid predicate a replicable non-hierarchical pattern of growth which could not but create a certain tension between the New Town and the old, but, in its consistent elaboration over the next century, grid development ensured a progressively westward shift in the city's centre of gravity during which time it became more and more difficult to identify this 'centre' as anything other than a rather tenuous prolongation of street activity threaded through the expanding urban network.

Thirdly, the somewhat surprising absence of George Square, which by the end of the century would become 'the city's *Grande Place*',[33] must be remarked. Its western boundary may be said to exist in the continuation of Queen Street but its eastern limits of Frederick Street–Glassford Street[34] do not appear in the McArthur plan grid; the northern extension of Miller Street actually traverses its subsequent centre. Either *The Glasgow Magazine* map of 1783 belatedly records Barry's *earliest* intentions for the Ramshorn area development, in which case it would seem that first thoughts did not envisage a large open public square, or—and this seems more likely—what is presented is simply a somewhat sketchy and no doubt ill-informed attempt to show the public that plans were afoot for the controlled expansion of the city.

Finally, the 1783 version of the McArthur plan presents the grid network *in outline only*, with no indication of how building development should proceed. There is no sign of the closely-packed built-up city blocks of later years and, indeed, it was not until the later 1780s, as Hutcheson Street and Great Glassford Street opened up more direct links to the

Trongate, that building developments along the chequer-board lines of 'those streets called the New Town were carried on with alacrity'[35] and the Council's investment began to yield a return. But one very extensive courtyard building evidently did already exist north of Ingram Street on the edge of the New Town. Occupying most of the block immediately east of the proposed junction of John Street and Ingram Street, this was a 'large quadrangular tape manufactory',[36] a two storey structure erected in 1743 on ground 'in the Ramshorn yard'[37] sold by the patrons of Hutchesons' Hospital to the Inkle Factory Company. Can it be entirely fortuitous that its form, so prominent on plan, is so peculiarly fitted for the grid pattern being imposed on the Ramshorn expansion? Does its form not also perhaps provide a cue for the scale and disposition of subsequent building development?

Answers to some of these dilemmas are to be found in the Barry plan published in 1782, the year before *The Glasgow Magazine* printed its gridded version of McArthur's earlier map. This Barry 'Plan of the City of Glasgow, Gorbells Caltoun and Environs', authorised by the Council in August 1780 (Figure 3.3), incorporates his latest intentions for the Ramshorn development, intentions he was soon to implement for, on the 14th of August, 1782, the Council minutes recorded that

> The committee appointed upon the Ramshorn grounds are of the opinion that there should be formed two streets, each 60 feet wide, running from east to west, at right angles to Queen Street . . . That there should be three streets running from north to south and parallel to Queens (*sic*) Street, one of 40 feet wide in the middle between the Incle factory and the church yard, another of 60 feet wide at the west end of the Incle factory, and the third of 60 feet wide at the same distance east from the head of Miller Street as Queen Street is to the west of it . . .[38]

An attempt has thus been made to produce a regularised, although not quite uniformly dimensioned, grid at the heart of which, as Barry's plan shows, George Square makes its appearance. Moreover, the Ingram Street inkle factory (it would not be demolished until the middle of the nineteenth century) has proved to be a significant factor in the new plan. Bounded on three and not merely two sides by the grid, the configuration of the factory block co-incides with that of the emergent street network. Negotiations entered into in 1785 between the proprietors of the inkle factory and the city council confirmed this relationship which appears to have been intended by Barry in his earlier proposals for the Ramshorn development and which had been shown on 'the original plan approved by the council, now mislaid and amissing . . .'[39]

But Barry has also shown the grid built up in solid unbroken street frontages similar to those of the factory and quite unlike either the close-packed *lands* of the mediaeval town or the detached mansions and villas of early Georgian development. While these black bands certainly do not represent building completed by 1782, their intention is clear enough: they underline, as it were, the fundamental architectural implications of the grid-iron plan. Here, in other words, is the simple formal idea of the courtyard block, its four uninterrupted street facades to be coherently conceived either on the basis of the subdivided whole, that is to say the street block, or the repetitive aggregated part, the individual feu unit. In the light of the elevational difficulties of unification and scale subsequently faced by the tenement builders it is perhaps significant that these earliest grid developments were frequently designed as unified sequences of individual 'one family'[40] terraced dwellings. Just as the tenement (defined, that is, simply as a flatted property of three or four storeys with a common close access) had already existed for some considerable time as an isolated building type in the mediaeval and early Georgian *milieus* of the city, so the urban grid continued to be developed without any immediate need to invoke what, under the greater pressures of nineteenth century expansion, was to become its later most familiar architectural expression. For the moment, the aspirations of the well-to-do moving in to the 'New Town' to escape the overcrowding of the old—increasingly unacceptable as much because of the enforced social overlap which life there entailed as for the density and varied quality of its buildings—demanded, if not the salubrious independence of the detached Georgian town house, then at least that aggrandizement by association, physical and metaphorical, which co-ordinated terraces or centrally pedimented street block designs afforded. However plainly interpreted, such were the forms and intimations of George Square. The 'full-blown' tenement solution of block and court had not yet appeared. Nevertheless, though their conjunction was as yet delayed, by the 1780s both urban form and building type were already in existence.

During the last decade of the eighteenth century, as building went ahead in and around George Square, the final portion of what today is known as the Merchant City was also being completed. The focus of this 'infill' development between Ingram Street and the Trongate was Wilson Street. From it, in much the same way as earlier expansion had taken place along the Trongate, a number of parallel streets ran north and south. Furthermore, not only was Wilson Street, like the Trongate, substantially broader than those streets which ran perpendicular to it, but its width was deliberately constricted at its west and east ends. Street frontages returned at these narrowed entries stressing the containment of the space (Figure 3.4). Thus, despite the creation of a rectilinear pattern consistent with the surrounding streets, the development could not, strictly speaking, be described as a grid. The decision to contrive a sense of urban enclosure in Wilson Street and the very fact that the development had to be carried out within an already established perimeter combined to produce a townscape of closed rather than open views. Following the precedent of the old Ramshorn Church at the end of Candleriggs and the recently built Cunninghame Mansion (1779) which now stopped the perspective west along Ingram Street, several of these new street vistas were architecturally accented with particular care, some with buildings of the highest quality.

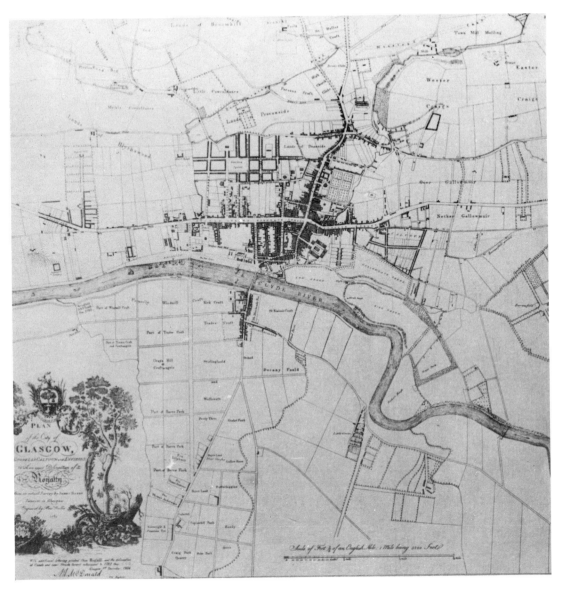

3.3 *Barry's map 1780.*

But if the open grid could not appear, the original street architecture—some of which was almost as splendid as these *points-de-vue*—could certainly be described as tenemental, at least in the limited sense referred to above. The Adamesque buildings of Wilson Street put up by Robert Smith, a builder acting for 'a wealthy company in England',[41] were especially fine examples. Tall four storey flatted properties, they were designed in the contemporary quasi-palatial Edinburgh manner rather than

167

3.4 *Muirhead Bone sketch of Wilson Street.*

the plainer local idiom—appropriately enough perhaps since, rather than lining the repetitive open-ended defiles of a grid streetscape, they confronted what, by virtue of its generous breadth and perceptible enclosure, constituted a grand inward-looking Neoclassical 'square', wholly unique in Glasgow.

On a plan of the city published in 1804 (Figure 3.5) in the second edition of Denholm's history of Glasgow,[42] and based on a survey carried out in that same year, increasingly rapid expansion on all fronts is becoming apparent. As well as the intense development of the Merchant City and George Square 'New Town', there are signs of growth in the east in Calton, in the north at Townhead, and in the extreme west at Anderston. The city's first grid-iron plan seems more securely anchored in the east by the continuation of George Street into Duke Street (1794)[43], and there are strong indications that a westward encroachment on the Lands of Blythswood is underway: in the Meadowflat, Camperdown Place has been named, the route passing along the south side of George Square (present day St. Vincent Street) has been extended westward, and the lines of Union Place (present day Union Street), Mitchell Street (unnamed) and Gordon Street are all coming into existence. By far the most geometrically coherent areas of growth are, however, the three gridded suburbs planned on the flat farmland south of the river.

168

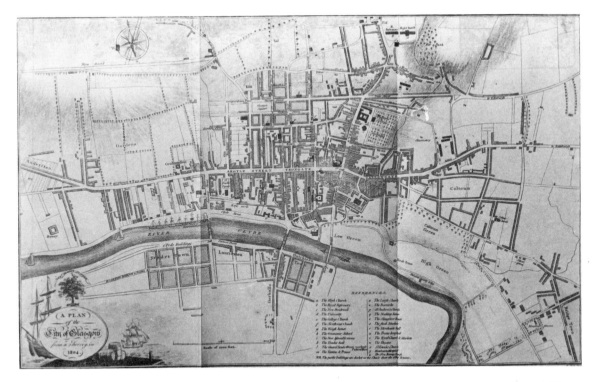

3.5 *Denholm's map, 1804.*

But here all is not as it seems. What appears to be an insistent drawing-board rigour, with only the slightest inflection to take account of the bend in the river or the old settlement of Gorbals, is in fact the concretization of an earlier pattern of tenure. The street grids have not been arbitrarily imposed but, as Kellett has shown[44] (Figure 3.6), actually follow and derive from the old field pattern. The transition is already apparent in Barry's 1782 map where a rectilinear arrangement of circulation is emerging west of Gorbals. With a convenient logic boundaries have become routes, an abrupt mutation which seems to confound the familiar categories of Kevin Lynch's urban analysis. And yet because in the Lynchian taxonomy both edges and paths are 'linear elements',[45] it is perhaps not surprising that speculative planning should effect this simple transition. At any rate, Trades Town, Laurieston and Hutcheson Town together comprise the second phase in the growth of the Glasgow grid.

It is particularly interesting that the directional ordinates of the first grid were not ignored. One of the striking aspects of the 1804 plan is the parallelism that exists between the Trades Town network of streets and the rectilinear pattern established north of the river over the previous century. Clearly this is the product of conscious planning hinged around the line of the New Bridge (present day Glasgow Bridge) which since 1771 linked the south bank via Jamaica Street to the city's main east-west axis of Trongate–

169

Argyle Street. The connection was not at once exploited but, in 1791, 'according to a plan prepared by John Gardener, land surveyor',[46] the Glasgow Trades House began to lay off the streets and steadings of the new suburb of Trades Town. The first eight blocks, occupying Windmill Croft, were disposed symmetrically around the crossed axes of Kingston Street and Centre Street.[47] Fittingly named, the latter is shown protruding south, clearly intended as the backbone of further growth into the lands of Trades Croft and Gray's Hill.

Along the eastern margin of Trades Town, 'Eglinton and Bridge Streets, marking the boundary between the lands belonging to Hutcheson's Hospital and the Trades House, were laid out at joint expense'.[48] The Hutcheson patrons did not, however, undertake any development in the adjacent Kirk Croft property but some distance to the east beyond Gorbals village where in 1792, they had purchased land south-east of the Old Bridge

> for the accommodation of a town, which the patrons had resolved to lay off on their division of the Gorbals lands; to be called *Hutchesone* (sic), in honour of the founders of the hospital, the principal street of which was named *Adelphi Street*, for the two brothers; and the next street *Hospital Street*.[49]

Begun in 1794 in by now typical 'foursquare' Glasgow manner, 'upon a regular plan, and laid out into a number of right lined streets',[50] Hutcheson Town produced the first major shift in the city's grid system—a 20° cant to the east. But, if conformity with the grand grid of the New Town, which had been maintained in Trades Town, was lost in Hutcheson Town, a strong riparian parallelism reinforced by the line of the Old Bridge and a new Saltmarket Bridge was, nevertheless, achieved. Although this new bridge was destroyed almost immediately by the floods of 1795 and an intended cast iron footbridge 'from a most ingenious design, drawn by Mr. P. Nicholson, architect'[51] does not seem to have been realised, in 1803 a timber bridge was 'thrown across the Clyde at the foot of Saltmarket Street.'[52] By 1830 the Hutcheson Bridge had been built and the canted grid was extending rapidly east towards the 90° swing in the river's course.

Last of the three cross-river suburbs to be projected (about 1800) was that undertaken by the speculator James Laurie on land purchased from Hutcheson's Hospital patrons. A map (Figure 3.7) included in the *Glasgow Directory* 'corrected till July 1803', shows these Kirk Croft lands between Trades Town in the west and Gorbals in the east still entirely undeveloped. Denholm's 1804 map does, however, record the completion of Carlton Terrace (1802–04) along the river bank and indicates the first signs of a street network co-incident with the Trades Town grid. Although the layout of the Laurieston streets seems still somewhat indecisive on the 1804 map, not only can the line of distant Buchanan Street be picked up as the central avenue of the new quarter across the river but Nicholson's 'pair of identical palace-fronted terraces'[53] are evidently meant to flank this same axis. By 1830, Portland Street and Abbotsford Place had indeed confirmed

170

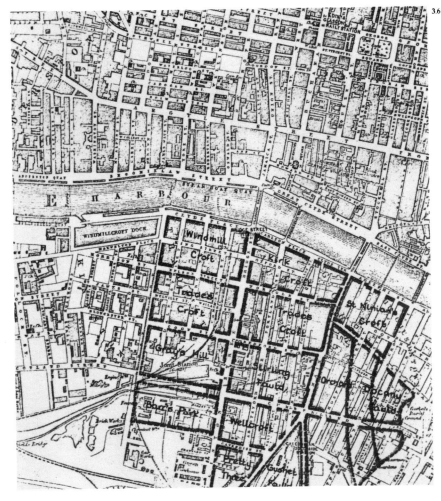

3.6 *Kellett's map of tenure pattern south of the river.*

its importance and building had been extended as far as Cumberland Street.

Early small-scale plans of the three new gridded suburbs suggest that unbroken street frontages to the city block were once again envisaged. Each development was to be wholly residential and, apart from Carlton Place, flatted tenement properties were intended throughout. But despite these common qualities, significant differences did emerge. In Trades Town, for example, where the block size of 250 feet by 300 feet came coincidentally closest to the pattern set by the street network of the George Square 'New Town', blocks were divided into fourteen feus without service lanes, five plots lining each of the 250 feet long east-west sides (Figure 3.8). Although Denholm describes several streets 'already

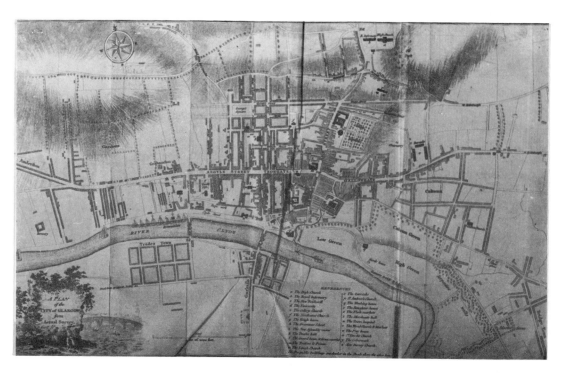

3.7 *Glasgow Directory map 1803*

built in handsome style',[54] whatever controls may have at first prevailed were not long sustained. Under growing industrial and commercial pressure, the almost square nature of the Trades Town block with its airy but prodigal 'back court' space soon submitted to a haphazardly mixed development which, in little more than a generation, turned a suburban village into 'a busy hive of manufacturing and engineering industry'.[55] The legal ease of translating a pattern of rural tenure directly into urban structure thus proved a deceptively convenient and specious procedure. Hutcheson Town, on the other hand, because of its much more economical elongated narrow block form—it measured c.150 feet by c.500 feet, although it too was without service lanes—remained substantially but not exclusively residential, well into the twentieth century. Thus, the geometry of the grid—rectangular rather than square—enabled the patrons of Hutcheson's Hospital to control land use, growth and appearance some-what more effectively and ensure a long-term future for their investment in urban housing. Even the very street frontages, as Worsdall notes, 'appeared more orderly than those of Tradeston, a uniform height of four storeys having been adopted almost from the outset'.[56]

The absence of service lanes in both the Trades Town and Hutcheson Town grids betrays something of the social nature of these new suburbs. A population of shopkeepers, clerks and independent craftsmen did not require the mews arrangements needed to accommodate either the

172

domestic servants or the physical accoutrements (as, for example, the horse and trap) which necessarily accompanied and supported a more middle class life style. In Laurieston, however, though the tenemental form persisted and the grid principle of planning was again applied, social aspiration ran somewhat higher—at least in the earlier phases of building. Not only was the quality of architecture grander and more dignified often with pedimented windows and splendid porches contributing to what McWilliam calls 'the climax of Glasgow's Georgian austerity'[57] but flats were larger and a subsidiary servicing network *was* integrated in parallel with the north–south alignment of streets in which the elongated block reached over 650 feet. Laurieston, in fact, was 'generally tenanted by genteel people of the middle classes, who have their places of business, or attend to professional avocations in Glasgow'.[58]

In these three progressively sophisticated variations, the theme of the tenement block and court was for the first time extensively grafted into the Glasgow grid. In due course the propensity of the spatial order of the grid for still further adaptation became evident under the pressures exerted by the increasingly rapid industrialisation of the nineteenth century city. As foundries, factories, warehouses, and finally railways bit into the fabric of the suburbs south of the river, the large residential populations of Trades Town, Hutcheson Town and Laurieston become almost exclusively working class. The spatial order of both architectural and urban form—tenement and grid—thus early proved readily amenable not only to contemporary differences but also to subsequent metamorphoses of social order.

A similar co-incidence of street block and tenement building type, in which the social premise was from the start proletarian, soon also occurred in the small manufacturing village of Bridge Town which was growing up on the south-east edge of the city. Until the last quarter of the eighteenth century, the lands of Dalmarnock 'lay in run-rig'[59] but, after the opening in 1777 of a bridge leading across the river to the Royal Burgh of Rutherglen, settlement intensified and the suburb took its name, Bridge Town. Denholm's map records this ribbon development, no doubt mainly single or two-storey weavers' housing, extending along the line of Main Street from what is now Bridgeton Cross to the bridge. As the textile and leather industries prospered, the working population increased further and four years later (1808) Fleming's 'Map of the City of Glasgow and Suburbs' (Figure 3.9) shows the tenement grid appearing, particularly on the east side of Main Street between Muslin Street in the north and Trafalgar Street near the river. It is interesting that, although the grid network introduced in Bridge Town did vary, it approximated in part to that at Trades Town, similar dimensions producing the same almost square block with its large inner court, uneconomical in strictly residential terms. Unlike Trades Town, however, but in common with most of the city's expansion east of Glasgow Cross, Bridge Town was from the start essentially working class in character. Housing being only one of manufacturing industry's needs,

3.8 *Tradeston feu map.*

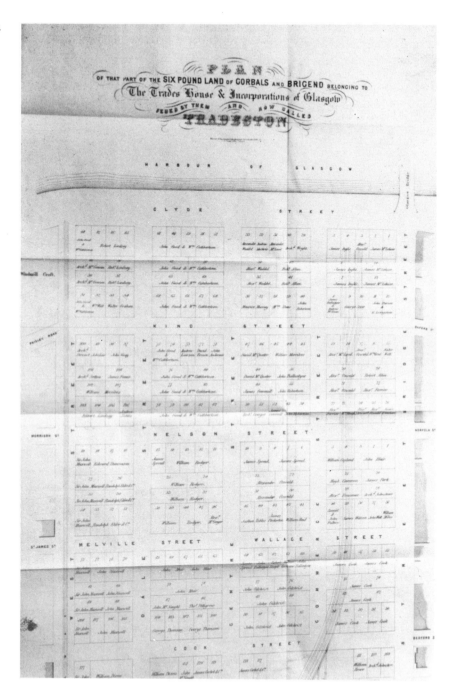

174

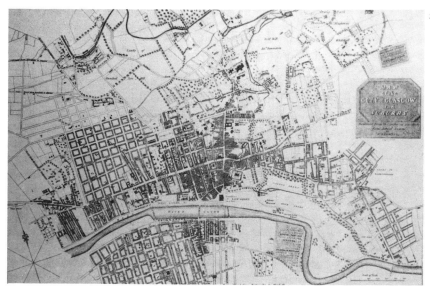

3.9 *Fleming's map 1808.*

the suburb was thus readily subjected to uncontrolled mixed development, 'the locality being literally studded with public works'.[60]

Trades Town, Hutcheson Town, Laurieston and Bridge Town were all peripheral developments. Their importance lies in the planned integration of the grid with tenemental housing which they exemplify. Their expansion could not, of course, physically affect central Glasgow but neither did the townscape or architectural character of that expansion make any immediate impact on the centre. Nevertheless, there too the grid was already spreading. The city magistrates, having acquired the lands of Meadowflat beyond the first 'New Town', began to project the lines of the streets on the north and south sides of George Square westward in that direction. At the same time Gordon Street made its appearance on the west side of Buchanan Street and Mitchell Street, Union Place and Alston Street pushed north from Grahamston. Then, with the potential ordinates of an extended grid established, the development of the vast 470 acre Blythswood Estate began. It was here, west of the Meadowflat lands, that the city's Second New Town, the counterpart of Edinburgh's already celebrated New Town, was to take shape. But in Glasgow development was to proceed not as a civic venture but as a private speculation.

Judging the moment ripe for profit, Major Archibald Campbell decided to feu off the Blythswood Annexation lands, hitherto entailed to his family. Holding the estate in fee as outright owners, he and his trustees were able to feu the lands freely and had soon concluded several increasingly remunerative transactions with a succession of enterprising but frequently over ambitious speculators keen to exploit the pleasant rising grounds of the estate for residential development. So profitable were these arrangements that in the fifty years from 1799 to 1849 the family's annual rental income from the Blythswood Annexation lands had risen from £223.1.3 to a prodigious £25,000.[61] While the Campbells prospered, many of those who had purchased land hoping to benefit from the city's expansion were ruined in the venture; Harley, Cuthel, Cooke, Garden and Burns all failed to hold on long enough to capitalise on their investment. Nevertheless, whatever the personal setbacks, development went ahead.

From the time of the earliest conveyances of estate property in 1800 until the end of the first decade of the new century, transactions between the Campbell trustees and William Harley, 'Merchant in Glasgow', are recorded time and time again in the voluminous chartularies of the Blythswood estate. Purchasing plot after plot, Harley was soon the dominant new proprietor. 'Senex', writing in *The Glasgow Herald* a generation later, greatly admired this enterprise and went so far as to give Harley himself the credit for the quality of the Blythswood development.

> . . . he tastily laid off and improved the whole of the grounds which he had feued. In short, Mr. Harley may be considered as the founder of the present New Town of Glasgow upon the Annexation lands.[62]

But did William Harley conceive any part of the street plan of the Blythswood New Town? It is most unlikely. Feus granted in March and April 1803,[63] some three months or so before the first transaction recorded between Harley and the Campbell trustees, already define rectangular plots of ground on the north of the estate bounded by Sauchyhall Road (now Street), Hill Street, Scott Street and Renfrew Street and on the south of the estate bounded by Argyle Street, Pitt Street, Douglas Street and Cadogan Street, which indicate the prior existence of a gridded network. Most—although not all—of Harley's own feus are similarly rectangular in form, notably the substantial purchase dated 16th January 1808,[64] in which the five plots, each about 300 feet by about 270 feet comprising *in toto* that portion of the network between Sauchiehall Street and Bath Street stretching from Nile Street (present day West Nile Street) in the east to Mains Street (present day Blythswood Street) in the west, were disponed. Who but the superiors of the estate, the Campbell family, would be responsible for the delineation of this grid? But when was the grid first established? And by whose hand?

A wholly satisfactory answer to these questions cannot yet be given. What can be said, however, is that the issue is closely bound up with the legal provisions, or rather prohibitions, of entail. In 1739 Colin Campbell of Blythswood had entailed the family estate in order to ensure that the inheritance would be maintained intact. This step, although preventing dissipation of the lands by succeeding heirs, carried with it certain difficulties for thereafter 'an heir in possession had no power at common law to sell . . .'[65] Just over half a century later this restriction seems to have become intolerable. Doubtless determined to exploit the economic potential of ground which lay in the immediate path of Glasgow's planned expansion westwards during the last quarter of the eighteenth century, the

Campbells succeeded in bringing a private Act of Parliament[66] which annulled the fetters of the entail and thus permitted the sale or feuing of the Blythswood lands, the money raised being invested in the aggrandizement of the family's other major estate holding at Renfrew. The year was 1792. In the same year James Barry, the city's favoured land surveyor, died and there appeared in the Council minutes a brief entry dated 9th August authorising

> . . . the lord provost and magistrates to employ Mr. Craig, architect in Edinburgh, to make a plan of the ground of Meadowflatt for building ground, as Mr. Craig is employed by Colonel Campbell of Blythswood to make a plan of his building ground in the neighbourhood of Meadowflatt, and it will be attended with considerable advantage to have the streets upon the two grounds uniform and corresponding with each other.[67]

This intriguing but alas solitary mention can surely only refer to James Craig (1744–95) the Edinburgh architect responsible for the plan of the capital's first New Town between 1766 and 1767. Craig's later years appear to have brought neither the acclaim nor the commissions that his early celebrity seemed to promise—allegations of arrogance and problems of debt cloud the picture—but it is fascinating to speculate that towards the end of his career he may have found the opportunity to translate his Edinburgh conception into the scaled-down more constrained context of Glasgow. No plan of Blythswood New Town, either in whole or in part, carries the name of James Craig; none antedates 1800; while all the plans subsequent to that date, whether those of individual feus attached to the legal documents or those larger surveys which progressively recorded the subdivision of the estate as a whole,[68] were drawn up by the Campbells' estate surveyor William Kyle (Figure 3.10). Nevertheless, *mutatis mutandis*, there are certain similarities between Craig's Edinburgh plan and the street network of Blythswood which cannot be dismissed as mere coincidence.

The nature of the Blythswood layout was, of course, largely determined by a number of pre-existent limiting factors to some of which reference has already been made. Two long roughly parallel but widely separated routes crossed the estate from east to west: in the north Sauchyhall Road and in the south Anderson Walk or Argyle Street. At right angles to these running south to north was Buchanan Street in the city's Meadowflat land on the eastern edge of the Blythswood estate. Projecting westwards across Buchanan Street, extending the south and north limits of George Square, the beginnings of St. Vincent Street and West George Street (then Camperdown Place) had been planned. All these routes lay in potentially orthogonal relationship, while the development of the first New Town, carried out by a city Council upon whose plans for expansion the Campbells' sudden good fortune depended, already provided guidelines for the dimensions of the street block. Moreover, as Barry's 1782 plan shows, the field pattern of the estate lands was based on a roughly similar

177

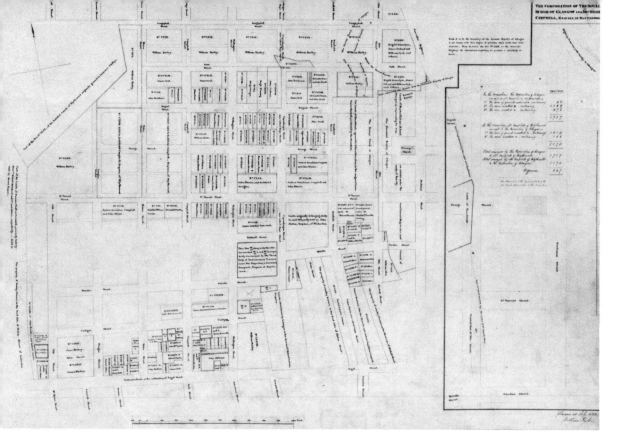

3.10 *Blythswood estate feuing map.*

north-south/east-west system. In short, all factors pointed to the adoption of a grid-iron plan, a layout which would, of course, offer the most convenient basis for feuing.

It seems reasonable to assume that this grid had come into existence, at least as a projected feuing pattern for speculative development, before 1800. If, in fact, James Craig did delineate it as early as 1792, its immediate implementation must have been hindered by a number of related events. In the first place Colonel John Campbell of Blythswood, at whose instigation the private Act of 1792 had been obtained, died and was succeeded by his brother Archibald Campbell in 1795.[69] Craig himself died in the same year. Furthermore the negotiations with the city over the co-ordination of development in Meadowflat with that in the Blythswood lands were delicate and, inevitably perhaps, slow. Complicated by the location of the Campbell family mansion of Enochbank, which lay frustratingly on the eastern marches of the estate, the whole venture necessitated not only carefully executed exchange of marching land but a decision by the family about its future home. In due course, feuing on the basis of the grid-iron plan did go ahead, although at first only along the north and south sides of Sauchyhall Road and immediately north of Argyle Street, but Archibald Campbell initially retained the Enochbank ground and purchased for himself two large plots on the crest of Blythswood Hill. By 1810 the Enochbank ground has passed into Harley's hands and the

178

city council was negotiating with both Campbell and Harley to lay down the extended lines of St. Vincent Street and George Street (present day West George Street) continuing westward through 'the respective properties of the said parties until they communicate with the streets leading northward from Argyle Street and the Anderston road: either already formed or to be formed' and also 'to open up and form Nile Street'[70] (present day West Nile Street). Both the Enochbank lands and the reserved hilltop site were thus bisected by George Street which, since 1807, had been accented at its eastern end in Meadowflat by William Stark's St. George's Church steeple.[71] Did Archibald Campbell contemplate marking the western skyline with a new town house set on the elevated ground at the opposite end of the new street? The precedent of Edinburgh, where in 1767 Sir Laurence Dundas has seized the opportunity to feu from the city 'an Area in the East Square'[72] at the eastern end of Edinburgh's George Street axis on which to erect his own house, may once more be apposite. In the event, however, no such conjectured aspirations were realised in the city, Blythswood House was built instead at Renfrew in 1821 on the estate which the disentail Act of thirty years earlier had expressly commended for enlargement, and feus on Blythswood Hill were finally released to be laid off a year or two later as Garden Square (present day Blythswood Square).

Fleming's 1808 map shows the full surprising extent of the disciplined grid which had been placed across the Blythswood Estate. Far more comprehensive than anything similar yet introduced in the city, the network of 'Building Ground' spread across the hills from Argyle Street in the south to Cowcaddens, almost three quarters of a mile to the north, and from Pitt Street in the west to Nile Street where the Blythswood lands abutted Meadowflat feus. Only the earlier line of Gordon Street and the oblique cuts of Mitchell Street, Union Place and Alston Street, which followed some slanted boundaries in the configuration of the old rural tenure, deviated from the almost mechanical perfection of the grid. Yet although the block size which appeared was consistently close to 250 feet by 200 feet and thus similar to those blocks established around George Square and Trades Town, there were several important respects in which this third phase of the Glasgow grid differed from its predecessors in the east and south of the city. It is these differences which hint strongly at the influence of Edinburgh.

For the first time, for example, the Glasgow grid had been applied to a sloping site. Even so the clash of geometry with topography was not without its own perceptible order. A certain affinity prevailed between the pattern of the contours of Blythswood Hill and the ordinates of the street grid: where the slope was gentler, i.e. in the east-west direction, the streets were more widely spaced; while, as the contours came more closely together in the north-south axis, so, too, did the streets which ran in parallel. Thus not only is it the case that 'the hill gives a real shape to the rigidly geometrical layout'[73] but the layout itself, in the subtle spacing of its

179

streets, whether achieved by accident or design, gives real shape to the experience of the hill. The steeper streets are shorter, the gradual slopes longer and more leisured, an arrangement designed at least as much for the convenience of the labouring horse, as the strolling citizen. Though the lie of the land is consistently more level in the east-west direction, the scale of the street blocks much greater, and a dominant axial route creates a measure of internal focus, the relationship of plan and topography at Edinburgh is nevertheless comparable—a grid set on a hill, its regularly channelled network of circulation and view implying infinite extension into the landscape.

The longer east-west dimension is also the line followed by a series of parallel service lanes which penetrate through almost every block of the Blythswood development. The existence of these lanes produces a second quality which, on the one hand, distinguishes the Blythswood grid from that around George Square or across the river in Trades Town or Hutcheson Town, and on the other, provides a further point of similarity with Craig's Edinburgh plan. In this latter respect, however, the Glasgow grid is a much reduced interpretation without the more sophisticated mews arrangements that Craig had been able to contrive within a grid block which, though similar in the ratio of its ordinates, is in fact some four times larger in area than its Blythswood counterpart. Only the smaller blocks to the north and south of St. George's Square (present day Charlotte Square) and St. Andrew's Square approximate to the dimensions of the grid in Glasgow. Nor do the buildings in Blythswood New Town face out from the block 'in a manner four-square' for they are orientated almost exclusively to the north and south. It must be said, however, that this rule did not apply so rigorously in later developments on the north of the estate over Garnethill to Shamrock Street (feued 1829). Nor was it at first in any way relevant to the area west of Blythswood Square (built 1823) beyond Pitt Street where, as late as c.1845, if Pagan's view (Figure 3.11) may be regarded as contemporary, only a few isolated villas had been raised.[74] Nor was the two-directional principle intended to apply south of St. Vincent Street where a plan (Figure 3.12) drawn up in 1820 showed 'The Town of Blythswood extended agreeably to The Design of James Gillespie, Esq., Architect'.[75] This plan, almost certainly prepared by James Gillespie Graham (1776–1855) who was then at work on the design of Blythswood House, Renfrew (1821) and the development of the Moray Estate to the west of Craig's New Town in Edinburgh (1821) was no doubt meant to record the superiors' intentions for that part of the Annexation lands between St. Vincent Street and Cadogan Street still largely unfeued at that date. Although never realised they present an interesting proposal which, again not uninfluenced by events in Edinburgh, combined the ideas of housing on all four sides of the block with that of the characteristically middle class service lane passing east-west through the subdivided back court.

The nature of the urban grid can never, of course, be satisfactorily

VIEW FROM NORTH WEST CORNER OF BLYTHSWOOD SQUARE, GLASGOW.

3.11 *View NW from Blythswood Square (Pagan 1847).*

3.12 *J. Gillespie (Graham) map of Blythswood, 1820.*

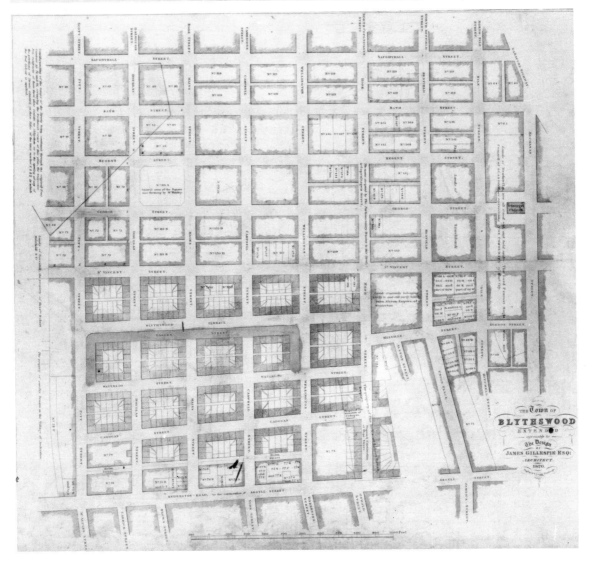

specified merely as a matter of block size and the provision or absence of a secondary service network. Some comment on the building type or types adopted is necessary also for, in determining the spatial order of the city, these formal aspects are always indissolubly linked. In this third aspect, Blythswood was conceived *not* in tenements but in terraced ranges or closely packed aggregations of houses 'linked to each other, gable to gable'.[76] It, therefore, followed the example of George Square itself, rejecting the more traditional precedent of the three- or four-storeyed flatted properties common in the older centre, in some of the lesser streets of the first 'New Town' and in the Trades Town and Hutcheson Town suburbs. And once again the solution has its similar if considerably grander Edinburgh parallel. In almost all cases, the gradient of the Blythswood streets, though never excessive in the east-west direction, provoked awkward but attractively idiosyncratic variations in the architectural syntax of the Neoclassical language. Block facades were unified by familiar formulae—the palatial Palladian schema (Adelaide Place) (Figure 3.13), the raising or projection of end pavilions (Bath Street, Blythswood Square) (Figure 3.14) consistent detailing of cornices, porches, etc. (Douglas Street, West George Street) (Figure 3.15)—but many of these formulae were infracted to adapt to the contingent topography.

Success or failure in the application of such formulae depended to a large extent upon the talent of the various architects commissioned to design series, terraces or whole blocks of housing. But results were also strictly controlled through legally binding feuing conditions. For since 'a superior who has been heir of entail in possession retains the right to enforce building restrictions after he has become fee simple proprietor'[77] it was still possible for Archibald Campbell and his trustees to determine the planning and architectural constraints within which development might take place. This they did, being careful to ensure compatibility with the city's expansion in Meadowflat. Streets 60 feet wide from building to building, were to be causewayed 'like the streets of the city of Glasgow of the breadth of 40 feet'. Pavements were to be made up 'in the same manner as the pavements of the city of Glasgow'.[78] Houses, which had to be erected within a specified number of years, could not be built higher than four storeys being limited to a front wall height of 52 feet above street level. Ashlar stonework and slated roofs were specified. Dormers and mansards were forbidden. Most important of all, by the inclusion of a *ius quaesitum tertio* in the feuing writs, the right to enforce these conditions was available not only to the superior but to adjoining and cross-street proprietors. Thus development was carefully, and for a time effectively, controlled.

It was this third and most geographically extensive phase of the Glasgow grid which, despite all the changes in scale, style and function which have affected its architecture since, left the Victorian city centre with its lasting rectilinear network of hilly communications. Yet, paradoxically, except for some later developments on its northern end and western margins, the

182

3.13 *Adelaide Place, Bath Street.*
3.14 *Blythswood Square.*
3.15 *Douglas Street.*

block and court arrangement of the flatted tenement which the nineteenth century would in due course turn into the archetypal Glasgow building, was scarcely to be found. On the contrary, Blythswood seems 'plainly imitative of Edinburgh's New Town':[79] the length to breadth ratio of the residential block, the secondary services network, the north- and south-facing terraces which predominate, the formal unification of street frontages by end pavilions and centre pieces or—more often in Glasgow because of the greater slopes in both ordinates of the grid—the stepped 'gable to gable' aggregations of one-family houses; in short, the very relationship of street network to the hill and the application of certain architectural schemata. All is reminiscent in some degree of Craig's plan and the housing which subsequently lined its streets. Of course, there are important differences; notably the stronger internal focus achieved at Edinburgh by a marked axial relationship between terminal squares and the increase in the size and scale of the capital's architecture. Nonetheless, the similarities are striking and cannot be accidental.

Fundamentally, the idea of setting a grid on a hill was the same. Below and beyond, particularly to the north and south, the landscape opened up to the view. Ruskin, who could see almost nothing in Edinburgh but 'square-cut stone—square-cut stone—a wilderness of square-cut stone forever and ever'[80] was as usual perceptive in the midst of prejudice. For him the open grid of Edinburgh's New Town offered *natural* relief from the grey austerities of classicism:

> As you walk up or down George Street, for instance, do you not look eagerly for every opening to the north and south, which lets in the lustre of the Firth of Forth, or the rugged outline of the Castle Rock?[81]

Funnelled down the 'square-cut' streets, the eye might survey the world beyond in more senses than one, for the openness of the grid to the landscape was as much a matter of putative propriety as visual prospect. Or so it was in Glasgow where no such ramparted margins as Princes Street or Queen Street had ever been raised to defend a social élite. While the quality of the landscape viewed from the Blythswood hills was neither so dramatic nor so romantic as that afforded by the splendid setting of Edinburgh's New Town between Forth and Castle, the advance of the Glasgow grid was less hierarchical, more consistently regular and thus more business-like. Whatever its similarities to the Edinburgh layout may perhaps betray in terms of comparable if muted social pretension, the layout of the Blythswood New Town in the end had none of the allegorical implications of the capital's streets—'an ideogram of the United Kingdom of England and Scotland',[82] as McWilliam has described them. On the contrary, it was unexceptional but practical: *in fine*, the Glasgow grid meant business.

Nor was there so much calculated grandeur in the Neoclassical architecture of Glasgow, although the emulation of the capital in this respect too can hardly be doubted. Denholm describes the houses of

Union Place (present-day Union Street) as 'lofty and elegant, with sunk stories and pallisades, similar to those in the new town of Edinburgh',[83] from which admiration for the architecture in the east may reasonably be inferred. Indeed, aspirations may sometimes have reached higher still. Leighton's picture of the Blythswood New Town is of 'numerous new streets and ranges of buildings of considerable architectural beauty . . . the houses of which are on the English plan . . .'[84] For all that, the quality of Glasgow's terraced architecture was restrained and modest, and it seems as if the combination of a more mercantile temperament and the rigorously repetitive discipline of the city's regular grid, far from aping the inflected social and spatial order of an increasingly Anglophile capital, may have precluded the excesses of *parvenu* cultural pretension. While 'the making of classical Edinburgh' proceeded in unquestionably grand manner, the platted grid of Glasgow filled up in less inflated, more anonymous style. First came the prepossessingly plain terraces of Blythswood and then, from the 1840s, the blocks and courts of tenement architecture. It was this later but lasting conflation of urban structure with building type which would create the characteristic townscape of the inner suburbs.

By 1830 the grid network east of Blythswood Square had already been largely built up in elegant terraces and co-ordinated sequences of stepped Georgian housing. Land on the northern and western sides of the estate was as yet, however, much less densely developed; there, only a few detached mansion houses and some isolated terraces stood on the green gridded plots between Sauchiehall Street and Shamrock Street. But, as the eastern edges of the Second New Town started to succumb to those commercial forces which had already swamped much of the originally residential character of the First, and the relentless pressure of the city's expanding population continued to increase, significant changes began to appear in the Blythswood townscape. By the 1840s then, on Garnethill, the one-family house model had been abandoned; in its stead, 'whole ranges of tenements'[85] lined the streets of the grid.

As the demand for houses continued unabated,

> there was need of another suburb to house the bulk of Glasgow's expanding upper middle class, so that those who built for it were compelled to turn to the area beyond Blythswood, further to the west.[86]

This 'suburb' was in fact that congeries of suburbs which gradually became Glasgow's West End.

Beyond the limits of the Annexation lands—and even before the fields west of Blythswood Square had been built up—Woodside Crescent (1831) and Newton Place (1837) were laid out, beginning a terraced development similar in its architectural qualities and street-and-lane plan to those in the Blythswood New Town. Spreading along both sides of Sauchiehall Street, by mid-century it had reached Kelvingrove. Terraced development remained the dominant pattern at Queen's Crescent (1840), on Woodlands Hill (1842-) and along Great Western Road (1849-), the main artery of

West End growth since 1841. But in none of these areas was housing disposed on a grid-iron plan. At Hillhead, however, the grid did reassert itself. Simpson writes that 'Hillhead was platted on a grid system in about 1850'[87] but a decade earlier seems a more likely date as the city map (Figure 3.16) prepared in 1842 by George Martin, Civil Engineer and Surveyor, already shows a fully developed rectilinear street network. Moreover, when building began around the middle of the century the terrace form, so dominant in the Georgian era, was subtly transmuted back into the flatted tenement. Granby Terrace, Hillhead Street (1856), its windows rhythmically grouped to articulate the long street wall, established a pattern which, later, further varied by subtle modulations in the elevational plane by decorative cornices, aedicules and string courses, and by bay or oriel projections, became the formal basis for all the remarkable permutations of the Victorian tenement facade.[88] Over the next few decades this pattern was to be repeated all around the spreading city in a number of localised suburban street grids.

If it can be said that there is a fourth phase of the Glasgow grid, it is, then, a prolonged one and must be found in these discrete residential districts—Hillhead, Partick, Kinning Park, East Pollokshields, Ibrox, Govanhill, Hyndland—stitched into the expanding urban fabric between the 1850s and the 1890s. What perhaps permits the identification of such a phase, despite the half century time span and scattered incidence, is the fact that while the terrace had disappeared the tenement block and court principle, with or without service lanes, had everywhere been finally wedded to the rectilinear street network.

*   *   *

All manner of precedents for the adoption of grid-iron planning in Glasgow may be suggested. Apart from the immediate example of Edinburgh the platted plan was common practice in Scotland throughout the eighteenth century. Since the union of 1707, which first saved and in time greatly stimulated the Scottish economy, particularly its agriculture and textile trade, reviving prosperity could be measured by the appearance of numerous planned towns and villages. McWilliam describes a wealth of such settlements, some two hundred, in fact, in many of which the plan is a conventional grid:[89] market towns (Crieff, 1731), estate villages (Ormiston, 1735), agricultural towns (Keith 1750; Huntly, 1765; Grantown-on-Spey, 1766), ports and fishing towns (Fochabers, 1775); industrial plantations, many of them in effect 'clearance towns'[90] (Archiestown, 1760 and 1783; Stanley, 1785; Newcastleton, 1793). Nor, of course, is the grid an eighteenth century phenomenon. Not far south of the border, for example, at Whitehaven in Cumbria—the very port from which the merchants of Glasgow had had to charter their vessels in the seventeenth and early eighteenth centuries—a small but rectilinear network of streets had been laid down during the 1660s as the basis for an expansion fostered by

186

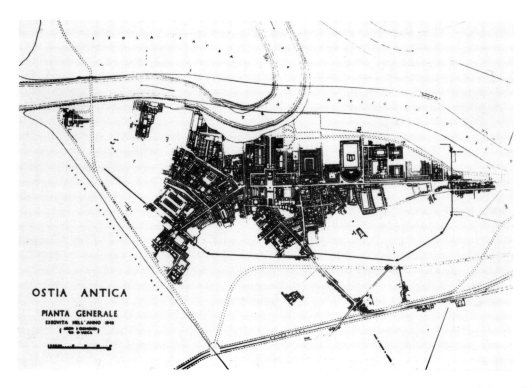

coaling and shipbuilding. The author of this plan was Sir John Lowther whose membership of the Royal Society and friendship with Wren and his contemporaries may explain something of the rational order he introduced at Whitehaven. Some years later it was Robert Hooke (1635-1703), a fellow of the Royal Society from 1663, who provided Lowther with 'a Designe of church and estimate'.[91] More significantly, Hooke's lost plan for the rebuilding of London, which the city's lord mayor and council of aldermen had approved and thought worthy of presentation to the King and which Lowther may have known, was 'a perfect grid, it streets running absolutely straight from east to west, north to south'.[92] In producing this design, Hooke, unlike Wren or Evelyn, had spurned the grand manner which applied in many contemporary French and Italian approaches to city layout; he may, indeed, have been more familiar with the rather more mechanical less hierarchical methods of Dutch, German and Scandinavian planners. The problem is not one to be solved here. But it is typical of those countless dilemmas of source and influence which must arise in any attempt to track down the origins and variants of the grid-iron plan.

The task is endlessly ramified. Perhaps indeed, it is not worth the candle for, ultimately, by whatever route, the trail can be pushed back through the streets of Renaissance ideal cities to the built precedents of classical times: the castral plan of fourth century BC Ostia (Figure 3.16) or the

3.16 *Ostia, castral plan.*

systematized fifth century BC layouts of Piraeus, Thourioi and Miletus (Figure 3.17). And despite the separation of centuries, even millenia, how easy and yet how strange to fancy that these ancient paradigms may be recognised in Glasgow: the *cardo* running north-south from the cathedral to the river, intersected at the mediaeval cross by the east-west *decumanus* of Gallowgate-Trongate; the repetitive cellular Hippodamian street block aggregated freely in the potentially limitless regularity of the Blythswood New Town.[93] Perhaps, as Le Corbusier's quasi-mystical invocation of *le lieu de l'angle droit*[94] proposes, this recurrent coincidence of vertical and horizontal has a universal validity not only in the re-presentations we make of our world but in our very perceptions. Do we not 'judge every object by analogy with our own bodies'?[95] Arnheim has no doubts:

> Man experiences the space he lives in as asymmetrical. Among the many directions of three-dimensional space along which he theoretically can move, one direction is distinguished by the pull of gravity: the vertical.[96]

Vertical and horizontal are the frame of reference for spatial consciousness.

Such musings produce only the most generalised justification. They take us a long way from the hard-headed speculations of the Trades House, the Hutcheson patrons and the Campbell trustees. As far, it might be said, as the raw 'counting house satisfaction'[97] of the Glaswegian is from the paramount concern of genteel Edinburgh society for *bon ton*. For if the Glasgow grid is in any sense a philosophical manifestation, it is not so much a matter of the emulation of this or that precedent in a quest for borrowed glories as a pragmatic reflection of a town on the make. Fundamentally, wherever it appeared, whatever specific formal influences may be suggested or subsequently proved, the Glasgow grid was a product of geodesic, legal and financial convenience.

The new street pattern might derive directly from the old divisions of the fields as in Trades Town and Laurieston, or it might be largely imposed upon the landscape as in the First and Second (i.e. Blythswood) Towns. But, for whatever reason, its regular and repetitive networks, relieved by no more than three significant inflections—George Square, St. George's Church and Blythswood Square, of which the two last can certainly be regarded as 'second thought' intrusions[98]—proclaimed no hierarchy and produced no focus. What they did do was to ensure a series of servicable bases for feuing. Similar literally mundane systematizations served well in Holland where 'not only the city, but even the land around it was a man-made creation',[99] in Ireland where the plantations were 'laid out on straight-forward grids' by colonial speculators 'making the best of their investment'[100] and, of course, in America where Jefferson's Land Ordinance of 1785 summed up a century of grid planning by extending the logic of the method to its practical and utopian infinity (Figure 3.18).

Glasgow's grids, with none of the self-conscious territorial ambitions of the Jefferson approach (though it may not be entirely irrelevant to

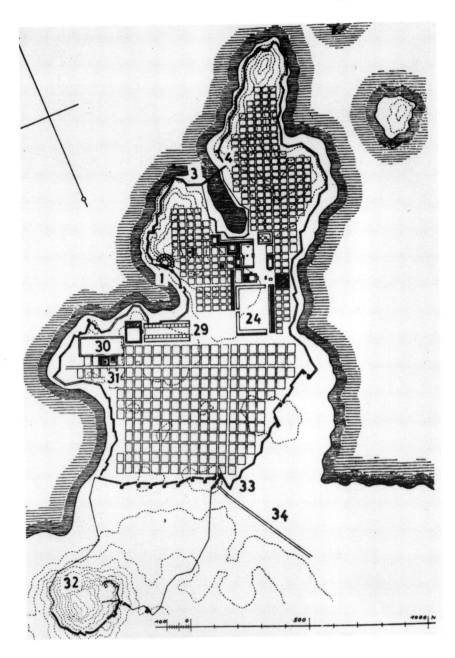

3.17 *Miletus plan.*

conjecture some other transatlantic planning influences between what were after all close trading partners) were, nevertheless, regularised enough to permit their integrated but free expansion. Trades Town and

189

3.18 *Jefferson's Ordinance grid.*

A SECTION OF LAND—640 ACRES.

A rod is 16½ feet.
A chain is 66 feet or 4 rods.
A mile is 320 rods, 80 chains or 5,280 f!
A square rod is 272¼ square feet.
An acre contains 43,560 square feet.
* "   "   160 square rods.*
* "   "   is about 208¾ feet square.*
* "   "   is 8 rods wide by 20 rods long,*
*   or any two numbers (of rods) whose*
*   product is 160.*
25×125 feet equals .0717 of an acre.

80 rods.

10 chains. 330 ft.

5 acres. 5 acres

20 acres.   5 ch. 20 rods

80 acres.   660 feet. 10 chains

40 acres.

CENTER OF   20 chains.   1,320 feet.

SECTION.

Sectional Map of a Township with adjoining Sections

36	31	32	33	34	35	36	31
1	6	5	4	3	2	1	6
12	7	8	9	10	11	12	7
13	18	17	16	15	14	13	18
24	19	20	21	22	23	24	19
25	30	29	28	27	26	25	30
36	31	32	33	34	35	36	31
1	6	5	4	3	2	1	6

160 acres.

40 chains. 160 rods or 2,640 feet.

Laurieston, hung as it were from bridge connections, reflected earlier development across the river. The north and south sides of George Square tied the First New Town into the pattern of subsequent growth across the Blythswood estate. In such ways the major central network of the city grew without hindrance in the north, south and west. Here and there, deflections occurred—at Hutcheson Town, beyond Charing Cross and in Townhead—and, as expansion continued throughout the second half of the nineteenth century, smaller more confined grids filled the wedges between the old and new radial routes.

In all these developments a number of factors—the clash of grid with grid or grid with radial, the interplay of street pattern and topography, the architectural fluency with which designs were able to interpret the language first of the Georgian terraces and then of the increasingly ubiquitous tenement—combined to create the Glasgow cityscape with its special sense of place. The places which resulted from this interplay were essentially incidental, chance products in the disposition of tenure. The imposed pattern remained abstract and aggregative. The grid was bound-

190

less, without limit and also without centre. It was a concept at once colonial and democratic, as both the examples of ancient Greece and contemporary America had shown. Benevolo, pondering the wider social and cultural impact of this paradox on the late eighteenth century, writes

> Thus the Cartesian network, which guaranteed the measurability of visible forms in the traditional artistic and scientific system, was generalised so as to become applicable on any scale, well beyond the limits that could be embraced by the human eye . . . but with this generalisation the boundaries of traditional culture were overstepped, for they had been linked precisely to the anthropomorphic scale of human sight and movements, and a completely new cultural universe opened up.[101]

In this new universe 'urban development was a process which was analogous to democratic development'.[102] Where Jefferson had legislated to establish 'a physical grid as a social equaliser'[103] and later designers, such as Ildefonso Cerda in Barcelona, would consciously articulate this same co-incidence of spatial and social order in their theory and practice, in Glasgow the process grew from within. The formally contrived enclaves of *place* or circus or axial boulevard were largely rejected and, prompted by a mercantile pragmatism which, too hard-headed for symbolic affectation and too busy to dream of utopias, had adopted the platted plan ostensibly as a practical feuing device, the grid advanced with an egalitarian indifference extending as much to function as to landscape. Yet this precisely expressed the city's view of the new universe: the grid delineated a capitalist world, aggressively colonial in its potential for limitless replication, yet at the same time neither aristocratic nor paternalistic but, in its cellular centre-less organisation, democratic. The grid was indeed the concretization of the Glasgow utopia. The regular 'Cartesian network' adapted easily to residential, commercial or industrial needs; it absorbed middle and working class populations alike; it spread across the flat meadows south of the river; it marched up and across the hills of Blythswood from Clydeside to Cowcaddens (Figure 3.19). By 1830 the pattern was assured; no other city in the country had acquired such a uniform and acquisitive structure as the basis of urban change. Meanwhile, society 'stood on the brink of a political change—and one at least as pregnant for the future as any other aspect of the shifting world. Within two years the Great Reform Bill would have become law, and the first step gingerly taken towards giving political representation to the middle classes'[104] whose wealth was building Glasgow. As the social order began to change, the uncompromisingly equitable geometry of the Glasgow grid, virtually without inflection or hierarchy *pari passu* enfranchised an equivalent order of townscape.

But the new universe was also one in which the abandonment of a closed 'anthropomorphic' perception threatened the more humane qualities of urban living. There *were* some intimidating prospects of repetitive boredom in which the grey walls of rather poorly designed tenements—as, for example, at London Road, Argyle Street or Scotland

191

3.19 *Mid-nineteenth century City map.*

Street—stretched further than the eye could see. But, in the main, architectural skill and an irregular topography combined to create places which, while similar, were never the same. In the tightly defined, often steep, perspectives of the grid, the use of a centralising palatial model to unify facades—so appropriate on the open squares of the Edinburgh New Town or, indeed, the Georgian barracks—became as inappropriate an architectural solution as the processional route or axial focus had been irrelevant in town planning terms.[105] Instead, the design of the Victorian tenement like the Georgian terraces which had preceded it, was based on an additive unit often brilliantly assembled and modulated in rhythmic relationships of window spacings, decorative mouldings and rustication. This time, however, the unit was that of the horizontal flat, not the vertical house, though groupings of these flats around a common stair and close were in turn placed side by side within the controlling dimension of the street block. Thus, built up from individual flat to close unit to street block, the architecture of the nineteenth century acquired a new aggregated identity.

The tradition of classical hierarchy, already eschewed in a planning grid whose neutrality rendered it both infinitely and regularly extensible and,

192

as is pointed out elsewhere in this collection of essays, *'freely* susceptible'[106] (my italics) to all manner of economic pressures, was now even more irrevocably rejected in this cellular configuration of the tenement block and court. The rules of Georgian classicism could no longer apply, and while, as Gomme and Walker have shown, the rules were more and more ingeniously stretched and some imaginative aberrations of the classical system were certainly devised by architects such as Wilson and Thomson struggling to come to formal terms with the elevational problems of the flatted facade or the block corner, such solutions could not entirely conceal the underlying absence of hierarchical order. In effect, a revolution had occurred: orthodox classical composition disintegrated.

Revolutions have their positive and negative consequences. As to the former, it has certainly been convincingly demonstrated that the reversion to the aggregating part as the basis of formal composition liberated architectural style from its thraldom to the *ancien régime* of Renaissance-Baroque graded integration.[107] In this respect the advent of high density urban housing merely added a late functional conviction to those formal changes which had already undermined traditional architectural order. Less attractive, on the other hand, is the proposition that this ostensibly liberating focus on the part, a 'democratisation' of form made at the expense of the structured whole, led in time to the monotonous concatenations of modernist design—in much the same way, perhaps, as the democratised society of the modern welfare state has too often seemed to disappear in the endlessly mirrored perspectives of offices and corridors that make up the dehumanising environment of Kafka's urban nightmare. Such a contention cannot be lightly dismissed for the spatial potential of the cellular matrix, the generalised 'Cartesian network' of plan, section and elevation, can readily become, as Benevolo implies, a frightening and alienating prospect. But unreservedly to accept that this criticism can be related to the Glasgow tenement and grid is to ignore that factor stressed at the start of this essay—the humanising interplay of building type and urban structure. For it is not only irregular topography and architectural skill which provide the townscape of so much of the nineteenth century city with its special character, but the very nature—the perceptible form—of the block and court. Buildings are not isolated units; streets are not abstract patterns. Tenements are 'four storeys, built in rectangles . . . '[108] This scale is apprehensible and negotiable; the flat has its own identity within the close, the close within the block. The significant fact is that both the spatial and the social order of tenements and grid *are* 'linked precisely to the anthropomorphic scale of human sight and movements . . . ' Tenements and grid are, indeed, formally additive but not without structure; they are classless but not without community. Perhaps it is relevant to adduce Smout's general assessment of Glasgow culture to describe the 'completely new cultural universe opened up' by the specific developments this essay has been discussing: tenements and grid are 'at once intimate and intellectual, but in no sense exclusive . . . '[109]

193

REFERENCES

1. Hanley, C., *Dancing in the Streets*, Paisley, 1972, p. 13.

2. Hind, A., *The Dear Green Place*, London 1968, p. 19. I have, of course, used the phrase in a more metaphorical sense than that of Hind's source.

3. Muir, E., *Scottish Journey*, Edinburgh, 1979, p. 153.

4. ibid., p. 109.

5. Worsdall, F., *The Tenement, A Way of Life*, Edinburgh, 1979, p. 88.

6. MacDiarmid, H., In the Slums of Glasgow in Grieve, M. and Scott, A., Eds, *The Hugh MacDiarmid Anthology*, London, 1972, p. 200.

7. Worsdall, op. cit.

8. MacDiarmid, Reflections in a Slum, op. cit., p. 287.

9. Le Corbusier, *Towards a New Architecture*, London, 1976, p. 194.

10. Gourlay, C., *Elementary Building Construction and Drawing for Scottish Students*, Glasgow, 1903.

11. Sant'Elia, A., Manifesto of Futurist Architecture, *Lacerba*, Florence, 1914, in Apollonio, U. Ed., *Futurist Manifestos*, London, 1973, p. 170.

12. Worsdall, F., Four Hundred Years of the Glasgow Tenement, *The Scottish Art Review*, Glasgow, Vol. XIV, no. 3, 1974, p. 4.

13. Robinson, P., The Tenement Story, Unpublished dissertation awarded RIAS Thomas Ross Prize, 1979.

14. Robinson, P., Scotland's High Living, *The Scottish Review*, Glasgow, no. 18, May 1980, p. 10.

15. Gomme, A. and Walker, D., *Architecture of Glasgow*, London, 1968.

16. McIlvanney, W., *Laidlaw*, London, 1979, p. 39.

17. Hanley, C., op.cit., pp. 13-15.

18. Niven, D., *The Development of Housing in Scotland*, London, 1979, p. 15.

19. Denholm, J., *The History of the City of Glasgow*, Glasgow, 1804, p. 111.

20. see *The Glasgow Magazine and Review* . . . , Glasgow, Vol. 1, 1783, p. 234.

21. Annan, T., *Photographs of Old Closes and Streets of Glasgow 1868/1877*, New York, 1977.

22. McUre, J., *A View of the City of Glasgow* . . . , Glasgow, 1736, p. 133.

23. 'Senex', *Glasgow Past and Present*, Glasgow, 1884, Vol. 2, p. 381.

24. *Views and Notices of Glasgow in Former Times*, Glasgow, 1848, p. 115.

25. Denholm, J., op.cit., p. 135.

26. Defoe, D., *A Tour thro' the Whole Island of Great Britain* . . . , quoted in MacGregor, G., *The History of Glasgow*, Glasgow, 1881, p. 304.

27. 'Senex', op.cit., p. 122.

28. ibid., p. 123.

29. *Views and Notices* . . . , op.cit., pp. 113-115.

30. Renwick, R., *Extracts from the Records of the Burgh of Glasgow with Charters and other Documents*, Glasgow, 1913, Vol. VII, 1760-80, p. 475.

31. Renwick, ibid., Vol. V, 1718-38, p. 375.

32. *The Glasgow Magazine and Review* . . . , Glasgow, Vol. 1, 1783, p. 464.

33. Gomme and Walker, op.cit., p. 57.

34. Note that Frederick Street has become North Frederick Street and Glassford Street is now South Frederick Street. Present-day Glassford Street was originally known as Great Glassford Street.

35. Denholm, J., op.cit., p. 116.

36. *Views and Notices* . . . , op.cit., p. 115.

37. MacGregor, op.cit., p. 310.

38. Renwick, op.cit., Vol. VIII, p. 61.

39. *ibid.*, p. 157.

40. Denholm, op.cit., p. 135.

41. Pagan, J., *Sketches of the History of Glasgow*, Glasgow, 1847, p. 104 quotes 'Senex', *The Glasgow Herald*, 18th Oct. 1843.

42. Denholm, op.cit.

43. Renwick, *Glasgow Memorials*, Glasgow, 1908, p. 26.

44. Kellett, J.R. *Glasgow, A Concise History*, London, 1967, p. 14.

45. Lynch, K., *The Image of the City*, Cambridge, Mass./London, 1972, p. 47.

46. Crawfurd, G., *A Sketch of the Rise and Progress of the Trades' House of Glasgow*, Glasgow, 1858, pp. 185-186.

47. These streets were originally named after the fourteen incorporated trades but soon lost those names.

48. MacGregor, op.cit., p. 377.

49. 'Senex', op.cit., Vol. 1, p. 141.

50. Denholm, op.cit., p. 144.

51. ibid., p. 145.

52. Cleland, J., *Annals of Glasgow*, Glasgow, 1816, Vol. 1, p. 40.

53. Gomme and Walker, op.cit., p. 72.

54. Denholm, op.cit., p. 146.

55. 'Senex', op.cit., Vol. 1, p. 65.

56. Worsdall, op.cit., p. 77.

57. McWilliam, C., *Scottish Townscape*, London, 1975, p. 124.

58. Pagan, op.cit., p. 134.

59. 'Senex', op.cit., Vol. 2, p. 27.

60. Pagan, op.cit., p. 135.

61. 'Senex', op.cit., Vol. 1, pp. 319-325.

62. ibid, p. 321.

63. *Chartularies of the Blythswood Estate,* general series of feus granted on the lands of Blythswood, Glasgow; First Trustees, 1800-1845, Vol. 1, p. 524 (Strathclyde Regional Archives, TD 234/43).

64. ibid., Vol. 7, p. 301. Note that plot sizes are to centre line of adjacent streets and should not be confused with block sizes.

65. Walker, D.M., *Principles of Scottish Private Law,* Oxford, 1970, p. 1272.

66. 'An Act for vesting those parts of the Lands and Estate of Blythswood . . . ', House of Lords Record Office, 32 George III, Chapter 40, Private.

67. *Council Act Book,* commencing Nov. 1791, ending Oct. 1793, Vol. 35, p. 173 (Strathclyde Regional Archives, C1.1.40).

68. Feuing plans of the Blythswood estate (various dates) are held by Strathclyde Regional Archives, Glasgow; the Royal Commission on the Ancient and Historical Monuments of Scotland, Edinburgh; and by Hacking and Paterson, Estate Agents, 1 Newton Terrace, Glasgow.

69. 'Genealogy of the Family of Campbell of Blythswood', 1847 (Strathclyde Regional Archives, TD 234.91.10).

70. Renwick, op.cit., Vol.X, p. 64.

71. ibid., Vol. IX, p. 574. Stark's elevation only was selected. No plan being regarded as satisfactory, James Cleland was appointed to draw up plans, specifications and to supervise the work. This minute also records that 'it was determined by a vote of the council, that the said new church should be erected on the west side of Buchanan Street, opposite to and fronting George Street, and not St. Vincent Street, as had been formerly proposed'. On 26th August 1806, some eight months earlier, the Committee appointed to consider siting had recommended 'the west termination of St. Vincent Street'.

72. Youngson, A.J., *The Making of Classical Edinburgh,* Edinburgh, 1975, p. 84.

73. Gomme and Walker, op.cit., p. 73.

74. Pagan, op.cit., Plate XIV, p. 113 (facing).

75. Strathclyde Regional Archives, TD234.2.

76. 'Senex', op.cit., Vol. 2, p. 244.

77. Walker, op.cit., p. 1275.

78. *Chartularies of the Blythswood Estate*, op.cit., Vol. 7, p. 301.

79. Simpson, M.A., 'The West End of Glasgow 1830-1914', in Simpson, M.A. and Lloyd, T.H., Eds, *Middle Class Housing in Britain*, Newton Abbot, 1977, p. 46.

80. Ruskin, J., *Lectures on Architecture and Painting*, London, 1907, p. 61.

81. ibid., p. 2.

82. McWilliam, op.cit., p. 79.

83. Denholm, op.cit., p. 138.

84. Leighton, J.M., *Swan's Views on the Banks of the Clyde from Glasgow to Greenock*, Glasgow, 1832, p. 4.

85. 'Senex', op.cit., Vol. 1, p. 156.

86. Simpson, M.A., in Simpson and Lloyd, op.cit., p. 47.

87. ibid., p. 60.

88. Gomme and Walker, op.cit., pp. 186-189. This chapter is by far the best formal analysis of the tenement fabric.

89. McWilliam, op.cit., pp. 86-108.

90. Bell, C. and R., *City Fathers*, Harmondsworth, 1972, p. 228.

91. Colvin, H., *A Biographical Dictionary of British Architects, 1600-1840*, London, 1978, p. 430.

92. Bell, op.cit., p. 70.

93. It should perhaps be stressed that this is indeed fancy; no military origins or conscious emulation of such classical precedents are suggested.

94. Le Corbusier, *The Modulor*, London, 1954, *passim*.

95. Wölfflin, H., *Renaissance and Baroque*, London, 1964, p. 77.

96. Arnheim, R., *The Dynamics of Architectural Form*, Berkeley, 1977, p. 32.

97. Hind, op.cit., p. 70.

98. St Andrew's Square being outside the gridded area of central Glasgow has been discounted. St. Enoch's Square, terminating the southern end of Buchanan Street and thus potentially related to the Laurieston grid across the Clyde might have been added. 'Senex', op.cit., Vol. 1, 1884, p. 162, reports a 'new square at the west end of Gordon Street' which was apparently under consideration in 1849 as 'another distinquishing feature in our city architecture'; no such development took place.

99. Benevolo, L. *The Architecture of the Renaissance*, London, 1978, Vol. 2, p.817.

100. Bell, op.cit., p. 67.

101. Benevolo, op.cit., Vol. 2, p. 1027.

102. Miller, B., in Ildefonso Cerda, an Introduction, *Architectural Association Quarterly*, Vol. 9, no. 1, London, 1977, p. 12.

103. Hayden, D., *Seven American Utopias, the Architecture of Communitarian Socialism, 1790-1975*, Cambridge, Mass. 1979, p. 20.

104. Smout, T.C., *A History of the Scottish People, 1560-1830*, London, 1971, p. 517.

105. As the end of the nineteenth century approached and the architectural abilities of the tenement designers reached a peak, less clearly codified more liberal stylistic approaches were adopted. Using the Scots Baronial idiom, for example, the corners of the tenement block received that special accentuation which their location in the 'open' context of intersecting streets had long merited.

106. Reed, P.A., 'Form and Context: a study of Georgian Edinburgh', companion essay in this collection. pp. 115-153

107. Kaufmann, E., *Architecture in the Age of Reason*, New York, 1955.

108. Hanley, op.cit., pp. 13-15.

109. Smout, op.cit., p. 390.

The School as Machine: Working Class Scottish Education and the Glasgow Normal Seminary

Thomas A. Markus

The first essay in this collection shows how deviations from the norm in the form of physical, mental or moral sickness were regarded as important threats to the order of society even before the Industrial Revolution whose beginnings coincided with fear of public disorder aroused by the French Revolution. So these threats were combatted with extra vigour in Scotland, as in the rest of Europe, by the end of the eighteenth century. The institutional, legal and philanthropic means which were used were designed to deal with *actual* disorder. Not surprisingly similar instruments to deal with *potential* disorder came later—in the first quarter of the nineteenth century. This period saw the first moves to provide systematic and universal education for the urban population—an aim that was not in fact achieved till the 1872 Act. However, a variety of urban and rural schools existed in the early nineteenth century which were offering significant sections of the population basic education in reading, writing, arithmetic and religion; in some cases other academic subjects were also available, and a number of schools offered teaching in spinning, sewing and other 'useful arts'. These institutions were financed and run by the Kirk, Burghs, charitable bodies and private individuals—the latter engaging in this activity as a profitable enterprise. The range of schools enabled the children of the older, landed gentry and the newer, professional and merchant classes, to pursue studies through the grammar schools and Academies and then the Universities to fit them for political, military, professional and manufacturing roles. They also enabled the factories to draw on a more or less literate body of workers for skilled and semi-skilled jobs; and for one section of the urban poor—a section which in proportional terms shrank during the first thirty years of the nineteenth century—to obtain a basic education. The seekers of this education (or, rather their parents, for the children were often reluctant recipients) saw this as a means of moving out of poverty and the labouring class and into the artisan, skilled or managerial sectors of commerce and industry. Its providers saw it as a means of providing moral fibre (through religious instruction), practical skills and basic literacy—all of which were essential ingredients in the formation and preservation of civil order, a productive labour force and a politically compliant population. The fulfilment of both sides' expectations led to an unconscious pact, one of whose important instruments was the range of school buildings in which its consequences were acted out. The participants in this pact included the Kirk; the city authorities, the charities, politicians (Tory, Whig and Radical) and even early workers' movements (as can be most clearly seen in the limitations of reading and enquiry which were tolerated in the libraries of first Mechanics' Institutes) each of which had their own objectives.

The Scottish educational tradition sprang from the Reformers' practical concern with establishing the Parish as the centre of spiritual life, a strong voice by the laity, and what Smout calls a 'stern and visionary social theology'[1] embedded in *The Book of Discipline* of 1560. Augustine's City of God served as a model, so that the duties of State and Church were clearly defined and inter-related into a theocracy. Education was pivotal in this scheme of things. A nationwide network of Parish schools was to be set up in the country each with its own schoolmaster, and Grammar schools and colleges in the Burghs, in each of which the poorest could receive free education. The county Parish schools were to serve all children between five or six and eight. The town Grammar schools would teach the town children from five to eight as well as those and the country children from eight to twelve. Latin was to be the most important subject for those over eight. Selected pupils from twelve to sixteen would then proceed to colleges or high schools in the more important towns beyond which the most gifted would proceed to University. The Reformers were fortunate in being able to build on an existing tradition of pre-Reformation Song, Burgh or Grammar schools which existed in most larger towns; but lack of finance and trained schoolmasters hampered the fulfilment of the plan. Often ministers doubled as schoolmasters and Smout believes that there was little advance in educational standards before 1600.[2] In 1616, however, a Privy Council decree to provide a school in every Parish was passed, backed by a further one in 1633 which laid the duty of financing it on the heritors. They were able, however, to evade this duty quite successfully till the passing of 1646 Act which was intended to force them, under penalty, to provide this support; this was further reinforced by the 1696 Act which was the last major educational legislation until the Act of 1803, establishing a minimum stipend and a house for the schoolmaster of every Parish, but this did not apply to Burghs. It is worth noting that legislation for the first one hundred and fifty years after the Reformation was concentrated on financial and property matters—the content of education being considered safely left in the hands of the Kirk.

Although finance was difficult to obtain till the 1696 Act, Scotland nevertheless established a national system of education by the end of the seventeenth century superior in scope and coverage to that of almost any other country in Europe. The graded system of Parish school, Burgh grammar school, a high school or college, leading to one of the Universities, was available to all of adequate ability and free to the poorest. It is true that in the Highlands this continuum was not so widely available as in the Lowlands, and also, that by the end of the eighteenth century, the growing urban centres were falling far behind the country and the older Burghs in provision of basic education for the new industrial working class. It will be seen that Stow and others estimated that only a minority of working class urban children received any kind of education in the first decades of the nineteenth century. Such provision as existed was of several kinds.

The first were the Burgh schools, financed largely by the Town Councils and in whose government the Kirk had less influence than in the rural Parish schools. Since these were often Grammar schools, with Latin central in the curriculum, admission presupposed a sound primary education which was increasingly difficult to obtain in the towns for children of the poorest section of the population. Thus during the late eighteenth century both primary and secondary education began to be more class-bound than it had been earlier. Secondly there were Charity schools for the various religious groups—Kirk, Dissenting and, later, Free Church. 'Adventure' or 'venture' schools were the third type—private establishments which charged fees and were run as profit-making enterprises. These were often housed in squalid premises and offered only the most rudimentary instruction given by unqualified and untrained teachers. Fourthly the Sunday or Sabbath schools resulting from the movement popularised by Robert Raikes of Gloucester after his first school was set up in 1780. The movement, although initially opposed by the Kirk as potentially seditious, quickly caught the Scottish imagination, with its strong emphasis on fundamentalist Bible teaching and close links to Parish churches. In order to teach the Bible, reading had often first to be taught and hence the Sabbath schools early became a useful addition to the educational resources.

Out of the Sabbath School movement grew the Sessional Schools set up in Edinburgh as a result of serious riots on New Year's Day, 1812. Prevention of such disorder was thought to lie in the religious education of the very young. So it was decided that every city Parish would set up a Sabbath school but on finding that it would be impossible to teach the Bible to most children as they could not read it was agreed to set up a Sessional school (for a group of city Kirk Sessions) in a suitably converted house in Leith Wynd in 1813. The educational innovator in the school from 1819 onwards was John Wood, ex-Sheriff of Peebles and an Edinburgh lawyer. His teaching methods, the design of his first purpose-built school of 1824, the relationship of his work to that of Stow and others and his involvement in teacher training are discussed later.

The other important school type in Scotland was the 'industrial' or 'spinning' school whose ideology goes back into the seventeenth century and which was closely connected with English types. As these schools are related to such experiments as Owen's at New Lanark and other Scottish educational and industrial projects, and since they also contain the educational and ideological pedigrees of the later nineteenth century workhouse and pauper schools, it is necessary to give an account of their development.

In principle the industrial school in both England and Scotland had been a concrete expression of the perceived relationship between production, pauperism and education for a 'useful' life long before the Industrial Revolution. Armytage says that the seventeenth century industrial or apprentice school was an 'allotrope' of the contemporary charity school.[3]

The ideology behind both demanded the support of pauper children at an economic rate and the provision, through the system, of trained, submissive and cheap labour for agriculture and other productive enterprises. In 1628 Sir William Borlase founded St. Martin's Free School to teach twenty-four boys and girls to knit, spin and make lace. In 1642 a similar school was founded at North Lydbury, Shropshire, for girls to learn spinning wool and flax, and another in 1670 at Bridlington for wool carding, knitting and spinning.

Thomas Firmin, in his *Some Proposals for the Employment of the Poor* in 1681 outlines a scheme of work-schools and tried to set up a self-supporting technical school for boys of four and five to learn spinning and reading. John Bellers' *Proposals for Raising a Colledge of Industry* (1696) which Robert Owen reprinted in full in *A New View of Society* has already been mentioned in Essay 1 as being a model for his own Utopian schemes. 1696 also saw the establishment of the Board of Trade, which a year later, received a report from John Locke proposing the establishment of working schools in every parish for *all* children between three and fourteen. The inculcation of regular work habits was seen by Locke as giving children an indelible practical 'mark' in the same way as he saw intellectual and moral education as filling a natural mental void—the child's mind being like 'an empty cabinet', 'a white paper void of all characters' and 'without any ideas'.[4] By 1698 the first workhouse was established in London and the 1723 General Act for the Relief of the Poor resulted in the setting up of a number of workhouses with charity work schools.

In Scotland the seventeenth century schools were sometimes attached to linen and woollen manufactories—for instance that set up in Peebles in 1633 and similar ones in Dundee, Aberdeen and Glasgow.[5] In 1641 an Act was passed proposing the setting up of boys' schools for spinning, weaving and cloth manufacture in all Burghs but few were actually created under it. Another Act of 1661 made similar provision with equally little success. In 1726 the Board of Trustees for Scottish Manufactures also proposed spinning schools for children from eight to fourteen, but again it resulted in only a few projects. Acts of 1747 and 1752 included education amongst their provisions, allowing for spinning schools on estates, ten of which were set up, at such places as Inverness, Stornoway and Dunblane. When, in 1784, the estates forfeited in 1745 were restored such schools were handed over to the SSPCK[6] which had its own programme of charitable industrial education.

The Society in Scotland for the Promotion of Christian Knowledge (SSPCK) was influenced by, but independent from, the English SPCK which was founded in 1698. One of the SPCK's chief aims was the establishment of charity schools for the religious and secular education of the poor. 'Secular' meant manual work and crafts—such as spinning, knitting and cobbling. Throughout the eighteenth century its schools were set up in England—even by 1754 it claimed to have two thousand and forty four, many of which had, or were 'industrial' schools. The combination of religion and production exactly paralleled the Bridewells which have been described in Essay 1. Children were thus able to be formed for a specific role in the social structure, in a way which was analogous to the *re*formation of criminals for the same role.

The SSPCK was formally set up in 1709 with Presbyterian rather than Anglican support. Initially its aims were both anti-Catholic and anti-Gaelic—both being associated with the more remote areas of the Highlands and Islands. However by 1767 the proscription on Gaelic was abandoned and Bibles in that language were printed. By 1758 the Society had one hundred and seventy six schools in the Highlands although the number declined in the next twenty years. But many of these schools taught apprentices in various trades such as blacksmithy, shoemaking and agriculture to the boys and spinning, knitting and sewing to the girls. In 1763 the Society had twenty spinning schools in which, apart from work, the Bible and the Catechism formed the daily curriculum.[7] In addition to these a number of employers in the spinning and mining industry set up their own schools, often financed by employees.

The characteristic attitudes to these industrial schools survived into the early nineteenth century and shaped the judgment of the new generation of schools then being set up as can be seen in, for instance, the Reports of the Society for Bettering the Condition of the Poor. Thomas Bernard's introduction of 1809 to a selected set of reprints of the Society's Reports[8] states that the industrial schools have to teach Piety, Virtue and Industry. The connection is constantly made between education and crime reduction, a calculus according to which schools are an *investment*; and Scotland is consistently held up as an example of how proper legal provision for education '. . . brought many thousands of dissolute and noxious poor into a state of civil order', bringing '. . . morality and good government'[9] at a time when in Europe '. . . anarchy, insubordination, and infidelity . . . civil disorder and dissolution' prevailed.[10] Children are to be prepared '. . . for a useful situation in life;—such as assist and promote industry, prudence, and domestic economy in the cottage of the poor;—or which, in case of public or private misfortune, prevent their domestic plan of economy from being destroyed'.[11] And a keystone of the policy for these schools was the complete or partial self-sufficiency that could be attained by the sale of goods produced by the children. A number of industrial schools are described in Bernard's volume, including the famous one in Kendal set up in 1799, and using Bell's 'Madras' system (one variant of the monitorial method described later) by 1808 for teaching its one hundred and twelve children aged from three years old upwards. Another typical late eighteenth century industrial school described is that for sixty boys and girls in Bamburgh. In it the main schoolroom is stated to be 40 feet long by 20 feet wide; it is occupied by jersey spinning machines whilst the (hand) flax spinners are on a gallery along one side of the room 'erected . . . so that the mistress has a full view of the whole number at once'.[12] The unification of production under surveillance with an adjacent smaller classroom for an hour's instruction a day is a reproduction of the contemporary spinning mill and has a spatial structure which will be seen to have been repeated for another half century in schools which no longer have an explicit production function.

By the opening of the nineteenth century Scotland was still ahead of England *nationally* in the provision of rural Education—in the Parish Schools in the Lowlands and the SSPCK and other charity schools in the Highlands; and in the provision of a reasonably democratic network of educational institutions in the towns for the children of the merchant, the professional and the skilled artisan classes. These included the Burgh schools, Academies, colleges and universities. They were more widespread, cheaper and available to a wider section of society than their counterparts in England, but nevertheless the system became increasingly one serving the middle classes. In the rapidly growing urban centres the children of labourers, and of unskilled and semi-skilled workers, fared no better than those in England and had little access to any systematic formal education.

Awareness of the social and economic problems being created by the presence of a mass of uneducated urban youngsters—and fear of a future mass of uneducated, unruly, and rebellious and criminal urban poor— created a number of educational and political reform movements in Britain which had strong Scottish connections and which linked Scottish and English thought. The Scottish educational developments and their school-building programme cannot be separated from these wider educational movements, nor those movements from earlier philosophical streams.

We have noted how, independent of the religious or political thought, the philosophical conviction grew that the minds and behaviour of children were eminently formable and malleable—and that the very shape of society itself could be altered by these means. Rousseau's *Émile* was the best known popular expression of this concept. This conviction grew out of the philosophy of Descartes and Hobbes; Locke's attack on 'innate ideas'; and the development of an empirical, secular, materialist and rationalist explanation of phenomena, of sense perceptions and of the mind. From this tradition grew the first psychological theories such as the 'associationism' of David Hartley (1705–1757). Based on a model of the nervous system, his theory led to the idea that the environment gave rise to stimuli which caused physiological changes which, in turn, resulted in ideas and thus formed the mind. These ideas 'associated' in a certain way as a result of the sequences and grouping of stimuli and hence their proper organisation could 'form' a child's mental development. Simon holds that Hartley's '. . . influence on educational thought, on philosophy itself, in the late eighteenth and early nineteenth centuries cannot be exaggerated'.[13]

These ideas were taken up most enthusiastically by Joseph Priestley the chemist, who had a life-long interest in education. He was connected with Matthew Boulton's Lunar Society (which met on nights of full moon!). Boulton through his partnership with James Watt and William Small (formerly Jefferson's tutor and Franklin's friend) and contact with Joseph Black the chemist, David Hume the philosopher and Adam Smith the economist, was part of a scientific and philosophical network with American and strong Scottish connections. Priestley's various educational enterprises suffered, with others, a temporary setback after the French Revolution and the general suppression of Radical movements. But these ideas were to re-emerge in the early nineteenth century with even greater force as the Radical challenge to both the Tory and the Whig establishment in the form of a kind of educational determinism which could, and should, be designed to produce a society not of the old (Tory) aristocracy, land owners and Church, nor of the new (Whig) liberals who wished to preserve the same social structures and educate society into acceptance of it, but of middle class values which truly reflected certain ideals of democracy, science, industry and reason.

The leader of the political Radicals was James Mill, (father of John Stuart Mill) who worked closely with Jeremy Bentham, the philosophical Radical and Utilitarian, in the cause of the extension of the franchise, prison reform and education. Mill developed Hartley's associationist ideas in the realms of emotional states, aesthetic sensations and moral feelings, all of which he tried to explain in terms of sensations of pain and pleasure. He was closely associated with the Quaker William Allen in the Lancasterian school movement, described below, and founded the (Radical) *Westminster Review*. His ideas were influential in Scotland through his contributions, starting in 1808, to the *Edinburgh Review* established by Henry Brougham, Francis Jeffrey and Sidney Smith. However, although he remained linked to the more radical Whigs, especially Brougham, he later violently attacked the *Edinburgh Review* and its politics. Together with Brougham and Joseph Wilson he was instrumental in setting up in Westminster in 1819 the first English infant school. Mill was also one of the main propagandists and thinkers whose work was essential to the passing of the 1832 Reform Act. In the first post-Reform Parliament seven Radical MPs were elected, and they introduced the 1833 Education Act which made £20,000 available for '. . . erecting School Houses for the Education of Children of the Poorer Classes in Great Britain'. None of the money went to Scotland that year, but from 1834 to 1837 an annual sum of £10,000 was paid and two years later the Privy Council Committee—'The Committee of Council on Education'—was set up, with an annual building grant of £30,000 part of which was available to Scotland. Thus Mill influenced Scottish education by legislative means too.

The most influential theoretician in educational reform of the period was Jeremy Bentham, philosopher, politician, jurisprudist and designer of the Panopticon prison plan described in Essay 1. He was closely associated with James Mill (and with his son, John Stuart, who was profoundly influenced by Bentham's writings and personality); with Francis Place another member of the London Radical Group and with Henry Brougham and William Allen. When in 1815 Place could find no school for educating his own nine children Bentham immediately offered his own garden as a site for a 'Chrestomathic' school, 'a new system of instruction in the higher branches of learning, for the use of the middling and higher ranks of life'.[14] Bentham set about developing 'the architectural, administrative and pedagogic plan'. With his customary total (or totalitarian, Utopian) thoroughness this starts with a new philosophy of knowledge tabulated in an 'encyclopaedic table' of logical sequence and usefulness, 'in the order in which they (the subjects) are most usefully taught'. The curriculum was to be practical, intellectual and scientific, with emphasis on a systematic learning order, from the basic and simple (such as the three Rs and various branches of modern science), to the intermediate (history, geography and spoken languages), to the final stage (medicine and mathematics). Classics and 'dead' languages are to be eschewed unless needed for one of the learned professions. Clearly influenced by Hartley's ideas, Bentham places great stress on the need for systematic and logical teaching, exhibition of models, pictures, samples and machinery, the use of proper experiments, and continuous examination and tests to assess the rate of absorption of knowledge.

The management of the school was to be on the 'monitorial' principles developed by Bell some fifteen years earlier—which are described below. It is strange that Bentham should have opted for the Establishment Bell rather than the Dissenting Lancaster. One may assume that the greater systematisation of the former suggested to him greater efficiency. Nevertheless *in general* Bentham was a Lancaster supporter. The building (Figure 4.1) for his garden was designed by James Bevans, whose work on prisons and lunatic asylums is noted in Essay 1. It was to be twelve-sided, with a master at the centre and six monitors in a ring around him, each controlling one of the six radial segments of pupils, arranged in concentric rings on a floor sloping up towards the edge of the building with the characteristic teaching 'circles' marked on the floor at the periphery. Windows were to be high, so that children were not distracted from learning, and the familiar 'place capturing' principle was to be used, whereby children sit in places allocated according to proficiency and attainment, moving and changing places every time they advance in front of or drop behind other pupils in the continuous competitive tests. Children were to be 'set', as in today's comprehensive schools, whereby they could be in a different class for each subject according to attainment. A total of *nine hundred* boys was to be taught by the one master! In 1816 Bentham's original idea for invisible, central inspection—so as to beget 'the sentiment of an invisible omniscience'—was still alive and well, thirty years after its first appearance. 'The principle of central and complete inspection, which a simple architectural contrivance affords, has been proved so wonderfully to augment the powers of superintendence, that it cannot fail materially to improve the influence of the teacher in a seminary of instruction'.[15]

Bentham had already applied such ideas in 1794 to an infant school in a

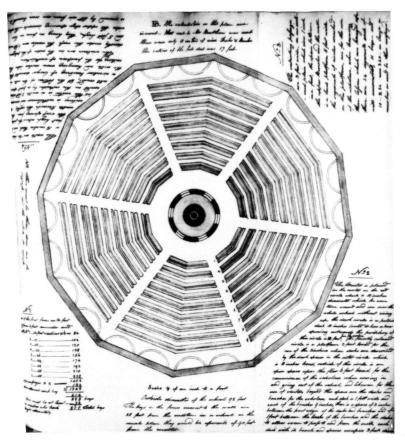

4.1 *James Bevans's design for a Chrestomathic school in Jeremy Bentham's garden, Queen Square Place, London, 1815,*
 (a) ground floor plan
 (b) section

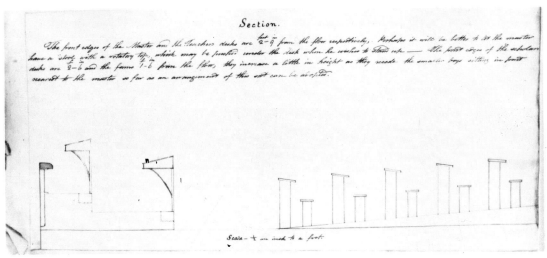

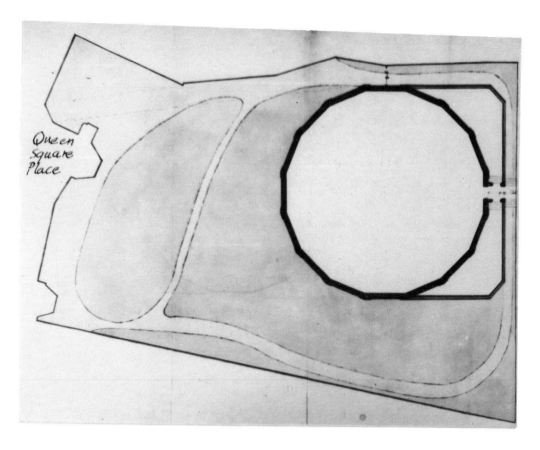

Queen
Square
Place

4.1 *(c) site plan.*

Nursery Panopticon, next to a Panopticon prison, situated at the centre of a semi-circle of cottages for fallen women. This was probably the 'Northotrophium' for 'The Innocent offspring of clandestine love'.[16] The Chrestomathic mechanistic educational and architectural model was never built (a second site, in Leicester Square, was rejected) but it had immense influence on rationalist-idealist philosophy of the nineteenth century. Circular and polygonal schools, preceding and subsequent to Bentham's scheme *were* however erected. One was the Wimbledon School of about 1773 (Figure 4.2); another was a Bell School in Bath—the new Bath District School in the grounds of Weymouth House, built for the National Society in 1816 designed by the Bath architect John Lowder (Figure 4.3). Little is known about this building, demolished for a new school in 1896. It is said to have accommodated one thousand children—boys on the ground floor and girls on the first; but, being a National School, it was run on the monitorial system and may well have followed Bentham's design of a central teacher's location.

The monitorial system is a central invention of Enlightenment ideology applied in an industrial context. Its role in Scottish thinking is as important as in that of almost every educational innovator of the first half of the nineteenth, century—Establishment or Dissenting; Tory, Whig or Radical, Socialist Utopian or philanthropic humanist, English or Scottish. The

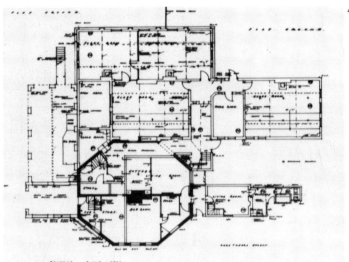

4.2 *Octagonal school, Wimbledon, c1773.*

literature of the movement is filled with both contemporary and later disputes about the first use of the system. It is now accepted that Andrew Bell, a Scot born and educated in St. Andrews, who took Church of England Orders and went as Army Chaplain to India, hit upon the idea in 1789 whilst acting as superintendent to the male orphan asylum in Madras. He trained an eight year old boy to act as monitor and teach the younger and less educated children and became convinced of the economy of such a method of education at just about the time that Samuel Bentham in Russia had invented a similar industrial process in which the scarce skilled workers could supervise hundreds of unskilled ones. In the hands of his brother Jeremy this flowered into the Panopticon. On Bell's return to London he published in 1797 *An Experiment in Education* in which he propounded the monitorial system. It was applied to a parish school, St. Botolph's in Aldgate, the following year. Possibly independently Joseph Lancaster, a Quaker, developed a similar 'system' opening up a one-room school in Borough Road, London, in 1801 and publishing his book, *Improvements in Education,* in 1803.

The two systems ran in parallel, and in competition. Lancaster's system made more rapid headway at first but he got into financial difficulties and had to be rescued by two other Quakers, William Allen and Joseph Fox in 1808. At this stage both Establishment and Dissenting churchmen supported his ideas and he obtained the patronage of George III, the Queen and the Princesses. Fox and Allen in 1808 set up the Royal Lancasterian Society which, in 1810, was reconstituted as The Institution for Promoting the British System for the Education of the Labouring and Manufacturing Classes of Society of Every Religious Persuasion—a title shortened in 1818 to the British and Foreign Schools Society. The Lancasterian movement spread rapidly in Britain and Europe and the

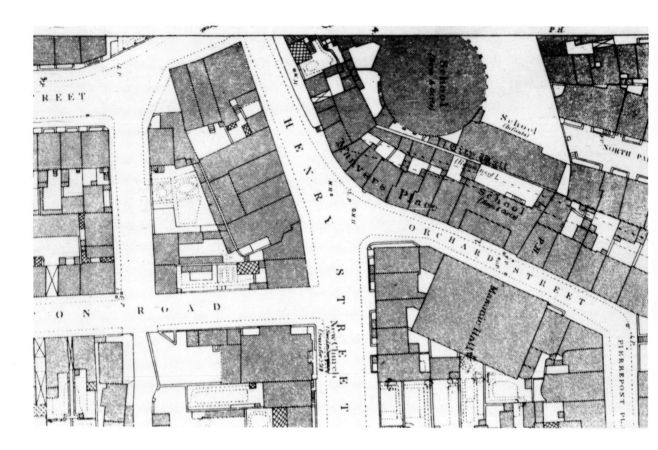

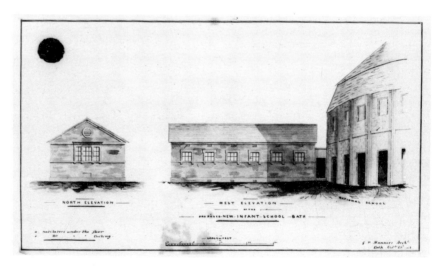

4.3 *Bath District 'National' School,*
Weymouth House, 1816;
architect John Lowder,
(a) site plan, from Ordnance
Survey map, 1886
(b) perspective sketch by G.P.
Manners, architect, 1843

212

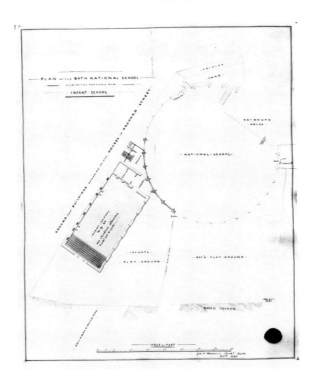

(c) part-plan by G.P. Manners, architect, 1843.

supporters of Bell's system became concerned at its success since, as a Dissenting body, it appeared to undermine the educational efforts within the Church of England. This was the very reason why not only Whigs, but Radicals such as Bentham, Mill, Place and even agnostics such as Owen supported it. So the Establishment supporters in 1811 set up a competitive body under the aegis of the S.P.C.K.—The National Society for the Education of the Poor in the Principles of the Established Church throughout England and Wales. This was totally committed to a curriculum based on Established religion and the Bible. After incorporation in 1817 it took over a number of Bell's and other charity schools and founded new ones in cities and towns. With the advantage of S.P.C.K. and the Church of England support it grew rapidly, raised substantial sums and provided not only buildings but books, equipment and teachers. The British and Foreign and the National (as it soon became known) systems differed chiefly in their degree of adherence to the formal doctrine of the Church of England, although the Bible and religion played a central role in both. But their buildings had minor, but significant, differences too.

Bell's system made little headway in Scotland, although he tried hard to introduce it North of the Border. Lancaster's system, however, spread into and in Scotland very quickly—partly because its religious basis was looser (although its educational methods were more rigid) and hence more adaptable to the doctrines of the Kirk, and partly because it lent itself readily to various shades of Scottish humanist, rationalist and Enlightenment interpretations of education.

There was a Lancasterian Society in Edinburgh by 1815 and elsewhere in Scotland within a few years. Cockburn says that the first Lancastrian (sic) school 'was a long low wood and brick erection, stretched on the very top of the Calton Hill; where it was then the fashion to stow everything that was too abominable to be tolerated elsewhere'.[17] The school was, in his opinion, 'abominable' to the alliance of Tories, the Kirk and the Episcopalians—all successfully 'crushed' by the Edinburgh Whigs. But his complaints of siting were not ironical; we have seen, in Essay 1, that he had earlier complained that 'it was a piece of undoubted bad taste to give so glorious an eminence to a prison' to site the new jail on Calton Hill.[18] In Glasgow events moved almost as fast as in England; a Lancasterian Society was set up in June 1810 '. . . for the purpose of Educating and Instructing the Children of the lower classes of the community at a cheap rate or gratis, for those who could not afford a small fee'.[19] Two teachers were engaged the same year and sent to Lancaster's school in London for training, and three 'extensive' buildings were erected—at Calton, Anderston Walk and the Gorbals. Figure 4.4 shows these in block plan form as they existed in 1821. Only the one in Calton was called 'Lancasterian'; that in Anderston Walk being described as a school for 'the New System of British Education' and that in the Gorbals simply as a 'Public School'.

Interest in the Lancasterian cause, and the Bell *versus* Lancaster debate, was kept alive in Scotland chiefly through the medium of the *Edinburgh Review*. In 1807 a review appeared[20] of a book published by Lancaster in the previous year—*Outlines of a Plan for Educating Ten Thousand Poor Children* etc; each school was to contain seven hundred to a thousand children. Each child was given a ticket according to achievement—when he is surpassed by another, the ticket is handed over; if a child moves from one class to another on account of achievement or lack of it, the respective *monitors* of the two classes also exchange tickets; these tickets are accumulated and exchanged for prizes. 'The boys who obtain the prize, commonly walk around the school in procession, holding the prizes in their hands, and an herald proclaiming before them, "These good boys have obtained prizes for going into another class" '. The *Review* comments on the importance of monitors, as part of the plan for achieving 'cheapness'; the significant military parallel is drawn between them and non-commissioned officers in the army, and the hopelessness of trying to govern an army entirely by captains, majors and colonels is pointed out. The education the poor thus receive '. . . probably renders them more tractable and less ferocious'. As for cheapness, 'A boy learns reading, writing and accounts, for fourteen shillings, who would, in hedge-breaking, or picking pockets, cost the country double the money in the same time'. It will be seen that Owen, Stow and others use precisely the same cost-

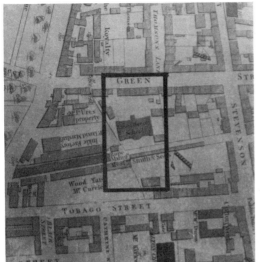

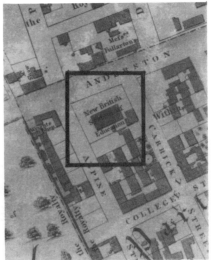

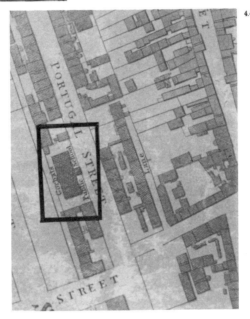

4.4 *The first three Glasgow Lancasterian schools, c1810, shown on Fleming's map in 1821,*
(a) Calton
(b) Anderston
(c) Gorbals.

benefit analysis of social economy in propagating schools and industrial settlements.

The economic motive and the economy of effort in having only one master is allied to the model of the school as a *machine*. Bell maintains that a master who was 'able and diligent, could, without difficulty, conduct ten contiguous schools, each consisting of a thousand scholars . . . Like the

215

steam engine, or spinning machinery, it diminishes labour and multiplies work, but in a degree which does not admit of the same limits. For unlike the mechanical powers, this intellectual and moral engine, the more work it has to perform, the greater is the facility and expedition with which it is performed, and the greater is the degree of perfection to which it is carried'.[21] So the machine obeys a dream of perpetual motion and is not subject to the laws of entropy. Thomas Bernard, writing a year later, applies Adam Smith's doctrine of the division of labour even more directly: 'The man who first made practical use of the *division of labour* gave a new power to the application of corporal strength, and simplified and facilitated the most irksome and labourious operations. To him we are indebted for "the greatest improvement in the productive powers of labour, and for the greater part of the skill, dexterity, and judgment, with which it is anywhere directed or applied" (quoting from *The Wealth of Nations*) . . . But that man, whatever was his merit, did no more essential service to *mechanical*, than Dr. Bell has done to *intellectual* operations. It is the division of labour in his schools, that leaves the master the easy task of directing the movements of the whole machine instead of toiling ineffectually at a single part. The principle in manufactories, and in schools is the same'.[22] Even as humane a writer as Coleridge referred to the monitorial system as 'an incomparable machine . . . a vast moral steam engine', although he may have been moved to praise Bell's system by perceiving the positive human relationships which it would generate between older and younger children rather than by its economy and efficiency.[23]

The plans of the early monitorial schools reflect a number of these ideologies and images; there is large, central open space, expressing unity and used chiefly for religious instruction of the whole school, this being in both Bell's and Lancaster's schemes the central, unifying discipline. In the centre, or around the edges, according to the two varieties, are subdivisions of identical areas, supervised by the monitors, for separate groups or classes. Bell articulates a complex hierarchy of teachers (all children) below the master, analogous to the industrial hierarchy of degrees of skill and supervisory power. Beneath the master, in a larger school, are the following ranks: usher, sub-usher, teacher, assistant teacher and finally tutor.[24] Above the master, and having a non-teaching role, is only the superintendent, who would normally be the minister in charge of the Parish, '. . . whose scrutinising eye must pervade the whole machine'. The image of this central supervising *eye* is present in the school itself; the master '. . . from his place . . . overlooks the whole school, and gives life and motion to every member of it'. So the role is both surveillance and *energizing*—an image which Bentham had fully developed in the Chrestomathic School and the Panopticon. The system became even more refined in the internal hierarchy of the pupils' spatial arrangements. The classes in Bell's schools were arranged in the centre of the schoolroom in squares or U shapes, each pupil being located according to progress and being moved around by the 'place capturing' method. Having been thus

216

ranked, the genius and the idiot are paired, in equal and opposite locations, 'First and last should be opposite to one another, the rest at equal distances and the opposite sides equal; and the teacher to stand where he can see and have command of the whole class'.[25]

Figure 4.5 shows a plan and interior of the National Society's Baldwin Gardens Model School, near Gray's Inn Road, established about 1811. The school is divided into two rooms, one for six hundred boys and the other for four hundred girls. The plan and the perspective show the writing desks and benches against the outside walls, with the writing children facing *away* from the body of the schoolroom, and the central part of the space with loose benches which can be arranged in various formations. In this particular plan they are arranged in double and triple rows in the boys' portion and in parallel rows in the girls', set out for a sewing class. Much of the teaching was carried out with the children standing in their 'classes' in the open space. An alternative arrangement of the benches was in U-formations for each class, with a central table in each U for the monitor. The teacher's table is seen on the central axis in the girls' room, from which, through the opening in the dividing wall, the whole school is under surveillance.

The typical Lancaster school is represented in Figure 4.6 which shows the model school at Borough Road. Here the arrangement is the opposite of the Bell (or 'Madras') layout. The centre of the room is occupied by *fixed* benches and writing desks in long parallel rows. The edges of the room are left free and marked with semi-circles on the floor, where classes of children can stand, each with its monitor, facing the wall on which lesson cards and sheets were hung. The master's desk is on a raised platform on the central axis, and the whole floor slopes up from the master's platform at a slope of 1 in 20, to ensure that all the children are visible. In the picture the master is seen on the right; 'the general monitor of order' standing on a stool in the centre, and each class monitor at the end of a row in which sit the children for whom he is responsible. Robson, the greatest English school architect of the later nineteenth century, illustrates a typical early Lancaster school in plan and section (Figure 4.7), showing the sloping floor.

The monitorial schools contain a number of significant spatial and formal representations of the social structure of the schools. They are highly centralised; the space and furniture is laid out to suit the hierarchical structure of the various ranks of monitors; there is little subdivision of space by solid walls into rooms—and considering that up to a thousand children might be simultaneously occupying the single large space, the effectiveness of the discipline can be appreciated. The model is the church or church hall and the spinning room of the early mills.

It was in the spinning mills of Scotland that one of the most imaginative educational experiments was made—and one that was to influence David Stow both directly and by other, indirect, paths. Robert Owen, industrial entrepreneur, political philosopher and educationalist in 1799 married the

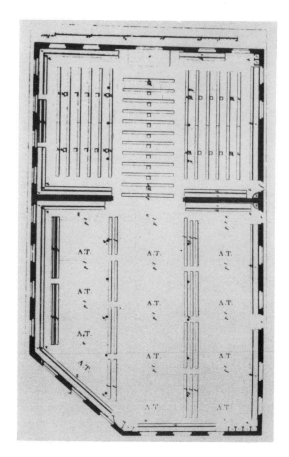

4.5 *National Society's school in Baldwin Gardens, London; early nineteenth century drawings,*
 (a) plan
 (b) interior view.

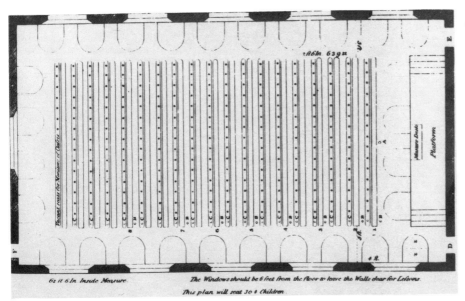

4.6 *British and Foreign School Society's model school, Borough Road, London; early nineteenth century drawings,*
    (a) plan
    (b) interior view.

daughter of David Dale, co-founder with Richard Arkwright of the industrial village and mills at New Lanark and in the same year he and his partners of the Chorlton Twist Company, Manchester, acquired the entire enterprise. He at once set about improving the mills, extending them, improving housing, food supplies and starting a programme of elementary public health and domestic economy in the village. He not only started to

219

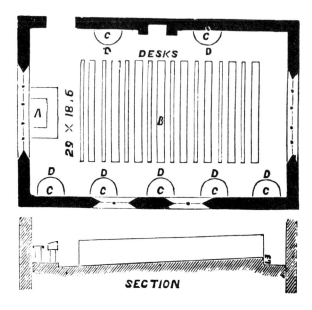

reduce the established (and widely accepted) use of pauper apprentices, eventually eliminating it completely, but raised the minimum age for work in the mills and started infant and primary education. His partners in the venture changed, in 1810, to a group of Glasgow merchants and financiers. But these, as his earlier ones, were suspicious of his social, political and educational views and practices and gave him little encouragement and only limited scope for practical execution of his ideas. However, after severe financial difficulties which came to a head in 1812, Owen found a new set of partners in 1814, when he and they acquired full ownership of New Lanark at an auction.

The new partners were all well-known in politics, Radical philosophy and education. They included Jeremy Bentham, and the two Quakers William Allen and Joseph Fox. The role of all three in the Lancasterian movement and educational reform has already been described and it therefore is not surprising that Owen received from them far greater encouragement and support than from his earlier set of strictly commercially-minded partners although Allen was the only one of the new partners to take an active interest in the running of New Lanark after 1814. In the pursuit of new capital, and to avoid bankruptcy, Owen wrote a pamphlet in 1812: *A Statement Regarding the New Lanark Establishment.* He took it to London in that and the following years hoping that the combination of business acumen and social reform which it expressed would attract the right kind of partner and adequate capital—but it failed to do so until 1814. In it he expresses the early crystallization of his educational and social philosophy and describes in detail the New Institution for the Formation of Character which had been planned as early as 1809.[26] The structure was complete in 1813 but Owen lacked capital for its internal fitting out till 1816, when it was opened. New Lanark also contained a less famous, and less well documented School which, it is thought, had been established later than the Institution, but before 1819.

The Institution has three floors. Initially the basement (ground floor at the back, as the land slopes) was a store cellar for the mills. The ground floor contained a communal kitchen and canteen, together with some indoor space for the infants; and the first floor a large, oblong room—140 feet by 40 feet—which had a triple function as school room, lecture hall and church. Figure 4.8 shows the plan and external elevation of the building. The ground floor eating room was also to be used three nights a week for dancing by young adults and the space was made available by raising the dining tables to the ceiling by means of pulleys. The top floor was to be divided by benches into reading and arithmetic classes on the Lancasterian principle; girls were to be taught to sew, cut-out and 'make useful family garments'; and they were also to work in the communal kitchen 'to learn to cook cheap and nutritious food, and to clean and keep a house neat and in order'. The boys were taught manual exercises in the 'drill-ground'—which also served as the infants' playground—and '. . . as much of the principles of military tactics as would enable them, with a little previous practice, at any future period of their lives, aided also by sentiments they would acquire, to render the most effectual defence of their country'. The combination of health, instruction, militarism and patriotism was the beginning of Owen's practical Utopianism. The top floor room was later evidently divided into two—both parts used as school, lecture room and church. The smaller room now contained a gallery on columns, which appears in the famous print of the school interior (Figure 4.9). This was used both by visitors to the school and by musicians; as well as this Owen's son mentions 'in his biography another 'gallery' which went round three sides of the larger room and it must be assumed that these galleries were in the form of raised platforms or stepped seats.[27] This room also had a pulpit at one end, used by the minister of whichever sect used the space for services, by lecturers and by the schoolmaster.

The School (Figure 4.10), a three storey building of similar plan, was of later date—perhaps about 1817—and seemed to extend both the cooking and eating facilities of the Institution and the educational ones.

The Institution was heated by a warm air system which fed the heated air to the top through the hollow cast-iron columns in the centre of the building which appear on the ground floor plan. This was no doubt an adaptation of the stove and warm air heating system first developed by Strutt in his Belper mill, and used in the Derby Infirmary designed and equipped by Strutt between 1806 and 1810. The group of Radicals who

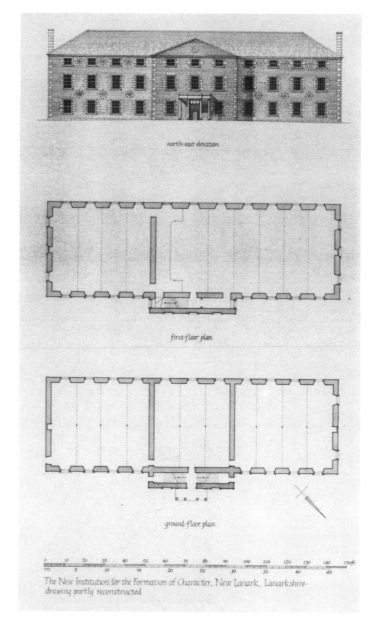

4.8 *Robert Owen's New Institution*
for the Formation of Character,
New Lanark, 1809-16,
  (a) ground and first floor plans
    and elevation
  (b) exterior view.

north-east elevation

first-floor plan

ground-floor plan

The New Institution for the Formation of Character, New Lanark, Lanarkshire—
drawing partly reconstructed

MR OWEN'S INSTITUTION, NEW LANARK.
(Quadrille Dancing.)

4.9 *New Institution, New Lanark, nineteenth century interior view of schoolroom.*

met in the Birmingham Lunar Society and the Derbyshire Philosophical Society included in their membership and contacts then or earlier not only Strutt, but Jeremy Bentham, Robert Owen, James Watt, Josiah Wedgewood and Matthew Boulton. The exchange of technical experience was surprisingly rapid—and its transfer between industrial buildings and hospitals, schools, asylums and prisons effected through the involvement of the same set of entrepreneurs, philanthropists and Utopians in both industry and social institutions.[28]

It appears that Owen employed one master and about ten male and female 'assistants'—these were probably youngsters in their teens, their work being based on the monitorial model of Bell and Lancaster. Owen was certainly enthusiastic about the Lancasterian system of *spatial* organisation which appeared to him to '. . . constitute on the whole a better manner for instruction . . . than those of Dr. Bell, although some of the details introduced by the latter are also very deserving of adoption'.[29] He is however critical of both in the amount of attention they pay to the *manner* of education rather than the *matter*; accusing them of inadequate attention to rational principles, and decrying especially the dogmatic and over-simplified theological and moral training their pupils received, as a result of which memory is all they require in '. . . this mockery of learning'.

In his autobiography Owen describes how he appointed the first master

223

4.10 *School, New Lanark, c.1817,*
(a) ground and first floor plans and elevation
(b) exterior view.

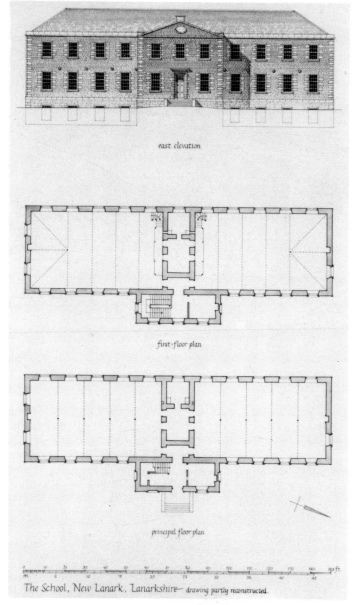

east elevation

first-floor plan

principal floor plan

The School, New Lanark, Lanarkshire— *drawing partly reconstructed.*

and mistress—James Buchanan and Molly Young—at the New Institution. The former is described as a '. . . poor, simple-hearted weaver . . . who had been previously trained by his wife to perfect submission to her will . . .' However he made up for this, in Owen's view, by his love of the children, patience, and willingness to be instructed by Owen for teaching in '. . . the first national infant school that had ever been imagined by any party in any country'. The latter was about seventeen years old on appointment '. . . who of the two, in natural powers of the mind, had the advantage over her new companion'.[30] These disparaging remarks about Buchanan, and Owen's later denigration of his work, may have been prompted by personal motives or by Owen's resentment of the fact that Buchanan acted as an unwitting instrument in establishing Wilderspin as the pioneer of infant education, by moving to London and taking Owen's ideas with him.

Henry (later Lord) Brougham, Whig, prominent *Edinburgh Review*-er, educational reformer and friend of Owen, Bentham, Mill and most Radical thinkers and the less orthodox Whig politicians, decided, in 1818, to set up an infant school in London, modelled on Owen's ideas and system which Owen claims he (Brougham) had experienced first-hand by visits to New Lanark,[31] though Rusk denies this.[32] Buchanan became the first teacher in Brougham's infant school in Westminster. Owen states that his services were requested by Brougham—a request to which he agreed 'Most willingly, for I have pupils who can take his place without any injury to the school'. However it is more likely that Buchanan quarrelled with Owen and left of his own volition. In 1820 the second London infant school was founded in Spitalfields by the evangelical Joseph Wilson who employed Samuel Wilderspin as his first master.

Wilderspin visited Buchanan's Westminster school and much of his early training was acquired from that source. He acknowledged this in his early publications, including *On the Importance of Educating the Infant Poor* (1823). However by the thirties he was repudiating this and claiming to be the inventor of the infant training system. His methods were unorthodox for the times; he used dancing, movement and play in both the schoolroom and the playground—the latter being a direct influence from Owen's work at New Lanark. Religion, natural history and other subjects were taught using objects, pictures and coloured illustrations, and discipline was based on moral persuasion and did not have submission as its central aim—a difference from Owen's and other early experiments which McCann[33] notes is due to the liberating influence of not having to prepare children directly for the labour market in mills. Figure 4.11 shows the plan and interior of the Spitalfields School. There are several important features to note. First, the presence of the 'teaching posts', as in the monitorial schools, for gathering groups of children around pictures and other illustrations; second, a stepped gallery at one end; third, a 'Classroom'; and fourth, the enclosed playground entered from the schoolroom, the door to it leading from that end of the room where special provision was made for visitors to sit and observe the lessons.

The gallery is commonly held to be Wilderspin's invention. In 1832, he wrote that in order to teach a group of children *together* in the large *school-room*—a method which he had already introduced into the *class*room and which was in distinction to the small group, or individual teaching by monitors in the schoolroom— '. . . I then made various experiments with seats, but did not succeed, until, at length, the construction of a gallery, or succession of steps, the youngest occupying the lower and the eldest the higher, answered the desired end'.[34]

But we have already seen that something very similar existed on three sides of the top floor schoolroom of the New Institution. It was also Owen's influence, no doubt transmitted by his ex-master Buchanan, that inspired Wilderspin to treat the playground as a central item in the scheme of things. The classroom was however, apparently, Wilderspin's completely original invention; '. . . the class that has done first is taken into a separate room, where the children have each another lesson, though in a different way from the first, for in what we call the classroom the children . . . being formed into a square . . . all say their lessons together'.[35] This use of the classroom for what was later to be called the 'simultaneous system' preceded the use of the gallery, by which he introduced the same method back into the schoolroom. By 1824 the Infant School Society was founded and Wilderspin was employed in propagating the teaching methods throughout the land. In 1836 this was superseded by the Home and Colonial Infant School Society which continued the work of training infant school teachers.

Wilderspin's work was well known in Scotland. One of the people influenced was John Wood, who in 1819 more or less by accident became the master of the Kirk Sessional School founded in Edinburgh in 1813, at first in a converted house in Leith Wynd and, from 1824, in a purpose-built school in Market Street. The Ordnance Survey map of 1852–4 shows the building as 'St. Mary's School—Roman Catholic' (Figure 4.12) and it also appears on Shepherd's print of 1831 with a symmetrical facade of two small towers and a large, mullioned central window. This window must have lit the main schoolroom over the 'gallery' which is shown on the plan. There must be some doubt however whether this gallery was part of the original structure. Stow, in 1836, praised Wood's 'intellectual' system, which, if it had '. . . added objects, pictures of objects, *a gallery* and a playground . . . would be complete'.[36] Wood used the monitorial system, with two monitors for each class of 30 children—one for teaching and one for discipline.[37] Religious instruction found its way into almost all the teaching, and all class books contained substantial moral and religious material. The Sessional schools spread rapidly in Scotland; Dundee had one in 1833, Perth in 1834[38] and by the same date Glasgow had six. By 1850 there were over one hundred, educating about twelve thousand children.[39] In general the standards in the Sessional schools were low, punishment was by the tawse, and equipment limited. However as early as 1826 the Church of Scotland was using the Market Street School as a training school for its teachers to be sent to the Highlands, thus

4.11 *Samuel Wilderspin and Joseph Wilson's Spitalfields infant school, London, 1820,*
(a) interior view
(b) ground floor plan.

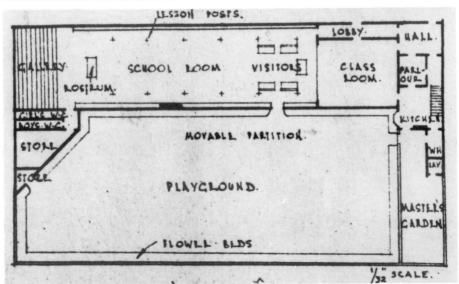

anticipating by two years Stow's first model infant school, also used for training.

Wilderspin's infant education movement spread to Scotland directly also. He visited Glasgow, Edinburgh and most of the larger towns in the twenties and early thirties and several schools based on the Spitalfields model were established. In Edinburgh an Infant School Society was set up in 1829[40] and within about a year opened its first school in The Vennel (off

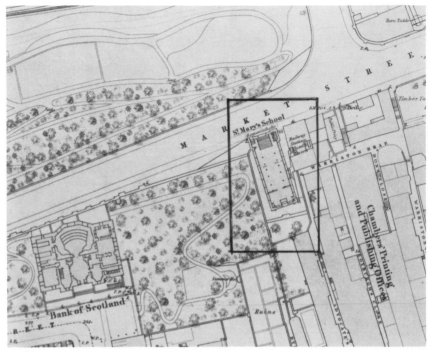

228

the Grassmarket) as shown on the 1852–4 map (Figure 4.13). Its founders had been inspired by Stow's work at the Drygate School in Glasgow. Their building was designed free of charge by 'Mr. Hamilton'. Whether this was Thomas Hamilton (1784–1858) designer of Edinburgh Royal High School or David Hamilton (1768–1843) designer of the Glasgow Normal Seminary, discussed below, it has not been possible to determine. The school has a gallery and was opened by Wilderspin himself. Since before 1832 he already had a gallery in his London School, it is more than likely that this was part of the original scheme.

But Scotland by this time had its second infant school innovator, also influenced by both Wood and Wilderspin, in the person of David Stow. Stow was born in Paisley in 1793 and early came under the influence of a strong religious education. At the age of eighteen, in 1811, he moved to lodgings in Glasgow, within walking distance of his father's business where he had started work. This walk led him daily through some of Glasgow's worst slums in the Saltmarket area. He deplored the living conditions, especially the total lack of provision for children's education which he saw basically as an absence of *moral training*. In 1816, after various earlier attempts, he set up a group of Sabbath Schools and started to teach in them. Although he recognised these as useful—'. . . through their instrumentality many individuals have been saved from ruin, and are, at this moment, useful members and ornaments of society'—he also notes that '. . . the training of one day in seven, as an antidote to the contaminating influence of the rest of the week . . .' is inadequate. So he proposed in about 1827 to '. . . look abroad for some more efficient moral engine'—and this was to be '. . . the infant school system conducted upon Bible principles'.[41] The first Glasgow Infant School Society for providing full-time teaching was set up late in 1827 and the first infant school opened in 1828 in a converted house in Drygate. (There is considerable variation given by Stow and his disciples as to the date of this School, and the most thorough chronology is that of Rusk[42] which is followed here). From the start Stow regarded it as a *model* for demonstration and for the training of pupil teachers. At first one month was the minimum training period but it was soon extended to a minimum of six and an average of eight months.

Stow was well aware of many Continental systems of education which had preceded his Drygate Model School; he also acknowledged the example of Sheriff Wood, of Edinburgh '. . . to no private individual is the cause of education more indebted than to Sheriff Wood for his disinterested exertions'.[43] He also commends Bell's and Lancaster's monitorial systems which, contrary to James Scotland's view, [44] he did not at first treat with 'resolute opposition': '. . . mutual instruction by monitors . . . is equally valuable to the scholar and to the master . . . (and) forms a very important feature of the Infant School'.[45] Later it was apparently also adopted in his Model Juvenile School. However by 1839 he is opposed to the monitorial system 'No monitors. Monitors can only teach facts—they cannot develop or train'.[46] He also knew of the work of Pestalozzi whose influence in Britain was significant and whose emphasis on presentation of lively images through objects and pictures, and discovery as a way of learning, had also influenced Owen but only after 1818 when Owen visited Pestalozzi's famous school at Yverdun in French Switzerland, his own basic principles having been already independently formulated by 1816. He commends also the Prussian and French experiments of the first decades of the nineteenth century. Above all he owed and acknowledged a great debt to the methods developed by Wilderspin. Stow concedes that Wilderspin's physical training is 'complete'; his intellectual method 'a great improvement on the old systems he had to contend with at the commencement' but capable of many improvements; but 'in the Religious department, the instruction given . . . is very incomplete'.[47] He blames the failure on the attempt to teach an undogmatic Christianity designed 'to offend no sect' (Wilderspin himself was a Swedenborgian), consisting mainly of Scripture history. He is even more outspoken about Owen's efforts, which he regarded as 'chiefly gymnastics and other physical exercises, accompanied by a certain amount of intellectual instruction by means of pictures'. But its chief defect was a failure to give *moral training*— being 'nearly destitute of any cultivation of one of the most important parts of our moral nature, viz. the religious affections and habits'.[48]

Stow's Training System had moral training as its central structure. By this he meant not only Biblical, Scriptural education, but also ' . . . the prevention of bad, and the formation of good habits' which was to be allied to physical and intellectual formation. Stow believed in the *tabula rasa* character of the infant mind. It was only the power of systematic *training* in habits of obedience to moral rules, started at the earliest age, which could overcome the 'pestilential atmosphere . . . (and) the contaminating influence of evil example'[49] which he saw growing all around him in Glasgow. Obedience was to be obtained without the use of physical punishment and other sanctions could be used, for instance the culprit's name could be written on a large slate in the view of all pupils. Stow also believed in mixed classes and saw the mutual influence of the sexes as a 'humanising influence'.

In common with Radicals, philanthropists and Utilitarians, Stow saw investment in education as a means of reducing crime and the cost of prisons and policing; for the infants otherwise grow up ' . . . breathing . . . such a pestilential atmosphere' that from the ranks of ' . . . the third or lowest moral class in the moral scale' (the first and second remain ill-defined) ' . . . at a future period, our bridewells, jails, and convict-ships will be replenished . . . '[50] He estimated that there were five to six thousand infants in this category in Glasgow in 1834. His calculus then concludes with adding the cost of Glasgow Jail, the Bridewell, which he believes will shortly need expansion due to the rapid increase in crime, the new House of Refuge, the Glasgow Police Establishment, and the *London* Police—a total cost of about £300,000.[51] It is interesting to recall that Owen, of whose secular and rationalist ideas Stow was so scathing, had argued in precisely

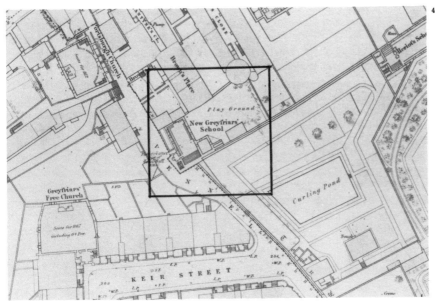

the same way to the County of Lanark in 1821, when in proposing his 'Plan' for a Utopian factory commune, he maintained that it would be an instrument for avoiding 'the dreaded crisis of violence'.[52] A colleague and landowner, Mr. Hamilton, who proposed to let 500-700 acres of his land for such an establishment, saw it as a means ' . . . which would supersede the necessity for erecting a Bridewell for the Country'.[53] Owen was doubtful about actually admitting criminals into the establishment, which should, at first ' . . . be formed for the relief of the industrious among the working classes'. It may also be accessible to ' . . . the middling and higher classes of society'[54]—a tripartite class division which Stow seemed to echo. It is also worth noting that even in Owen's rationalist/Utilitarian Utopian 'parallelograms' he proposed to have the juvenile and infant schools 'in the line of buildings to be erected across the centre of the parallelogram, in connection with the *church and places of worship*' (author's italics). If Owen could not make this disconnection it is interesting that Stow *did* do so (as far as layout was concerned) with the single exception of the 1834 'Parochial Establishment' mentioned below.

Two fundamental educational, as distinct from moral, ideas formed the basis of Stow's fully developed system: 'Sympathy of numbers' and 'Picturing out'. By the former he meant the mutually beneficial effect of large numbers of children working together—this ' . . . social sympathy may prove the very means of moral improvement' in constrast to the ' . . . concentrated masses of human beings (in) large cities and factories . . . (which) afford peculiar facilities and encouragement to vice'. So the supposed bane of large cities and factories can be 'turned morally and *consequently* politically, into great national blessings' (author's italics).

Stow's text indicates that this sympathy of numbers consists in acquiring obedience and orderly behaviour by being trained into a group where conformity is a supreme virtue. So the unruly mobs of cities, 'at present producing evil habits, ought to be laid hold of in our educational system as an instrument to good'.[55]

Together with his fear of and repulsion for the city, in its uncontrolled state, goes Stow's idealised picture of nature and rural society; the rural parochial schools of Scotland had '. . . rendered her peasantry at once intelligent and moral'.[56] Later describing the garden, flower beds and fruit trees which should be planted in the playground of his schools, there is the constant inference of the innocence of nature.

'Picturing out' consisted of the use of simple analogy, question-and-answer, ellipsis and pictorial representation; learning by rote was anathema. Before elaborating on Stow's other methods the development of his school buildings has to be traced.

The 1828 Drygate school (Figure 4.14) was a converted house but it already had features which were to last throughout the Stow system—notably the playground which Stow regarded as the 'uncovered school-room'. Its recommended size was 50 feet by 90 or 100 feet. It was to be 'a little world of real life' where mental, moral and physical character is best developed and '. . . consequently where moral habits can be best formed'. The resolution of small, everyday quarrels and conflicts and respect for plants and fruit trees would teach honesty; the fact that children did not steal or even touch these desirable objects showed that '. . . moral teaching in schools would be the *cheapest* police'.[57] Wilderspin, whom Stow visited as early as 1820, through Owen's influence *via* Buchanan, had already emphasised this role of physical exercise and outdoor play. But physical exercise was also a means of preparing children's attention when they returned to the gallery: 'to prepare them for receiving the intellectual and moral lessons to which they are called—just as military drilling prepares the soldier for instant obedience and prompt action at all times'. In the playground the children also 'learn to sing . . . and to sit, stand, walk etc., in order and in healthful comfort and regularity'.[58] Stow extends the role of surveillance of the children in the playground, so much so that the master eating his lunch in the classroom has to see the children through a special window and should, occasionally, join in their play. Surveillance, too, was morally based on a constant reminder that 'Thou God seest me'. At Drygate and in later schools he used the circular swings seen in Figure 4.14; the children waiting their turn 'form a circle, and count a given number to some lively tune, or sing a moral song or rhyme.'[59] Such swings also seem to have been Wilderspin's invention.

A Mr. and Mrs. Caughie were appointed master and mistress at Drygate and Wilson of Spitalfields was contacted to send someone to train them. Needless to say it was Wilderspin who was chosen and came in May 1828. Whilst he was in Scotland he lectured on his methods in the Glasgow Trades' Hall and visited the towns mentioned earlier. On some of his visits,

For Training Infants, and Practising Normal Students—1826.

No. I.—First Model School,

4.14 *David Stow's first school in Drygate, Glasgow, 1828.*

such as that to Dumfries, Caughie accompanied him with a group of the Drygate children who were 'publicly exhibited'. In Edinburgh his lectures and the demonstrations in the Waterloo Rooms were such a success that the Edinburgh Model Infant School already described was set up.

By 1829 two purpose-built Stow schools were under construction in Glasgow, both in St. John's parish—the Marlborough Street School, opened in that year, and the Chalmers Street Infant School Establishment and Female Sewing School, opened in 1830. This is illustrated by Stow in an 1834 publication (Figure 4.15)[50] which shows a schoolroom 46 feet by 26 feet, the same size as that given for Marlborough Street. The description states that above it is a Juvenile School and a playground, with swing posts, flower borders and latrines shown for each. However on the 1860 Ordnance Survey map (Figure 4.16) the Juvenile playground is occupied by another building which is probably the Sewing School and it is quite likely that Stow's illustration is an idealised or 'model' plan.

The building programme was now vigorous for the next few years. In 1832 an Infant School was opened in John Street, St. David's Parish. In the same year the Model School and the Caughies moved from Drygate to a new school in Steel Street, the Saltmarket—but the 1860 map does not show it. By 1834 a school in Cowcaddens, Barony Parish, had also been set up.

233

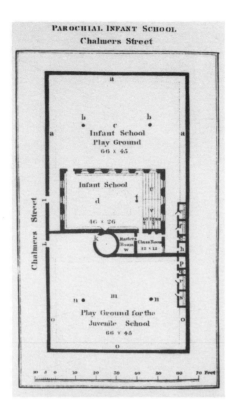

PAROCHIAL INFANT SCHOOL.
Chalmers Street

By 1833 the system had been extended to Juvenile Schools for children from six to twelve or fourteen years old. The first one was erected also in St. John's Parish, in Annfield Street, and put under the care of John Auld, master. Stow illustrates this school (Figure 4.17), and the map of 1860 also shows it. It had an 'English' and a 'Commercial' School—that is, an academic and a practical stream.

Basically both the infant and the juvenile schools adopted the same plan—a large school room, with a gallery at one end, a smaller and attached classroom (on the Wilderspin model) in which the master can 'examine each class separately, after being under monitors in the school-room' and after being taught as a whole or half class in the gallery, and a playground. The classroom had to open both from the schoolroom and the playground and there was also a door opening directly from the playground into the classroom. Thus the children moved from monitors in the schoolroom, to the master in the classroom and out into the playground, supervised by the master through the classroom window; and then back into the schoolroom. 'This rotary movement continues until the prescribed time allotted to that part of the system is exhausted'.[61] This is a good analogue to the central inspection and production principles of the Benthams' Panopticon establishments.

The gallery as a teaching device was basic to Stow's system. By 1834 it is

234

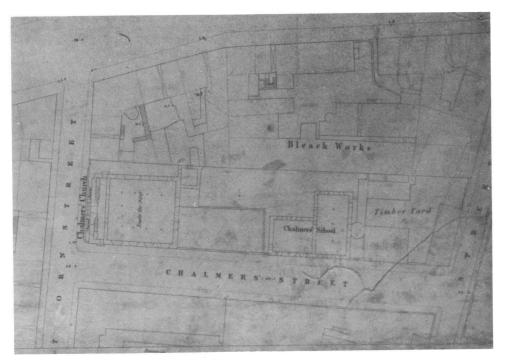

4.16 *Chalmers Street Infant School shown on Ordnance Survey map, 1860.*

described in detail, and in 1836 illustrated, with exact specifications of dimensions for infants and juveniles (Figure 4.18). It had to be large enough to seat all the pupils as this '. . . enables the children to fix their eye more easily upon the master . . . and . . . enables . . . the master . . . to observe and direct more perfectly every movement of the children'. 'The social principle is concentrated in the gallery, and greatly more influential than when the children are seated around a schoolroom, at desks, or on scattered forms; the attention of all is secured; all receive one lesson, and all learn'.[62] This was direct criticism of the monitorial system of individual and small group teaching, although as we have seen Stow supported it and used it when necessary. Writing was done on fixed benches and desks against the two long walls of the schoolroom. It was important for the teacher to have *total* control—not only of vision but of hearing '. . . every word spoken by the master or scholars is more easily heard by all when thus seated'.[63] It was here that the 'simultaneous' method which was so influential in later British classroom systems of the nineteenth century became firmly established.

In 1834 a Glasgow Educational Society (called the Educational Association in its first year) was formed, in parallel with the existing Infant School Society, to propagate more widely both the infant and juvenile methods. At its inaugural meeting Professor Welsh of Edinburgh University gave the Address which concerned itself chiefly with the need for

235

4.17 *David Stow's Annfield St. John's*
Juvenile School, Glasgow 1833,
  (a) ground floor plan
  (b) Ordnance Survey map
1860.

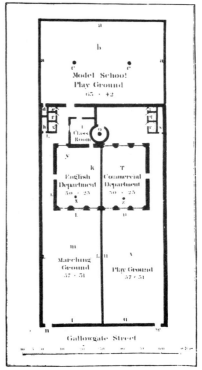

PLATE 4

PAROCHIAL JUVENILE SCHOOL
Annfield St Johns

Model School
Play Ground
65 × 42

Class
Room

English
Department
50 × 25

Commercial
Department
50 × 25

Marching
Ground
57 × 51

Play Ground
57 × 51

Gallowgate Street

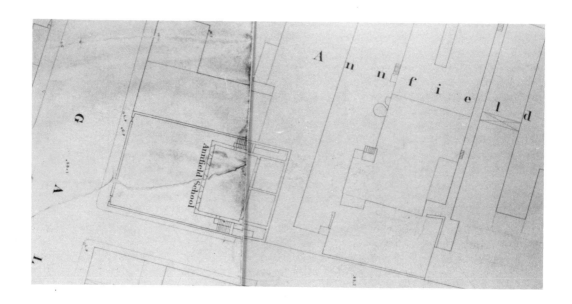

Annfield School

organised teacher training, many of the ideas being based on the Prussian methods which he had recently seen in action. From this point on the movement for professional training of teachers in Scotland gathered momentum. The Society set itself the target, in 1835, of setting up a 'Normal Seminary' (the word 'normal' being used in the Continental sense of a norm or rule being instituted to form a standard model for imitation and reproduction). Its object was to teach both 'the theory of teaching' and to give training '. . . in the practice of it'.[64] This distinction between theory and practice precedes a fundamental division around which much British higher education was built in the nineteenth century. For the training purpose, model or demonstration schools had to be included in which the teachers could learn their craft under the director's supervision. By 1835 normal training schools were already in existence in various forms in England, Scotland and on the Continent. Both the National School Society, in its school in Westminster, and the British and Foreign School Society at Borough Road were training teachers in the Bell and Lancaster systems respectively as was Wilderspin at Spitalfields and we have seen that Wood's Sessional School in Edinburgh became a training school for the Church of Scotland as early as 1826. Moreover, the Prussian training system was well known. All this is acknowledged in a Society publication of 1835, although elsewhere Stow was inclined to claim total originality for his Seminary. Its real innovation was in the formalisation of theory and practice and in the recognition that by simply assisting a master, young teachers would be incompletely prepared.

From the start it was intended to include in the Seminary a model juvenile and infant school, a commercial school for boys and a 'female school of industry'. The Committee selected Mr. Auld's St. John's, Annfield Juvenile School and Mr. and Mrs. Caughie's Saltmarket Infant School of St. Andrew's Parish, as the two which should be transferred to the Seminary, and they appointed John McCrie as Rector. In 1836 a site at the West end of Cowcaddens in Dundas Vale was acquired. David Hamilton, Glasgow's foremost classical architect of the day, was appointed as designer—but so far no details of his appointment, fees or drawings have been discovered.[65] The foundation stone was laid in November 1836 —so Hamilton must have worked at great speed and it was part-completed by 1837; but he did have a head start in the detailed specification which Stow published in the first, 1836, edition of his *Training System* (a popular and influential work which by 1853 had run to nine editions). According to Gildard[66] 'a considerable time' elapsed between the completion of the two wings, containing all the teaching accommodation of four schools, and the centre block of offices and shared accommodation. It is possible that this with its clock tower was executed by his son James Hamilton.

Hamilton had not only built, by this time, the Royal Exchange (1827) and the Exchange Square (1827-1830) but was also designer of St. John's Church, Bell Street (1819)—a Tudoresque building, now demolished— which was the church of the Parish in which several of the early model schools were established and where Stow worked closely with the minister, Doctor Thomas Chalmers. Chalmers was the leader of the Evangelical party in the Kirk and deeply involved in poor relief, education and politics. He tried to prove, in Glasgow, that the poor could be maintained by voluntary contributions, mainly from the poor themselves! He left Glasgow and, in 1832 became Moderator of the Church of Scotland. He was a staunch Tory, personal friend of Walter Scott's and defender of the property rights of the landed gentry. His influence on Stow was probably through his religious convictions rather than directly through his political allegiance.

Both Hamilton and Stow lived in Buchanan Street and it is likely that they will have been acquainted and also that Hamilton worked for the Society as an act of charity, charging no fees. In this involvement with charitable and institutional design he would have been following the examples of earlier Scottish architects—Robert Adam, Robert Reid and William Stark being the best known. In England Soane, Elmes, Wyatt and others had adopted the same practice. Such work offered designers more scope of grand manner solutions than was available in daily practice; involvement in philanthropic and charitable work was an essential link with potential private and public clients; and it may also have been motivated by a desire to find public expression for a conscience sensitive to social misery.

The Normal Seminary, which still exists virtually in its original form on the corner of New City Road and Garscube Road in Cowcaddens, is a building of three-storeys and a heating basement, with a central clock tower or 'steeple' between two wings over the entrance block. The wings enclose a court (Figure 4.19). The two main floors are tied by a shorn-down major order of pilasters of slightly Tuscan character. The front and end pavilions on the sides have arched, key-stoned, windows (Figure 4.20). The two symmetrically disposed main entrance gates (Figure 4.21) show strong neo-classical forms. Most of the building is shorn of all but essential detail; the entrance porch, however, with its four square columns, and the central tower with its four diagonal scrolls and two coupled pilasters on each face, are invested with finely executed detailing and more elaboration, characteristic of Hamilton's classical work, which achieve a focus of attention on the central axis. The tall arched windows between the pilasters have a somewhat anaemic look which does not, however, rob the building of general robustness.

The plans illustrated here are reconstructions of how the accommodation was probably arranged, and of the most likely type and location of internal fittings. On the ground floor were located the juvenile and infant schools, one in each wing, with the 'private seminary' (that is, fee-paying commercial school) and female school of industry located over them on the first floor. The central block probably contained the janitor's house and the director's offices on the ground floor; the library and a students' room on the first floor; and the art studio on the top floor. There was also a

238

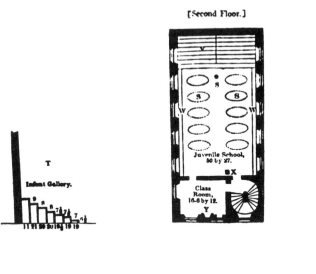

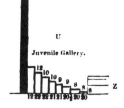

[Second Floor.]

Juvenile School, 80 by 27.

Class Room, 16-6 by 12.

Infant Gallery.

T

Juvenile Gallery.

U

Z

10 20 30 40 50 60 70 80 90 100 feet.

4.18 *David Stow's design for a typical Juvenile schoolroom and recommended sections for a Juvenile and an Infant gallery, 1836.*

museum of 'natural and artificial objects, articles of manufacture and commerce, and a few models of machinery'; but it is difficult now to determine its location in the building. Each of the two ground floor schoolrooms had its own gallery, and three adjacent galleried classrooms. The two upper schoolrooms were probably basically the same as those on the ground floor but with only two schoolrooms, as the rear end was occupied by the juvenile and infant masters' houses. Each of the four schools had its own playground. The first floor circulation allows direct communication between the wings without passing through the central block; this is achieved by means of an ingenious cantilevered wooden gallery (Figure 4.22). The heating was from a basement furnace with warm air ducts to the main apartments (Figure 4.23) and the schoolrooms had wooden columns at the centre of the span which were adjusted in the basement, over the sleeper wall supports, by means of wooden wedges (Figure 4.24)—a system identical to that used in cast iron by Strutt in his Belper North Mill in 1804 (Figure 4.25).

In the first edition of the *Training System* (1836) Stow produces not only an exact specification of the system and the curriculum, but also drawings of model schools for various sizes of city sites and various requirements. In none of these does a church appear. This represents a significant change over two years, for in 1834 he was proposing a central church between the infant and the 'English' (ie higher academic) juvenile school with a

4.19 *David Stow's Glasgow Normal Seminary, 1836; architect David Hamilton,*
   (a) reconstructed ground floor plan
   (b) reconstructed first floor plan
   (c) reconstructed second and attic floor plans.

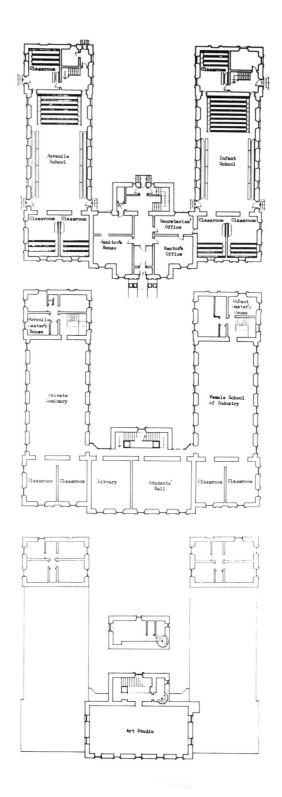

240

4.20 *Glasgow Normal Seminary*
  (a) exterior view showing nineteenth century appearance of front elevation
  (b) side elevation
  (c) aerial view
  (d) front porch.

juvenile commercial school attached, to form a 'Parochial Institution' (Figure 4.26); 'we connect the church with the schools, both to show how ground may be saved, and also, because such forms (sic) one of the most important parts of the machinery for moral training'.[67] The central church was a common feature in European hospitals, schools, prisons and asylums and, even though Stow abandoned this metaphoric-symbolic plan, the Normal Seminary and many of his model designs still maintain a central architectural feature of ecclesiastical form and within the schoolrooms it is difficult to avoid the analogy between master's desk and altar, gallery and pews.

The frontispiece of the 1836 work shows a two-storey school which in plan, is basically one wing of the Normal Seminary (Figure 4.27). 'The elevation . . . is not intended to exhibit any particular style of architecture, for it is the plainest possible'.[68] The book also includes plans for a larger version of the same with specific instructions about the connections between schoolroom, classroom and playground. Only a brief description and outline section of the galleries is given—already seen in Figure 4.18; in later editions these are much amplified. For instance, by 1845[69] the female school of industry gallery is fully described and by 1853 backed up with a view of a solitary girl on the gallery at her sewing (Figure 4.28) and by detailed sections of both infant and juvenile galleries (Figure 4.29). Even the first edition contained interior views (Figure 4.30) of both schools with the gallery in use. In one, children are shown facing the wall on fixed benches, writing. By 1845 more elaborate model schools were included

242

(Figure 4.31) and by 1853[70] there is even a Gothic version, in Sherbone (sic), Dorset, designed by R.J. Withers in 1849 (Figure 4.32). In the same text is illustrated a high building for a cramped city site—the London and City Lane Moral Training Schools (Figure 4.33). Here he recommends an open arcaded ground floor for the infant playground, two middle floors for the two schoolrooms and a flat, asphalted roof for the juvenile playground.

Stow's work had widespread influence in the middle of the century—throughout Britain and indeed further afield. His motto, taken from the Book of Proverbs—'Train a child in the way he should go and when he is old he will not depart from it'—was placed on a heraldic emblem over a scroll with the words 'The Training System' in the main entrance hall of the Seminary (Figure 4.34). Its sense is in a direct line of descent from Locke-Hartley-Priestley-Rousseau-Owen-Bentham environmental rationalism; a concept of mental development based on the mechanical analogy of the clock—which, once constructed, adjusted and wound up, proceeds to work without deviation. This belief was so strong that no detail of the environment could be left to chance—everything had a formative role in the initial character. The 'association of ideas' was an early social theory which tried to deal in a positive way with urbanisation and population density. For whilst Stow was at his most active the whole sanitary reform movement under Chadwick, the work of Engels, the early work of Dickens and the numerous Select Committees on urban affairs were highlighting the most dramatic effects of physical and social squalor and misery. Stow saw this for himself, but he believed that through early educational

4.23 *Glasgow Normal Seminary; basement warm air furnace.*

4.24 *Glasgow Normal Seminary,*
 (a) *ground floor wooden column*
 (b) *basement column supported by wooden wedges.*

4.25 *Strutt's Belper North Mill, Derbyshire, 1804; basement column supported by cast iron wedge.*

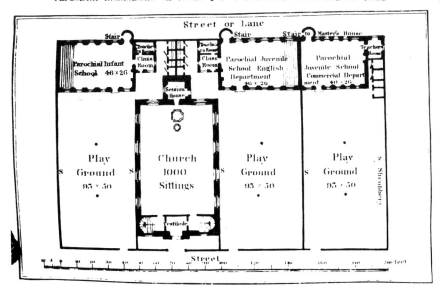

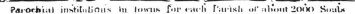

4.26 *David Stow's 'Parochial Institution', 1834: ground floor plan.*

4.27 *David Stow's Model School, 1836; ground floor—Infants; first floor—Juveniles,*
   (a) exterior sketch
   (b) ground floor plan (NB discrepancy between sketch and plan in number of windows).

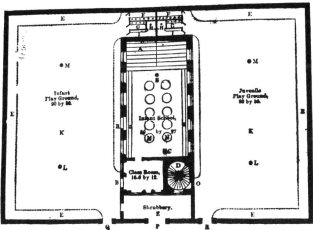

245

The small table holds scissors, wires, books, etc., and each upright post suspends work bags for two girls.
NOTE.—With or without the small tables for the girls' work, etc., this Gallery is very suitable for a Senior Department.

SECTION, GALLERY, PLATE 10.—FEMALE SCHOOL OF INDUSTRY.

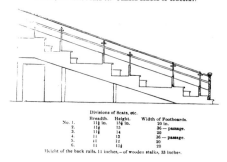

Divisions of Seats, etc.

No.	Breadth. of Seats.	Height.	Width of Footboards.
No. 1.	11½ in.	15½ in.	20 in.
2.	11½	15	36 — passage.
3.	11½	14	20
4.	11	13	36 — passage.
5.	11	12	20
6.	11	11½	20

Height of the back rails, 11 inches,—of wooden stalks, 33 inches.

No. 7.—GALLERY—INITIATORY OR INFANT DEPARTMENT.

GALLERY.—JUVENILE DEPARTMENT.

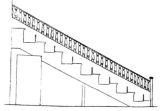

INITIATORY OR INFANT GALLERY.			JUVENILE GALLERY.		
Height of Seats.	Breadth of Seats.	Breadth of Footboard. feet on floor.	Height of Seats.	Breadth of Seats.	Breadth of Footboard. feet on floor.
Bottom.			Bottom.		
1 7 in.	9 in.	15 in.	1 9 in.	11 in.	16 in.
2 7½	9	15	2 9½	11	16
3 8	9	15	3 10	11	16
4 8½	9½	15	4 11	11	16
5 9	9½	15	5 11	11	16
6 9	10	15	6 12	11	16
7 9½	10	15	7 14	11	Backs of children supported by the wall boarded 2 feet 3
8 10	10½	15			or 2 feet 6 inches high above seat.
9 11½	11	Backs against			

wall, boarded 2 feet high above seat.

Height of the open railing, not solid board, for resting the back—Infant, 9 inches; and Juvenile, 10 inches. The open railing, 10 or 11 inches high, inclined backwards 1½ inches at the top, deducts a little from the width of the footboard or passage behind. For side half step, see Plate No. 4.
N B.—The footboard is sunk the thickness of the wood behind the small railing, by the seat before being raised by a one-inch board. If the School-hall does not admit of 8 seats for the Juvenile, or 10 for the Initiatory, the middle heights may then be deducted. For the top or bottom heights. For the working plan of the Juvenile Gallery, see Plate No. 11, also the height of seats, breadth of footboard, height of railing for backs, etc. A Gallery with fewer than seven steps does not admit of an under passage, and a narrower room than 26 feet does not admit of a passage at all. A Juvenile Gallery of six steps for a small school only 18 feet wide, without an under passage for caps, etc., according to Plate No. 11, we have seen erected for £7 7s.
Height of side railings from top of bottom seat, 2 feet 4 inches.

4.28 David Stow's 1853 design for a teaching gallery for a 'Female School of Industry'.

4.29 David Stow's 1853 designs for infant and juvenile galleries.

4.30 *David Stow's interior views of*
    (a) an Infant schoolroom
    (b) a Juvenile schoolroom.

[Interior of an Infant School.]

[Interior of a Juvenile School.]

247

4.31 *David Stow's 1845 designs for alternative Training Schools,*

    (a) elevation and ground floor plan, for the Highland Society

    (b) elevation and ground floor plan for a Village School

    (c) elevation and ground floor plan for a 'Small Training School' with Master's house

    (d) alternative ground and first floor plans for (c) when site is limited.

NOTE.—These Schools do not cost much more than Plates No. I. and II. ; but they occupy a larger space of ground. This Plan might be a good platform for a small Normal Training Seminary, the upper floor to be used as Class Rooms for the Students—the centre forming a hall. The Senior or advanced department has a play-ground behind the buildings. Wherever front ground can be had, this will be found an imposing and very economical plan. The building is of stone. The belfry is of wood, and only cost between £5 and £6.

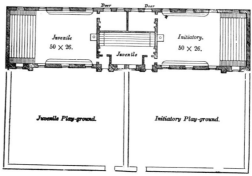

GROUND PLAN OF PLATE No. 4.

a Junior Division, 20 by 28. **The Play-Ground,** in two divisions, may be in front or back of building. *b* Advanced Division, 46 by 28. *c* Juvenile Class-Room. *d* Infant Department, 46 by 28. *e* Infant Class-Rooms, 14 by 12. *Upper Floor*—**Master's Houses and School of Industry.** The Water-Closets are placed at each end of the building.

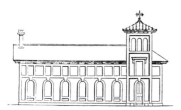

No. 11.—Village Training School, with Master's house above and small School of Industry, or Infant's below and Juvenile above.—Play-Ground enclosed in front.

The ground plan of the two rooms (covered and uncovered) is the chief point to be attended to. Every person will of course please his own tastes to the building—cottage, Grecian style, &c.

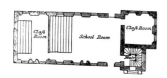

Ground Plan of Juvenile Training School.
Nos. 2, 4, 5, and 6, are more convenient than this.

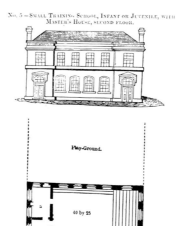

No. 5.—SMALL TRAINING SCHOOL, INFANT OR JUVENILE, WITH MASTER'S HOUSE, SECOND FLOOR.

A Class-room, 16-6 by 12.
This is understood to be on the line of a street, or placed only a few feet backwards.

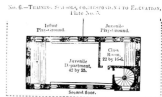

No. 6.—TRAINING SCHOOLS, CORRESPONDENT TO ELEVATION, Plate No. 5.

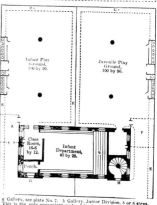

a Gallery, see plate No. 7. *b* Gallery, Junior Division, 5 or 6 steps. This is the only convenient mode of having two Training Schools for 120 or 150 children each, when the width of the ground does not permit the erection of the building as in plate Nos. 2 and 3. Nos. 2 and 4 are decidedly the preferable plans for two Schools, with play-ground on either side.

248

formation this population density could become something creative, moral and productive. It could even surpass the dream of rural innocence: 'However highly in the moral scale, therefore, agriculturalists may be elevated, the inhabitants of a large town may be raised still higher'.[71] The production model would achieve this: regularity, order and surveillance, classification—'. . . the children must be classified, both in regard to their ages and attainments'—and organised work processes—'. . . education is pursued with more efficiency when there is a proper subdivision of labour, on the part of the teachers, and of classification in regard to the ages of the scholars'. The product would not only be docile, orderly and decent but also highly productive: the curriculum '. . . ought to have a useful solid tendency, such as will fit them (the children) to become good servants— good mechanics—good tradesmen—good fathers—good mothers, and respectable citizens. The intellectually cultivated christian mechanic is the best safeguard of our nation, and his moral worth is the very salt and leaven of civil society '. . . whilst his female counterpart is being prepared for the role of 'Frugal housewife, attentive sister or help to an aged parent'.

With the 1843 Disruption in the Church of Scotland Stow joined the Free Church, together with his old friend Doctor Chalmers and four hundred and seventy ministers of the Church of Scotland. He was forced to leave the Normal Seminary and moved into a new institution and building a short distance away—the Free Normal Seminary (Figure 4.35) opened in 1845, which may have been the work of Charles Wilson. Education and learning now carried a more popular, romantic image, in the form of turrets, battlements and Tudor windows, thus making the link with a national rather than a remote, classical culture.

The tiny Government grant made to school building in 1833 was the start of more serious involvement in national education. The Parliamentary proposals for setting up a national scheme for teacher training, in which Brougham took a prominent part, foundered in 1838, chiefly due to entrenched opposition from both Established Church and Nonconformists. But in 1839 a Select Committee of the Privy Council *was* set up, though Church opposition grew even more vehement. The Committee's most enlightened act was to appoint Dr. Kay (later Kay-Shuttleworth) as its first secretary. Kay was a Manchester physician who had firsthand experience of cholera during the 1832 epidemic. This convinced him that housing, sanitation and education were the real answers to combat urban squalor and disease. In the same year as the epidemic he published a major work on working class living conditions in Manchester[74] which, in detail of observation and acuteness of comment, equals Engels' work of 1845.

Under the Poor Law Reform Act of 1834 a minimum of three hours' instruction a day for children in workhouses was prescribed. Kay was appointed Assistant Poor Law Commissioner in East Anglia in 1835, and in London in 1838. He was then, and later, particularly committed to improving the education of pauper children and travelled widely in Britain and on the Continent to study the most modern methods. He was increasingly disillusioned with the monitorial system and impressed with what he saw in Scotland, especially the work of Wood in Edinburgh and Stow in Glasgow (although the latter made limited use of monitors). When, after his London appointment, he started experiments in the famous Norwood workhouse school, he imported Alexander Wilson as headmaster from Dalkeith where he was teaching, after being trained by Wood. It was the fame of this establishment, at home and abroad, which made him a strong contender for the post of secretary to the new Committee. It is worth noting that it was taken for granted that the most relevant experience for public *educational* policy was seen as the Poor Law, the workhouse and urban disease. In 1840 Kay opened a teacher training college in Battersea on his own initiative which, later became the first of a number of Church of England training colleges—there were twenty-two by 1845.

The Committee of Council published an immensely important document in 1840, being its Minutes from 1839-40 with *Appendices and Plans of Schoolhouses*.[75] In the explanation of the numerous plans for schools varying in size from one for thirty to one for four hundred and fifty children, the Committee makes a strong bid for plans designed for the 'simultaneous' system which Kay so admired in Scotland. In order to nip criticism in the bud from both the religious groups dedicated to the monitorial (or 'mutual instruction') systems, he argues for a 'mixed method' in which both class and monitorial groups can be used for the juvenile department. The plans illustrate a number of fixed benches and desks arranged on stepped platforms (a development of the gallery but coupled to the Lancasterian precedent) and one set of parallel desks for each class, the total number of classes varying from two to eight. For the infants the plan is basically Stow's. However, to undermine criticism even further, the Minutes illustrate, for each plan, alternative layouts based on both Bell and Lancaster modes of teaching. Figure 4.36 is the design for a medium sized school for eighty children, without an infants' department; Figure 4.37 for a school of three hundred juveniles and one hundred and fifty infants. The Minutes also illustrate the designs for an enormous Normal School and Orphan House for three hundred juveniles and one hundred and fifty infants which included residential accommodation for the children, staff and for about eighty pupil teachers. The chapel and main lecture auditorium are on the central axis.

Kay was still active in the same directions with the Poor Law Commissioners, to whom he submitted an illustrated report in 1839 on the design of workhouse schools, which the Commissioners published in their *Fifth Annual Report* (1839). One design is for eight hundred (!) people, adults and children, including a school for the latter (Figure 4.38). The chapel and dining hall are on the central axis, there is an old persons' wing, a wing for idiots and various workshops. Only the previous year, in their Fourth Annual Report (1838) the Commissioners had produced similar designs (by the architect Sampson Kempthorne of London) and

4.32 *Stow school in Sherbone (sic, Sherborne?) Dorset, 1849; architect R.J. Withers, elevation and ground floor plan.*

No. 12.

Initiatory Play-Ground.
For Infants—
120 by 60.

WEST ELEVATION.

Juvenile Play-Ground.
Boys and Girls—
120 by 60.

SOUTH ELEVATION.

No. 12.—BACK GROUND.

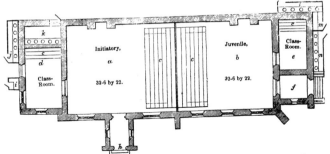

This Elevation was drawn by R. J. Withers, Esq., Sherbone, architect, and executed at Sherbone, Dorset, in 1849, for small British Schools. We have retained the same proportions of the building, but altered the arrangements of the ground plan to suit the Training System, with galleries, class-rooms, etc. They will each accommodate 80 scholars.

We would prefer that the 'South Elevation' should be in front, as in Plates Nos. 1 and 2, *having play-grounds on either side*, but we give the Elevation as executed, to show how easily ordinary schools may be converted into training ones.

Our readers will also find several very tasty Elevations in the publications of the Lords' Committee of Council—easily convertible into Moral Training Schools.

a Initiatory Training School. *b* Juvenile Training School. *c* Galleries. *d* Initiatory Class-room. *e* Juvenile Class-room. *f* Entrance to Juvenile Department. *h* Entrance to Initiatory Department. *i* Retiring place for Boys. *j* Water-Closet for Boys—Infants. *k* Do. for Girls—Infants. *l* Do. for Girls—Juvenile. *m* Retiring place for Boys. *n* Water-Closet for Girls.

Cost of building, exclusive of the site, £550.

N.B.—A square pannelled ceiling is found cooler in summer, and warmer in winter, than hanging ones as this is. The pannelling of a ceiling tends to prevent an echo.

Two Circular Swings may be placed in each play-ground, also gymnastic posts. Flower borders, 3 to 4 feet broad, on at least two sides of the ground. The division of the two play-grounds may be boarded 5 feet high, and planted with evergreens, etc.

251

4.33 *David Stow's design for the London and City Moral Training Schools, 1853, elevation, ground, first ('ground'?) floor and roof plans.*

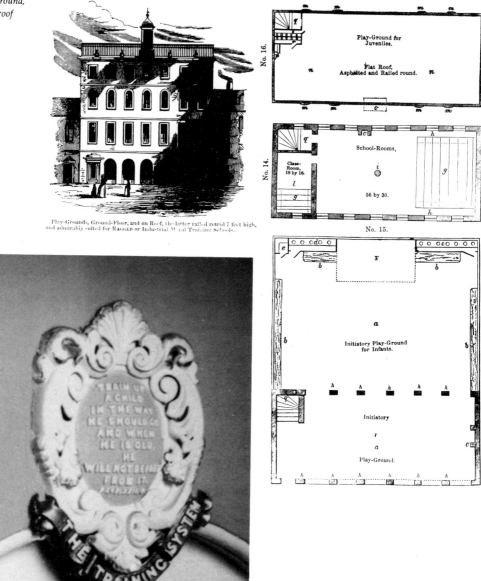

No. 13.—LONDON AND CITY LANE MORAL TRAINING SCHOOLS,
ON A LINE WITH THE STREET OR LANE, OR RECEDING 5 OR 6 FEET BACKWARDS.

No. 16.

Play-Ground for Juveniles.

Flat Roof, Asphalted and Railed round.

No. 14.

Class-Room, 18 by 16.

School-Rooms,

56 by 30.

No. 15.

Initiatory Play-Ground for Infants.

Initiatory

Play-Ground.

Play-Grounds, Ground-Floor, and on Roof, the latter railed round 7 feet high, and admirably suited for RAGGED or Industrial Moral Training Schools.

4.34 *Motto of the Training System on heraldic emblem in entrance hall of the Glasgow Normal Seminary.*

252

4.37 *Design for a school for three hundred juveniles and one hundred and fifty infants, 1839-40; Committee of Council on Education.*

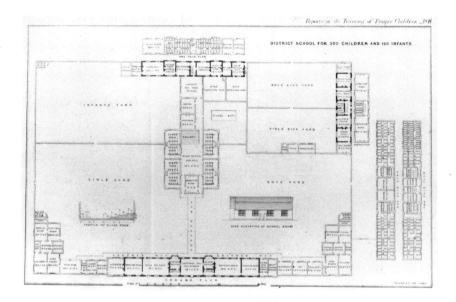

4.38 *Poor Law Commissioners' proposal for a workhouse school, 1839,*
(a) isometric
(b) ground floor plan.

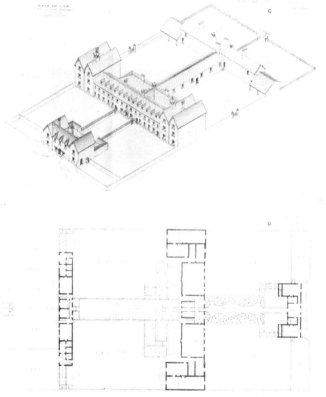

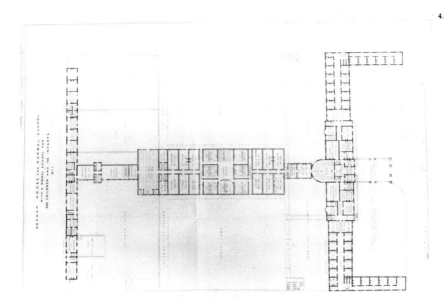

4.39 *Poor Law Commissioners'
proposal for an 'Orphan House
and Normal School' (workhouse)
for four hundred and fifty
children, 1841.*

Kay is critically but positively responding to those schemes. In 1841 the Commissioners prepared a special report on the *Training of Pauper Children* and their model school for three hundred juveniles and one hundred and fifty infants is, once again, an amalgam of the galleried and classroom systems which had been developing on a smaller scale for over forty years (Figure 4.39).

These industrial and workhouse schools result from the acceptance by the State of full legal and financial responsibility for institutions which had hitherto been the province of a range of religious and philanthropic bodies. Thus the close relationship between religion and ideology on the one hand and social doctrine on the other was carried over into official policy which has survived till today with little alteration in its fundamental structure as is reflected, for instance, in the 'approved' curriculum.

The buildings and institutions became larger and more comprehensive, catering for all ages from infants to the aged in all aspects of life—religion, work, education and leisure. The links between poverty, morality, disease and lunacy were not only accepted as part of the social order, but scientific and clinical claims were being made for social causality in such deviancy. Insanity was thought to be class-related and due to lack of education: 'The moral causes of insanity will naturally affect the rich and educated differently to the poor and uneducated . . . The lower orders, who ought more generally to be exempt from the concomitant of wealth and indolence, that is disease, unhappily provoke it by their excesses'.[76] Thus the denial of the work ethic by the rich through 'indolence' and the poor through thriftlessness ('excesses') are both moral choices and therefore to be condemned.

These total institutions were therefore centred on work. There were two kinds of products from them: objects, which could be sold to support the enterprise, and people, who could be sold on the labour market. The close cohesion and hierarchical order among both inmates and staff, and the centralisation of control, is modelled on the central power source of the factory or mill, the fixed relationship between the parts of the machine and the role-specialisation of the various grades of workers. Appeal to the notion of a huge 'family' or 'community' gave this machine a human face in its external image and was a 'moral' instrument for the maintenance of internal order. Economy of scale, achieved through the vast scale of operation, was equivalent to mass-production and argued in the Town Halls on a cost-benefit basis. The educational machine had now been extended to a microcosm of society— the fragmented sections of which are coerced into a productive unity.

REFERENCES

1. Smout, T.C., *A History of the Scottish People, 1560-1830,* Glasgow, 1979, p. 7.

2. Ibid.

3. Armytage, W.H.G., *Four Hundred Years of English Education,* Cambridge, 1964, p. 42. I have used his work as a secondary reference for some of my seventeenth century examples.

4. Locke, John, *Essay Concerning Human Understanding,* first edition, London, 1689-1690, Woozley, A.D., Ed., London, 1964, book 2, chapter 1, section 2, p. 89.

5. Scotland, James, *The History of Scottish Education,* London, 1969, Vol. 1, p. 102.

6. ibid., p. 103.

7. ibid., pp. 101-103.

8. Bernard, Thomas, Preface to *Of the Education of the Poor;* etc., London, 1809.

9. ibid., p. 260.

10. ibid., p. 96.

11. ibid., p. 64.

12. ibid., pp. 193-194.

13. Simon, Brian, *Studies in the History of Education 1780-1870,* London, 1964, p. 45.

14. Bentham, Jeremy, *Chrestomathia,* London, 1817. Also Burston, W.H., *James Mill on Philosophy and Education,* London, 1973, pp. 69-72.

15. Bentham, Jeremy, *Proposals for Establishing in the Metropolis a Day School;* etc., London, 1816. Pamphlet in Place Collection, British Library, Vol. 60.

16. Evans, Robin, Bentham's Panopticon; an Incident in the Social History of Architecture, *Architectural Association Quarterly,* 3,2, April/July 1971, pp. 34 and 37.

17. Cockburn, Henry, *Memorials of His Time,* Edinburgh, 1856, pp. 271–272.

18. ibid., p. 240.

19. Cleland, J., *Annals of Glasgow,* 2 Vols., Glasgow, 1816, Vol. 1, p. 258.

20. *Edinburgh Review,* 1807, p. 61 et seq.

21. Bell, A., *The Madras School, or Elements of Tradition,* London, 1818.

22. Bernard, op. cit., pp. 35–36.

23. Coleridge, Samuel Taylor, *Lay Sermons,* in *Collected Works of S.T. Coleridge,* White, R.J., Ed., London, 1972, p. 41; and *Notebooks,* Cockburn, K., Ed., London, 1973, paras 4181–4182.

24. Bell, A., *Instruction for Conducting a School etc.,* 2nd edition, London, 1809, pp. 9–10.

25. Bell, A., *Manual of Public and Private Education etc.,* London, 1827, p. 20.

26. Owen, Robert Dale, *Threading My Way, Twenty-seven Years Autobiography,* 1874, p. 77.

27. Owen, Robert Dale, *An Outline of the System of Education at New Lanark,* Glasgow, 1824, p. 29.

28. Bruegmann, Robert, Central Heating and Forced Ventilation: Origins and Effects on Architectural Design, *Journal of the Society of Architectural Historians,* XXXVII, 3 October 1978, pp. 144–145.

29. Owen, Robert, *A New View of Society,* 1816, in Silver, Harold, *Robert Owen on Education,* Cambridge, 1969, Fourth Essay, p. 134.

30. Owen, Robert, *Life of Robert Owen,* 1857, in Silver, op. cit., p. 64.

31. ibid., p. 65.

32. Rusk, R.R., *The Training of Teachers in Scotland,* Edinburgh, 1928, p. 25.

33. McCann, P., Popular Education, Socialization and Social Control: Spitalfields 1812–1824, in McCann P., Ed., *Popular Education and Socialization in the Nineteenth Century,* London, 1977, p. 23.

34. Wilderspin, S., *Early Discipline Illustrated; or the Infant System Progressing and Successful,* London, 1832, p. 5.

35. Wilderspin, S., *On the Importance of Educating the Infant Children of the Poor*, London, 1823, pp. 18–19.

36. Stow, David, *The Training System,* etc., Glasgow, 1st edition, 1836, p. 7.

37. Wood, J., *Account of the Edinburgh Sessional School,* 1st edition, Edinburgh, 1828 and later editions, 1829, 1830 and 1833.

38. Scotland, op. cit. Vol. 1, p. 280.

39. *General Assembly of the Church of Scotland, Education Committee Report,* 1851.

40. *First Report of the Edinburgh Infant School Society,* Edinburgh, 1832.

41. Stow, op. cit., p. 57.

42. Rusk, op. cit.

43. Stow, op. cit., p. 7.

44. Scotland, op. cit., Vol. 1.

45. Stow, op. cit., p. 2.

46. Stow, David, *National Education; Supplement to Moral Training and the Training System* etc., Glasgow, 1839, p. 22.

47. Stow, *The Training System* (1836), op. cit., p. 5.

48. ibid., p. 6.

49. Stow, David, *Moral Training* etc., Glasgow, 2nd edition, 1834, p. 35. No first edition is known although Stow claims in *National Education,* p. 8, that it was published in 1831–2.

50. ibid., p. 35.

51. ibid., p. 67.

52. Owen, Robert, *Report to the County of Lanark of a Plan for Relieving Public Distress* etc., Glasgow, 1821, Prospectus, p. 1.

53. ibid., p. 65.

54. ibid., p. 66.

55. Stow, *The Training System,* (1836), op.cit., p. 61.

56. Stow, *National Education,* op.cit., p. 18.

57. Stow, *The Training System,* (1836), op.cit., p. 136.

58. Stow, David, reported in *History and Principles of Stow's Training System;* etc., Glasgow, 1852, p. 100.

59. Stow, *The Training System,* (1836), op.cit., p. 137.

60. Stow, *Moral Training,* op.cit.

61. Stow, *The Training System,* (1836), op.cit., p. 122.

62. ibid., p. 69.

63. ibid., p. 69.

64. ibid., p. 61.

65. Gildard, Thomas, 'An Old Glasgow Architect on Some Older Ones', paper read to Architectural Section of the Philosophical society of Glasgow, 13th December 1894, in *Proceedings of the Philosophical Society of Glasgow,* Vol. XXVI, 1894–95, Section VIII, pp. 97–127. Also Stow, *The Training System* (1836), p. 62, footnote.

66. ibid., p. 103.

67. Stow, *Moral Training,* op.cit., p. 287.

68. Stow, *National Education,* op.cit., p. 27.

69. Stow, *The Training System,* 6th edition, Glasgow, 1845.

70. Stow, *The Training System,* 9th edition, Glasgow, 1853.

71. Stow, *Moral Training,* op. cit., p. 286.

72. Stow, *The Training System,* (1836), op.cit., pp. 172–3.

73. Stow, *The Training System,* (1836), op.cit., pp. 175–6.

74. Kay, James Phillips, *The Moral and Physical Condition of the Working Classes Employed in the Cotton Manufacture in Manchester,* London, 1832.

75. *Minutes of Committee of Council on Education; with Appendices and Plans of School-Houses 1839–40,* London, 1840.

76. Skultans, Vieda, *Madness and Morals; Ideas on Insanity in the Nineteenth Century,* London, 1975, pp. 37–38. Extract from Burrows, G.M., *Commentaries on Insanity,* London, 1828, pp. 9–10 and 18–20.

Versions of Scottish Pastoral: the Literati and the Tradition 1780–1830

Andrew Noble

> . . . that tendency to domesticate the issue which has always been the great curse of Scottish life and letters.
>
> *Hugh MacDiarmid*

In his seminal *The Country and the City* Raymond Williams, by analysis of the complex interconnections of English literature and social history, has rendered a salutary account of the distorting manner in which certain literary modes have been employed in representing rural life both in terms of its own nature and for the purpose of making distinct, false contrast between rural and urban modes of experience. Crucial in Williams's treatment of his theme is that period of particularly rapid transition in the latter part of the eighteenth century and early nineteenth century which saw the final disintegration of the remnants of feudal order and the ascendancy of the new, energetic values of agrarian capitalism. Williams's work represents with clarity and conviction the manner in which traditional pastoral form was manipulated by a wide range of writers at the behest of commercial power to disguise in this period the acquisitive politics and harsh economic facts of agricultural transition and 'improvement'. He defines this literary activity thus:

> 'Pastoral' means, we are told, the simple manner in which general truths are embodied or implied; even a modern proletarian industrial novel can be pastoral in this sense! But while as a critical procedure for understanding, say, Spenser, this is fair enough, its extension is absurd, and the absurdity has a point, there has been an effective and voluntary congealment at the point of significant historical transition, from a feudal to a bourgeois world.
>
> . . . For the pastoral of the courts and of the aristocratic houses was not, as it came through, the really significant development. Isolated in time and in status, its modes and realities are quite understood. What is much more significant is the internal transformation of just this artificial mode in the direction and in the interest of a new kind of society: that of a developing agrarian capitalism. Neo-pastoral as a court entertainment is one thing, neo-pastoral in its new location, the country-house and its estate, is quite another.[1]

Correctly emphasising the innovative importance of the English aspects of this experience, Williams pays some attention to Anglo-Scottish writing in this period but not to the Scottish experience in itself. Thus he detects in James Thomson a highly influential British figure in creating the post-Spenserian, false paradigms of rural experience which, at best, disguised the true nature of things and, at worst, grossly flattered established power. The following essay is, consequently, an attempt to analyse and explore the degree of discrepancy between the pastoral illusion and rural reality as it existed in Scottish writing about the Scottish situation. A particular value in such a task arises from the fact that, as we shall see, Scottish historians still tend to read rather naively many of the literary texts purporting to deal with this crucial period in Scottish history when, if not in scale then in intensity, Scotland's rate of change matched that of England. Such a reading of the literature is also intended to shed some helpful light on the vexed and complex question regarding the comparative social conditions existing in the two countries at this period. At the least, it should qualify the fairly widely held belief that the Scottish experience of change was significantly less painful.[2]

The corollary to Williams's discussion of false pastoralism as a mode of dealing with rural life is that a deceitful and not merely a simplistic contrast is created regarding the superiority, physical and moral, of rural to urban life. With the appearance of the industrial city, the traditional village becomes enormously attractive. Such a corollary also holds good in Scottish writing. Given that by far the most significant demographic fact in late eighteenth century Scotland was urbanisation accompanied in the West by early industrialisation, the absence of contemporary tales of its two cities, Edinburgh and Glasgow, is quite remarkable. Cockburn, as we shall see, was characteristic in his sentimental nostalgia for the Old Town and his dislike of what he considered was the sparse, ascetic architecture of the New where he lived his practical day-to-day life. His solution was to go as often as possible to his suburban Gothic retreat, Bonaly, where suitably attired he played at farm labour and fantasised that in *his* kingdom, at least, the continuity of the national life maintained itself. Scott's Abbotsford represents a more extravagant version of the same strategy. The contemporary Scottish city does not exist in Scott's novels. When, as he rarely does, he attempts to convey the dramatic change from agrarian to urban life in Scotland that was going on all around him (a change which caused him a level of anxiety which he dreamed of releasing in violence) Scott's fictional descriptions were kept safely distanced by the employment of melioristic generalisation. The following passage from *Rob Roy*, is most characteristic of his employment of an Augustan tone in an inappropriate historical context:

> It is always with unwillingness that the Highlander quits his desert and at this early period it was like tearing a pine from its rock to plant him elsewhere. Yet even then the mountain glens were ever-peopled, although thinned occasionally by famine or by the sword, and many of their inhabitants strayed down to Glasgow . . . there formed settlements . . . there sought and found employment, although different, indeed, from that of their native hills. This supply of a hardy and useful population was of consequence to the prosperity of the place, furnished the means of carrying on the few manufactures which the town already boasted, and laid the foundation of its future prosperity.[3]

Rob Roy is as close to urban commerce as Scott allowed his fiction to come. The great fictional exponent of the Whig interpretation of history, Scott desired to verify the theories of Hume and Smith which had predicted that a new economic order entailed a new harmonious psychological and social order. Thus, unlike the great Romantic writers of his age, he evaded contemporary social detail such as means of production, education and living conditions because of the degree of suffering and squalor which they presented as evidence contradictory to these progressive theories. In life as opposed to art he was, however, deeply anxious not about the condition of the Scottish common people but about their potential to threaten the stability of the state. As I have suggested elsewhere, Scott's fiction is not concerned with Jacobitism but Jacobinism.[4] His frequently violent personal fantasies led him to consider that a Highland host should be let loose among the restless Lowland working class at the times of the Radical troubles in 1819. At the time of the 'battle' of Bonnymuir he envisaged himself, mounted and sabre equipped, riding down what in actuality was to prove pathetically few Radicals. Like the rest of the Edinburgh literati, Scott's lack of literary treatment of urbanisation and industrialisation did not stem from ignorance but from a desire to create a literary *cordon sanitaire* round these areas. Density of population, especially in a disaffected and unemployed condition, nurtured revolutionary potential.

In such rare moments as literary good taste allowed a member of the Edinburgh literati to report conditions of urban poverty, his attitude was hardly Orwellian. In the *Noctes Ambrosianae* created with such extraordinary skill by Professor John Wilson, 'Christopher North', in the second and third decades of the nineteenth century, those occasions when the slums of Edinburgh and Glasgow are recorded, are done with a Scotch rhetoric created from equal portions of Calvinistic sermonising and Gothic sensibility. These are the places of the rightfully condemned; the fallen poor who will menace the virtuous and even the State. Also, as in this discussion describing the horrors of the Old Town, they stand as eloquent testimony to the opposed allegedly pure virtues of Scottish rural life— innocence as compared to experience.

> Thank God, Mr North, the fresh airs o'heaven blow through your shepherd's hut, and purify it frae a'pollution. Things hae really come to a queer pass when towns' bodies, leevin in shops and cellars, and garrets and common stairs, and lanes and streets that, wi' a' their fine gas lamp-posts, are pestilential wi' filth and foulzie; and infested wi' lean, mangy dowgs, ruggin out stinkin banes frae the sewers; and wi' auld wives, like broken-backed witches, that are little mair than bundles o' movin rags, clautin among the bakiefu's o' ashes; and wi' squads o' routin or spewin bullies o' chiels, staggerin hame frae tripe-soopers, to the disturbance o' the flaes in their yellow-tinged-lookin blankets; and wi' anes, and twas, and threes, o' what's far waur than a' these, great lang-legged, tawdry, and tawpy limmers, standin at closes, wi' mouths red wi' paint, and stinkin o' gin like the bungs o' speerit-casks, when the speerit has been years in the wudd; while far and wide over the city (I'm speakin o' the Auld Town) you hear a hellish howl o' thieves and prostitutes carousin on red herrings and distillery-whuskey, deep down in dungeons aneath the verra stanes o' the street; and faint far-aff echoes o' fechts wi' watchmen, and cries o' "murder, murder—fire, fire" drowned in the fiercer hubbub o' curses, ending in shouts o' deevilish

lauchter—I say—What was I gaun to say, sir? something about the peace and pleasantness o' Mount Benger, was't no? and o' the harmless life and conversation o' us shepherds amang the braes, and within the murmurs o' the sheep-washing Yarrow.

North. I hope it was so—for that dark picture needs relief.

Shepherd. An it shall hae relief. Wad it no be relief to rise, at Mount Benger, just a wee bit dim, dewy half-hour afore the sun; and when a' the household were yet asleep in the heaven o' morning dreams, to dauner awa down to the soun' o' the waterfa', that ye skently see glimmerin in the uncertain twilight?

North. And so leap in upon the Naiad before she has braided her tresses, or arranged the cerulean folds of her flowing cymar.

Shepherd. Wad it no be relief to see green glittering Nature becoming distincter and distincter, far and wide over the vale and braes, and hills and mountains, till ere you can finish the unpremeditated prayer that God's beautiful creation has breathed into your heart—Earth and Heaven are in broad daylight, and, solemn thocht! anither morning is added to the span of man's mortal years?

Tickler. "O rus!"

Shepherd. A' the larks are awa up wi' their sangs to heaven—a' the linties are low down in the broom wi' theirs—sic is the variety o' instinct amang the bonny creturs that live in nests! And the trouts are loupin in the water, and the lambs are running races on the braes, and gin I were there to see, perhaps the wild swan is amang the water-lilies of St Mary's Loch, or say rather the Loch o' the Lowes, for that is a lonelier water, and farther up amang the shadows o' the hills.

North. A morning landscape, by Claude Lorraine!

Shepherd. Returnin back hame, the wife and weans are a' at the door,—and isna my wee Jamie a fine fallow, wi' his licht-blue cunnin een, and that bashfu' lovin lauch, when he sees his father—and that saft and low forest voice, that gars me, every time I see the blessed face o' him, thank God for his goodness, and my heart overflow wi' what is surely happiness, if there be sic a thing as happiness on this inexplicable earth?[5]

While Wilson could happily never wholly suppress his talent for irony and parody, this malicious contrast between country and town was incessantly employed in Edinburgh-inspired Scottish writing from the latter part of the eighteenth century. It allowed the Scottish middle and upper classes to evade the social realities of the poor and, even more disturbingly, enforce dogmatic political attitudes. In this false antithesis, what Williams has cogently described as a policy 'to promote superficial comparisons and to prevent real ones', the image of country life was even more contrived and artificial than the horrors of the Glasgow and Edinburgh slums were exaggerated.[6] Perhaps the most significant proof of this is the ferocity with which Edinburgh's literary critics, in particular Jeffrey in *The Edinburgh Review*, assaulted the new English Romantic poetry (especially that of Wordsworth) which sought to describe the conditions of deprivation and deracination among the host of rural poor. T.S. Eliot's wise remark concerning Wordsworth—'it is Wordsworth's social interest that inspires the novelty of form in verse, and backs up his explicit remarks upon poetic diction; and it is really this social interest which (consciously or not) the fuss was all about'[7]—is nowhere more true than in the context of early nineteenth century Edinburgh.

Wordsworth's poetry displayed the personal and social dissolution caused by agrarian crisis: the havoc which was wreaked on people when they are both uprooted and left without hope; the dark, deliberately obscured face of progress and improvement. Not simply the common people but the suffering of the common people is a theme for him of the highest seriousness. As Geoffrey Hartman has cogently remarked:

> It was not, as recent scholarship has shown, Wordsworth's humble subject matter that caused the trouble. The magazines of the time (equivalents of our *Ladies' Home Journal* and *Saturday Evening Post*) were full of Christian sentiment about Crazy Kate or the fate of the common soldier or the starving robin. They were true of their age, the age of sensibility, and reflected the taste of a growing class of bourgeois readers. What mostly scandalised the latter were Wordsworth's strange moods of exaltation: the way he inflated a trite or private happening as if it contained a truth never before perceived. He sinned against that iron clad law of literary and social decorum which limited the poet's role to putting before his public "What e'er was thought, but ne'er so well express'd." For, in Wordsworth, the novelty seemed to lie in the quality of the thought rather than the quality of the expression. The expression, indeed, was obviously flat; and whereas in the ordinary run of magazine verse the manner helped to raise the matter, here was a poet who overtly disdained the yeasty virtue of style.[8]

To demonstrate Wordsworth's poetry of dissent, to reveal the general lack of such poetry in Scotland in that age, and to show what the Scots grew so irate over, the following lines from *The Excursion* are most apposite:

> You may remember, now some ten years gone,
> Two blighting seasons when the fields were left
> With half a harvest. It pleased heaven to add
> A worse affliction in the plague of war,
> A happy land was stricken to the heart,
> 'Twas a sad time of sorrow and distress.
> A wanderer among the cottages,
> I with my pack of winter raiment saw
> The hardships of that season. Many rich
> Sunk down as in a dream among the poor,
> And of the poor did many cease to be,
> And their place knew them not. Meanwhile, abridged
> Of daily comforts, gladly reconciled
> To numerous self-denials, Margaret
> Went struggling on through those calamitous years
> With cheerful hope. But ere the second autumn
> A fever seized her husband. In disease
> He lingered long, and when his strength returned
> He found the little he had stored to meet
> Was all consumed. As I have said, 'twas now
> A time of trouble: shoals of artisans
> Were from their daily labor turned away
> To hang for bread on parish charity,
> They and their wives and children, happier far

Could they have lived as do the little birds
That peck along the hedge-rows, or the Kite
That makes her dwelling on the mountain rocks![9]

It is not without irony that Wordsworth should have made the narrator of this part of *The Excursion* a Scottish pedlar, albeit one working in the Lake District, because it was this poem that brought about Jeffrey's most infamous denunciation of the English poet. One of the most significant obsessions of Scottish critical thought in the early nineteenth century as it was expressed through the cosmopolitan organs of *The Edinburgh Review* and *Blackwood's Magazine* was with what they conceived of as Wordsworth's aesthetic irregularities and malpractices in attempting to create a poetry representative of contemporary common life. In this convoluted quarrel the denunciation of any degree of comparability between Burns and Wordsworth was a fact of central importance. Jeffrey began the process with a relatively moderate and Whiggish, if misleading, account of this in 1808 but by 1817 the attack had reached the intense, personalised pitch so beloved of Blackwood's Tories. Wordsworth is described thus:

> . . . A man who, if it be true that he possesses poetical genius, most certainly possesses no other quality in common with Robert Burns: a retired, pensive, egotistical *collector of stamps* . . . one that seems to be completely overflowing with envy, malignity, and a thousand bad passions . . . a melancholy, sighing, half-parson sort of gentleman, who lives in a small circle of old maids and sonneteers, and drinks tea now and then with the solemn laureate.[10]

Suspect though such Scottish review criticism is concerning Wordsworth, however, one of its themes demands consideration as possibly pertaining to more than national and personal prejudice. It was constantly reiterated by the Scottish reviewers that Wordsworth knew nothing of Burns since he knew nothing of Scotland. From this they deduced that Wordsworth's poetry of rural distress was not applicable to Scotland since the Scottish peasantry were not only more loyal than their English counterparts but were not exposed to the degree of agrarian disruption prevailing in the South. Consequently Scottish literature did not need to evolve new forms or, worse, debase poetry to convey such harsh realities. Revealingly the Scotch reviewers, both Whig and Tory, saw themselves as custodians of an English literary tradition of fixed, normative values where rules of literary genre were also rules of social class.

This Edinburgh antipathy to the new English poetry should also serve warning of the often too easy acceptance that after the Union the intrusion of English language and literary forms into Scotland was the essential cause of the downfall of the Scottish literary tradition. The truth is much more complex. What literate Scotland did was to import certain genteel, sentimental English modes, in themselves heavily influenced by French neo-classicism, which were not characteristic of the mainstream of the great English tradition. When they came to deal with the great English writers the literati either sentimentalised or suppressed them. Swift suffered the latter and Shakespeare suffered both these indignities.[11] The condition that Louis Bredvold describes as evolving in eighteenth century English literature was to prove true in even more damaging respects in upper-class Scottish writing. Bredvold believes that the tough, masculine style of the great English writers of the earlier part of that century, with their satirical, irreverent, dissenting attitudes, gave way to a sentimental conformity:

> In this disillusionment as in their politics, the satirists were old-fashioned. When they are viewed against the setting of the history of literature and thought of the whole eighteenth century, they appear as survivors of a dying era. Even as they were at work, they were challenged by what seemed a more modern spirit, a more sympathetic and comforting way of looking at human nature. The 'softness of the heart' Steele intimated in his preface to *The Conscious Lovers* (1723), is a greater merit than the 'hardness of the head'. In the early years of the century this spirit flourished in Whig literary circles, very obvious in Steele, more subtly pervasive in Addison. As the century progressed it gradually prevailed everywhere; in spite of the declared opposition of Fielding and Johnson and Burke, the 'new sensibility' dominated in poetry, drama and fiction. The same change was going on in France and the rest of Europe. La Rochefoucauld was replaced by Vauvernargues; Rousseau attacked Molière and drenched Europe in sentiment.[12]

Because of Edinburgh, the partial vacuum in Scotland resulting from the Union and the accident of rugged Highland landscape and a 'primitive' society within relatively easy access, perhaps no European society was more flooded by this lachrymose tide than Scotland. Perhaps no European country had less need of the kind of compensatory fantasies and politics which it provided.

Whether or not the endemic sentimentality of late eighteenth century art was a necessary prelude to what Morse Peckham has defined as High Romanticism, it hardly evolved in Scotland beyond the stage of verbosity and deliberately inchoate emotion.[13] James Beattie's *The Minstrel* influenced Wordsworth but no comparable Scottish Romantic poet appeared. Scottish middle class literature, therefore, either took to excess English sentimental writing; unintentionally parodied it so that MacKenzie renders Sterne without any of the Irishman's extraordinary, convoluted intelligence and knowing wit; or bowdlerised robust writers such as Fielding. (Smollett is a partial exception to this). Walter Scott might privately write that 'I can by no means think that the coarseness of an ancient romance is so dangerous to the public as the mongrel and inflammatory sentimentality of a modern novelist'[14] but this did not stay that ever-moving hand from giving him the cash he needed and his vast public what it wanted. Despite his own best instincts and desires, Scott editorially expurgated in deference to the growing force of respectability, the vital, violent and passionate elements from both the traditional Scottish material and from the later English writers, Dryden and Swift. He both titillated this audience with 'primitive' violence and assured it of its own sensible probity. Edwin Muir's remark on Scott's abuse of tradition is applicable to almost all the Scottish middle-class writing of that age of which, rightly, Scott is considered the paragon:

> The eighteenth-century English novel was a criticism of society, manners and life. It set out to amuse, but it had a serious intention; its criticism, however wittily expressed, was sincere, and being sincere it made for more civilised manners and a more sensitive understanding of human life. Scott marks a definite degeneration of that tradition: after him certain qualities are lost to the novel which are not recovered for a long time. The novel becomes the idlest of all forms of literary art, and by a natural consequence the most popular. Instead of providing an intelligent criticism of life, it is content to enunciate moral platitudes, and it does this all the more confidently because such platitudes are certain to be agreeable to the reader. It skims over every aspect of experience that could be obnoxious to the most tender of prudish feelings, and in fact renounces both freedom and responsibility. Scott, it seems to me, was largely instrumental in bringing the novel to that pass; with his enormous prestige he helped to establish the mediocre and the trivial.
>
> How much of the moral responsibility for this rests on him and how much on his age, which was awakening to gentility, it is probably impossible to determine. The fact remains that all that Scott wrote is disfigured by the main vice of gentility: its inveterate indifference to truth, its inability to recognise that truth is valuable in itself. No doubt there have been countless genteel writers in the history of English literature. But Scott was the first writer of really great powers to bow his knee unquestioningly to gentility and abrogate his responsibility. As a result the tradition of English prose fiction was devitalised for more than half a century.
>
> When we turn to his influence on Scottish literature we find the same story. There were not many genteel Scottish writers before Scott; there have not been many ungenteel ones since. His gentility can be seen in his *Border Minstrelsy* which he loved and yet could not but Bowdlerize. But the difference he introduced into Scottish poetry can be seen most clearly by comparing his own poems in the ballad form with the old ballads themselves. It is pretty nearly the difference between
>
> > I lighted down my sword to draw,
> > I hacked him in pieces sma',
>
> and
>
> > Charge, Chester, charge! On, Stanley, on!
> > Were the last words of Marmion,
>
> the difference between a writer fully conscious that he is dealing with dreadful things and one who must make even carnage pleasing and picturesque.
>
> Scott was a man of great genius and of enormous inventive powers. But has any other writer of equal rank ever misused his gifts and indefatigably lowered the standards of literature with quite such a clean conscience?[15]

Scott promulgated and vulgarised the economically progressive theories of the Scottish Enlightenment by embodying them into adventure stories. This required a certain evasive handling of his material. As Muir points to his treatment of violence, so we can see similar methods adopted in his representation of common life. The following passage from his *Journal* goes to the heart of that method:

> I saw the poor childs funeral from a distance—Ah that Distance! what a magician for conjuring up scenes of joy or sorrow, smoothing all asperities

reconciling all incongruities veiling all absurdness softening every coarseness doubling every effect by the influence of the imagination. A Scottish wedding should be seen at a distance the gay bound of the dancers just distinguished amid the elderly groupe of the spectators—the glass held high & the distant cheers as it is swallowed should be only a sketch not a finished Dutch picture when it becomes brutal & boorish. Scottish psalmody too should (be) hea(r)d from a distance—The grunt and the snuffle and the whine and the scream should be all blended in that deep and distant sound which rising and falling like the Eolian harp may have some title to be called the praise of our maker,—Even so the distant funeral the few mourners on horseback with their plaids wrapped around them. The father heading the procession as they entered the river and pointing out the ford by which his darling was to be carried on the last long road—not (one) of the subordinate figures in discord with the general tone of the incident—the presence of the mourners seeming just accessories and no more to the general purpose of the procession this is affecting—to be in the midst of the bustle is incongruous and unpleasant from the contradictions which it involves.[16]

Since evasion is so much part of all of us, it would be wrong to criticise Scott as a man. Art, however, cannot be so inclined. Its business is with life's very contradictions. This passage is like nothing so much as a sentimental Victorian painting. Nor has it the toughness of eighteenth century pictorial prose with its grasp of and relish for low life. Equally, it is romantic in the worst sense and uses romantic concepts deceitfully as in the image of the safely distanced Eolian harp. The safe distance, in fact, is its purpose. Pain and vulgarity are kept at arm's length. Behind the distaste there is also a degree of fear. Sentimentality such as this has a manifestly complex relationship to the objects of its attention and apparent enthusiasm. Morse Peckham has given a remarkable account of the preponderance of sentimentality in the latter part of the eighteenth century which is germane to Scott and the Scotland he represented. Peckham explains the nature of this lachrymose phenomenon, which he saw as arising from the breakdown of Enlightenment values and aspirations, thus:

An important consequence for students of literature was the steady development in intensity and quantity of sentimentalism. Its original source was the necessity to discharge the tension consequent upon the affirmation that the world is radiant with order and value which any mind free from superstition, tyranny, and priestcraft could arrive at for itself, and the inconsistent perception that it is not. An aesthetic stimulus came to be valued for its power to discharge that tension in tears and enthusiasm. Further the more the basic instability became apparent, the more necessity there was to fall back upon an emotional affirmation of order, value, and identity as qualities structured in the real world. From this point of view Ossian was a typical late Enlightenment phenomenon.[17]

Throughout Europe we have an aesthetic deification of the peasant and savage produced simultaneously with the destruction of such groups and races. With terrible irony, Rousseau's doctrines, as they were assimilated by bourgeois society, achieved precisely the reverse of their conservationist intention. Thus in Scotland Burns as peasant is posthumously made a national symbol while, Cobbett suggests, economic conditions on the land deteriorate. No sooner are the Highland Clearances enacted than nineteenth century Scotland starts to define itself through a superficial Celtic symbolism. Scottish public celebrations are highly revealing. Burns suppers commence in the very early nineteenth century where the Edinburgh literati, whose actual patronage to the Bard had been derisory, gluttonously ate and drank to his memory, to the rural pieties he represented and, not least, to the democratic unity of the Scottish people. This was outdone in both comedy and pathos by George IV's visit to Edinburgh in 1822 where in a capital draped in tartan (the king's twenty-one stone was swathed in a natty pink) a 'nation' pledged its allegiance to a Hanoverian king. Walter Scott in a frenzy of excited activity organised the whole charade and so forgot himself as to sit on a glass and deeply cut his backside. Perhaps the Lowlanders were covertly celebrating Cumberland's memory.

The intention to implant rural and Highland stereotypes in Scottish consciousness was essentially intended to promulgate a pseudo-national identity on the basis of the notion that Scotland was not a country undergoing the social stresses inherent in rapid urbanisation and industrialisation. Edwin Muir has noted that this can be accurately detected in the decline of Scottish literature and folk song into the sentimentality of the Kailyard. In his marvellous *Scottish Journey* he described the phenomenon thus:

> 'Annie Laurie' was really the first great public milestone on Scotland's road to the Kailyard and the window in Thrums, and its popularity showed that that road was predestined. Two things mainly contributed to set Scotland, an eminently realistic country, on such a path: the breakdown of Calvinism, a process salutary in itself, but throwing off as a by-product an obliterating debris of sentimentality, and the rise of an industrial system so sordid and disfiguring that people were eager to escape from it by any road, however strange. The flight to the Kailyard was a flight to Scotland's past, to a country which had existed before Industrialism; but by the time the flight took place Industrialism itself had sucked that tradition dry of its old vigour; it was no longer of importance except as a refuge from the hard facts of Scottish town life.[18]

While such chronic symptoms did not appear until later in the nineteenth century, the roots of the Kailyard run deep. Elements of it certainly exist in Burns but to understand it fully we must appreciate the literary warfare waged by the literati against their own tradition and the poets from the common people who, in the eighteenth century, represented that tradition. This theme runs from MacKenzie, through Jeffrey and *The Edinburgh Review* to that deadly duo, Lockhart and Wilson, in *Blackwood's*. Edwin Muir believed that such a class struggle was more important in a Scottish rather than an English context because Scottish writing had, unlike English, so frequently come from the people.

> It is a thing worth noting that the one or two great poets whom Scotland has produced have been men in the ordinary sense uncultivated. Excepting Scott, those of whom we know anything have sprung from peasant or humble

stock; and there was even before Burns, who set a fashion, a tradition of peasant poetry and a belief that an artificer of Scottish song might most congruously be a plowman or a weaver. In poets of this degree, so scarce in English literature, Scottish poetry has almost always been prolific; and against the solitary figure of Bloomfield it can set Fergusson, Ramsay, Tannahill and a host of others, the worst of whom are sentimental, and the best, if minor poets, most authentically poets. Outside these, among her imaginative prose writers, Scotland has shown a disposition for common or even mean conditions.[19]

MacKenzie's longevity made it possible for him to know Ramsay, Fergusson and Burns. Ramsay who both resurrected elements of traditional Scottish literature and combined them with genteel elements (one of his collections is revealingly entitled *The Tea Table Miscellany*) was the only one, personally and poetically, with whom MacKenzie felt at ease. In the last years of his life he wrote a set of notes for a memoir (Scott inherited them) in which he summed up his sense of poetic value. The main theme running through his aesthetic is the nature of pastoral poetry. On the face of it, MacKenzie seems to endorse a realism in Scottish eighteenth century pastoral poetry—a movement away from the enamelled artificiality of Italian models;

> We had from imitation of Italian models, an infusion of Arcadian sentiment and Arcadian characters at the time to which I allude, before Allan Ramsay (who is not, however, free from it) first, and in much superior style, Burns shewed us a better sort of lyrical poetry. Before then we had our *Corydons*, our *Alexises*, our *Sylvias*, and our *Amintas*.
>
> . . . I suggested to Burns the idea of his writing a pastoral after the manner of *The Gentle Shepherd*, and he seemed to relish the idea much. Yet I know not if he could have taken time and bestowed attention on any great work; he felt strongly the passions as well as the manners of a particular character; but it is questionable if he could have constructed a drama consisting of a combination of characters, woven into a well arranged plot and carried on to a natural conclusion. He was the poet of impulse and was unwilling to study for excellence.[20]

As well as the didactic condescension, the slur on Burns's sense of craft which was of the first order, the misunderstanding of Burns's dramatic powers—*The Jolly Beggars* would, of course, be beyond the pale—this impression that the rejection of artificial classicism entailed a genuine desire for the sort of realism that traditional poets like Fergusson and Burns were capable of is quite misleading. Irritated and provoked in his old age by the appearance of Wordsworth and the Lake School MacKenzie propounded the following rules which not only ran counter to the new English poetry but to his own native tradition:

> Opposite to (the fault I have mentioned) is another which seems to me to prevail in modern poetry, namely, the *ultra simple* (if I may use a political epithet), which some poets of great genius, and particularly one illustrious member of the Lake School, has brought into notice and indeed into favour. This is never above using any word or expression which it thinks appropriate to the person or thing described, however vulgar or coarse. The legitimacy of

5.1 *Engraving of a painting by D.
Octavius Hill of Mossgiel, the
farm rented by Burns and his
brother in 1784.*

this modern pretension to poetical excellence requires a little consideration. It will be admitted that everything that is natural is not poetry, of which the very essence seems to be a certain elevation and elegance of language above the standard of ordinary life. Nobleness and dignity are the attributes of poetry. These may belong to the feelings and the sentiments of inferior persons, but the language in which those feelings and sentiments are to be conveyed seems to require a certain degree of elegance and elevation if it is to be entitled to the denomination of poetry. Language is the dress of thought, and a decency in its apparel seems indispensable if we would avoid disgust, or wish to attain pleasure in their association. The elevation of common and mean objects by the language in which they are described is certainly more congenial to the spirit of poetry and gives much greater delight to the reader of poetry, than the introduction of such objects in the plainer and coarser garb in which the everyday communications of ordinary life they are clothed. The majesty of Virgil could give grace to the meanest object of a farmyard which Theocritus, but for the noble language in which he wrote, would be found to want, and which, if literally translated into a language less refined, would create a feeling of displeasure or disgust . . .

Poetry selects picturesque images amidst the vulgar accompaniments which surround them. A cottage room has many pieces of furniture of which the description would be offensive rather than pleasing; but Cartwright has selected one circumstance in describing his cottage room, which is picturesque elegant, and which is strictly appropriate to the humble apartment. In describing the dawn of the first morning light he says;

> The rising sun its silver ray
> On the plain wall in diamonds threw.

We see the lattice with its little diamond-shaped panes, and feel the rural charm of the place with all its simplicity and unambitious peacefulness.[21]

MacKenzie's aesthetic values are the consequences of a restrictive sense of social propriety which would debilitate poetry. The Lake School is so treated. The common people are wholly condescended to: *provided* that they do have certain 'feelings and sentiments' these need to be translated into an appropriate poetic diction. As well as condescension on MacKenzie's part there is, if not fear, a degree of anxiety regarding these self-same people. Scott's genteel perspective was, as we have seen, achieved by keeping a safe distance. MacKenzie, when he focuses on detail, looks not simply for items which, like the lattice window, bespeak rural charm but also endear themselves by their 'unambitious peaceful-ness'. In all such pastoral writing what is repeatedly stressed is this element of contentment essential to the life of country people and envied by those burdened by urban care. The real meaning of this image and the message it conveyed was an apprehensive need to conceive of the country people as politically dormant. So conceived, they could then act as models for or studied contrasts to other social groups. Poets of the people also had to know their place. Scott, MacKenzie and the Edinburgh literati treated Burns with, at best, condescension. As Fairchild has remarked:

To the sedater Brahmins of the Blair-Robertson-MacKenzie type, the plebian Burns was a literary curiosity to be regarded with amiable superciliousness.

They had no real understanding of him, nor he of them.[22]

If Edinburgh society treated Burns badly, the earlier Robert Fergusson (whose poetry is as much located in the city itself as Burns's was in Ayrshire) was dealt with even more harshly. Part of Fergusson's poetry derives from Ramsay's competent, 'aiten reed' versions of English pastoral poetry such as Gay's. As John Speirs has remarked:

> Where his verse is weakest, if occasionally charming, is where it is related as a Scotticised variety to the eighteenth-century Spenser of English verse, as in the hybrid *Farmer's Ingle* (which in some way anticipates the *Cottar's Saturday Night*), or, more often, the eighteenth-century Milton of *Lycidas, L'Allegro* and *Il Penseroso* the latter combines easily with the pastoralism. Even *Auld Reekie,* one of Fergusson's best poems, weakens appreciably from the point where the eighteenth-century pastoral Milton becomes audible. But from Ramsay and his predecessors Fergusson inherited also living Scots verse conventions (the Scots verse epistles and elegy, and the mode of his *Hallow Fair* and *Leith Races*) that had been given a new lease of life; and his most significant and best work is an extension of these Scots conventions. If the first half and more of *Auld Reekie* may be said to be the Scots equivalent of anything English, it is of the Augustan verse of Pope and Swift which incorporates their most active actual interests.[23]

These lines from *Auld Reekie* demonstrate Speirs's case and make obvious MacKenzie's antipathy. While Fergusson could write poetry of Virgilian charm, as prescribed, these lines with their sense of the tangible and seamy are truer to him and to the Scottish poetic tradition:

> Whan feet in dirty gutters plash
> And Fock to wale their fitstaps fash;
> At night, the macaroni drunk,
> In pools and gutters aft-times sunk:
> Heh! what a fright he now appears,
> Whan he his corpse dejected rears!
> Look at that head, and think if there
> The Pomet slaister'd up his hair!
> The cheeks observe:– Where now cou'd shine
> The scancin glories o' carmine?
> Ah, legs! in fain the silk-worm there
> Display'd to view her eident care:
> For stink, instead of perfumes, grow,
> And clarty odours fragrant flow.[24]

Fergusson's relationship with the spirit of Swift and Pope was a natural one because the irreverent, 'flyting', ironically comic and reductive idiom of the native Scottish poetic voice merges naturally with the best of English Augustan satire. At best the Scottish imagination does not suffer pompous fools gladly. Fergusson wrote a poem for which MacKenzie never forgave him called *The Sow of Feeling*. Fergusson's amatory, declamatory pig, awaiting the butcher's knife, in a masterful monologue parodies the sentimental conventions of eighteenth century pastoral which MacKenzie had exploited.

276

Ah, Luxury! to you my being owes
Its load of misery,—its load of woes!
With heavy heart I saunter all the day;
Gruntle and murmur all my hours away!
In vain I try to summon old desire
For favourite sports,—for wallowing in the mire:
Thoughts of my husband, of my children slain,
Turn all my wonted pleasure into pain!
How oft did we, in Phoebus' warming ray,
Bask on the humid softness of the clay?
Oft did his lusty head defend my tail
From the rude whispers of the angry gale;
While nose-refreshing puddles streamed around,
And floating odours hailed the dung-clad ground.[25]

While Fergusson was able to keep feeling of this kind at laughing arm's length, Burns, whose poetry was 'curiously divided between MacKenzie and Fergusson', was sometimes incapable of so doing. When it actually intruded into his life it produced even more grotesque results.[26] The sentimental Burns was wholly acceptable to the pontificating MacKenzie. The other poet, the lyrical realist with unruly erotic and political desires was to be denied. In his memoirs MacKenzie could not resist the *ad hominem* attack on both of them while using the respectable Allan Ramsay as a moral contrast:

> There were three native poets, all of talents and genius, but the difference in their fates and conduct was occasioned by the company they kept. Allan Ramsay was originally a barber in the country; he came to Edinburgh and got into the business of a bookseller, publishing his first volume, *The Evergreen,* in 1724. He occupied the shop at the end of the Luckenbooths, afterwards Creech's. Having by his good conduct and liveliness got into very respectable society, he lived happily and died leaving a family well enough provided for.
>
> Fergus(s)on, dissipated and drunken, died in early life, after having produced poems faithfully and humourously describing scenes of Edinburgh of festivity and somewhat of blackguardism. He wrote about 177(3).
>
> Burns, originally virtuous, was seduced by dissipated companions, and after he got into the Excise addicted himself to drunkeness. Tho' the rays of his genius sometimes broke through the mist of his dissipation; but the habit had got too much power over him to be overcome, and it brought him, with a few lucid intervals, to an early grave. He unfortunately during the greatest part of his life had called, and thought, dissipation *spirit,* sobriety and discretion a *want of it,* virtues too shabby for a man of genius. His great admiration of Fergus(s)on showed his propensity to coarse dissipation. When he allowed his mind its proper play, he produced poetry of a very high cast, full of tenderness and sometimes sublimity; he had much more of the *vivida vis* than either of his predecessors. (*Vide* a great deal more of him in former sheets).[27]

Vicious and dishonest as it is (Fergusson's tragic end is particularly misrepresented) this is mild compared to what was to follow in the character assassinations brought to a fine art by later Scottish sentimental critics. Burns is valued to the degree he is capable of translating the life and language of the people into forms appropriate to the New Town drawing room. The situation was not uniquely Scottish. As Raymond Williams has pointed out English poets like Clare, Bloomfield and Stephen Duck were exposed to the same destructive pressures.[28] Erratic patronage wherein extravagant praise was followed by neglect and coercive instruction based on emasculating neo-classic theories of form and diction frequently led them to mistake their own genius and turn from a poetry of bitter, vivid fact to the 'creeping humility' inherent in celebrating the alleged dominion of benevolence. The tendency to instability and neurosis in these men is not to be wondered at. Moved from their own community, partly by their own ambition, they ended belonging to none. As Fairchild has remarked concerning the confusion of impulse and nature in Burns:

> The coarse physical realism of the peasant which he was and the gay irresponsibility of the person of quality which he aspired to be entered into a disastrous combination. The selfishness and lack of chivalry which marked his relations with women are not surprising in a man of impulse who was almost always able to convince himself that his impulses were good.[29]

Burns was perhaps more volatile and recognition-seeking than his English counterparts. Also the pressure to write in English and the sentimental culture he was exposed to in Scotland was more harmful. As Fairchild has remarked: 'it was a self-approving indulgence of the emotions not a discipline of the spirit'.[30] Burns's letters, in particular, mix a physical and spiritual realism with posturing derived from sentimental fiction.[31] That part of him which was eager to please struck the attitude of the sentimental peasant poet. This was the Burns who could write: 'For my part, my ambition was, and still my strongest wish is, to please my Compeers, the rustic Inmates of the Hamlet'.[32] More harmfully it was this Burns who could, uncharacteristically, write 'The Cottar's Saturday Night' which was to become a kind of social and political Ark of the Covenant for bourgeois Scotland whereby a version of rural life (as real as Norman Rockwell) was seized on as social realism. In particular it fed the Establishment's compulsive desire to be assured of the political placidity of the common people and, most importantly, as we shall see, of their loyalty in time of war.

> From scenes like these, old Scotia's grandeur springs,
> That makes her lov'd at home, rever'd abroad:
> Princes and lords are but the breath of kings,
> 'An honest man's the noble work of God:'
> And *certes*, in fair Virtue's heavenly road,
> The *Cottage* leaves the *Palace* far behind:
> What is a lordling's pomp? a cumbrous load,
> Disguising oft the *wretch* of human kind,
> Studied in arts of Hell, in wickedness refin'd
> O Scotia! my dear, my native soil!
> For whom my warmest wish to Heaven is sent!
> Long may thy hardy sons of *rustic toil*
> Be blest with health and peace and sweet content!

And O may Heaven their simple lives prevent
From *luxury's* contagion, weak and vile!
Then howe'er *crowns* and *coronets* be rent
A *virtuous Populace* may rise the while,
And stand a wall of fire, around their much-lov'd Isle.[33]

That this side of Burns has been grossly exaggerated 'by a critical sentimentality which in itself descends from the most spurious aspects of his own thought'[34] is an unhappy but hardly original comment about Burns's posthumous Scottish and, indeed, international reputation. Much more disconcerting is the fact that contemporary Scottish history can still radically misinterpret the literary evidence of the eighteenth century largely because Burns's life and work is still interpreted at this superficial level. Thus, in his relatively recent volume in *The Edinburgh History of Scotland,* William Ferguson presents lack of protest in Burns's poetry as a central proof of the generally beneficent development of Scottish society in the latter part of the eighteenth century:

> On the whole (apart from the isolated incident of the Galloway Levellers) the breakdown of the old social order in Lowland Scotland does not seem to have caused great hardship. Partly this was due to the slow and irregular pace at which the changes were affected, and partly it was because those displaced from the land were readily absorbed by the rise of industries, with the consequent formation of villages and the growth of towns. And so in Lowland Scotland the term 'agrarian revolution' touches no chords in the folk memory. There is no vestige in Burns' works of the 'Deserted Village' theme or of the bitter lamentations that later anathematised the Highland Clearances. The simple truth seems to be that the benefits of agrarian improvements were shared by all classes of Lowland Society. In spite of spiralling prices the real wage of agricultural labourers increased over the period; their diet was better; famine was unknown and, but for the bad year of 1799, by the end of the century all but unthinkable. Better living conditions led to marked improvement in health and vigour.[35]

That marked and measurable improvement took place in the course of the eighteenth century in Scotland is indisputable. That it took place in quite such a harmonious way seems most improbable. Rancour and discontent was of the essence of Burns's character both concerning his own lot and that of the community he came from. Missing this central fact, Ferguson consequently does not deal with the detailed documentary evidence that Burns provides in his private letters, with the more complex problem of the literary strategies Burns had to adopt to embody this dissent in his *public* poetry and, finally, Burns's sympathetic involvement with the French Revolution both as a factor in itself and for what it tells us about the state of Scottish political consciousness in the last decade of the eighteenth century. In a letter of 1783 Burns wrote:

> I shall only trouble you with a few particulars relative to the present wretched state of this country. Our markets are exceedingly high; oatmeal 17 and 17d pr peck, & not to be got even at that price. We have indeed been pretty well supplied with quantities of white pease from England &

elsewhere, but that resource is likely to fail us; what will become of us then, particularly the very poorest sort, Heaven only knows.—This country, till of late, was flourishing incredibly in the Manufactures of Silk, Lawn & Carpet Weaving, and we are still carrying on a good deal in that way but much reduced from what it was; we had also a fine trade in the Shoe way, but now entirely ruined, & hundreds driven to a starving condition on account of it.— Farming is also at a very low ebb with us. Our lands, generally speaking, are mountainous and barren; and our landholders, full of ideas of farming gathered from the English, and the Lothians and other rich soils in Scotland; make no allowance for the odds of the quality of the land, and consequently stretch us much beyond what, in the event, we will be found able to pay. We are also much at a loss for want of better methods in our improvements of farming: necessity compels us to leave our old schemes; & few of us have opportunities of being well informed in new ones. In short my dear Sir, since the unfortunate beginning of this American war, & its unfortunate conclusion, this country has been, & still is decaying very fast—

Even in higher life, a couple of our Ayrshire Noblemen, and the major part of our Knights and Squires, are all insolvent. A miserable job of a Douglas, Heron & Co's Bank, which no doubt you have heard of, had undone numbers of them; and imitating English, and French, and other foreign luxuries & fopperies, has ruined as many more.[36]

Thus Burns as a very young man had a comprehensive grasp of the unstable economic patterns so characteristic of the age; the effect on manufacture and diet; the inequity and iniquity of the financial methods of agricultural improvement when applied to second or third rate land such as he himself had to farm and, finally, the decadence of the aristocracy. Scottish attention to this side of Burns has been spasmodic. Garrulous sentimentality needed a social sense quite other than the bleak, harsh domestic and working conditions Burns actually experienced. These lines from *The Vision* are by no means the most quoted:

> There, lanely by the ingle-cheek,
> I sat and ey'd the spewing reek,
> That fill'd wi' hoast-provoking smeek,
>   The auld, clay biggin;
> And heard the restless rattons squeak
>   About the riggin.
>
> . . . Had I to guid advice but harket,
> I might, by this, hae led a market,
> Or strutted in a Bank and clarket
>   My Cash Account;
> While here, half-mad, half-fed, half-sarket,
>   Is a' th' amount.[37]

Not encumbered by Scottish blinkers, the English Romantic writers who visited Scotland and who both admired and identified with Burns saw more clearly this grim privation. Thomas De Quincey, no stranger to life's lower levels, wrote that 'I felt that upon him, amongst all the children of labour, the primal curse had fallen heaviest and sunk deepest'.[38] Not Eden but the terrible aftermath was the peasant's lot. Lest this seem too melodramatic, the witness of an American, Nathaniel Hawthorne is apposite. When he came to Britain as the American consul in Liverpool he expeditiously visited Ayrshire to see for himself the actual conditions in which the poet had lived. He was horrified by its squalor and stink and this account of Mauchline Farm is a fair example of his general response. One virtue of Hawthorne's report is that he was still close enough in time in the 1850s to perceive conditions similar to those prevailing in Burns's own life-time:

> The whole house was pervaded with a frowzy smell, and also dunghill-odor; and it is not easy to understand how the atmosphere of such a dwelling can be any more agreeable or salubrious morally than it appeared to be physically. No virgin, surely, could keep a holy awe about her while stowed higgledly-piggledy with coarse-natured rustics into this narrowness and filth. Such a habitation is calculated to make beasts of men and women; and it indicates a degree of barbarism which I did not imagine to exist in Scotland, that a tiller of broad fields, like the farmer of Mauchline, should have his abode in a pig-sty. It is sad to think of anybody—not to say a poet, but any human being—sleeping, eating, thinking, praying, and spending all his home-life in this miserable hovel, but, methinks, I never in the least knew how to estimate the miracle of Burns' genius, nor his heroic merit for being no worse man, until I thus learned the squalid hindrances amid which he developed himself. Space, a free atmosphere, and cleanliness have a vast deal to do with the possibilities of human virtue.[39]

Interpreting Burns is notoriously difficult because of his self-dramatising tendencies. Hawthorne's image accords, however, with a great deal of his own testimony as regards his early farm experience which he described as 'the cheerless gloom of a hermit with the unceasing moil of a galley slave'.[40] His brother Gilbert, less rhetorically, affirms this state of affairs: 'the very poorest soil in a state of cultivation . . . To the buffetings of misfortune we could only oppose hard labour, and the most rigid economy. We lived very sparingly.'[41] Professor John Weston delivers this account of the grim minutiae of the farm life and toil;

> They lived in a stone, thatched house, along with their stock, no bigger than the mud cottage with a turf roof Burns was born in. It was heated by peat dug by themselves from the muirs. They were forced by lack of cash, not by ignorance, to use the old style farming, that is, dunged infield and unmanured outfield, both used without rest until exhausted. Their old 'Scotch plough' was a heavy wooden monster thirteen feet long for cultivating rocky ground, with only a bit of iron in the sock and coulter. It was drawn by four horses and made a v-shaped rut. For their harrow they probably could not afford iron teeth and instead used wood pegs hardened by fire. Their £40 rent had to be paid by selling oats, and maybe a little barley, peas and beans, and butter (from one or two cows). Oats were cut with a sickle, threshed with a flail, winnowed by wind, and ground daily on a knocking stone. They tethered (not having fences) a sufficient number of sheep and grew enough flax to make their own clothes. They grew no hay for winter forage, using straw and wild bog hay cut with a sickle. They ate nothing but skim milk, oats, cabbage and maybe potatoes; and when there

was none of that they starved. The little lime they used to make the soil less sour, they bought because they had no kiln to burn it themselves. They hauled it on sledges or in creels or horseback, because they had no cart with wheels.[42]

As *The Vision* indicates such conditions are eloquently present in Burns's best poetry. Present, too, is protest against them and against the conditions of agrarian crisis prevailing in Ayrshire and, indeed, throughout Britain in Burns's lifetime. Burns, for fear of loss of patronage and other reprisals, had often allegorically or ironically to disguise this dissent. Wordsworth, a witness to the power of the agrarian crisis to dispossess people, had no doubt Burns clearly wrote of it. A poet capable of a couplet like 'To lie in kilns and barns at e'en/when banes are crazed and bluid is thin' understood with terrible intimacy the suffering of the times.[43] Burns had a sense—partly ironic and partly self-deprecatory—that he lived in a world where only 'rich folk hear and see' but he devised methods of subverting this, the chief of which was, partly influenced by Swift, the creation of personages who conducted ironic monologues. As in his marvellous 'Address of Beelzebub' this can burst forth as poetry of unsurpassed dissent. Perhaps because he was not dealing with his native Ayrshire but with feudal abuses in the Highlands he felt he could speak here more directly. He still uses an ironic persona, here the very devil himself, but it is a poem quite remarkable for the virulence of its anger and its keen sense of cruel and degrading detail:

> BUT, hear me, my lord! Glengary hear!
> Your HAND'S OWRE LIGHT ON THEM, I fear:
> Your FACTORS, GRIEVES, TRUSTEES an' BAILIES,
> I canna say but they do gailies;
> They lay aside a' tender mercies
> An' tirl the HALLIONS to the BIRSIES;
> Yet, while they're only poin'd, and herriet,
> They'll keep their stubborn Highlan spirit.
> But smash them! crush them a' to spails!
> An' rot the DYVORS i' the JAILS!
> The young dogs, swinge them to the labour,
> Let WARK an' HUNGER mak them sober!
> The HIZZIES, if they're outlins fausont,
> Let them in DRURY LANE be lesson'd!
> An' if the wives, an' dirty brats,
> Come thiggan at your doors an' yets,
> Flaffan wi' duds, an' grey wi' beese,
> Frighten awa your deucks an geese;
> Get out a HORSE-WHIP, or a JOWLER,
> The langest thong, the fiercest growler,
> An' gar the tatter'd gipseys pack
> Wi' a' their bastarts on their back![44]

In the light of this evidence both from Burns himself and his most perceptive critics and commentators Ferguson's claims about not only a lack of bitterness in Burns' poetry but a lack of justified bitterness is extraordinary. Ferguson's error seems to stem from an ignorance of the poetry which leads to an arbitrary division of it from Burns as political radical and the bitter conflict between that radicalism and the Scottish establishment particularly in the last decade of the eighteenth century. Burns is not to be understood only in the context of the painful reality of rural life and the exploitative growth of agrarian capitalism he must also, as Crawford cogently points out, be seen as deeply influenced by the French Revolution.[45] We cannot understand the life and *letters* of late eighteenth and early nineteenth-century Scotland without understanding the degree of obsession with revolutionary France. As Cockburn recorded:

> Everything rang, and was connected with the Revolution in France; which, for above twenty years, was the all in all. Everything, literally everything, was soaked in this one event.
> Yet we had wonderfully few proper Jacobins; that is, persons who seriously wished to introduce a republic into this country, on the French precedent. There were plenty of people who were called Jacobins; because this soon became the common nickname which was given, not only those who had admired the French liberation, but to those who were known to have any taste for any internal reform of our own. There was a short period, chiefly in 1793 and 1794, during which this imputation was provoked by a ridiculous aping of French forms and phraseology, and an offensive vaunting of the superior excellence of everything in that country. But the folly, which only appeared in a few towns, was very soon over, cured by time, by the failure of the French experiment, and by the essential absurdity of the thing itself; and it had never been patronised by a single person of sense and public character or influence.[46]

Cockburn's sense of the discrepancy among the ruling and property owning class between the real and the imagined threat of radical insurrection is revealing. It is impossible to gauge accurately the authenticity of their public response to fear of revolution. The danger was seemingly exaggerated on occasion to justify the increase of political repression. As a poem of the period noted:

> There can be no harm in giving alarm,
> And scaring the people in strange apprehensions;
> By brewing the storm, we avoid a Reform,
> And securely enjoy all our places and pensions.[47]

The forces at the disposal of Tory Scotland were far in excess of any challenge the Radicals could mount. The Edinburgh Jacobin trials of 1793–4 under Braxfield were, as E.P. Thompson has shown, corrupt to a degree not realisable in England.[48] When it came to actual conflict in 1819 at the so-called Battle of Bonnymuir it was no contest. Authority in Scotland over this period tended to be both given to militaristic role-playing (Cockburn is highly revealing in the boyish joy of Scots of his class in donning warrior garb against the threat of French invasion and insurrection) and a much more inflexible, even sadistic, desire to punish scapegoats who were, allegedly, corrupting the populace.

Given not only Burns's temperament, his politics and, above all a creative power which allowed him immediate communication with a mass audience, the situation was fraught with danger for him. Burns's enthusiasm for the French Revolution is well known. The incident of his sending carronades to France, captured in his role of exciseman, is well known. Less commented on is the purity of his revolutionary aspirations and his unnerved response to the situation his radical gestures got him into. In a recent book Robert D. Thornton has attempted to explain and defend Burns as revolutionary.[49] The book is mainly a study of an extraordinary figure, William Maxwell, a Scottish doctor who had not only sent daggers to the Revolutionaries but participated in the execution of the King. Maxwell returned to his native country and was Burns's doctor in Dumfries in the last years of the poet's life. He is considered responsible for the sea-bathing 'cure' of the poet's last days so may not altogether have shaken off his homicidal tendencies. Thornton's thesis—on highly tenuous evidence—is that, though Maxwell appeared to be a conforming, rehabilitated general practitioner, he remained an ardent revolutionary to the end. Consequently he postulates that he and Burns, despite their disguises—(Burns by this time was in militia uniform) kept to the end their revolutionary integrity. That one can keep secret one's deepest beliefs without self-damage, especially for a *poet,* is doubtful. Thornton's own new evidence of Burns's increased drinking in these last days seems to point to a growing feeling of humiliation and self-disgust. The poet's own words to Mrs. Dunlop suggest this: 'I too, Madam, am just now Revolution-mad . . . mine is the madness of an enraged Scorpion shut up in a thumb-vial'.[50] What is certain is that, unable to disguise a truly revolutionary poetry in either irony or allegory, Burns kept it hidden. It is relatively recently that 'The Tree of Liberty' has been finally attributed to him. Nothing less like the pietistic loyalty of 'The Cottar's Saturday Night' could be imagined:

> But vicious folks aye hate to see
>   The works o' Virtue thrive, man;
> The courtly vermin's banned the tree,
>   And grat to see it thrive, man;
> King Loui' thought to cut it down,
>   When it was unco sma', man;
> For this the watchman cracked his crown,
>   Cut aff his head an a', man.

> . . . Let Britain boast her hardy oak,
>   Her poplar and her pine, man,
> Auld Britain ance could crack her joke,
>   And o'er her neighbours shine, man.
> But seek the forest round and round,
>   And soon 'twill be agreed, man,
> That sic a tree can not be found,
>   'Twixt London and the Tweed, man.[51]

Verse of this kind was anathema to the literati. The scepticism of Enlightenment thought was designed not for mass consumption so as to encourage the overthrow of established institutions but for new urbane élite who were to take over these institutions. The Edinburgh Whigs were the true inheritors of the values of the Enlightenment and a central theme of Jeffrey, in particular, in *The Edinburgh Review* was precisely the anxious, aggressive desire to make sure, as he saw it, that literature should not be used to provoke a popular insurrection. Burns was by this time dead but his ghost was not laid. In particular, his work had to be divorced from the English Romantic poets who, Jeffrey believed, were a threat to the stability of the state. Wordsworth, in particular, he discerned as a poetic Robespierre who would burst from his unhealthy seclusion to infect the masses.

Jeffrey's analysis of what he defined as Wordsworthian megalomania was Johnsonian. Anyone who sought not the checks and balances of urban civility but sought seclusion was of doubtful character. Wordsworth was, in fact, held up as an example of the poet as demagogue. Latent in such poetic licence lay more tangible forms of insurrection:

> Many a generous rebel, it is said, has been reclaimed to his allegiance by the spectacle of lawless outrage and excess presented in the conduct of the insurgents; and we think there is every reason to hope, that the lamentable consequences which have resulted from Mr. Wordsworth's open violation of the established laws of poetry, will operate as a wholesome warning to those who might otherwise have been seduced by his example, and be the means of restoring to that ancient and venerable code its due honour and authority.[52]

As perhaps befits an Edinburgh lawyer, what Jeffrey sought to do was employ the authority of law to confine and condemn English Romantic poetry. His world view and that of his large, propertied audience was one of a rigidity which arose from a mixture of class interest and fear. The *Lyrical Ballads* and *The Edinburgh Review* appeared almost simultaneously but two more contrasting attitudes could not be imagined. From the first Jeffrey saw the new English poetry as a political and social threat. His early review of Southey's *Thalaba* defined a position regarding what he conceived of as this Romantic menace in a manner which was not to change:

> A splenetic and idle discontent with the existing institutions of society, seems to be at the bottom of all their serious and peculiar sentiments. Instead of contemplating the wonders which civilisation has created for mankind, they are perpetually brooding over the disorders by which its progress has been attended. They are filled with horror and compassion at the sight of poor men spending their blood in the quarrels of princes, and brutifying their sublime capabilities in the drudgery of unremitting labour. For all sorts of vice and profligacy in the lower order of society, they have the same virtuous horror, and the same tender compassion.[53]

Jeffrey's thought, in all its aspects, is preoccupied with defining stability and stasis as pertaining to all aspects of reality. Or, it could be said, he was preoccupied with the question of authority. In contrast the English Romantics believed that society was in a state of critical transition and that the imaginative writer must respond accordingly. The weight and quality of modern literary and historical scholarship would tend to confirm the latter view. What writers like Raymond Williams and E.P. Thompson point to is the growth of capitalism which brought with it new, disruptive methods of economic practice and work. With this significant change in the balance of society went a pursuit by this burgeoning class of its own advantage to the extent that even the Law (the Game Laws provide a particularly pertinent example) was changed and adapted for its benefit. Far from Romanticism expressing 'a splenetic and idle discontent' it was the voice of documentation and justice. As Wordsworth wrote:

> . . . In Britain ruled a panic dread of change;
> The weak were praised, rewarded and advanced;
> And, from the impulse of a just disdain,
> Once more did I retire into myself.[54]

The anomalous position of the Scottish ruling class was that it both wrought change and held itself not responsible for its consequences. The essential attraction of *The Edinburgh Review* was that in the fields of law, economics and literary criticism it dispensed in a bright, witty manner a rationalisation of the prejudices of its audience. Jeffrey, far more than Wordsworth, was a manipulator of public consciousness. His activities were designed to prove either the virtues of the property-owning class or the vices of its alleged enemies. Moral accountability was dispensed accordingly. Laissez-faire economics were at one and the same time held to be universally beneficial and amoral since the market was a mechanism. This, conveniently, made redundant certain virtues the New Testament held to be essential in the conduct of the rich towards the poor and removed the burden of even attempting to integrate moral choice and economic practice. Very much a product of Enlightenment thought, Jeffrey's belief in the mechanical nature of how things functioned extended well beyond the sphere of economics. He saw the mind as mechanism and, in consequence, as a process that worked by association. We knew what we knew by a process of habit—in modern parlance, we are programmed—and Jeffrey deduced from this that knowledge was a static, received thing. Thus civil law was a *final*, comprehensive statement of good and evil which need, happily, take no account of a deteriorating environment as a cause of disruption or criminality. Thus, too, the forms, content and our responses to literature were conditioned by its tradition. Jeffrey, therefore, went to considerable pains to define this tradition in order to prove that the new poetry was a malign, mutated form which should be discarded as not conforming to established practice. This, as we have seen, is what Hartman meant when he said that Wordsworth 'sinned against the iron clad law of literary and social decorum' which limited the poet's role to putting before his public 'What e'er was thought, but ne'er so well express'd.'[55] Jeffrey's aesthetic censorship was ultimately social and political. His sense of the English literary tradition—of which he was the self-appointed guardian—was inevitably trivial. Since poetry had to be

286

made incapable of representing social reality not only had the recognised verse of his own age to be merely sentimental but the master spirits of the past had to be reduced to a similar status. Jeffrey's version of Shakespeare is particularly revealing: 'He has pointed out that fond familiarity with beautiful forms and images, that eternal recurrence of what is sweet and majestic in the simple aspects of nature, that indestructible love of flowers and odours, and dews and clear waters, and soft airs and sounds, and bright skies and woodland solitudes, and moonlight bowers which are the Material elements of Poetry.'[56] This is not quite the ingredients of *King Lear* in its agonised appraisal of the moral responsibility of power. Art, with such materials as Jeffrey's to work with, is emasculated. Not content with this, however, Jeffrey also manufactured theories of genre and language to buttress further his position. The given law of poetic genre was also the given law of class genre. Therefore, a poetry which took the condition and feelings of the common life seriously was, in Jeffrey's terms, impossible. His is an elaboration and extension of MacKenzie's position. This, it should be remembered, is the aesthetic theory of a man who self-admiringly defined himself as Whig and reformer:

> Now the different classes of society have each of them a distinct character, as well as a separate idiom; and the names of the various passions to which they are subject respectively, have a signification that varies essentially according to the condition of the persons to whom they are applied. The love, or grief, or indignation of an enlightened and refined character, is not only expressed in a different language, but is in itself a different emotion from the love, or grief, or anger, of a tradesman, or a market wench. The things themselves are radically and obviously distinct; and the representation of them is calculated to convey a very different train of sympathies and sensations to the mind. The question, therefore, comes simply to be—which of them is the most proper object for poetical imitation? It is needless of us to answer a question, which the practice of all the world has long ago decided irrevocably. The poor and the vulgar may interest us, in poetry, by their *situation*; but never, we apprehend, by any sentiments that are peculiar to their condition, and still less by any language that is characteristic of it. The truth is, that it is impossible to copy their diction or their sentiments correctly, in a serious composition; and this, not merely because poverty makes men ridiculous, but because just taste and refined sentiment are rarely to be met with among the uncultivated part of mankind; and a language, fitted for their expression, can still more rarely form any part of their ordinary conversation.[57]

The Romantics also thought, though in quite another fashion, that the situation of the poor was ridiculous. Inbuilt in Jeffrey's attitude, again an Enlightenment inheritance, is a theory of evolution which asserted the superiority of his 'civilised' and refined group. While Scottish eighteenth century intellectuals might sentimentally dabble with Highland and pastoral self and national images there was an accompanying and controlling fear of regression. In Jeffrey there is, in fact, contempt and fear of the lower classes as not only threatening political disruption but of dragging civilised achievement backwards. Jeffrey feared that the adult condition which he believed his society has attained might be lost in the childish state inherent in socially inferior persons. One of his most repeated protests against the Romantics, Wordsworth in particular, was that their poetic diction was both an expression of and invitation to such regression. Infantilism was its essential mode of speech and society was thereby threatened. Wordsworth linguistically offended the law of literary progress:

> But what we do maintain is, that much of the most popular poetry in the world owes its celebrity chiefly to the beauty of its diction; and no poetry can be long or generally acceptable, the language of which is coarse, inelegant, or infantine.
> . . . the new poets are just as great borrowers as the old; only that, instead of borrowing from the more popular passages of their illustrious predecessors, they have preferred furnishing themselves from vulgar ballads and plebian nurseries.[58]

From the evidence such as this, it is clear that dealing with Burns as man and poet would cause Jeffrey severe problems. In his 1808 review of Cromek's *Reliques of Robert Burns* he dealt with these in a deviously talented fashion.[59] His account is seminal not only for Burns's emasculated nineteenth-century reputation but for the version of the life of the Scottish peasantry as promulgated in the subsequent writing of that century. A fundamental aesthetic distinction, which is also a moral and political distinction, was drawn by Jeffrey between the compliant sentimentalist and the rough, licentious man of the people. Burns's love poetry is largely dismissed as being in ill-taste and socially presumptuous since it is 'seldom accommodated to the timidity and "sweet austere composure" of women of refinement.' His more overtly political satire is similarly discounted: 'They seem to have been written, not out of playful malice or virtuous indignation, but out of fierce and ungovernable anger'. Indeed they were. With some truth Jeffrey saw Burns as infected by the 'romantic' self-indulgence of the age, but his analysis of this leads him to a wrongheaded evaluation of the poetry and a wilful legal and political prescription:

> This pitiful cant of careless feeling and eccentric genius, accordingly, has never found much favour in the eyes of English sense and morality. The most signal effect which it ever produced, was on the muddy brains of some German youth, who left college in a body to rob on the highway, because Schiller had represented the captain of a gang as so very noble a creature . . . Akin to this most lamentable trait of vulgarity, and indeed in some measure arising out of it, is that perpetual boast of his own independence, which is obtruded upon the readers of Burns in almost every page of his writings. The sentiment itself is noble, and it is often finely expressed; but a gentleman would only have expressed it when he was insulted or provoked; and would never have made it a spontaneous theme to those friends in whose estimation he felt that his honour stood clear. It is mixed up too in Burns with too fierce a tone of defiance; and indicates rather the pride of a sturdy peasant, than the calm and natural elevation of a generous mind.
> The last of the symptoms of rusticity which we think it necessary to notice in the works of this extraordinary man, is that frequent mistake of mere

exaggeration and violence, for force and sublimity, which has defaced so much of his prose composition, and given an air of heaviness and labour to a good deal of his serious poetry. The truth is, that his *forte* was in humour and in pathos—or rather in tenderness of feeling; and that he has very seldom succeeded, either where mere wit and sprightliness, or where great energy and weight of sentiment were requisite.[60]

Jeffrey's diagnoses of 'the symptoms of rusticity' always lead to the discovery of a malignant source when they give evidence of a personality other than that of the moderate, enlightened gentleman and bespeak a political possibility other than the one desired by the Whig élite. What was needed to smoothe such alarms was to display Burns's best power of 'tenderness of feeling' employed in presenting peasant life. Thus Jeffrey wrote:

We have said that Burns is almost equally distinguished for his tenderness and his humour:– we might have added, for a faculty of combining them both in the same subject, not altogether without parallel in the older poets and ballad-makers, but altogether singular, we think, among modern critics. The passages of pure humour are entirely Scottish,—and untranslateable. They consist in the most picturesque representations of life and manners, enlivened, and even exalted by traits of exquisite sagacity, and unexpected reflection. His tenderness is of two sorts; that which is combined with circumstances and characters of humble, and sometimes ludicrous simplicity; and that which is produced by gloomy and distressful impressions acting on a mind of keen sensibility. The passages which belong to the former description are, we think, the most exquisite and original and, in our estimation, indicate the greatest and most amiable turn of genius; both as being accompanied by fine and feeling pictures of humble life, and as requiring that delicacy, as well as justness of conception, by which alone the fastidiousness of an ordinary reader can be reconciled to such representations. The exquisite description of 'The Cottar's Saturday Night' affords, perhaps, the finest example of this sort of pathetic. Its whole beauty cannot, indeed, be discerned but by those whom experience has enabled to judge of the admirable fidelity and completeness of the picture.[61]

Jeffrey's stress on Burns as a singular modern talent for representing rural life was, of course, directed at the English Romantics. Nothing in Wordsworth could compare with 'The Cottar's Saturday Night' and even if Burns sometimes employed a 'ludicrous simplicity' it was not the kind of mental defection discoverable in Wordsworth:

Our other remark is of a more limited application; and is addressed chiefly to the followers and patrons of that new school of poetry, against which we have thought it our duty to neglect no opportunity of testifying. Those gentlemen are outrageous for simplicity; and we beg leave to recommend to them the simplicity of Burns. He has copied the spoken language of passion and affection, with infinitely more fidelity than they have ever done, on all occasions which properly admitted of such adaptation: but he has not rejected the helps of elevated language and habitual associations, nor debased his composition by an affectation of babyish interjections, and all the puling expletives of an old nurserymaid's vocabulary. Let them contrast their own fantastical personages of hysterical schoolmasters and sententious leech-gatherers, with the authentic rustics of Burns' 'Cottar's Saturday Night', and his inimitable songs; and reflect on the different reception which these personifications have met with from the public. Though they will not be reclaimed from their puny affectations by the example of their learned predecessors, they may, perhaps, submit to be admonished by a self-taught and illiterate poet, who drew from Nature far more directly than they can do, and produced something so much liker the admired copies of the masters whom they have abjured.[62]

Literary tradition, according to Jeffrey's definition, was an authoritarian premise he perpetually summoned to his aid in dealing with English Romantic poetry. Thus 'The Cottar's Saturday Night' is superior to Wordsworth not only in terms of its greater realism but because it derives its power from the paradoxical fact that the peasant Burns has a greater grasp of traditional literature than the middle-class Wordsworth. Hence there is no psychological regression in Burns since he comprehends the eternal value of 'elevated language and habitual associations'. This leads Jeffrey to declare, that the life of the peasantry has assimilated enough of the literary culture of their social superiors to make them politically reliable in times of foreign war and civil turmoil. These Scottish peasants are neither adequately represented nor corrupted by Wordsworth's dangerously regressive vocabulary. To read Burns properly is to be socially reassured:

> His epistles to brother poets, in the rank of farmers and shopkeepers in the adjoining villages,—the existence of a book-society and debating-club among persons of that description, and many other incidental traits in his sketches of his youthful companions,—all contribute to show, that not only good sense, and enlightened morality, but literature, and talents for speculation, are far more generally diffused in society than is generally imagined; and that the delights and the benefits of these generous and humanising pursuits, are by no means confined to those whom leisure and affluence have courted to their enjoyment. That much of this is peculiar to Scotland, and may be properly referred to our excellent institutions of parochial education, and to the natural sobriety and prudence of our nation, may certainly be allowed: but we have no doubt that there is a good deal of the same principle in England, and that the actual intelligence of the lower orders will be found, there also, very far to exceed the ordinary estimates of their superiors. It is pleasing to know, that the sources of rational enjoyment are so widely disseminated; and, in a free country, it is comfortable to think, that so great a proportion of the people is able to appreciate the advantages of its condition, and fit to be relied on in all emergencies where steadiness and intelligence may be required.[63]

Jeffrey's problem in dealing with Burns was caused by his awareness that he was dealing with a *Scottish* poet. His response here was governed by picque because he felt that increasingly the English looked on the Scottish language as a mere equivalent of 'the barbarous dialects of Yorkshire or Devon'.

Before proceeding to take any particular notice of his poetical compositions, we must apprise our Southern readers, that all his best pieces are written in Scotch; and that it is impossible for them to form any adequate judgement of their merits, without a pretty long residence among those who still use that language. To be able to translate the words, is but a small part of the knowledge that is necessary. The whole genius and idiom of the language must be familiar; and the characters, and habits, and associations of those who speak it. We beg leave too, in passing, to observe, that this Scotch is not to be considered as a provincial dialect, the vehicle only of rustic vulgarity and rude local humour. It is the language of a whole country,—long an independent kingdom, and still separate in laws, character and manners. It is by no means peculiar to the vulgar; but it is common speech of the whole nation in early life,—and with many of its most exalted and accomplished individuals throughout their whole existence; and, if it be true that, in later times, it has been, in some measure, laid aside by the more ambitious and aspiring of the present generation, it is still recollected, even by them, as the familiar language of their childhood, and of those who were the earliest objects of their love and veneration. It is connected, in their imagination, not only with that olden time which is uniformly conceived as more pure, lofty and simple than the present, but also with all the soft and bright colours of remembered childhood and domestic affection. All its phrases conjure up images of school-day innocence and sports, and friendships which have no pattern in succeeding years.[64]

With remarkable ease and celerity the fears concerning Wordsworth's poetic regression to earlier states are dismissed. Not only is Scotland sealed off from the intrusive English intelligence by virtue of the fact that the English cannot comprehend the language (the native tongue becomes the first line of defence on the Tweed) but a return to a Scottish childhood is of a quite different order of experience than the return to an English one.

What Jeffrey unwittingly demonstrates is the abuse of the native language with regard to the creation of this destructively immature personal and national predicament. The linguistic confusion and erosion which took place in Scotland after the Union created a situation in which the anglicised middle-class could indulge themselves and exploit their social inferiors. It allowed them the verbal licence to switch from an English derived mode of ratiocination and command (*not* the essential nature of the English language) to a dialect of false innocence and insincere populism. Despite causing a subconscious insecurity and, perhaps, a sense of inferiority with regard to England—making the Anglo-Scots the willing servants of Westminster—this was within Scotland a highly convenient dualism. Thought and feeling did not creatively interact but were compartmentalised. Literature, poetry in particular, became a kind of false consciousness and not the most intense form of verbally incarnating conscience. Given over to providing illusion, it repressed awareness of the nature of the real and, consequently, left unhindered the pursuit of the material goals of the class for which they spoke. As well as evading spiritual self-scrutiny, such regression into prelapsarian states allowed one to see less anglicised social inferiors as children who were either to be objects of benevolent condescension or ruthless discipline. In

Scott and Scotland written in 1936, Edwin Muir clearly revealed the sorry nature and implications of this forked tongue:

> The loss of civilisation is bound up with the loss of language; for no civilisation can exist without a speech in which it can express both its thought and its passion: without an adult tongue, for there can be no maturity except through a working relation between feeling and thought . . .
>
> Anyone, indeed, who chose to enter into this problem of Scottish dialect poetry from the psychological side, could make out a good case for the thesis that Scottish dialect poetry is a regression to childhood, an escape from the responsibility of the whole reason to the simplicity and irresponsibility of the infant mind.
> infant mind.
>
> . . . To most of us who were born and brought up in Scotland dialect Scots is associated with childhood, and English with maturity. This may be a regrettable fact, but it must be accepted; for there is no Scots language to which we can pass over from the restricted and local province of dialect: there is only English. When, therefore, having foresaken dialect speech and its associations of thought and feeling, we turn back to it again, we plunge in spite of ourselves into the simple world of childhood, with its emotions untouched by thought, its sanctioned irresponsibility and endless false hopes.
> . . . A nation in which the mind is divorced from the feelings will act with hot savagery at times, and with chill insensibilty at others; and the loss of Scottish civilisation, of Scottish unity, is the only thing that can explain the peculiarly brutal form which the Industrial Revolution took in Scotland, where its chief agents are only conceivable as thoughtless or perverted children.[65]

That the Industrial Revolution in Scotland was marked by such barbarism would have been wholly unsurprising to William Cobbett because his vision of the preceding Agrarian Revolution recorded on the basis of his 1832 tour of that country was of a nation which was self-destructively mechanistic in terms of social theory, the application of that theory and in the savage new methods of work and instruments of production. Cobbett's *Tour in Scotland; and in the Four Northern Counties of England in the Year 1832* is the most severe of all the English Romantic critiques of Scotland.[66]

Raymond Williams observed that Cobbett's contribution to our understanding of England lay in his 'persistent social questioning and observation'.[67] The same is true of his perception of Scottish life. Cobbett could compare Scottish agrarian conditions with those in England, America and Ireland. What struck him so forcibly about Scotland was that, in relation to England and America conditions were significantly worse:

> God did not make the land for the few, but for the many. Civil society invented property; but gave it not that absolute character which would enable a few owners to extirpate the people, as they appear to be endeavouring to do in Scotland. Our English law effectually guards against these of so villanous a disposition; it gives all men a right of maintenance out of the produce of the earth: it justly gives the necessitous poor a claim prior to that of the owner of the land.[68]

Even more acute than in England, too, was the discrepancy between the fertility of the land and the poverty of the mass of the people who lived on it. Cobbett frequently refuted earlier English notions about the poverty of Scottish soil. He saw in the Lothians and the Clyde Valley arable land of unsurpassed quality. Indeed, he felt it far better than anything he had seen in America. He considered that the working and living conditions of many of the Scottish peasants he observed rendered them 'worse off than the negro by many degrees'. It may be argued that although Cobbett was employing comparative methods, he was too violently prejudiced regarding both the Edinburgh literati and the social philosophy characteristic of so many Scottish thinkers to see Scotland clearly. He was certainly outraged. Jeffrey's treatment of him in 1811 had not been forgotten. Jeffrey with his obsession with rigid form had denounced Cobbett's desire for electoral reform as unbalancing the fixed, delicate balance of the constitution. Cobbett's response had been characteristically harsh: he had no faith in the actual reforming capacities of the Edinburgh Whigs and saw them as pursuing change only in so far as it benefitted themselves:

> I cannot say but I have a sneaking kindness for them. They have done a great deal of good in lashing the boobies and bastards that are fastened upon the public; but what has long appeared to me evident is, that they want to supplant them, and fasten themselves upon us; rather than which I, for my part, would have to maintain the boobies and bastards, who, being somewhat gorged already, are likely to suck our blood less unmercifully than those northern leeches would.[69]

Besides being enraged with the abstracting, quantifying and dehumanising nature of Scottish social thought Cobbett believed that it was not confined to Scotland but, as a form of crude dynamic change (along with physically violent baillies) was exported to England to wreak havoc there. He undertook his Scottish tour to analyse the puzzling quiessence of the people and because:

> I, even I, had strong feelings excited in my mind against Scotland generally (always expressly making great exceptions) by the scoundrelly *"feelosofers"*, who preached up a doctrine tending to cause the people of England to be treated like cattle; even I could not make out how it was, that Scotland should spew forth so many of these monsters.[70]

To understand the nature of Cobbett's answer to his own question, we must understand not simply the analogies he drew with the Irish situation but, even more strongly, the degree to which his analysis of Scotland was governed by his profound admiration for the veracity of Jonathan Swift's style and vision. That there is a connection between a loss of national integrity and an excess of destructive ratiocination and mechanisation is implicit in Swift. In this century Edwin Muir has made explicit the possibility of such a connection as a central factor in the decay of Scottish society:

> A nation without a central organ to give it unity, a merely discarnate nation

such as Scotland, is far more defenceless against the mechanical and purely materialistic forces of civilisation than any integral group could be. All that it can oppose to those forces is floating tradition; and a tradition that has no concrete symbol to embody it soon fades, and presently there is nothing but the isolated individual and the operation of mechanical forces but a name and memory. That has not yet happened to Scotland, but it has been happening for the last hundred years; and it probably helps to explain why so many Scotsmen have excelled in engineering and business, and so few have done anything remarkable in the humane arts. Having a nation only in name, they inevitably become servants of pure undifferentiated 'progress' at its most impersonal and its least humanly significant, servants of a thing that acknowledges no national boundaries, even one's own, that indeed scarcely acknowledges humanity, though created to serve it. So Scotland has earned the reputation of being a nation of engineers, servants of the machine. In other words, it has suffered more from the development of industrialism, from the effects of the industrial revolution, than any other part of the British Isles. It has suffered more, and both physically and spiritually, because against the rage of that revolution it could oppose nothing but the mere idea of a nation, an imagination that could do nothing to shield it.[71]

Cobbett saw the disintegration of traditional Scottish power in terms similar to that defined in Swift's *Modest Proposal*. His first sight on coming to the Border was two wholly different groups in transit. One was itinerant poor moving South in search of work. The other was a stream of heavily laden carts moving towards English markets. He connected this with greedy landowners and degenerate Scottish aristocracy seeking both the highest prices and the pleasures of London and Paris to the chronic detriment of their own people. Like Ireland, Scotland had 'a stupid and unnational nobility'. It was infected by what he called the imperial mentality of the 'pro-consul' whereby one served a foreign master in order to further one's own ends. This could also exist in terms not simply of greedy, economic individualism but also in terms of the development of fractious social philosophies as rationalisations of this greed. One of Scotland's worst exports to England, according to Cobbett, was a certain kind of ratiocinative, authoritarian thinker. If the common heart of the Scottish people was sound its over-developed head was manifestly unhealthy:

> Be assured, gentlemen, that this journey to Scotland was not at all necessary to convince me of the intelligence and virtues of Scotchmen, against whom, in general, I never had a prejudice in my life, and, had none to be removed. In speaking of the perverse and renagado *pretended philosophers,* who, like similar reptiles in the distant provinces of the Roman Empire, have gone to the seat of government to sell their own country and help to enslave ours, I have been obliged to designate them by naming the part of the kingdom from which they came; but I have invariably said, at the same time, that I imputed not their disposition to the people of Scotland, whose oppressions, whenever I shall have the power, I deem it my duty to remove to the utmost of that power; and, in some measure, my journey to Scotland, by the great knowledge that it has enabled me to acquire, will assist me in the performance of the duty.[72]

Cobbett has all Swift's savage indignation for the brutal imposition of abstraction upon human community. In Scotland itself Cobbett saw elements of Swift's Laputa made tangible in the new threshing machines causing severe unemployment and in the severely functional architecture of the new farm buildings (designed to sever the older, milder relationships obtaining between master and men). He detected, like Blake, something demonic in the desire to impose rational models and patterns. Behind this abstract and 'progressive' state of mind he believed there existed a compulsive desire for a power that dehumanised everything it touched. Squalor and poverty abounded but it was made infinitely worse for Cobbett because he saw it as the consequence of the authoritarian excesses of the leaders—aristocrats, landowners, clerics and the intelligentsia of this new order. The houses of the common people bespoke outer dereliction (they were not characterised by the rooted, English cottage garden) and inner squalor. The level of alcohol consumption indicated a deeply depressed populace. Conditions varied but nowhere reflected the abundant fertility of the environment:

> Before I quit LANARKSHIRE, it is right for me to observe, which I do with great pleasure, that the working people are treated much better here than in the LOTHIANS; that the farms are smaller, the occupations numerous, the proprietorships not a few; that the farmservants are frequently in the farmhouses, and that the 'boothie' system is by no means so prevalent. Though, mind, small farms have been here moulded into large ones within the last thirty or forty years; cottages have been swept away in very great numbers; the people have been huddled together in great masses; and that every one of these masses has to exist under the continual scowl of a barrack. As to agriculture, LANARKSHIRE is a very fine county altogether; it has a due mixture of orchards, woods, corn-fields and pastures.[73]

Despite Cobbett's delight in the fecundity of Lanarkshire most of his autumn journey was—compared to what rural life could be—a season in hell. No relation appears to the pervasive pastoral dream in the Scottish writing which was, mainly in *Blackwood's*, exactly contemporary with this: exhausted by work, deprived even of the dignity of possessing their own cutlery, life for the itinerant labour force living in the bothies was thus described by Cobbett:

> The custom here is for men to plough with a pair of horses; to go out at daylight; come in at twelve o'clock, and stay in till two; then go out again and plough till night; and I have seen many of them at plough till sunset.
> I went to the 'boothie' between twelve and one o'clock, in order that I might find the men at home, and see what they had for their dinner. I found the 'boothie' to be a shed, with a fire-place in it to burn coals in, with one doorway, and one little window. The floor was the ground. There were three wooden bedsteads, nailed together like the births in a barrack-room, with boards for the bottom of them. The bedding seemed to be very coarse sheeting with coarse woollen things at the top; and all seemed to be such as similar things must be where there is nobody but men to look after them. There were six men, all at home; one sitting upon a stool, four upon the sides of the births, and one standing talking to me. Though it was Monday, their

beards, especially of two of them, appeared to be some days old. There were ten or twelve bushels of coals lying in a heap in one corner of the place, which was, as nearly as I could guess, about sixteen or eighteen feet square. There was no back-door to the place, and no privy. There were some loose potatoes lying under one of the births.[74]

Cobbett was aware of the hostility of Scottish critics towards him and of the inner divisions in Scottish writing between those who bore witness to what he recognised as truth and those who promulgated the literary falsehoods of the Establishment. Thus taking the opportunity to pay his respects to Burns's widow in Dumfries, he remarked that it was 'a mark of my admiration of the talents of her late husband, one single page of whose writing is worth more than a whole cart load that has been written by WALTER SCOTT'.[75] Unfortunately, Cobbett seems not to have been aware of the one living Scottish writer whom he might have found to be a kindred spirit. Like Burns, James Hogg came from the common people, though he was a shepherd rather than a small farmer. As volatile but less rancorous than Burns he was an equally inept businessman. Both natural writers, a life of prudent toil must have been desperately trying to them. Little wonder that Burns's last wish was to be financially independent so that he could devote himself to his art. Commercial need, a frequent desire for social conviviality and involvement in Edinburgh's condescending literary circles distorted and reduced Hogg's output. His one work of genius is, of course, *The Confessions of a Justified Sinner*. Significantly, this brilliant psychological excursion set in Scotland reflects very little sense of place. Edinburgh is touched upon as a place of potential mob violence and sinister obscurity while the rural lodgings Colwan finds frequently display extreme poverty and hardship but locale remains a peripheral element in the novel. Hogg's article written in 1832 called 'On the Changes, Amusements, and Condition of the Scottish Peasantry' however demonstrates his capacity for intelligent social analysis.[76] His view did not verify Cobbett's vision of near total impoverishment in the bothy system since he recognised that the peasant and servant class were 'better fed, better clothed, and better educated than the old shepherds and hinds of my first acquaintance; but they are less devout, and decidedly *less cheerful and happy*'.[77]

Hogg gives very precise reasons for the loss of the conjunction of probity and pleasure in the life of the Border peasantry. He points to an erosion of social relationships between masters and men expressed in the disappearance of 'one for the pot' poaching and a new, local warfare conducted between scroundrelly, semi-professional gangs of poachers and corrupt gamekeepers. More significantly, despite an evident improvement in diet and work distribution, he attributes the deterioration in the quality of rural life to the breakdown of the 'family' group to which both farmer and servant had belonged.

> Formerly every master sat at the head of his kitchen table, and shared the meal with his servants. The mistress, if there was one, did not sit down at all,

but stood at the dresser behind, and assigned each his portion, or otherwise overlooked the board, and saw that every one got justice. The master asked a blessing, and returned thanks. There was no badinage or idle language in the Farmer's hall in those days, but all was decency and order. Every night the master performed family worship, at which every member of the family was bound to be present, and every Sabbath morning at least, and the oldest male servant in his absence took that duty on him. The consequence of all this familiarity and exchange of kind offices was, that every individual family formed a little community of its own, of which each member was conscious of bearing an important part. And then the constant presence of the master and mistress preventing all ebullitions of untimely merriment, when the hours of relaxation came, then the smothered glee burst out with a luxury of joy and animation, of which we may now look in vain for a single specimen. But ever since the ruinous war prices made every farmer for the time a fine gentleman, how the relative situations of master and servant are changed! Before that time every farmer was first up in the morning, conversed with all his servants familiarly, and consulted what was best to be done for the day. Now, the foreman, or chief shepherd, waits on his master, and, receiving his instructions, goes forth and gives the orders as his own, generally in a peremptory and offensive manner. The menial of course feels that he is no more a member of a community, but a slave; a servant of servants, a mere tool of labour in the hand of a man whom he knows or deems inferior to himself, and the joy of his spirit is mildewed. He is a moping, sullen, melancholy man, flitting from one master to another in hopes to find heart's ease and contentment—but he finds it not; and now all the best and most independent of that valuable class of our community are leaving the country.[78]

Compared to Cobbett's account, the damage being wrought by this significant change in relationships was more psychological than physical. Self-respect declined in proportion to the degree the servant felt himself to be the mere object of his master's designs. On both sides money became much more important in defining the nature of the relationship. For Hogg there was in all this an undoubted element of a paradise lost but it was a genuine sense of loss partly because it bespoke an awareness of the deterioration of sexual relationships which were, if not innocent, healthily knowledgeable. As contact between master and men became strained so did that between men and women. Hogg clearly understood the sad consequences of sexual repression:

In short, though the manly sports of the country, such as wrestling, leaping, racing on foot, putting the stone, archery, and numberless others, may, in some few places, be on the increase, still the young men have these violent exercises to themselves; and since the extermination of the penny-weddings, kirns, and family-dances, the peasantry have not an amusement in which the sexes join; and this sort of abstraction is the first thing that tends to demoralise society, and to stamp the character of man with a more rude and repulsive tint. Youth and manhood combined require some principle of excitation, and when that of female beauty is withheld from them, they must descend to a worse, the glass and the boisterous mirth.[79]

Cobbett would have wholly agreed that it is precisely 'this sort of abstraction that tends to demoralise society'. He, like Swift, saw it as a multilevelled threat percolating down from a diseased, hyper-rational mind to infect every level of life. Like Cobbett, Hogg saw a loss of liberty as the fate of the Scottish peasant at the beginning of the nineteenth century:

> The gradual advancement of the *aristocracy* of farming, if I may be allowed the expression, district after district being thrown into large farms, which has placed such a distance between servants and masters, that in fact they have no communication whatever, and very little interest in common. The master's eye is never upon them, and of course they have no opportunities of ingratiating themselves with him or with his family; but are subjected to all the caprices of a menial like themselves. The ancient state of vassalage was a delightful bond compared to this. It is a state of absolute slavery, with only one amelioration, namely the liberty, at each term, of selling themselves to the highest bidder. This last, with its concomitant evils, already stated, I consider as the principal cause of the radical change which you have observed, and of which you were pleased to make the inquiries at me.[80]

A principal symptom of the change for Hogg was a decline in traditional folk music. 'On looking back, the first great falling off is in *song*. This to me, is not only astonishing but unaccountable. They have ten times more opportunities of learning songs, yet song singing is at an end, or only kept up by a few migratory tailors.'[81] For Hogg this certainly bespoke a loss of social amiability but also, more crucially, a decline of consciousness due to a deterioration in feeling. The new work represented a fundamental shift in attitude towards a mere sentimentality:

> By dint of hard pressing, a blooming nymph will sometimes venture on a song of Moore's or Dibdin's (curse them!) and gaping, and half-choking, with a voice like a cracked kirkbell, finish her song in notes resembling the agonies of a dying sow.
> The publication of the Border Minstrelsy had a singular and unexpected effect in this respect. These songs had floated down on the stream of oral tradition, from generation to generation, and were regarded as a precious treasure belonging to the country; but when Mr Scott's work appeared their arcanum was laid open, and a deadening blow was inflicted on our rural literature and principal enjoyment by the very means adopted for their preservation.[82]

What we have seen Edwin Muir describing as the popular sentimental music characteristic of Kailyard Scotland and the onset of industrialisation, begins, according to Hogg's testimony, with the decline of a certain quality of rural life. Sentimentality, of course, was not the exclusive preserve of the upper class. They used it exploitatively but both rich and poor employed it, with varying degrees of self-awareness, to conceal from themselves the painful reality of their situation—albeit very different kinds of pain. On the one hand it was a compensatory fantasy to obscure responsibility and on the other it was false antidote to a sense of social and personal dereliction. Muir, in his poetry, was also aware of this earlier shift in values within the rural community:

Till Scott and Hogg, the robbers, came
And Nailed the singing tragedies down
In dumb letter under a name
And led the Bothy to the town.[83]

Whether Hogg was as culpable as Scott of this chronic dilution of traditional material is highly questionable. What is true, however, is that Hogg's connection with *Blackwood's* and, in particular, his friendship with Professor John Wilson ('Christopher North') led to the employment of Hogg's own persona in justifying the insincere pastoral vision of Scotland promulgated by that organ. In the second and third decades of the nineteenth century with Scotland undergoing convulsive change, *Blackwood's* projected a national image not simply of stasis but torpor. This was frequently justified by recourse to the testimony of Scotland's peasant poets:

> Scotland has better reason to be proud of her peasant poets than any other country in the world. She possesses a rich treasure of poetry, expressing the moral character of her population at very remote times; and in her national lyrics alone, so full of tenderness and truth, the heart of a simple, and wise and thoughtful people is embalmed to us in imperishable beauty. If we knew nothing of the forefathers of our Scottish hamlets, but the pure and affectionate songs and ballads, the wild and pathetic airs and music which they loved, we should know enough to convince us that they were a race of men strong, healthy, happy and dignified in the genial spirit of nature. The lower orders of the Scotch seem always to have had deeper, calmer, purer and more reflecting affections than those of any other people—and at the same time they have possessed, and do still possess, an imagination that broods over these affections with a constant delight, and kindles them into a strength and power, which, when brought into action by domestic or national trouble, have often been in good truth sublime.[84]

This is not Wilson but Lockhart, perhaps the supreme pourer of such snake-oil prose on Scotland's troubled waters. As an antidote to the uncertainty of the times Lockhart brought to a climax the process of creating a false national historical consciousness that had been evolving since 1707. William Ruddick, at best ingenuously, described Lockhart's vision as having 'an anti-urban, primitivist bias'. In his introduction to *Peter's Letters to his Kinsfolk*, Ruddick also noted that:

> But the book's final climax is the extended account of a country sacrament, the scene of natural pious feeling and a natural reverence for traditions; pure direct feelings and the dignity of venerable institutions and human age. For all its concern with the present *Peter's Letters* finally achieves a Wordsworthian vision of pastoral simplicity and innocence: the vision which Lockhart was to strive for again and again a few years later in his novel *Adam Blair*. In it assertion of the absolute necessity of understanding the arts and institutions of a country within the context of its historical development, *Peter's Letters* is clearly a work of the nineteenth century: post Wordsworth, post Scott pointing ahead towards Carlyle and Ruskin.[85]

It is hard to know where to start in dealing with such a miscomprehension of Scottish Toryism as manifest in Lockhart and *Blackwood's*. At the very least, Mr. Ruddick should have availed himself of what Wordsworth and Carlyle actually thought of Lockhart. Lockhart debased the currency of both the Scottish tradition and of high European Romanticism in order to create or rewrite a kind of literary-cultural Scottish history amenable to inculcating a sense of complacency and torpor. Rather than face actual and growing problems of social change, especially the industrial city, one could escape into this dreamland. What Ruddick refers to as Lockhart's awareness of the 'self-renewing traditionalism of Scott and folk-culture' is highly suspect. Lockhart's hagiography of his father-in-law was partly based on his own self-aggrandisement and had the intended effect of confusing Scott's abortive fictions with the essence of the Scottish literary tradition. Lockhart debases Romantic thought and art to create a synthetic Scottish image. Thus the misty luminosity of Turner's versions of Edinburgh becomes a sentimental fog to enshroud the city from realistic scrutiny. Scotland seems in these accounts a land without significant urban life when, in fact, a vast movement in population into the industrial West of Scotland was underway. Glasgow is treated thus:

> It appeared to me, upon the whole, that the Glasgow manufacturers conduct matters with more attention to the comforts of those they employ, than most of their brethern elsewhere . . . I was assured, at least, that there prevails in this place nothing of the vile custom of unceasing labour by day and by night, which has been, with so much noble passion, described and branded in the words of the Wanderer. After being confined for hours to the steam-heated atmosphere of these places, my ears dingling with the eternal rock and buzz of wheels and spindles, and my eyes fretted and inflamed with the flakes of cotton every where flying about; and in spite of all that I have said, my spirits being not a little depressed by the contemplation of so many thousands of poor creatures shut out in their captivity from
>
> > The gentle visitations of the sun
> > And in these structures mingled, old and young,
> > And unripe sex with sex, for mutual taint,
>
> . . . my spirits being somewhat saddened with all these poisonous sights, and sounds and reflections, I readily embraced the proposals of my friend—that we should walk forth, namely, into the fields, and refresh ourselves with breathing the unpolluted air of heaven, till the hour of dinner.[86]

Wordsworth's *Excursion* is here evoked but not in terms of its power as social commentary but as a prelude to escape to the open air. The Scottish middle class were intent on such escapes.

Cockburn, in a private context, acts out the same desire and false assumption as does Lockhart in attempting to fabricate public consciousness. His holiday jaunts from Edinburgh were not to genuine freedom but, as has been suggested, to a self-indulgent mock Gothic country house where he could play at agricultural work, suitably attired, and fantasise about belonging to an earlier, less worryingly complex Scotland. The simulated feudal architecture represented nostalgia for a lost nation but it did not represent any desire to renew older forms of paternalism. Like Lockhart, Cockburn's position was only superficially that of the great Romantics. Bonaly, his country home was knowingly created as a suburban defamation of a certain kind of conservationist Romantic thought which began with Goldsmith's *Deserted Village*.

> But, realising the profanations of Auburn, I have destroyed a village, and erected a tower, and reached the dignity of a twenty-acred laird. Everything, except the two burns, the few old trees, and the mountains, are my own work, and to a great extent of my own hands. Human nature is incapable of enjoying more happiness than has been my lot here; where the glories of the prospect, and the luxury of wild retirement, have been all enhanced by the progress of my improvements, of my children and of myself. I have been too happy, and often tremble in the anticipation that the cloud must come at last.[87]

Cockburn's fear was deeply implanted in the sub-consciousness of property owning, entrepreneurial Scotland. Lockhart sought to simulate a state of national unity by means of a debasement of Romanticism in such a way that it becomes falsifying in pictorial, verbal and architectural form. Hence his vision of Abbotsford. These superficial symbols of alleged integration referred to a traditional Scottish unity which could be seen most clearly in the *unchanged* nature of the loyal Scottish peasantry. It was not too difficult to distort Wordsworth to fit such a pattern. Indeed as Wordsworth grew older he became, not a genuine conservative but a member of the sentimental, authoritarian establishment. A radical poetry such as that of Keats could not be so dealt with. This, in part, explains the extraordinary virulence of Lockhart's attack on Keats and the Cockney School:

> Such a fire of contumely, kept up on this most conceited knot of superficial coxcombs cannot fail to produce ere long the salutary effect of entirely silencing their penny trumpets of sedition and blasphemy—to say nothing of their worthless poetry . . . They are by far the vilest vermin that ever dared to creep upon the hem of the majestic garment of the English muse.[88]

Hazlitt, the master spirit of the Cockney School, believed that the demonic, religious fanaticism of the past had been resurrected in *Blackwood's*:

> Instead of slow fires and paper caps fastened round the heads of the victims, we arrive at the same end by a politer way of nicknames and anonymous criticism. *Blackwood's Magazine* is the modern version of Fox's *Book of Martyrs*.[89]

He saw Scottish Toryism as petrified, in both senses of the word. Its fear led to a desire for absolute stasis. The partial achievement of this statis led to an increased degree of fear because the pressure of social discontent had also been increased. Lockhart knew of English and German conservative social theories. Indeed Schlegel is freely translated to suit the devious ends of *Peter's Letters*. The essential element of such theories which

5.2 *Engraving of a painting by D. Octavius Hill of the Braes of Ballochmyle.*

was continuity of organic growth was, however, discarded. In such pseudo-conservatism the creativity of both artist and society was denied. What one got was the production of simulated art which was, by definition, without creativity and anti-intellectual. Although they endlessly borrowed from the great Romantic artists men like Lockhart and Wilson in reality envied and even hated them. Hazlitt, specifically defining Scott and Scottish Toryism, clearly understood this:

> A Tory may be a poet, but no Tory can be a philosopher; for he has not even the capacity of conceiving an abstract proposition. As his conclusions have no principle of truth or justice to rest on, but mere prejudice and interest, so their are no means, however unfair, venal or contemptible, of which he will not avail himself to keep up the delusion in his own mind, or to impose on the folly of mankind. A nick-name is the *ne plus ultra* of Tory logic. Why? Because it implies a strong degree of mechanical hatred and contempt, without assigning any reason for it. What anything *is* in reality, or what it *ought to be* in justice, are questions alien to Tory faculties; for they only consider (from narrowness of understanding and from sordid selfishness) what it *has been,* or how it can be made to last in order to plague the world, and to serve themselves and their patrons.[90]

Lockhart was not a fool but he was both envious and sycophantic.[91] He felt he had done the state some service. That service, given the state of Scotland, was inevitably corrupting. He had to create a false symbology of the past in order to obscure the fissures of the present. He was also quite aware of what he was doing. Visiting Abbotsford he discerned a symbol produced by a national imagination similar to his own. Scott, the Border Laird, kept an extravagantly garbed piper. All, however, was grist to Lockhart's Scottish historical mill:

> It is true, that it was in the Lowlands—and that there are other streams upon which the shadows of the tartan might fall with more of the propriety of mere antiquarianism, than on the Tweed. But the Scotch are right in not now-a-days splitting too much the symbols of their nationality; as they have ceased to be an independent people, they do wisely in striving to be as much as possible a united people.[92]

Lockhart, like so many Scottish writers before and after him, was both victim and agent of this national paradox. Genuine art cannot be created from such a state of inner division exacerbated as it was by an economic theory which increased such division. What is produced is sentimental fantasy, the strongest component of which is the appeal to a mythical, pastoral past of tranquility and obedience. An already tenuous Scotland, with Lockhart's prescient Victorian sentimentality, becomes thoroughly unreal:

> All enlightened foreigners have been impressed with a sense of the grandeur of such a national character, but they have failed in attributing it to the right cause. The blessings of Education have indeed been widely diffused over Scotland, and her Parish Schools have conferred upon her inestimable benefits. But there is such simplicity and depth of moral feeling and affection in her peasantry—such power over the more agitating and tumultuous

passions, which, without weakening their lawful energies, controls and subdues their rebellious excitement—there is an imagination so purely and loftily exercised over the objects of their human love—that we must look for the origin of such a character to a far higher source than the mere culture of the mind by means of a rational and widely-extended system of Education. It is the habitual faith of the peasantry of this happy and beautiful land, 'that has made them whole'.

. . . It is the heart of the people, not merely their external character, of which we speak, though that too is beyond all comparison the most interesting and impressive of any nation in the world. It would require a long line of thought to fathom the depth of a grey-haired Scottish peasant's heart, who may have buried in the churchyard of his native village the partner of a long life, and the children she had brought to bless it. Time wears not out from his heart any impression that love has once graven there; it would seem, that the strength of affections relying on heaven when earth has lost all it valued, preserved old age from dotage and decay. If religion is most beautiful and lovely in the young, the happy, and the innocent, we must yet look for the consummation of its sublimity in the old, the repentant, and the resigned, and both may be seen

> In some small kirk upon its sunny brae,
> When Scotland lies asleep on the still Sabbath-day.[93]

It seems the most extraordinary contradiction that the cosmopolitan, sceptical, energetic dreams of less than a century before had shrunk to this pietistic, Sabbatarian torpor. What this essay has been discussing, however, is the nature of the evasions and paradoxes in the thought of the Scottish Enlightenment which made such an outcome inevitable. Implicit in the unresolved problem of authentic nationality is a decline in imagination. Without that core all secondary, functional powers of the mind turn destructive. Hence the paradox that a country given over to 'progress' can end desperately clinging to regressive make-believe.

304

REFERENCES

1. Williams, Raymond, *The Country and the City,* London, 1975, p. 33.

2. I would here recommend the reader to Dr. T.M. Devine's Social Stability and Agrarian Change in the Eastern Lowlands of Scotland, 1810–1840, *Social History,* Vol. 3, No. 3, October, 1978, pp. 331–345 which deals with the tangible elements in Scottish agriculture (e.g. kind and consequent rotation of crops) which led to a situation somewhat different from that prevailing in England.

3. Scott, Walter, *Rob Roy,* London, 1896, p. 154.

4. Noble, Andrew, MacChismo in Retrospect, *The Bulletin of Scottish Politics,* No. 2, Spring 1981, pp. 72–81.

5. North, Christopher, *Noctes Ambrosianae,* Edinburgh, 1860, Vol. I., pp. 174–5.

6. Williams, op.cit., p. 71.

7. Eliot, T.S., Wordsworth and Coleridge, *The Use of Poetry and the Use of Criticism,* London, 1964, p. 74.

8. *Wordsworth: Selected Prose and Poetry,* Ed., Hartman, G., New York, 1970, p. xvii.

9. *Poetical Works of Wordsworth,* Ed., Hutchinson, Thomas, London, 1936, p. 597.

10. *Blackwood's Magazine,* Vol. II, October, 1817, p. 202.

11. See for example Jeffrey's review of Hazlitt's *Characters of Shakespeare's Plays* reprinted in *Essays from the Edinburgh Review* introduced by Hannaford Bennet, London, 1924, pp. 59–86. Even more revealing is Adam Smith's treatment of Swift in his literary lectures delivered at Glasgow University, *Lectures on Rhetoric and Belle Lettres,* Ed., Lothian, J., Edinburgh, 1963, p. 20.

12. Bredvold, Louis, The Gloom of the Tory Satirists, *Eighteenth-Century English Literature—Modern Essays in Criticism,* Ed., Clifford, New York, 1959, p. 15.

13. Peckham, Morse, *The Triumph of Romanticism,* Columbia S.C., 1969.

14. *The Letters of Sir Walter Scott,* Ed., Grierson, H.J.C., London, 1932, Vol. I, p. 221.

15. Scott and Tradition, *Edwin Muir—Uncollected Scottish Criticism,* Ed., Noble, Andrew, London, 1982, p. 209–210.

16. *Scott on Himself,* Hewitt, D., Edinburgh, 1981, p. 225.

17. Peckham, Toward a Theory of Romanticism: II. Reconsiderations, op.cit., pp. 30–31.

18. Muir, Edwin, *Scottish Journey,* Edinburgh, 1979, pp. 67–68.

19. Muir, Edwin, A Note on the Scottish Ballads, Noble, op.cit., p. 155.

20. Thompson, Harold William, Ed., *The Anecdotes and Egotisms of Henry MacKenzie,* London, 1927, p. 168.

21. ibid., pp. 162–3.

22. Fairchild, Hoxie, Burns, *Religious Trends in English Poetry,* Vol. II, New York, 1956, p. 52.

23. Speirs, John, *The Scots Literary Tradition: An Essay in Criticism,* London, 1962, pp. 110–111.

24. *The Works of Robert Fergusson,* Edinburgh, 1970, p. 344.

25. ibid., p. 182.

26. This theme is developed in some detail in Jack, R.D.S. and Noble, A. Eds, *The Art of Robert Burns,* London, (in the press, 1982).

27. *Anecdotes and Egotisms,* op.cit., p. 151.

28. Williams, op.cit., pp. 110–120.

29. Fairchild, op.cit., p. 44.

30. ibid.

31. See K.G. Simpson, Sterne and Burns: The Impulse of Wit, Jack and Noble, op.cit.

32. *The Letters of Robert Burns* (2 Vols.), Ed., De Lancey Ferguson, Oxford, 1931, Vol. I, p. 70.

33. *Burns—Poems and Songs,* Ed., Kinsley, James, London, 1971, *72,* p. 21.

34. Fairchild, op.cit., p. 50.

35. Ferguson, William, *Scotland—1689 to the Present, The Edinburgh History of Scotland,* Vol. 4, Edinburgh, 1968, p. 173.

36. *Letters,* Vol. I, p. 15–16.

37. *Poems and Songs, 62,* p. 81.

38. A Liverpool Coterie, *The Collected Writings of Thomas De Quincey,* Ed., Masson, David, Edinburgh, 1899, II, p. 137.

39. Hawthorne, Nathaniel, Some of the Haunts of Burns, *Our Old Home: A Series of English Sketches,* Cornell, 1970, Vol. V, pp. 202–203.

40. *Letters,* Vol. I, p. 108.

41. Quoted in Weston, John C., Robert Burns's Satire, Jack and Noble, op.cit.

42. ibid.

43. Epistle to Davie, A Brother Poet, *Poems and Songs, 51,* p. 50.

44. ibid., *108,* p. 205.

45. Crawford, Thomas, *Burns—A Study of the Poems and Songs,* Edinburgh, 1960.

46. Cockburn, Henry, *Memorials of His Time,* Ed., Forbes Gray, Edinburgh, 1945, pp. 64–5.

47. Quoted by Lucyle Werkmeister, *A Newspaper History of England 1792–93,* Lincoln, Neb., 1967, p. 142.

48. Thompson, E.P., *The Making of the English Working Class,* London, 1980, pp. 135–6.

49. Thornton, Robert D., *William Maxwell to Robert Burns,* Edinburgh, 1979.

50. *Letters,* Vol. I, p. 277.

51. *Poems and Songs, 625,* p. 722–3.

52. Review of Wordsworth's *Poems in Two Volumes, The Edinburgh Review,* Vol. XI, Oct. 1807, p. 231.

53. *The Edinburgh Review,* Vol. I, Oct. 1802, p. 71.

54. Quoted by E.P. Thompson, op.cit., p. 193.

55. Hartman, op.cit.

56. Jeffrey in Hannaford Bennet, op.cit., p. 62.

57. ibid., Review of *Thalaba*, pp. 66–7.

58. ibid., Review of *Poems in Two Volumes*, pp. 217–8

59. *Robert Burns: The Critical Heritage*, Ed., Low, Donald, London, 1974, pp. 178–195.

60. ibid., pp. 183–4.

61. ibid., p. 187.

62. ibid., p. 195.

63. ibid., pp. 194–5.

64. ibid., p. 186.

65. Muir, Edwin, *Scott and Scotland*, London, 1936, pp. 70–75.

66. Cobbett, William, *Tour in Scotland; and in the Four Northern Counties of England in the Autumn of the Year 1832*, London, 1833.

67. Williams, op.cit., pp. 135–140.

68. Cobbett, *Tour in Scotland*, op.cit., p. 108.

69. Cobbett, William, *Political Register*, XII, No. 15, 10th October 1807, p. 556.

70. Cobbett, *Tour in Scotland*, op.cit., p. 156.

71. Muir, Edwin, The Functionlessness of Scotland, in Noble, op.cit., pp. 106–107.

72. Cobbett, *Tour in Scotland*, op.cit., p. 193.
Cobbett's never less than abrasive style was raised to pugilistic heights when his mind not infrequently turned to his loathed tribe of 'Scotch *feelosofers*'. He was right to be somewhat apprehensive when advancing into Scotland for his earlier English *Rural Rides* is replete with enraged denunciations of Scottish social and political follies;

follies which, to him, seemed to take to extremes the social errors of the day. Not a little xenophobic, perhaps, he saw the intrusion of Scottish thinkers into English life as, at the very least, hastening the break up of its rural, organic structure. He did not share Hume's condemnation of feudalism as repressive since he saw it being replaced by repressions at least as great. He hated Adam Smith's laissez-faire economics and saw Walter Scott's endorsement of paper rather than gold currency as a further step towards degeneration. Perhaps his principal Scottish enemy was Dr. John Black who was the editor of *The Morning Chronicle*. Cobbett loathed his minatory social philosophy and, he believed Scotsmen, given power, tended to be mentally and physically authoritarian. Thus the Scots were, to his mind, the most extreme advocates of Malthusian dogma concerning population. This fact brought Cobbett into conflict with *The Edinburgh Review* and with the demographic attitudes of men like Chalmers and Colquhoun. See George Woodcock's Notes to *Rural Rides*, Penguin, London, 1973, pp.515–533. The following is a fair example of Cobbett's general tone when dealing with the Scottish establishment:

> The 'instructor' gives us a sad account of the state of the working classes in Scotland. I am not glad that these poor people suffer: I am very sorry for it . . . But I must be glad that something has happened to silence the impudent Scotch quacks, who have been for six years past, crying up the doctrine of Malthus, and *railing against the English poor laws*. Let us now see what they will do with their poor! Well, amidst all this suffering there is one good thing; the Scotch political economy is blown to the devil, and the Edinburgh Review and Adam Smith along with it. (Woodcock, p. 362).

73. ibid., p. 224.

74. ibid., p. 130.

75. ibid., p. 235.

76. Hogg, James, On the Changes, Amusements and Condition of the Scottish Peasantry, *The Quarterly Journal of Agriculture*, Vol. III, Feb.1831–Sept. 1832, pp. 256–263.

77. ibid., p. 256.

78. ibid., p. 258–9.

79. ibid., p. 262.

80. ibid., p. 263.

81. ibid., p. 256.

82. ibid., p. 257.

83. Muir, Edwin, Complaint of the Dying Peasantry, *Collected Poems, 1921–1958,* London, 1960, p. 262.

84. Lockhart, John Gibson, Some Observations on the Poetry of the Agricultural and that of the Pastoral Districts of Scotland, illustrated by a comparative view of the Genius of Burns and The Ettrick Shepherd, *Blackwood's Magazine,* Vol. IV, Feb. 1819, p. 521.

85. Lockhart, John Gibson, *Peter's Letters to His Kinsfolk,* Ed., Ruddick, William, Edinburgh, 1977, p. xxi.

86. ibid., pp. 165–6.

87. Cockburn, *Memorials,* op.cit., pp. 153–4.

88. *Peter's Letters,* op.cit., p. 111.

89. Hazlitt, William, The Spirit of Controversy, *The Complete Works,* Ed., Howe, P.P., London, 1933, Vol. 20, p. 309.

90. ibid., Illustrations of Toryism—from the Writings of Sir Walter Scott, Vol. 19, p. 288.

91. Muir, Edwin, The Scorpion, in Noble, op.cit., pp. 219–221.

92. *Peter's Letters,* pp. 131–132.

93. Lockhart, Some Observations . . ., op.cit., pp. 521–522.

Selected Bibliography

Recent Historical Perspectives on the Period:

Hobsbawm, E.J.   *The Age of Revolution.* London: Weidenfeld and Nicolson, 1962.

Thompson, E.P.   *The Making of the English Working Class.* London: Victor Gollancz, 1963, rpt. London: Pelican Books, 1980.

Williams, Raymond. *The Country and the City.* London: Chatto and Windus, 1973.

Contemporary Views of the Age:

Cobbett, William.   *Tour in Scotland and the Four Northern Counties of England in the Autumn of the Year 1832.* London 1833.

Cockburn, Henry.   *Memorials of his Time.* Edinburgh: Black, 1856.

In addition *The Edinburgh Review* from 1802 and *Blackwood's Magazine* from 1817 provide a wealth of interesting insights into the times.

Scotland:

Dickson, Tony.   *Scottish Capitalism: Class, State and Nation from before the Union to the Present.* London: Laurence and Wishart, 1980.

Lenman, Bruce.   *Integration, Enlightenment and Industrialisation: Scotland 1746–1832,* Volume 6 in *The History of Scotland.* London: Edward Arnold, 1981.

Smout, T.C.   *A History of the Scottish People 1560–1820.* Glasgow: Collins, 1969.

Edinburgh:

Daiches, David.   *Edinburgh.* London: Hamilton, 1978.

Fleming, John.   *Robert Adam and his Circle.* London: John Murray, 1962.

Youngson, A.J.   *The Making of Classical Edinburgh.* Edinburgh: Edinburgh University Press, 1966.

Glasgow:

Daiches, David   *Glasgow.* London: André Deutch, 1977.

Gomme, Andor and   *Architecture of Glasgow.* London: Lund Humphries,
Walker, David.   1968.

Worsdall, F.   *The Tenement, A Way of Life.* Edinburgh: Gordon Wright, 1979.

Architecture of the Enlightenment in general:

Kaufmann, Emil. *Architecture in the Age of Reason; Baroque and Post-Baroque in England, Italy and France.* Cambridge, Mass: Harvard University Press, 1955.

Rosenau, Helen. *Social Purpose in Architecture: Paris and London Compared 1760–1800.* London: Studio Vista, 1970.

Robert Owen:

Butt, J. (Ed.) *Robert Owen, Prince of Cotton Spinners.* London: David and Charles, 1971.

Owen, Robert. *A New View of Society and other Writings.* London: Dent, 335. Everyman's Library, nd.

Bentham:

Bentham, J., *Panopticon; or the Inspection House.* London: 1791.

Bentham, J. *Panopticon; Postscript.* Two volumes, London: 1791.

Institutions

Foucault, M. *Madness and Civilisation: A History of Insanity in the Age of Reason;* translated by Richard Howard. London: Tavistock Publications, 1967.

Foucault, M. *Surveiller et Punir: Naissance de la Prison.* Paris: Editions Gallimard, 1975.

Foucault, M. *The Birth of the Clinic;* translated by A.M. Sheridan. London: Tavistock Publications, 1973.

Hospitals:

Thompson, J.D. and Goldin, G. *The Hospital: A Social and Architectural History.* Yale: Yale University Press, 1975.

Prisons

Markus, T.A. The Pattern of the Law, *Architectural Review,* CXVI, October 1954, pp251–256.

Asylums

Skultans, Vieda. *Madness and Morals: Ideas on Insanity in the Nineteenth Century.* London and Boston: Routledge and Kegan Paul, 1975.

Education:

McCann, P. (Ed.) *Popular Education and Socialisation in the Nineteenth Century.* London: Methuen, 1977.

Simon, Brian. *The Two Nations and the Educational Structure 1780–1870.* London: Lawrence and Wishart, 1974.

Stow:

Stow, David. *Moral Training.* Glasgow: 1st edition 1836.

Acknowledgements

The Scottish Arts Council has made a publication grant, and both the University of Strathclyde and the Scottish International Education Trust have provided underwriting against publication costs. This generous help is gratefully acknowledged.

In addition the editor gratefully acknowledges a publication grant for the preparation of this book from the Carnegie Trust for the Universities of Scotland. This was originally granted to help with a larger work, which is still in preparation, but as much of the material for that has also been used here it would be ungracious not to acknowledge the Trust's help.

Each of the authors gave generously of his time to help his colleagues and the editor by comments, discussions, correction, suggested sources and critical development of ideas. Honor Mulholland fully participated in this process as assistant editor and also shouldered a substantial part of the sub-editing, proof reading and indexing burdens.

In the Department of Architecture and Building Science thanks are due to Ms Ellen Craig, Mrs Aileen Nuttall and Ms Teresa Sharkey for preparing the typescript; Mr Charles Brown for significant help in preparing photographs; and Ms Kathryn Young for preparing drawn illustrations. Two graduates of the Department, Robert Craig and Ian Brebner, allowed material from their 'Spatial Order and Social Order' 1981 dissertations to be used.

Professor John Butt and John Hume, of the University's Department of History gave valuable critical help and generously lent sources for some of the New Lanark figures.

Ms A H Williamson, of Jordanhill College Library, and the College's photographic technician Mr B Lochrin, gave valuable help in copying material from the College Library.

Mr J. Murray generously gave permission for the reproduction of two engravings of the Scottish landscape artist D Octavius Hill's paintings. Fifty of these plates are published in *The Land of Burns* (Glasgow: Richard Drew Publishing, 1981).

Below formal acknowledgement is made to individuals and organisations for permission to reproduce material in their possession. But, in addition, the following are to be specially thanked for arranging access to original drawings, assistance with references, and arrangements for reproduction of material in their collections:

Dr A R Bailey

Dr Stephanie Blackden, History of Medicine and Science Unit, Department of History, Edinburgh University

Mr Robert Bryant, City Archivist, Bath City Council

Ms C H Cruft and the staff of the Royal Commission on the Ancient and Historical Monuments of Scotland, Edinburgh

Mr David Dean, Director of Library Services, The British Architectural Library, London

Mr Richard Dell, Principal Archivist and the staff of Strathclyde Regional
    Archives, Glasgow
The staff of Edinburgh City Library, Edinburgh
Ms Susan Floate, Librarian, Royal College of Psychiatrists, London
Mr Robert Kilgour and Ms C Brooke, City of Edinburgh District Council,
    Department of Architecture
Ms Ludlow, Library of the Royal Faculty of Procurators, Glasgow
Mr Iain McIvor, Department of the Environment
Mr Colin McWilliam, Department of Architecture, Heriot Watt
    University, Edinburgh
Dr Makey, City Archivist, Edinburgh City Archives
Mr Andrew Miller and the staff of the Mitchell Library, Glasgow District
    Council
Mr Rattray, partner in Hacking and Paterson, Glasgow
Mr D J H Smith, County Archivist, Gloucestershire County Council
Ms Dorothy Stroud, Assistant Curator, Sir John Soane's Museum, London
Mr Duncan Torbet, Chief Librarian, City of Dundee District Council,
    Central Library, Dundee
Dr Alexander Walk

Permission to reproduce the figures listed has been given courtesy of
the following

Bath City Council	Figure 4.3
Anthony Blond Educational Limited, London	Figure 3.6
Mr Ian Brebner	Figure 1.77
Bristol Royal Infirmary	Figure 1.10
British Architecture Library	Figures 1.66, 1.73
The British Library	Figures 1.72, 1.74, 4.1
The British Library of Political and Economic Science	Figure 3
City of Dundee District Council, Central Library, Dundee	Figure 1.76
Collection of the City of Edinburgh	Figure 1 (and cover)
Mr Robert Craig	Figure 4.19
Edinburgh City Libraries	Figures 2.1, 2.2, 2.7, 2.8, 2.9
Edinburgh District Council, Department of Architecture	Figures 1.44, 1.45, 1.58, 1.59, 1.60, 1.63
The Free Press, New York	Figure 3.16 (E.A. Gutkind, *International History of City Development* Vol. IV)
Gloucestershire County Archives	Figure 1.75(b)
Mr John Hume, Department of History, University of Strathclyde	Figures 4.8(b), 4.10(b)
Jordanhill College Library	Figures 4.14, 4.20,(a), 4.36, 4.37, 4.38, 4.39

314

315

Index